After Slavery

New Perspectives on the History of the South

UNIVERSITY PRESS OF FLORIDA

Florida A&M University, Tallahassee
Florida Atlantic University, Boca Raton
Florida Gulf Coast University, Ft. Myers
Florida International University, Miami
Florida State University, Tallahassee
New College of Florida, Sarasota
University of Central Florida, Orlando
University of Florida, Gainesville
University of North Florida, Jacksonville
University of South Florida, Tampa
University of West Florida, Pensacola

AFTER SLAVERY

Race, Labor, and Citizenship in the Reconstruction South

Edited by Bruce E. Baker and Brian Kelly

John David Smith, Series Editor

University Press of Florida

Gainesville / Tallahassee / Tampa / Boca Raton

Pensacola / Orlando / Miami / Jacksonville / Ft. Myers / Sarasota

Frontispiece: Rice plantation workers in Georgetown County circa 1890.
Courtesy of the Caroliniana Library at the University of South Carolina.

Printed in the United States of America on acid free paper

This book may be available in an electronic edition.

First cloth printing, 2013
First paperback printing, 2014

Library of Congress Cataloging-in-Publication Data
After slavery : race, labor, and citizenship in the reconstruction South /
edited by Bruce E. Baker and Brian Kelly.
p. cm.—(New perspectives on the history of the South)
Includes bibliographical references and index.
ISBN 978-0-8130-4477-4 (cloth: alk. paper)
ISBN 978-0-8130-6097-2 (pbk.)
1. Slaves—Emancipation—United States. 2. Reconstruction (U.S. history, 1865–1877) 3. Slavery—United States—History. 4. African Americans—History—1863–1877. 5. African Americans—History—1877–1964. 6. United States—Race relations.
I. Baker, Bruce E., 1971– II. Kelly, Brian, 1958– III. Series: New perspectives on the history of the South.
E185.2.A34 2013
306.3'620973—dc23 2013007062

The University Press of Florida is the scholarly publishing agency for the State University System of Florida, comprising Florida A&M University, Florida Atlantic University, Florida Gulf Coast University, Florida International University, Florida State University, New College of Florida, University of Central Florida, University of Florida, University of North Florida, University of South Florida, and University of West Florida.

University Press of Florida
15 Northwest 15th Street
Gainesville, FL 32611-2079
http://www.upf.com

Contents

Acknowledgments vii
List of Abbreviations ix

Introduction 1
Bruce E. Baker and Brian Kelly

1. Slave and Citizen in the Modern World: Rethinking Emancipation in the Twenty-First Century 16
Thomas C. Holt

2. "Erroneous and Incongruous Notions of Liberty": Urban Unrest and the Origins of Radical Reconstruction in New Orleans, 1865–1868 35
James Illingworth

3. "Surrounded on All Sides by an Armed and Brutal Mob": Newspapers, Politics, and Law in the Ogeechee Insurrection, 1868–1869 58
Jonathan M. Bryant

4. "It Looks Much Like Abandoned Land": Property and the Politics of Loyalty in Reconstruction Mississippi 77
Erik Mathisen

5. Anarchy at the Circumference: Statelessness and the Reconstruction of Authority in Emancipation North Carolina 98
Gregory P. Downs

6. "The Negroes Are No Longer Slaves": Free Black Families, Free Labor, and Racial Violence in Post-Emancipation Kentucky 122
J. Michael Rhyne

7. Ex-Slaveholders and the Ku Klux Klan: Exploring the Motivations of Terrorist Violence 143
Michael W. Fitzgerald

8. Drovers, Distillers, and Democrats: Economic and Political Change in Northern Greenville County, 1865–1878 159
Bruce E. Baker

9. Mapping Freedom's Terrain: The Political and Productive Landscapes of Wilmington, North Carolina 176
Susan Eva O'Donovan

10. Class, Factionalism, and the Radical Retreat: Black Laborers and the Republican Party in South Carolina, 1865–1900 199
Brian Kelly

Afterword 221
Eric Foner

Bibliography 231
List of Contributors 255
Index 259

Acknowledgments

This collection grew out of two major conferences sponsored by the After Slavery Project, an international research collaboration funded by the (U.K.) Arts and Humanities Research Council and involving three of the contributors to the present volume—Bruce E. Baker, Brian Kelly, and Susan E. O'Donovan. The Ninth Wiles Colloquium brought a dozen leading scholars of U.S. emancipation to Queen's University Belfast for an intensive, three-day symposium on "Rethinking Reconstruction." Such an exceptional gathering could not have taken place without the encouragement of Professor David Hayton, then Head of School in History at Queen's, or the generous support of the Wiles Trust. The editors want to express their gratitude to the late Trevor Boyd and the Boyd family, to Catherine Boone at Queen's, and to successive head librarians John Gray and John Killen at Belfast's Linen Hall Library. We are grateful to Moon Ho Jung and Enrico Dal Lago for their incisive comments on two of the colloquium sessions, and to Richard Follett, Sharon Harley, Steven West, and all of the Wiles participants.

The second gathering was an even more ambitious undertaking, organized over a period of eighteen months from a distance of more than three thousand miles. With generous funding from the South Carolina Humanities Council, the Conference on Race, Labor and Citizenship in the Post-Emancipation South brought together more than 250 professional historians, journalists, archivists, curriculum specialists, trade union activists, and high school educators from twenty-three states in the United States and Canada, Ireland, and the United Kingdom, for twenty-four panels over three days. To put it simply, we could not have pulled off such a logistical challenge without the institutional support and the incomparable organizing skill and commitment of Simon Lewis and Lisa Randle of the Carolina Lowcountry and Atlantic World (CLAW) program at the College of Charleston. Anyone who attended the conference will remember it as a model of vibrant discussion and engaged scholarship, and we are extremely grateful to Lisa and Simon, and to Dave Gleeson, Steven Hahn, Mary Moultrie, Bernard Powers, Ken Riley, and Kerry Taylor for their help in making it such an extraordinary success.

Finally we wish to thank Professor John David Smith with the University Press of Florida, who early on saw the potential in bringing some of this work to a wider audience; to the anonymous readers who offered critical comments and confirmed his judgment; and to Sian Hunter, also at the press, who has guided the project through the labyrinth of modern publishing.

Abbreviations

AGO	Records of the Adjutant General's Office, 1762–1984 (National Archives)
ARI	Avery Research Institute
BRFAL	Records of the Bureau of Refugees, Freedmen and Abandoned Lands (National Archives)
CUA	Catholic University Archives
DUSC	Duke University, Special Collections
FHS	Filson Historical Society
FSSP	Freedmen and Southern Society Project
GDAH	Georgia Department of Archives and History
GHS	Georgia Historical Society
MDAH	Mississippi Department of Archives and History
NA	National Archives and Records Administration
NYHSL	New York Historical Society Library
NYPL	New York Public Library
OCC	Records of the Office of the Comptroller of the Currency (National Archives)
OR	The War of the Rebellion: A Compilation of the Official Records of the Union and Confederate Armies
RG	Record Group (National Archives)
SCDAH	South Carolina Department of Archives and History
SCHS	South Carolina Historical Society
SHC	Southern Historical Collection
USACC	Records of the United States Army Continental Commands, 1821–1920 (National Archives)

Introduction

BRUCE E. BAKER AND BRIAN KELLY

"In my youth, in my manhood, in my old age," Thaddeus Stevens reminisced as he rose in Congress to urge ratification of the Fourteenth Amendment, "I had fondly dreamed that when any fortunate chance should have broken up for awhile the foundations of our institutions" the nation's political leadership might seize the opportunity to "[free] them from every vestige of human oppression, of inequality of rights, of the recognized degradation of the poor, and the superior caste of the rich." Now, however, just fourteen months after Confederate surrender had sealed the end of slavery and—in the late President Abraham Lincoln's words—cleared the way for a "new birth of freedom," Stevens resigned himself to being "obliged to be content with patching up the worst portions of the ancient edifice." Already, well before the post-emancipation order had taken any definite shape in the former slave states, Stevens declared that his "bright dream had vanished 'like the baseless fabric of a vision.'"[1]

Stevens's dejection seems at first glance conspicuously out of step with the dramatic transformation unfolding before him: he was rising, after all, to lend support to the Fourteenth Amendment—acknowledged then and now as a landmark in American constitutional history and one of the enduring legislative achievements of the Reconstruction era, overturning the newly contrived "Black Codes" and extending citizenship to freed slaves formerly possessing only those rights granted at the discretion of whites. In the immediate circumstances surrounding the congressional debates, however, Stevens found grave cause for concern. A more root-and-branch overhaul of American democracy might have been possible if Lincoln's successor in the White House, Andrew Johnson, shared Stevens's vision, but the new president rejected calls for thoroughgoing reconstruction in favor of a more lenient approach to readmission of the former slave states that left them, in

Stevens's derisory appraisal, "as nearly as possible in their ancient condition." Throughout the previous summer, the Ohio-born journalist Whitelaw Reid observed, the nation's capital had been "filled with the late leaders in Rebel councils, or on Rebel battle-fields," who "filled all avenues of approach to the White House," keeping Johnson "surrounded by an atmosphere of Southern geniality, Southern prejudices, Southern aspirations." Faced with the prospect that "the seceders may soon overwhelm the loyal men in Congress," Stevens urged the "speedy adoption" of a compromise amendment that he could "not pretend to be satisfied with." "Take what we can get now," he urged fellow Republicans, "and hope for better things in further legislation."[2]

The weakening of the amendment through a series of concessions unsettled congressional Radicals,[3] but for Stevens and others this round of compromises portended a more comprehensive retreat. In the "plastic moment" following the end of the war, Reid had suggested, Washington could have "prescribed no conditions for the return of the Rebel States which they would not have promptly accepted." Former Confederates "expected nothing; were prepared for the worst; would have been thankful for anything," he wrote.[4] Faced with the energetic mobilization of freed slaves in pursuit of land and liberation, white Southerners may have viewed submission to federal authority as preferable to the unrestrained assertion of black aspirations. Through the summer and fall and into the early months of 1866, former slaves across the plantation South made plain their expansive understandings of what freedom entailed. For a while the egalitarian vision of committed Radicals matched these ground-level attempts to transform the region. Against a backdrop that saw freed slaves dividing out the plantations of their former masters, Stevens had reminded an audience in his home state of Pennsylvania that the rights of formal citizenship were meaningless without the independence that land ownership could bring. "It is impossible that any practical equality of rights can exist," he insisted in September 1865, "where a few thousand men monopolize the whole landed property."[5] Freedpeople demonstrated an intuitive grasp of this pragmatic relationship between land and freedom: "Gib us our own land and we take care of ourselves," a former slave in Charleston asserted, "but widout land, de ole massas can hire us or starve us as dey please."[6]

By early the following year, it had become increasingly clear that "the freedmen's dream of title to confiscated or abandoned land had been lost."[7] The planters' delegations that had made their way to Washington seeking an audience with Johnson found their efforts rewarded beyond their most optimistic hopes. The same president who had declared in early 1865 that "Treason must be made odious" and vowed that the "great plantations must be seized, and divided into small farms," not only brought a halt to federally sanctioned land reform; in a decision characterized by Freedmen's Bureau Commissioner Oliver Otis Howard as a "breaking of the [government's] promise,"[8] President Johnson overturned General Sherman's Special Field Orders, No. 15, ejecting freedpeople from the abandoned plantations they had claimed as their own along the Georgia and South Carolina coast and restoring the land to their returning ex-masters. Military officers and Freedmen's Bureau personnel sympathetic to the plight of former slaves did what they could to delay and obstruct the retreat; where they had the strength to resist, freedpeople attempted to hold onto what they had. Neither group could reverse the process, however, and in a war of attrition planters clearly had the upper hand. For many freedpeople and some of their allies in Washington, at least, passage of the Fourteenth Amendment revealed a glaring paradox: one of the high points in legislative triumph coincided with a sharp narrowing of the scope of freedom.

Thomas Holt's opening essay urges those of us who study Reconstruction to return to "the problem of freedom and citizenship." In its most simplistic deployment in modern popular discourse, "freedom" for African Americans is assumed to have been gifted, fully realized, at the moment of emancipation. But the anxiety felt by freedpeople and their allies in the summer of 1866 illustrates a more complicated dynamic: the meaning of freedom was vigorously, often lethally, contested in the years following the war's end; the struggle over its parameters followed a complicated and uneven trajectory; and the shifting, ever-provisional standing of the confrontation between former masters and newly freed slaves at any juncture reflected the balance of forces between these two main social forces and a long list of second- and third-string protagonists. The "concept of freedom has a history," as Holt insists—and we can trace its development both over the millennia and in the more chronologically restricted process of nineteenth-century slave emancipation. The slaves and their descendants were not mere ciphers in that evolution: by their forceful intervention they altered the meaning of freedom itself, "thrust[ing] themselves into a modern political habitus, into the world we still inhabit, and [linking] their story and struggles to our own."[9]

Scholars engaged in trying to complicate our understanding of slave emancipation and its relationship to freedom's modern history have moved along two main paths of inquiry over the past several decades. Many have been drawn to comparative methods, producing a rich historical literature on the shared and distinctive elements in post-emancipation societies across the Atlantic world and beyond. Eric Foner's 1983 essay, "The Anatomy of Emancipation," was seminal in demonstrating for North American scholars the fresh insights that a comparative framework might yield, but in the years since, his suggestive early work has been augmented by an impressive body of scholarship, the cumulative effect of which has been to establish "comparative emancipation" as a vibrant, growing field in the increasingly transnational discipline of history.

The logic of Holt's scholarship on Reconstruction moved toward the international perspective that he deploys in his essay here. His first book, *Black over White: Negro Political Leadership in South Carolina during Reconstruction* appeared in 1977, after the first wave of revisionist scholarship in the 1960s had crested. It was an important contribution to what Foner would later describe as "post-revisionist" scholarship on Reconstruction. While much other work highlighted the accomplishments and capabilities of African Americans during Reconstruction, Holt sought to answer the question of why African Americans in South Carolina, where they had the greatest numerical majority, just could not make change stick. Part of the answer, he suggested, lay in divisions within the African American community itself: divisions based on color, and class, and perhaps geography (though that is never stated as clearly). A comparative perspective underlay *Black over White*: why did some black legislators favor fundamental reform while others opposed it? Holt carried this instinct for comparison into his later work on Jamaica, and then into a jointly authored collection on post-emancipation societies that compares Jamaica, Cuba, Louisiana, and French West Africa. In his essay here, Holt carries the international and comparative frameworks he has used for more than three decades for considering slaveries and their endings backward in time, to the critical period when the modern idea of freedom was taking shape, and then forward to the present day.

The international framework advanced here by Holt and embedded in much of the recent scholarship is not entirely new, of course. Though it is a dimension of his work too often overlooked, W.E.B. Du Bois anchored his pioneering *Black Reconstruction* in an explicitly global perspective: for him, the struggles attending slave emancipation in the United States constituted a critical chapter in a wider story about race and global structures of labor exploitation at the dawn of the new industrial age. Academic historians are inclined—even trained—to react against the kinds of explicit comparisons Holt makes between the ostensibly distant and exotic social landscape of the late nineteenth century and our own age, but his observations on the persistence of unfree labor in the twenty-first century (and the attendant debates over who is entitled to the rights of citizens) resonate powerfully with Du Bois's framing of Reconstruction. "That dark and vast sea of human labor . . . that great majority of mankind," the latter wrote in 1935, "shares a common destiny . . . despised and rejected by race and color, paid a wage below the level of decent living[.] Enslaved in all but name" they gather up raw materials "at prices lowest of the low, manufactured, transformed, and transported," with the resulting wealth "distributed [and] made the basis of world power . . . in London and Paris, Berlin and Rome, New York and Rio de Janeiro." Looking out from the depths of our own global economic crisis, Du Bois's depiction of the exploitive relations between global capital and a racially stratified, multinational labor force seems more familiar than some scholars might want to acknowledge.[10]

Historians of American Reconstruction are not obliged to detail the planetary dimensions of every episode that figures in the struggles over emancipation—indeed, as most of the essays in this volume illustrate, critical insights can be gleaned from close study at the local level. But to return to the dilemma facing freedpeople and their allies in the summer of 1866, we should be mindful, at least, that the gap between emancipation's liberating promise—Stevens's "bright dream," the slaves' "jubilee"—and the harsh reality that settled over the South from the early 1870s onward is part of an important wider story with global dimensions.

The attempt to explain this disparity between promise and lived experience in historical terms has been one of the other central preoccupations in recent scholarship on Reconstruction and serves as the thread connecting the wide-ranging essays included here. The British historian W. R. Brock wrote perceptively in 1963 that the failure to remake the American South was "a part of the wider failure of bourgeois liberalism to solve the problems of the new age which was dawning." Just as in the British context formal equality under the law had proven compatible "with aristocratic privilege, an established Church, denial of suffrage to the masses, and the exploitation of low paid labour," so too in the United States the limits of the particular variant of freedom available to former slaves—and to many whites, for that matter—were circumscribed by the economic and social imperatives attending the newly emerging industrial order. Republicans "undertook to promote political equality in a society characterized by equality in almost nothing else," William McKee Evans reminds us. The experience of Reconstruction, Du Bois asserts in similar vein, exposed the fallacy in the "American Assumption" that "any average worker" could, through sustained effort, rise to the top, and in recent years a number of more tightly focused explorations of "free labor ideology" have tracked its sharp attenuation between a glorious zenith in the thick of the confrontation with proslavery forces at midcentury and its base adaptation to corporate power a few decades later.[11]

Comparative study of emancipation in the Atlantic world has lifted scholarship on the aftermath of slavery in the United States out of its former parochialism, but until recently the distinctive evolution of American historiography—and especially the aggressively racialized interpretation that dominated historical writing through the first half of the twentieth century—continued to shape the field. Du Bois launched the first comprehensive assault on what seemed, in 1935, a well-established and secure consensus, but in important ways he was compelled to construct his own interpretation on the terrain staked out by the so-called Dunning School.[12] If the "centerpiece" of its work was a "detailed [but] contemptuous portrait of the Republican state governments that flourished in the south for a time after 1867," Du Bois regarded a large part of his task as the vindication of these very same regimes. Here his conceptualizing of Reconstruction as labor history and his insistence on embedding it in a wider context of industrial transformation drove Du Bois well beyond an assault on the foundations of racist historiography, but others following in his wake remained focused on redeeming Southern Republicanism. In this work of "rehabilitation," Howard Rabinowitz observed, scholars "spent much of their time disproving the traditional characterizations" of the Republican Party—sometimes at the expense of a frank assessment of its shortcomings or a thoughtful explanation for its ultimate failure.[13] This defensiveness—the tendency among historians of Reconstruction in the postwar period to challenge its conclusions but work from within the framework laid down by the Dunning School—was inevitable, perhaps, but debilitating all the same.[14]

The forceful challenge launched by Du Bois and a small number of lesser-known historians caught little traction in or beyond academic circles before midcentury.[15] Early revisionist work by Howard K. Beale, and later John Hope Franklin and Kenneth Stampp, found a wider resonance. But when Eric Foner writes in the afterword to this volume that his *Reconstruction: America's Unfinished Revolution, 1863–1877* (1988) came after "an incredibly creative thirty-year period of scholarship on Reconstruction," he is referring in the main to work informed and often directly inspired by the emergence of the modern civil rights movement. The remarkable upheaval of the 1960s reshaped historical writing on the period in two important ways. Its most demonstrable effect was to undermine the racist foundations of the Dunning School. Infrequently acknowledged but no less important was the conceptual shift that these events encouraged—away from the concentration on political and economic elites underpinning "consensus" history and toward an expansive vision of social history "from below." Both of these trends were evident in the revisionist scholarship dating from the late 1960s, and their enduring influence is evident throughout this volume.[16]

Combining a sure command of the vast scholarly literature and easy fluency with the archival sources, Foner consummated the challenge to the Dunning School initiated by Du Bois a half century earlier and reinvigorated by the resurgent challenge to Jim Crow after the mid-1950s. But where Du Bois seems to have felt obliged to devote considerable effort to extolling the accomplishments of the Republican Party in the South, Foner adopts a more critical stance. Acknowledging both the party's achievements and the difficult context in which it maneuvered, he nevertheless shares the thrust of the "post-revisionist" critique, which attributes at least part of the blame for Reconstruction's collapse on the "cautious and unimaginative" bearing of the Republicans themselves. Paradoxically, the scale of Eric Foner's feat in crafting what Michael Perman has called "the mature and settled Revisionist perspective" on Reconstruction presents a conundrum for scholars eager to break new ground. The difficulties of mapping out a productive agenda for new research in the wake of Foner's achievement were plainly evident to Perman: if in the process of "conclud[ing] a phase of historiographical reconsideration" Foner's synthesis had managed to "reconcile controversies that had seemed impossible to settle," he wondered, "it does raise one unsettling question and leave it unanswered—what is left to be done?"[17]

Historians did not have to wait long for an answer. In his prize-winning *A Nation under Our Feet: Black Political Struggles in the Rural South from Slavery to the Great Migration* (2003), Steven Hahn offered a robust and compelling reinterpretation, demonstrating that there was life in the field even yet. Based, like Foner's work, on an extraordinary grasp of wide-ranging archival sources, Hahn called for a radical reframing of Reconstruction as a link in the long chain of continuities connecting black working-class aspirations from the late antebellum period to the upheaval brought on by World War I. Deeply skeptical of the "liberal integrationist" perspective he perceives in much of the post–civil-rights-era scholarship—and, implicitly, in Foner's interpretation—Hahn emphasized the durability of black agency, the centrality and resilience of kinship and community networks, and an enduring propensity toward black autonomy over a narrative constructed around the privileging of formal politics and African Americans' struggle for citizenship and assimilation.[18]

It remains to be seen whether *A Nation under Our Feet* will generate a new body of scholarship specific to Reconstruction where, after all, historians have long acknowledged the centrality of freedpeople's agency, the quest for autonomy, and the enduring (or intermittent) appeal of black nationalism.[19] For all its power in illuminating the inner world of an important strand of grassroots black politics, Hahn's focus leads away from exploring other neglected problems in the historiography of Reconstruction. The field has seen a steady output of studies emphasizing freedpeople's agency, but little acknowledgment until recently that there were limits to the former slaves' power to remake their world.[20] Likewise, while the historical record contains numerous examples of freedpeople's attempts to assert their autonomy, there are important arenas (formal politics, for example) where they pursued meaningful collaboration with whites, as in the ranks of the Republican Party or the Union League movement. In the highly polarized, often violent atmosphere of the mid-1870s, racial unity could be critical to the survival of freedpeople's communities, but this solidarity was complicated by the increasing social stratification pervading black neighborhoods across the South. "Class has been taboo in Afro-American history," Nell Painter wrote a quarter century ago. Scholars shied away from engaging with the problem of intraracial conflict, she asserted, "for fear of opening a Pandora's box of racial disunity,"[21] a reluctance that does not seem to have abated in the years since.

The After Slavery Project, a transatlantic research collaboration that organized the two conferences from which this collection grew,[22] developed out of a growing sense that even as W.E.B. Du Bois was being widely venerated as the progenitor of a new history of emancipation in the United States, his insistence on understanding Reconstruction as a critical chapter in *the history of the American working class* was lost sight of. If, as Holt has insisted elsewhere, "the social relations of labor constitute the starting point for any examination of the Afro-American experience,"[23] we thought it worthwhile to return to the set of class- and labor-related problems that had been too frequently neglected in much of the newer scholarship on Reconstruction. Wholly sympathetic to the call to place slaves and freedpeople at the very center of our understanding of this period, we were at the same time mindful of the constraints under which they struggled to remake their world, and were determined to acknowledge both the agency of freedmen and women in "making their own history" *and* the restrictions on their room for maneuver. After an extremely productive period of research for the wider field, we reasoned, it might now be possible to move beyond broad generalizations about "black life" in the Reconstruction South and begin to map the contours of a varied experience among freedpeople in diverse geographical and demographic settings, in a variety of crop cultures, and carrying into their struggles an uneven heritage of labor and political mobilization.

The result is a collection of research essays that do not necessarily speak to a single shared theme but are constructed around innovative approaches to some of the central problems of Reconstruction. One striking aspect of the collection is the sheer variety of local experience during Reconstruction: the possibilities open to freedpeople in early postwar southern Louisiana or Wilmington, North Carolina, are impressive when set against the harshly unfavorable context of Kentucky or upcountry South Carolina. With their adversaries across the region determined to root out "erroneous" and "exaggerated" notions of freedom, freedpeople's capacity to shape the postbellum order depended, Erik Mathisen and Gregory Downs suggest, on their ability to secure the support of influential whites. In Mississippi, former slaves (and whites) did this through "leveraging their loyalty in return for federal protection and civic rights," Mathisen argues, while in North Carolina, according to Downs, freedpeople practiced a "politics of territoriality," seeking powerful guardians in the state apparatus to compensate for their lack of power on the ground. Both essays compel us not only to think in new ways about the role of the state after emancipation but also to consider whether freedpeople's agency has been overstated in much of the recent literature.

Freedpeople may have looked to the Reconstruction state for protection and social advance, several essays suggest, but they were often bitterly disappointed by its indifference and ineffectiveness. If, as Foner has suggested, "the state had become . . . for a time[,] a battleground between former master and former slave,"[24] it mattered a great deal whether military commanders or state or federal officials were energetic in upholding freedpeople's new rights or acquiescent in the face of white attempts to resubordinate freed men and women. It mattered also whether federal authorities were able to assert their supremacy over local government, which often remained in the hands of bellicose Confederates long after they'd been swept from the battlefield. While black Mississippians were trying to attach themselves to a "powerful, centralized state" to shore up their claims to property, Downs argues that the machinery put in place to oversee Reconstruction in North Carolina was weak and ineffectual, an assessment very close to the one advanced by J. Michael Rhyne for Kentucky. Theirs are hardly novel judgments, but Downs's central argument goes one step further, attributing the failings of Reconstruction neither to racism among federal officials nor to black disaffection with the inadequacies of the free labor vision, but to bureaucratic inertia—to a lack of "efficacy." Intentionality doesn't figure in the balance sheet for Downs—a finding that sets his work off from the conventional wisdom permeating revisionist scholarship; the will was there on the part of Northern officials but, in his rendering, they lacked the power to guarantee a new dawn for black Americans.

In other settings across the South, freedpeople were either able to assert themselves more aggressively or their capacity to shape the new order changed over time. Often these variations had to do with a particular confluence of local conditions. The presence in New Orleans of a radicalized Afro-Creole artisan class, James Illingworth argues, invigorated links between urban workers and plantation laborers, and between slaves and freeborn men of color. Radicalism in southern Louisiana's sugar parishes moved back and forth between the city and the countryside, producing a cross-fertilization that deepened freedpeople's resistance in both spheres. Illingworth is interested in the role of the state as well, though in his rendering freedmen are not so much supplicating themselves to more powerful allies as taking advantage of the Radicals' ascent at Washington to confer legitimacy upon militant strikes and other forms of grassroots mobilization.

Plantation-rooted, plebeian radicalism seems to have found its way into the rice fields below Savannah, Georgia, by late 1868 as laborers there—both male and female—challenged the planters' prerogatives through the organization of a Loyal League, the launch of a series of strikes, and other acts of defiance. Jonathan Bryant cuts through the layers of misrepresentation and fear-mongering by which white conservatives—prominent ex-Confederates among them—tried to inflame the situation, revealing that at its core the much-hyped "Ogeechee insurrection" amounted to a labor dispute pitting radicalized laborers against ex-masters outraged at the "insolence" of their former property.

It was the proslavery citadel of Charleston, South Carolina, that most resembled antebellum New Orleans in containing both a large slave majority—based mainly on outlying cotton and rice plantations—and a numerically small but influential class of freeborn blacks and mulattoes. As Holt demonstrated in his important (but too frequently neglected) *Black over White,* intraracial relations took on a very different aspect in post-emancipation Charleston, where the gap between the city's "brown elite" and lowcountry plantation slaves persisted throughout Reconstruction. Brian Kelly traces some of these tensions between the high point of black laborers' mobilization in early Reconstruction and its denouement after 1877, suggesting that the restoration of white "home rule" was "felt most acutely by the predominantly working-class constituency whose grassroots mobilization powered the Radical project" in the immediate aftermath of Confederate defeat. The labor mobilizations that sent white elites in the southern sugar parishes and its cotton and rice belts into such a panic in the mid- and late-1860s would become rare by the mid-1870s, as conservatives returned to power in one state after another and the room for laborers' militancy narrowed or disappeared. The rice plantations below Charleston were exceptional, with labor militancy persisting even beyond Redemption.[25]

Freedwomen figure briefly in examinations of rice-field militancy in Georgia and South Carolina, but more prominently in the essays by Rhyne and Susan Eva O'Donovan. In Kentucky, a Union state where, paradoxically, jubilee arrived late and in hushed tones, families bore the brunt of white violence, and freedwomen and children seem to have been especially vulnerable. Returning Confederates and white wartime Unionists alike made it difficult for parents to "reclaim their children from former masters"; forced apprenticeship figured prominently among the grievances of the ex-slave community, calling into question both the authority and commitment of a Freedmen's Bureau steeped in Northern, middle class assumptions about the "legitimacy" of black family life. By O'Donovan's account, black Wilmington's rootedness and stability, the inheritance bequeathed by its antebellum black community to freedom's first generation, provided tangible protection to freedwomen and their families and "gave structure and strength to their 'earliest collective activities and formal organizations.'"

While Reconstruction offered opportunities to many, it brought disappointment to many more, both black and white. To understand why the South's "ancient edifice" of race and class privilege remained largely intact, it is not enough to uncover the various explanations for why the region's minority of African Americans were unable to transform it. We must at the same time account for why such a negligible proportion of the region's white majority were willing to cast their lot with the Republican Party. In the forcefully presented closing chapter of his *Black Reconstruction*, Du Bois exposed the racial malice animating those historians who had contributed to the flawed foundations of early twentieth-century Reconstruction historiography. But he noted also their class bias, pointing out that for all their attachment to white supremacy they had made "little attempt" to explore "the rise and economic development of the poor whites and their relation to the planters and to Negro labor after the war."[26]

The revisionist scholarship on which Foner built his new synthesis discredited popular and scholarly assumptions about black racial inferiority, but it made little substantial impact on our understanding of the predicament of poor whites, too often relegating them to the role of atavistic obstacles to black aspiration and primarily as members of the Ku Klux Klan. There have been some modest advances in recent years, though the late Armstead Robinson's lament that "historians [too] often assume the nonviability of biracial politics" seems no less valid today than it did when he wrote it more than thirty years ago. If in turning their backs on the possibilities of thoroughgoing reform the Republicans had let down their black supporters, as Kelly suggests in South Carolina, the same turn may have simultaneously closed off possibilities for building an active and engaged constituency among nonelite whites. In Georgia, Robinson concluded, the party leadership "expressed reservations about the largely working-class nature of their [bi-racial] coalition"; its decision to stake the party's hopes on the "'New South' commercial and industrial elite" around Governor Joseph Brown accelerated the Republicans' collapse among the white yeomanry.[27]

Michael Fitzgerald uses modern research resources to get a clearer profile of Ku Klux Klan membership in Reconstruction Alabama and to offer a tentative explanation for their motivations. A substantial part of the Klan's membership there appears to have been among the "downwardly mobile sons of middling slaveholders" rather than among the white rabble popularly associated with bitter-end white supremacy. Their expectations of mastership were dashed with the end of slavery, and the changes wrought by Reconstruction offered nothing to replace those hopes. More pertinent to Robinson's conclusions about Georgia, Bruce Baker explains why poor whites in the South Carolina mountains abandoned the Republican Party after an initial period of favorable consideration in the early aftermath of the war. Like their counterparts in North Carolina, white mountain Republicans in the Palmetto State found themselves the victims not so much of Democratic onslaught as the contradictory and self-defeating policies of their own party. As railroads supported by local and national Republicans disrupted traditional modes of subsistence, the party leaders dominating state politics increased taxes on these cash-strapped mountaineers to pay for the railroad bonds, and Republican federal revenue agents began arresting illicit distillers among the party's mountain constituency. The success of the Democrats' appeal by 1876 is hardly surprising, therefore, even without considering their open resort to racism.

The essays collected here suggest that Perman's concern that with Foner's 1988 synthesis Reconstruction had become a "finished revolution" was premature. And while Hahn's important study presents a compelling new synthesis organized around the quest for African-American autonomy, the field remains very much open, with critical problems unresolved and research on some key issues still surprisingly undeveloped. Recent scholarship looks to the influences on Reconstruction from beyond the South and outside the United States, just as it also extends its scope backward in time to the Civil War and ahead to the beginning of the twentieth century. If the work carried out by scholars through much of the twentieth century tried to establish once and for all the significant role of former slaves in shaping Reconstruction, there were outlying strands of scholarship that posed questions about other aspects of the period that were too seldom reflected in the dominant syntheses of the time. Historians today are following those threads in new directions, revealing their connections to stories we are already familiar with. In other cases, old topics yield new insights through the application of different techniques to sources (as in O'Donovan's innovative use of Freedman's Bank records to develop a profile of Wilmington's black community), or sometimes through simply asking novel questions. Perhaps it makes more sense to view Reconstruction historiography not as a field in search of a new synthesis, but as one which has at long last moved beyond the distractions imposed by the debate over Dunning, now reopened to a new generation of scholars and citizens who will bring questions of their own to this critical chapter in the American past.

Notes

1. Senator Thaddeus Stevens in Cong. Globe, 39th Cong., 1st Sess. (13 June 1866), 3148.

2. Ibid.; Reid, *After the War*, 314.

3. Stevens was mainly concerned with changes to the third section of the amendment, which in his words had been "wholly changed by substituting the ineligibility of certain high offenders for the disfranchisement of all rebels until 1870," a modification that "endanger[ed] the Government of the country, both State and national" and might "give the next Congress and President to the reconstructed rebels."

4. Reid, *After the War*, 296.

5. "Hon. Thaddeus Stevens on the Great Topic of the Hour. An Address Delivered to the Citizens of Lancaster, Sept. 6, 1865," *New York Times*, 10 September 1865.

6. Reid, *After the War*, 59. See also "Edisto Freedpeople's Committee to General O. O. Howard, Freedmen's Bureau," 20 or 21 October 1865, in *Freedom*, edited by Hahn et al., 440–41; Powell, *New Masters*, 101.

7. Syrett, *Civil War Confiscation Acts*, 151.

8. Johnson used the phrase "Treason must be made odious" as part of a stump speech he gave regularly on the campaign trail during the 1864 elections. See "Our Next Vice-

President; Speech of Gov. Johnson at Nashville," *New York Times*, 16 June 1864; Howard to Stanton, 24 November 1865, in U.S. Congress, *Message from the President*, 8.

9. See in addition to his essay here Holt, *Problem of Freedom*.

10. Du Bois, *Black Reconstruction*, 15–16. For further discussion of Du Bois's international perspective, see Cedric J. Robinson, *Black Marxism*, 185–240.

11. Brock, *An American Crisis*, 289; William McKee Evans, *Ballots and Fence Rails*, 251; Du Bois, *Black Reconstruction*, 182–85. On free labor ideology see Foner, *Free Soil, Free Labor, Free Men*; Montgomery, *Beyond Equality*; Heather Cox Richardson, *Death of Reconstruction*.

12. See Dunning, *Reconstruction, Political and Economic*.

13. McCrary, "Political Dynamics of Black Reconstruction," 51; Rabinowitz, ed., *Southern Black Leaders of the Reconstruction Era*; Moneyhon, "Failure of Southern Republicanism," 107.

14. The tendency is evident in Du Bois's early *Atlantic Monthly* article on the history of the Freedmen's Bureau. In places he concedes too much to prevailing Dunningite prejudices: former masters "were peremptorily ordered about," Du Bois contends, "and punished over and again, with scant courtesy from army officers," while bureau officials were "too often found striving to put the 'bottom rail on top,' [giving] the freedmen a power and independence which they could not yet use." While neither assertion would withstand much scrutiny today, their inclusion in an essay aimed at exalting the Freedmen's Bureau for having been "successful beyond the dreams of thoughtful men" demonstrates the pervasive influence of the Dunning School, even among those eager to challenge its dominance. Du Bois, "Freedman's Bureau," 354–65; quote from p. 362. Du Bois presented a more nuanced appraisal of bureau operations in *Black Reconstruction*, 220–30.

15. An exception is its resonance in Popular Front historiography. See Baker, *What Reconstruction* Meant, 125–44, and Kelly, introduction to *Labor, Free and Slave*, by Mandel (2007).

16. A quarter century ago Holt suggested that "the biases that left slaves, as people, out of the history of slavery were not simply racial. They more often had to do with what could be considered legitimate and illegitimate sources." He noted the "striking similarities in the problems of sources confronted by students of women's history, working-class history, or that of cultures that left no written records." See Holt, "Whither Now and Why?," 7.

17. Perman, "Eric Foner's Reconstruction," 74, 77–78.

18. Hahn, *A Nation under Our Feet*.

19. Holt wrote more than twenty-five years ago that "the nationalist orientation of so many fourth-generation scholars might involve a reaction to the negative implications of integration." See Holt, "Whither Now and Why?," 2. In some ways Hahn's study provides a useful corollary to recent scholarship on the "long black power movement." See for example Joseph, *Waiting 'Til the Midnight Hour*. For critical reviews of *A Nation under Our Feet* see Holt, "Review of *Nation under Our Feet*"; Kelly, "Review of *Nation under Our Feet*"; and Lichtenstein, "Roots of Black Nationalism?"

20. Peter Coclanis offers a robust, even caustic critique of the tendency to exaggerate agency in "Slavery, African American Agency, and the World We Have Lost." Exceptions

to this trend include O'Donovan, *Becoming Free in the Cotton South* and Downs, *Declarations of Dependence*. See also Rodrigue, "Black Agency after Slavery," 40–65, and Kelly, "Labor and Place," 653–87, and Follett et al., *Slavery's Ghost*.

21. Painter, comment on "The Difference Freedom Made," by Armstead L. Robinson, 83.

22. The After Slavery Project website is available at http://www.afterslavery.com. See the acknowledgments of this volume for details of the project-sponsored conferences.

23. Holt, "Whither Now and Why?," 3.

24. Foner, *Nothing but Freedom*, 3.

25. John Rodrigue finds a similar persistence in the Louisianan sugar parishes, culminating in the hard-fought 1878 strike. See Rodrigue, *Reconstruction in the Cane Fields*.

26. Du Bois, *Black Reconstruction*, 721.

27. Armstead L. Robinson, "Beyond the Realm of Social Consensus," 279, 283. See also his, "The Difference Freedom Made," 51–74.

1

Slave and Citizen in the Modern World

Rethinking Emancipation in the Twenty-First Century

THOMAS C. HOLT

On a Saturday evening, in April 1793, several hundred black slaves near the village of Trois-Rivières, on the French West Indian colony of Guadeloupe, rose in revolt against their enslavers, killing twenty-two of them. After laying waste to several of the properties, they organized themselves into quasi-military units, posted sentries to secure the estates, and sent a detachment marching toward Basse-Terre, the island capital. As they approached the town they encountered French soldiers, who having been alerted to the revolt, had set out to put it down. When the two groups came within firing range of each other, a soldier called out "Who goes there?" To which one of the blacks responded, "Citizens and friends!" A squad of French soldiers approached the slave rebels and began questioning them: Are you citizens? Are you patriots, they asked? "We are friends," a rebel replied, "we have come to save you, and hate only those aristocrats who want to kill you. . . . We want to fight for the Republic, the law, the nation, [and] order." Then followed an extraordinary scene, in which black slave rebels and French soldiers marched into the provincial capital as comrades in arms, shouting "Vive la République." Although it would take another half century before slavery was finally abolished in France's American empire, events that evening played a small role in setting the course for that emancipation. France abolished slavery permanently in 1848, in the midst of yet another revolutionary upheaval at home.[1]

If we were to fast-forward two centuries, we would find ourselves at the celebration of the 150th anniversary of that latter event. It was a celebration made even more notable because the French press subjected it to a rather bold scrutiny, pointing out, for example, that this was *the first time* that the anniversary of emancipation had been acknowledged in quite a while, possibly because it raised such embarrassing questions about the nation's founding traditions. For while citizens of France could be proud that their national revolution had lent decisive support to the slaves' resistance and the overthrow of colonial slavery, they must hang their heads in shame that with the revolution's unraveling, slavery had been reinstated just eight years later (in 1802) and allowed to endure for another generation. The French Revolution initiated liberty and citizenship for all, and yet in the end, it left millions in bondage.[2]

Correcting this neglect at long last, Jacques Chirac—the conservative president of the republic in 1998—marked the anniversary of emancipation by intoning a tribute whose themes many will recognize as echoes of Latin American historian Frank Tannenbaum's seminal work, *Slave and Citizen*. In his 1947 book, Tannenbaum had argued that the true measure of the severity of a slave system was the degree to which it recognized what he called "the moral personality" of the slave and thus smoothed the path to the ex-slaves' eventual acceptance as a citizen.[3] President Chirac invoked a similar gauge to assess French emancipation. In 1848, he declared, the emancipated slave passed rapidly to assume his role and identity as a "citizen" of France, a fluid transition for which the nation should feel proud; here was a fitting emblem for their nation's special capacity to integrate foreigners into "Frenchness." But when Chirac's bold words appeared in *Le Monde* the next day, they were juxtaposed with a cartoon of a black figure, with each hand manacled. On one side, a chain that had bound him to a white slave master, labeled "1848," was broken; on the other side, however, he was fastened to a departing airplane by an *unbroken* chain, labeled "1998." What this cartoon signified was the fact that at the very moment Chirac spoke, his administration was embroiled in a heated controversy over the nation's policy of deporting refugees from France's former African colonies. Even then a small group of these "sans papiers," as they were called (meaning those without legal entry documents), had barricaded themselves in a Catholic Church seeking asylum. Many others, however, were being rounded up daily and sent "home."[4]

Thousands of French people—along with a sprinkling of other nationals (including me)—took to the streets to protest this blatantly two-faced policy of Chirac's government. But, in fact, asylum and *manifestation*, were just the latest of many acts of solidarity with the beleaguered Africans. In his remarkable book, *A Colony of Citizens*, historian Laurent Dubois described a poignant public ritual in the little town hall of Pantin, a village just outside Paris, on 30 June 1997. The assistant mayor there, a Socialist and thus opposed to Chirac's government, donning the tricolor slash that is the emblem of the

Republic and of his official authority, received ten *sans-papiers*, one by one, into the hall of justice. There, two French citizens, who declared their wish to become godparents of these undocumented aliens, accompanied each of them. Though undertaken as a practical act aimed at facilitating resistance to deportation, the assumption of godparentage was also an act heavily freighted with symbolism. The alien was being taken into the family: both the personal family of his or her sponsor and the larger national family. In many ways, then, this act of adoption echoed the bold greeting and hopes of the rebels at Trois-Rivières two centuries earlier: to be "citizens" and "friends."[5]

Meanwhile, on the other side of the Atlantic and almost exactly three years before the *sans-papiers* controversy brought Jacques Chirac's conservative government to the brink of crisis, the *Los Angeles Times* broke a story about a sweatshop uncovered in El Monte, a suburb of Los Angeles, California. A group of more than seventy Mexican and Thai women were found working under conditions that the reporter could only describe as "slave-like." Deprived of physical mobility and effectively of actual wages, they labored to manufacture luxury goods for the shelves of some of America's most famous fashion emporiums—Macy's, Lord & Taylor's, and other retailers.[6]

What was especially striking about this incident, however, was that some weeks later a suit was brought on behalf of these workers based on the constitutional prohibition against "involuntary labor" under the Thirteenth Amendment.[7] Less than half a decade before America celebrated the dawn of the twenty-first century, therefore, a charge of slavery was being adjudicated in a federal court. *What next? Was it possible that a twentieth-century Dred Scott decision was in the making?* Would these undocumented, American *sans-papiers* be declared to have no rights that the native-born were bound to respect?

Fortunately, matters did not take that bizarre turn. But it has turned out that the 1995 Los Angeles case was simply the first of many such cases exposed over the waning years of the twentieth century. Almost every major American vendor of clothing was implicated at one time or another. The factories were found in hovels in forbidden corners of our major cities and in elaborate offshore installations, like the one uncovered in the American-controlled Marianas. In the latter location there was a further twist, suggesting a global, multinational character of such enterprises reminiscent of the days of the trans-Atlantic slave trade. For in the Marianas case, the factory—though on American soil—was being run by Chinese entrepreneurs, who brought in Asian labor from impoverished countries along the Pacific Rim. Meanwhile, much closer to home, other Chinese entrepreneurs—some U.S. citizens, some not—operated similar factories in the Sunset Park district of Brooklyn, New York.[8]

Invoking the emotionally charged phrase "slave trade" is not hyperbole, nor is the comparison intended as some kind of shock tactic. Often when we tender a comparison of something contemporary with slavery it is merely a rhetorical flourish intended to render the referenced practice beyond the pale, by associating it with something immediately recognized as archaic. In such cases, the rhetorical device relies on the assumption that our temporal distance from slavery will shock us into action. But, of course, it also assumes that we are no longer within the same historical field of reference as slavery. That is, that that bygone era shares nothing in common with the reality of our present.

By contrast, in many of these cases—as the legal suits invoking the Thirteenth Amendment attest—the association is quite literal. Workers toiled behind locked doors of hovels with unbelievable sanitary facilities. They had to get permission to go to the toilet, and did so under utterly humiliating surveillance. Although ostensible wage-workers, their wages were not only pressed toward subsistence levels but oftentimes were reduced further by various ploys (such as manipulating the time or not paying for production below the set quota), and those devices sometimes left the worker with no wages at all.[9]

It seems justified in this instance, therefore, to claim a more literal comparison rather than a rhetorical one. And not so much for its shock value—although that, too, would not be a bad thing—but rather to try to refine the questions we might ask of ourselves, to gain a more reflexive insight into some of the contradictions of our current moment, by the discursive act of distancing ourselves from that moment. One way to do this, perhaps, is to ask why such "anomalies" as slave-like labor should occur in our otherwise progressive democratic era, when the notion of an ever-expanding freedom is the staple of American political discourse. What if we propose the contrary, heretical notion that cases of labor exploitation like that uncovered in Los Angeles are of a piece with that seemingly ancient labor flow we know as the international slave trade and that our current moral and political dilemmas about its resolution are continuous with those that our predecessors confronted when trying to imagine the world that would follow upon the abolition of the slave labor system.

Like Thomas Jefferson's famous "firebell in the night," these revelations awaken us to the fault lines in our vaunted self-image of progress and modernity, to the archaic forms of human relations that are dogging our steps into the twenty-first century. They surely underscore the necessity for reflection and mobilization to correct the sins of our present—of our here and now. In a collection focused on nineteenth-century emancipation, however, they might suggest an opportunity—perhaps even an obligation—to refine if not recast our inquiries of that earlier moment. Therefore, I will be attempting to parse the complex meanings that I think these vignettes illuminate about the historical umbilical cord that links our present moment with that of those rebel slaves at Trois-Rivières two centuries ago; the multivocality of the declaration of godparentage by the French friends of the *sans-papiers* just a decade ago, which, I will argue, echoes down the centuries an essential aspect of citizenship in the modern nation-state; and most of all, something of the complex meanings, the antinomies of freedom and citizenship in the modern world, which first emerged in nineteenth-century emancipation campaigns and that persist in many ways into our present.

Freedom as a Problematic

My particular preoccupations here have grown out of my earlier work on slave emancipation; work in which I struggled to comprehend freedom as a conceptual and historical problem. It soon came to me that these were not just discrete problems soluble by ever more intensive research, but part of a larger *problématique,* though as yet a still undefined one. That is to say, as distinct from a *problem,* which is a question looking for an answer, a *problématique* (as I use the term here) is a terrain of inquiry or conceptual field for which the appropriate researchable questions may still need to be formulated.[10] Strictly—or formally—speaking the *problématique* provides the conceptual framework for the formulation of the problems. Of course, sometimes we are alerted to the need for a new conceptual schema in the first place because of empirical anomalies that demand answers. Either way, many of the most pervasive and enduring problems of the human experience—and the problem of race and gender come readily to mind—cannot and will not be solved simply by the accumulation of new facts. More often than not, their solution requires of us a radical and rigorous reexamination of those conceptual frames within which our empirical questions are posed. Reckoning with the problem of freedom and citizenship in the modern world is one such issue.

Certainly, when I began my own academic career, the *problématique* guiding studies of the Reconstruction period in the United States were very different. At that time, the study of the post-emancipation period had little of the incredible energy that then animated slavery studies. Enlivened by the various contemporary political controversies for which slavery was presumed to hold answers, historians dived into such tempests as that swirling around Daniel Patrick Moynihan's infamous claims about the weakness of black family traditions (which generally were presumed to date from slavery), or they took on the dubious arguments of others that slavery had destroyed any cultural basis for African American political solidarity and resistance and thereby compromised contemporary freedom struggles.[11]

By contrast, the freedom that followed slavery seemed relatively static as a field of inquiry. Contrasting sharply with slavery studies, which had been profoundly reshaped in the 1960s and 1970s by a comparative or cross-national perspective, studies of the post-emancipation era remained relatively provincial—hewing closely to the American national narrative. For students of slavery, it was merely the endpoint of a heroic struggle. While its temporal frame for many students of Reconstruction was as the distant prelude of the mid-twentieth-century civil rights movement. Its significance lay mainly in the legal precedents it established and the national promise it proffered that would finally be redeemed, belatedly, in our own time, one hundred years late: what Martin Luther King Jr. once referred to as *the unredeemed blank check of American democracy*. In a strange reversal of what one might have expected, therefore, the story of slavery took the uplifting form of a romance, while that of its aftermath was sketched in the more somber hues of tragedy and betrayal, in Langston Hughes's memorable phrase, a festering "dream deferred."[12]

But why, I asked, should one feel compelled to return to the days of slavery to address contemporary issues of African American life and culture, family and politics, ideology and belief? Surely what happened *after* slavery also mattered to the formation of our present. Somehow, in my view, to think otherwise seemed to freeze black folk in time—ever emergent from that prior formative moment. Indeed, many of my contemporaries went even further, skipping over slavery as well to find the roots of African America in an African past beyond memory. What was needed it seemed to me—though I hardly had the language to articulate it at the time—was to reexamine freedom itself, not just as an era in time, but as a conceptual whole, as a system of social relations in its own right, as a moment of formation relevant to the twentieth century and beyond. Indeed, one perhaps even more relevant than slavery to our present predicament. Much of the work I have undertaken over the intervening years has been aimed more or less at that larger goal. I'd like to sketch in bold strokes how further work in this vein might be imagined. How one might frame a study of emancipation that speaks to issues of freedom and citizenship in the twenty-first century.

Of Slavery and Freedom

"Freedom" is a word rife with ambiguity and contradiction, even in the more learned and careful discourse of scholars. Fortunately, we are now blessed with a considerable body of historical work—notably by David Brion Davis, Eric Foner, Ira Berlin, and others—with which to frame its problematic, to elaborate the conceptual architecture of the problem of freedom in the modern world.[13] What all of this work underscores, I think, is that the concept of freedom has a history, and thus it is not some innate, transcendent quality of the human spirit, floating above particular histories. It is important, then, that we recognize how slave emancipation in the nineteenth century marked a radical break in that history, a breach in the conceptual framework that reframed freedom's very conditions of possibility. The rebel slaves at Trois-Rivières sensed as much. When hailed by the French troops ("Who goes there!"), they answered, "citizens."

No longer slaves, not simply free men, but *citizens*. Thus they marked a caesura, a rupture in the long history of slavery in that forever after slave rebellions would move or would seek to move along that same trajectory. By 1947, as the title of Tannenbaum's seminal book suggests, this trajectory would announce itself as normal, expected, the only way to inhabit a true and meaningful freedom. This had not always been so, however.

Before the modern era, release from slavery was hardly tantamount to passage into freedom as we now understand it. One certainly did not become a citizen, or even a whole free agent in the arrangement of one's economic and social affairs. One simply moved into a niche within a social hierarchy—taking one's place along a kind of continuum of social status framed and anchored by lordship and bondage. Indeed, Orlando Patterson's broad survey of slave systems has enhanced our appreciation for how thoroughly the manumission of slaves in the premodern world was simply the other side of the coin of bondage.[14] In fact, successful slave governance everywhere continued to depend on the safety valve of manumission. (In much the same way that the management of prisoners today depends on the possibility of eventual parole.) James Madison, the fourth president of the United States and a prominent Virginia slaveholder, was quite explicit on the subject when he discussed the political calculus of slaveholding. Slavery could not survive without manumission, he wrote one of his relatives in December 1785, and the "fools" in the Virginia legislature bent on restricting the master's right to free his slaves were merely hastening the day of total emancipation. They believed that reducing the numbers of free blacks by making manumission more difficult would make them safe, he fumed, but their actions would reap exactly the opposite of the security they sought.[15]

Madison's insight is confirmed by the management of diverse slave systems throughout the hemisphere. Though often phrased as a master's bounty for faithful service, manumission was more often than not a reciprocal exchange transaction anticipating something in return, usually his or her future service and fealty. Thus even the foolish slaveholders of whom James Madison complained, who did not appreciate the utility of manumission as a safety valve in the workings of bondage, were probably well aware of its usefulness in enhancing labor exploitation. For example, there is ample evidence that ostensibly free manumissions in Brazil—which had the largest free black population in the hemisphere—were more often than not conditioned on the recipient continuing his or her labor service to the owner's estate and/or to his or her heirs. Indeed, such conditional manumissions became a favored legal ruse, enabling slave owners to pass on an inheritance that could not be legally seized for debt under Brazilian law. Far from being a radical break with slavery, therefore, this "freedom" was more a continued subordination and exploitation under different rules. All in all, one historian has concluded, black ex-slaves in Brazil did not become citizens, they simply became *ex*-slaves.[16]

It is now widely acknowledged that during the Age of Revolution, Western ideas about slavery and freedom were radically transformed. We also know, as Benedict Anderson has famously argued, that this era would witness a conceptual revolution in statecraft, one in which the very nature of the western nation-state—the very premise of what constituted a nation—was fundamentally altered.[17] These parallel developments intersected to reframe the meaning and import of freeing a slave.

Positing that the modern nation is not a historical given, but the product of social-historical processes, Anderson muses about the problem of rendering the new nation-state "emotionally plausible" as well as "politically viable," once the comforting hierarchies of aristocratic lineage had been stripped away. Given the sheer emotional novelty of the modern nation-state, therefore, the capacity to think and feel "nation-ness" only became possible through a radical change of consciousness, a changed sense of space and time, and thus of social relations. Separation from king and country required a new consciousness of "*we-ness*"—one premised quite literally on novel criteria: not ancient lineage and not obeisance and fealty to an aristocratic polity. People must now picture themselves as part of a physical and conceptual abstraction, their loyalties, allegiances, and social ties mediated not in face-to-face interactions or embedded in a political-religious hierarchical order. The nation must be *imagined* as a horizontal plane rather than a vertical ladder.[18] Thus, the relationship among those admitted within its bounded space was fundamentally transformed, with significant implications for decisions about who was in and who was outside.

This change not only had profound practical implications for the emancipation of slaves, it raised the stakes. Whether acknowledged by contemporaries or not, it posed Tannenbaum's question: Could the former slave also be a citizen? Were the qualities of character that made one suitable for subordinated, "cheap" labor an insuperable barrier to acceptance as an equal member of the polity? Of course, these questions were somewhat muted in many Atlantic world polities because most of their white population did not yet occupy equal standing in the political process. But over time, they rose to the surface of political discourse everywhere.

When the rebels on Guadeloupe demanded to be recognized as citizens, therefore, they thrust themselves into a modern political habitus, into the world we still inhabit, and they linked their story and struggles to our own. Their action reframed both how we might understand the stakes of their and other slave's bids for freedom and how we might articulate the tensions between labor recruitment and citizenship in our own historical moment, when the modern nation-state's need for the free movement of labor can be antithetical to the worker's claims to citizenship.

Of Freedom and Slavery

To explore this theme, let us return to my second vignette, the case of the "slaves" uncovered in those Los Angeles sweatshops, but taking this case not simply as rhetorical ammunition against contemporary capitalism but as part of a larger, more fundamental dynamic. The geopolitical conjunctures in this scenario are all too familiar to students of the evolution and destruction of the Atlantic slave labor system. As was the case with slave labor—and with the indentured labor of East Indian and Chinese immigrants recruited to fill the void in many American societies after slavery was abolished (Jamaica, Trinidad, Guyana, Brazil, and Cuba being, along with the United States, among the more prominent cases)—the fundamental rationale is the reallocation of productive resources, the movement of workers' bodies from areas of presumed low labor demand to those of high demand.[19] This development should not be naturalized, as some economists are wont to do, as abstract, morally cleansed notions like "supply and demand" often imply. There was not a natural-born population surplus in eighteenth-century West

Africa, for example, but rather a deliberate social dislocation in response to pressures and opportunities that came with the roughly simultaneous European penetration of Africa and the Americas and the impact this had on the respective indigenous economies and polities of those areas. Thus slavery in the Americas developed not as a *natural* outcome of an unbalanced land-labor ratio *demanding* workers; rather it arose from the perceived "necessity" to mobilize and manage a labor force to produce goods for which Europeans had "discovered" a demand.[20] We cannot stress too strongly, I would argue, that the creation of global relations of labor and consumption is to some extent constitutive of the advent of modernity. Indeed, the Atlantic slave trade was modernity's initial nexus, as it both stimulated and depended upon the coordination of a global movement of labor and new consumer goods.[21] A similarly complex nexus of production and consumption demands drives the current situation, which strongly suggests that that earlier Atlantic system prefigured the development of the twenty-first-century global economy. In some ways, then, the changes set in motion in the late twentieth century—that we have labeled globalization—is but the latest phase of that development.

These cases underscore the fact that labor under slave-like conditions is neither a turn of phrase nor an exaggeration, because such systems *depend* on the "command" of labor in all the possible meanings of that term.[22] "Cheap labor," as it is often designated, *gets to be cheap* through the application of a concrete repertoire of controls. Sometimes actual physical violence "cheapens" labor, and there are examples of this in reports from the contemporary sweatshops. But more generally, labor is rendered cheap and docile by systematic deprivation of the means to earn a living otherwise, by restrictions on its ability to organize and bargain collectively at the worksite, and by limiting its access to potential allies outside the workplace. And in a further step—as with African slaves in the eighteenth and nineteenth centuries and with Asian indentured laborers in the nineteenth and early twentieth century—these twenty-first century slave-like workers are racialized. By falling into the category of the stranger, the outsiders, the *"not-us,"* their very identity as humans with human rights becomes a question of debate and contestation rather than a given. Sometimes literally sequestered, hidden, and unreachable denizens in the recessed enclaves of our domestic spaces, sometimes rendered as shadowy figures or out of view in a distant, benighted land, they take on the stereotyped character of their ascribed spaces. Like the slaves of another era, whether objects of pity or of demonization, they are not possible agents of their own lives and thus their possibilities to be like or among us as equals becomes difficult to imagine. Thus one of the pressing problems of the twenty-first century is to find a way to re-imagine our national spaces so as to incorporate these now liminal figures, especially since—like the slaves of another era—it is us who have made them.

How did we "make" them? In the late 1960s, major industries in G7 countries seeking to establish operations in areas of "cheap labor," with less state regulation, moved production to offshore sites in developing countries, especially in the Caribbean basin and southeast Asia.[23] By the 1970s new financial service providers emerged, bringing new technologies and technical expertise that fostered innovations in the mobilization and management of capital. Associated with these developments also was the social-spatial phenomenon that Saskia Sassen has called "global cities," like New York, Tokyo, and London, the service centers of the global economy.[24] Bringing the sweatshop workers within the framework of Sassen's analysis of the rise of global cities suggests that this development was not some sideshow of the modern political-economy but linked to its main currents. They figure into the warp and woof of the fabric of modern life: workers—some undocumented, some legal; some fearfully exploited, some not; but all functioning in an informal economy not regulated by law.[25] Many are in sweatshops like those I have described making luxury and casual apparel to clothe our bodies. Others clean our houses and care for our children. They are found in the thoroughfares of the streets of our major urban areas, driving gypsy cabs or vending all sorts of merchandise. Their statuses and situation vary widely, but what they have in common is that they constitute a parallel class of "service" workers to the highly paid professional service sector manning the technology of the globalized economy. Arguably, they make the latter's very existence possible.

The scenario I have just described deviates from the iconographic image of the American immigrant that fills our school books and political stump speeches: poor but proud, living in nuclear households, struggling to climb the ladder of success. They might pass through wage labor for a while, as Abraham Lincoln so famously described it, but then they will acquire a little shop, and finally a lucky few would become secure bourgeois entrepreneurs. There is enough truth to this portrait to make it almost unassailable—and certainly unpatriotic to question it. But for every Korean storekeeper, one might find in the shadows of our global cities a different kind of entrepreneur, more like the Chinese small-factory proprietors in Sunset Park in Brooklyn, built on the exploited labor of other Chinese, illegal entrants struggling to find a secure place in the world as free citizens of their adopted nation.[26]

The human flow that brought them here, however, was set in motion by more distant dislocations in the economies of the countries from which they came, a great deal of that dislocation prompted by earlier European, Asian, or American investments in offshore production facilities. In many cases, recruitment into urban and rural wage-labor pools in their homelands preceded their migration to low-wage jobs in global cities like Los Angeles and New York.[27]

Another striking feature of our contemporary labor crisis is that the worker in question is more than likely to be a woman—whether found in a factory, a home, or a bordello.[28] Although well-known, this is a startling fact about contemporary, international labor flows that demands greater scrutiny, especially as it might inform the nexus between labor and citizenship I have sketched here. Although the gender ratio of this twenty-first-century international labor recruitment is exactly opposite that of the eighteenth and nineteenth centuries, I am convinced that bringing studies of the two moments into conversation could be mutually enlightening. Let us consider, to begin with, the fundamental reversals in the character of such labor over the period we are discussing and its implication for the prospects of the laborer becoming a "citizen" and "friend." As we know, although men predominated among the Africans transported in the original Atlantic slave trade by ratios of up to two to one, both men and women were crucial to slave-labor regimes—whether in southwest Georgia cotton plantations or on western Jamaican sugar estates. It was no accident, then, that a principal battleground after slavery was the recruitment and control of women's and children's labor.[29] The outcomes of that struggle varied. Sharecropping in the American South recaptured much of that labor eventually, while what Sidney Mintz called the "peasant breach" in Jamaica gave women and their families resources for continued resistance and a measure of control. In both places, however, women became a formidable force in the political sphere. They became de facto political actors even if not formally recognized as such.[30]

Our contemporary scene looks very different, however. As I have noted, women seem to be overrepresented in the new "cheap" labor force, which suggests that many of their menfolk (husbands, sons, fathers) may well have been thrust out of the labor force into positions of dependency, living on their women's remittances from first-world worksites or the out-sourced factories nearer home. Meanwhile, not only are their womenfolk's roles as workers rendered relatively invisible, so are their possible roles as political actors and citizens.

I must confess here that I am not at present prepared to go much beyond these rudimentary and trenchant observations. I thought it worth advancing them, nonetheless, because I believe that a deeper analysis of this phenomenon is sorely needed, and that it might just be mutually beneficial to students of nineteenth-century emancipation, on the one hand, and those exploring twenty-first-century labor migrations on the other. Recent studies of U.S. Reconstruction, in particular, have made us keenly sensitive to the interplay of gender, labor, and citizenship;[31] our own times could benefit from similar perspectives and insights. It may well be that the fact that the stranger knocking at our gate is often a young woman—often with continued ties to a distant homeplace—complicates our capacity to address her exploitation and our own culpability.

Workers and Citizens: The New Non-Citizen

Contemporary developments lend an entirely new perspective, I think, to the title Tannenbaum chose for his book: *Slave and Citizen*. Indeed, the notion that slaves actually became equal citizens anywhere certainly contributed to the skepticism with which Tannenbaum's thesis was greeted. Much of the scholarship since leaves little doubt that he overstated the case, to say the least. Nonetheless, his formulation, in my opinion, correctly frames the larger problematic of freedom in the modern world. Freedom, self-determination, security do not exist outside citizenship, and thus civic belonging was crucial to the realization of freedom after slavery. Ex-slaves everywhere recognized as much, even if many subsequent historians have not. Once again, our contemporary difficulties addressing issues of basic human justice, imagining and delineating human rights in a world of nation-states, re-imagining national formation, with all its attendant questions about boundaries, national integrity, and "belonging"—all this draws a bright red arrow back to those late-eighteenth and mid-nineteenth-century moments of Jubilee. There may be some utility in revisiting them in light of our present dilemmas.

Although sweatshop workers are but a tiny minority of American workers—their recent numbers in the United States are put at 200,000 give or take; though many millions more work abroad under companies with subcontracts to American firms—their plight nonetheless is more than emblematic of a larger class of the world's labor force (in Europe as well as America) who are effectively noncitizens in their places of labor.[32] Like the French *sans-papiers*, they are the strangers at the gate whose knock poses a profound problem for democratic governance. In many cases, like the *sans-papier*, they are less strangers than members of the extended national family, "returnees" coming to a "home country" they helped build, even if they have never seen it. In some cases, as with the quasi-colonial connections of the United States to its southern neighbors, the links are perhaps more, or less, politically complicated, but they still reflect the delayed social fallout from earlier projections of the vectors of American capital and military power outside its national borders. In either case, the connections are not simply historical, but part of the nature of modern capitalist economies, which are ever dependent on global capital flows and labor recruitment—here or there, which makes this phenomena of the *ostensible* stranger-at-the-gates one that is practically relevant because it is not likely to go away, and a moral imperative because it challenges fundamental notions about the meaningfulness of freedom in the contemporary world.

From the historical advent of the modern nation-state, during the Age of Revolution, the nation's very existence has turned on the question of "who belongs?" The very idea that national citizenship as such constitutes one's moral personality, one's moral claims to an equal humanity, has a divided history, however. According to one strand of thought, with the collapse of divine monarchies and the emergence of the modern state system, national belonging became a necessity to the constitution of one's being as a rights-bearing person. As the Hague Convention of 1930 declared, "every person should have a nationality." The point was driven home even more emphatically by Supreme Court Justice Earl Warren almost thirty years later: "Citizenship," he wrote, "is man's basic right for it is nothing less than the right to have rights." A "stateless person," he went on, would be deprived of any lawful claims to protection from any nation.[33]

This idea of neatly bounded states, made up of persons bearing neatly bounded bundles of rights still dominates our national imaginary. And, yet, work on citizenship and voting in the United States—by a broad range of legal scholars, political scientists, and historians—has shown the convoluted twists and turns in how the question of citizenship has been addressed and answered historically; and most important, it suggests that *no answer is ever final.* While on the face of it, citizenship would seem to presuppose an inside and an outside, members and nonmembers, the fact is that many nation-states have found it advantageous from time to time to allow dual citizenship. For example, it would have been totally disruptive to the new state of Lithuania, established in the wake of the collapse of the Soviet Union in 1989, to have not recognized the dual citizenship claims of the Russians in its midst. There are numerous other examples like this where national belonging is in fact fractured, parceled, and sometimes even ambiguous. While all nation-states recognize the necessity of adjudicating citizenship claims to ensure allegiance and national solidarity, therefore, they have actually deployed a bewildering array of strategies to achieve those goals.[34]

So where does this leave the worker rendered stateless today because of her undocumented entry into the nation? Well, there is another strand of thought, now well documented in the U.S. case, of noncitizen workers exercising at least some citizenship rights historically, including the right to vote. As the late constitutional scholar Alexander Bickel pointed out many years ago, the U.S. Constitution was actually written in terms of the rights of *inhabitants and persons* rather than citizens, a term that slipped into state and federal law much later. Noncitizens of all kinds exercised the right to vote in a number of states. Indeed, it was not until 1928 that *all* aliens were barred from voting in *all* states. And as Alex Keyssar has shown, the rationale for extending suffrage rights had less to do with high moral principles or political theory than with raw political necessities and opportunities, often generated by social crises and war.[35] By definition, the success of suffrage expansion required some group who already had suffrage rights finding some advantage in extending it to another that did not possess it. Moreover until the anti-immigrant panics of recent years, there have been numerous rights and benefits that noncitizens enjoyed along with citizens, including education, welfare, et cetera. Indeed, this is part of the reason that so many inhabitants were perhaps slow to naturalize as citizens.[36]

Conclusion

I will not attempt to go further here to suggest what political process might resolve our present difficulties in negotiating these issues, or even what form a proactivist agenda might take. More consistent with the spirit of this intervention, I would rather end with some thoughts on how we might begin to arrive at a different imaginary of "belonging" and inclusion—one that might form part of the conceptual grounding for that different politics. It will not be surprising to you, no doubt, that my imaginary forms in part around my reflections on the subjects I have been discussing throughout the essay—scenes of former slaves seeking entry within the public body of citizens, some of them, like the various American slave rebels during the Age of Revolution, even at the very moment of the inception of those new national bodies. They, too, we must remember were perceived as "cultural strangers" and outsiders despite being integral to the very making of the social-economies of those polities they now wished to enter. Though seemingly "over there" and "other," they were in reality very much a part of the "here" and the "us." True they were "different," because their social formation and lived experiences were different, but perceiving that difference as a threat was a *choice* that need not have been made.

Here I would like to share some reflections of a very different sort that I have found stimulating in thinking about this problem. In a book entitled *Democracy and the Foreigner*, Bonnie Honig suggests that contrary to conventional thinking, the foreigner has played a crucial role in the historical and literary imaginary about how to consolidate and reconstitute democratic societies—that is, communities constituted paradoxically by the a priori "given-ness" of membership and the "chosen-ness" of that membership. In a democratic polity, one is always already a member by birth, even as one repeatedly enacts the choice of membership through political participation, since the origins and sustenance of that polity lies in the freely bestowed consent of its members. And, yet, since such a community is defined solely by the fellowship of the beings within it, membership is *ever* subject to negotiation and renegotiation.[37]

Given this circumstance, the intrusion of the foreigner, or the outsider within, Honig argues, can be constitutive, and not just in the most obvious sense of affirming a foil against which its members' distinctive character can be identified. Instead, Honig takes us through an amazing and diverse array of texts in which the foreigner is actually the founder of the community or its source of revitalization, because that role can *only* be enacted by a nonmember, an outsider. Thus invoking biblical figures from Moses to Ruth in Israel, or from Jean-Jacques Rousseau's lawgiver in the *Social Contract* to Dorothy in *The Wizard of Oz*, Honig shows how outsider figures have founded, revitalized, or enabled community formation.

Honig's point is not simply literary; she wants to suggest this phenomenon as an ongoing, replicable principle of the growth and revitalization of democratic societies—that is to say, that it is not mere *tolerance* of the newcomer who brings difference in her wake, but the *necessity* of foreignness, of difference, to the continued health of the body politic. Democracy itself is a politics among strangers, she argues. Furthermore, democracy in our present moment requires not the myth of national kinship, but a cosmopolitan consciousness that assumes responsibility for the strangers both here and in other lands.

If this position has merit (and obviously I offer it thinking that it does) then we need to think anew, to re-envision how modern nations—so inherently dependent on the infusion of new peoples as labor—will be able to embrace them also as members of the polity, as citizens. Like those slave rebels who greeted the soldiers of revolutionary France in Guadeloupe some two centuries ago, calling out "We are citizens and friends," we might yet respond with the French revolutionary soldiers, "Welcome to our ranks."

Notes

1. Dubois, *A Colony of Citizens*, 23–25.

2. Cooper, Holt, and Scott, *Beyond Slavery*, 151–52.

3. Tannenbaum, *Slave and Citizen*.

4. *Le Monde*, 25 April 1998. See also Cooper, Holt, and Scott, *Beyond Slavery*, 151–52.

5. Dubois, *A Colony of Citizens*, 1–2.

6. George White, "Workers Held in Near Slavery, Official Says," *Los Angeles Times*, 3 August 1995; Bill Wallace, "70 Immigrants Found in Raid on Sweatshop: Thai workers tell horror stories of captivity," *San Francisco Chronicle*, 4 August 1995, A12.

7. On 9 November 1995, federal indictments were issued for ten of the Thai operators of the factory, charging them with involuntary servitude. Many of the El Monte victims later gained U.S. citizenship. Theresa Watanabe, "Home of the Freed," *Los Angeles Times*, 14 August 2008. "7 Thais Enter Guilty Pleas for Detention in Sweatshop," *New York Times*, 11 February 1996, accessed 15 April 2012, http://www.nytimes.com/1996/02/11/us/7-thais-enter-guilty-pleas-for-detention-in-sweatshop.html?scp=31&sq=El%20Monte%20case&st=cse.

8. For example, see Steven Greenhouse, "Suit Says 18 Companies Conspired to Violate Sweatshop Workers' Civil Rights," *New York Times*, 14 January 1999, accessed 15 April 2012, http://www.nytimes.com/1999/01/14/us/suit-says-18-companies-conspired-to-violate-sweatshop-workers-civil-rights.html?ref=northernmarianaislands; Bao, "Sweatshops in Sunset Park." The literature on the global webs connecting the American apparel industry with domestic and offshore sweatshops is extensive. See Ross, *Slaves to Fashion*; Bonacich and Waller, "Role of U.S. Apparel Manufacturers."

9. Ross, *Slaves to Fashion*; Bao, "Sweatshops in Sunset Park."

10. For more on this usage, see *Fiche méthologique préparée par Cécile Vigour—octobre 2006*, accessed 19 February 2011, http://www.melissa.ens-cachan.fr/IMG/pdf/Elaborer Problematique.pdf.

11. The official citation for the Moynihan Report is United States, Department of Labor, Office of Policy Planning and Research, *The Negro Family: The Case for National Action* (Washington, D.C.: Superintendent of Documents, 1965). For discussion of its role in the evolving "culture of poverty" discourse, see Rainwater and Yancey, *Moynihan Report and the Politics of Controversy*. For resonance in historical literature, see Elkins, *Slavery*.

12. Hughes's poem was originally published as "Harlem" in his collection of poetry entitled *Montage of a Dream Deferred*.

13. David Brion Davis, *Problem of Slavery*; Berlin, et al., *Freedom* (Vol. 1: *Destruction of Slavery*); Foner, *Reconstruction*. Also of interest is Foner, *Story of American Freedom*.

14. Patterson, *Slavery and Social Death*.

15. See Archibald Stuart to John Breckinridge, 26 January 1786, Breckinridge Family Papers, cited in James Madison to Ambrose Madison, 15 December 1785, n. 3, in Stagg, ed., *Papers of James Madison*, accessed 30 May 2012, http://www.rotunda.upress.virginia.edu/founders/default.xqy?keys=JSMN-search-1-1&mode=deref.

16. Kiernan, "Manumission of Slaves," 144–54. See also Schwartz, "Manumission of Slaves in Colonial Brazil." For a U.S. comparison, see Condon, "Manumission, Slavery, and Family," 127–57.

17. Anderson, *Imagined Communities*, 6–7.

18. Ibid, 19–22.

19. For example, see Jung, *Coolies and Cane*.

20. The land-labor nexus as explanation for slavery is an old idea of which a recent exposition is found in Green, *British Slave Emancipation*. For a different take on this historical development, see Holt, *Children of Fire*, 43–73.

21. The transatlantic links between labor and consumption are best explicated by Sidney Mintz in *Sweetness and Power*.

22. Even a cursory survey of contemporary accounts makes clear that the term "slavery" is not hyperbolic. For example, see Mireya Navarro, "In Land of the Free, a Modern Slave," *New York Times*, 12 December 1996, accessed 15 April 2012, http://www.nytimes.com/1996/12/12/us/in-land-of-the-free-a-modern-slave.html.

23. For examples, see Brooks, "Ideal Sweatshop," 91–111; Whalen, "Sweatshops Here and There," 45–68; and idem *From Puerto Rico to Philadelphia*.

24. Sassen, *Global Cities* and *Globalization and Its Discontents*.

25. Light, "From Migrant Enclaves to Mainstream," 705–37.

26. Bao, "Sweatshops in Sunset Park."

27. Whalen, "Sweatshops Here and There."

28. Tens of thousands of poor, would-be immigrant women from Third World and Eastern European countries have been subjected to sexual servitude according to U.S. and U.N. reports. For more on the human landscape of contemporary worker migrations, see U.S. State Department's periodic reports: accessed 2 June 2012, http://www.state.gov/j/tip/rls/tiprpt and http://www.gvnet.com/humantrafficking/USA.htm.

29. For examples, see O'Donovan, *Becoming Free in the Cotton South*; and Holt, *Problem of Freedom*.

30. Sidney W. Mintz, "The Rural Proletariat and the Problem of Rural Proletarian Consciousness," *Journal of Peasant Studies* 1 (April 1974): 91–324; Elsa Barkley Brown, "Negotiating and Transforming the Public Sphere."

31. Edwards, "'The Marriage Covenant Is the Foundation of All Our Rights'"; Bercaw, *Gendered Freedoms*; O'Donovan, *Becoming Free in the Cotton South*.

32. Ross, *Slaves to Fashion*, 36.

33. League of Nations, "Convention on Certain Questions Relating to the Conflict of Nationality Laws," accessed 2 June 2012, http://www.paclii.org/pits/en/treaty_database/1930/2.html. Justice Warren's dissenting opinion in Perez v. Brownell, 356 U.S. 44 (1958) can be found in (accessed 2 June 2012) http://www.caselaw.lp.findlaw.com/scripts/getcase.pl?court=US&vol=356&invol=44.

34. Aleinikoff and Kusmeyer, "Plural Nationality." See also Aleinikoff and Kusmeyer, ed., *From Migrants to Citizens.*

35. Keyssar, *Right to Vote.*

36. Ibid., table A12, 359–61. For an example of reticence to naturalize, see George J. Sanchez, *Becoming Mexican American: Ethnicity, Culture, and Identity in Chicano Los Angeles* (New York: Oxford University Press, 1993).

37. Honig, *Democracy and the Foreigner.*

2

"Erroneous and Incongruous Notions of Liberty"

Urban Unrest and the Origins of Radical Reconstruction in New Orleans, 1865–1868

JAMES ILLINGWORTH

In January 1866, Freedmen's Bureau agent William Dougherty reported on the radicalization and unrest among black workers in Algiers, a suburb of New Orleans, Louisiana. Contrary to Dougherty's advice, agricultural workers in the vicinity of Algiers were "delaying to make a permanent contract" with the planters, causing a serious labor shortage. Dougherty noted several reasons for the behavior of the freedpeople under his jurisdiction. In the first instance, he believed that the plantation workers were holding out for wages "at the rate of fifty cents per hour" because black longshoremen in New Orleans had recently been on strike for such a raise. Second, Dougherty attributed the recalcitrance of black workers to the presence of "freedmen recently discharged from the army" who he felt were possessed of "erroneous and incongruous notions of liberty." And third, the Bureau agent noted that plantation hands in the vicinity of New Orleans enjoyed the option of going "to the city to work on the levee and the steamboats," where wages were higher and "paid more frequently."[1]

Dougherty's report reveals important themes in the early history of Reconstruction in New Orleans. First and foremost, it shows that labor in the urban economy gave freedpeople the confidence and economic muscle to forcefully advance their own vision of the postslavery South. The clash between these expectations and the aspirations of returning Confederates would play a major role in the coming of Radical Reconstruction in New Orleans. Dougherty's report also demonstrates the leadership that black veterans were to play in the popular politics of early Reconstruction in New Orleans. Just six months after Dougherty wrote his report, it was the determination of black veterans in particular to reopen the Louisiana constitutional convention and win the right to vote that provoked the racial violence of the New Orleans Massacre, paving the way for congressional intervention in the South and the onset of Radical Reconstruction. Finally, Dougherty's report suggests the ways in which black urban working people were able to exert an influence over their rural counterparts, pioneering forms of protest such as the strike that would contribute to the radicalization of black workers in the countryside.

While historians have devoted relatively little attention to the particular experiences and contributions of the urban popular classes during the Civil War and Reconstruction, some rich scholarship does exist. Scholars of the antebellum South have frequently noted that cities such as New Orleans created major problems of control for the owners and employers of slave labor.[2] Although Steven Hahn's pathbreaking *A Nation under Our Feet* focuses primarily on the experiences and activism of rural African Americans, it also demonstrates the crucial role urban black men played in the politics of Reconstruction, particularly in the years immediately following the Civil War.[3] The most important study of post–Civil War urban radicalism remains Peter Rachleff's study of black labor organizing in Richmond, Virginia.[4] Recent works by David Cecelski and Thomas Buchanan show that black workers in the commercial South built organizing traditions that persisted through the antebellum period and extended into the 1860s and 1870s.[5] Michael Fitzgerald has shown how class divisions within the African American community produced a steady radicalization of the Reconstruction process.[6] Tera Hunter has revealed how black working women in Atlanta used the relative freedom of the postwar urban South to build a cohesive—and sometimes militant—working-class community.[7]

In this essay I build on the work of these scholars to show how the popular classes of one Southern city contributed to the coming of Radical Reconstruction. I identify two distinct phases in this process. First, popular mobilization in New Orleans contributed to the crisis of presidential Reconstruction in the summer of 1866. In the year immediately following the end of the war, the radicalization and mobilization of working people clashed with the reactionary expectations of many returning Confederates, resulting in social turmoil and an explosion of racial violence in 1866. The events in New Orleans, along with similar scenes in other Southern locales, helped convince many Northerners that President Andrew Johnson's Reconstruction policy had been far too lenient and was allowing the return to power of the former rebels. In this context, congressional Republicans seized control of federal policy in the South and inaugurated Radical Reconstruction. Second, in 1867 and 1868, black working people became a crucial factor in the formation of a new political bloc. Not only did their activism play an important role in pushing local Republicans in a more radical direction, but they also helped to connect what began as an urban movement to the black working people of rural Louisiana. In these years, therefore, the interplay between federal state intervention and urban working people's activism became the determining factor in the progress of change at the local level.

Presidential Reconstruction

The Union occupation of New Orleans and southern Louisiana, which began in April 1862, made this region a test case for the return of federal rule in the South. Union naval forces engaged in the blockade of southern ports needed bases of their own in order to refuel and take on provisions. Southern Louisiana took on a strategic importance in Lincoln's war plans, moreover: as Union commander Benjamin Butler later remembered, the president "was anxious that a fleet should go up the [Mississippi] river and open that great avenue of transportation."[8] Although it flowed from military necessity, however, the occupation of New Orleans and southern Louisiana unleashed a wave of political and social upheaval that Union authorities had neither intended nor anticipated. Most important, enslaved African Americans used the presence of Union troops as an opportunity to win their freedom and flocked to federal positions in their thousands. In a matter of months the threat of Confederate counterattack had forced Benjamin Butler to begin the enlistment of black troops. Union military authorities played an increasingly important role in mediating the relationship between white owners and black workers, to the point that slavery had all but dissolved by the middle of 1864.[9] At the same time, Abraham Lincoln's desire to create a loyal state government in Louisiana drove him to seek collaborators among the white working men of New Orleans in particular.[10]

If war and occupation had begun a process of revolutionary transformation in New Orleans, however, the advent of presidential Reconstruction signaled an abrupt change of course. President Lincoln had been moving in the direction of support for black male suffrage by the end of the war and had recommended that the government of Louisiana consider enfranchising at least some African American men.[11] Lincoln's successor, Andrew Johnson, believed that, whatever the evils of slavery and secession, only white men could rule the South, and he moved quickly to pardon former Confederates and restore local self-government in the conquered territories.[12] Louisiana had already experienced its own version of the transition from Lincoln to Johnson a little earlier in the year. In March 1865, Lieutenant Governor James Madison Wells assumed the state's executive office when the former governor, Michael Hahn, won the legislature's election for the U.S. Senate. Hahn, a representative of immigrant laborers and small businessmen in New Orleans, had led the moderate Unionist faction during the Civil War. Although he was no friend of black civil rights, Hahn had at least been willing to consider Lincoln's plea for limited black male suffrage.[13] Wells, by contrast, was a cotton and sugar planter from Rapides Parish in central Louisiana. He had been one of Louisiana's most active planter-Unionists during the Civil War and came to occupied New Orleans as an important representative of a potential alliance between urban and rural Unionists.[14] In this capacity he was the perfect candidate for lieutenant governor in the elections of 1864. But if Wells was a staunch Unionist, he was also an opponent of African American rights. At his inauguration on March 4, the new governor noted he would "call to my aid the best and ablest men of the State."[15] As it turned out, this meant that Wells would reach out to returning Confederates in an attempt to build a new white supremacist bloc between Democrats and Conservative Unionists.

Wells signaled his intentions with the appointment of Dr. Hugh Kennedy as mayor of New Orleans. According to one commentator, Kennedy was a "strong advocate of the rebellion, a man who favored oppression, who believed in elevating the aristocracy and degrading the laboring classes."[16] Once in office, Kennedy purged Unionists from the municipal police department and appointed Confederate veterans in their places. The result was a wave of police repression against people of color in New Orleans.[17] In August, the Provost Marshal General for Freedmen, Captain Andrew Morse, wrote to John Mitchell, mayor of Jefferson City in the New Orleans suburbs, reminding him that "slavery being abolished the laws and regulations which then discriminated between white and colored persons are now null and void." In this context, Morse felt obliged to admonish Mitchell for the actions of his police officers, who had arrested "colored men in their own premises without any just cause."[18] The situation in New Orleans was replicated in rural areas of the state: from New Iberia to Baton Rouge, Confederate veterans had engaged in a campaign of repression against the freedpeople.[19]

The actions of white police officers soon led to a sharp clash between Mayor Kennedy and the federal authorities in New Orleans. First, Major General Banks returned from his campaign against Mobile and removed Kennedy from office. When Banks's superior, Edward Canby, accepted Kennedy's protests and restored his position as mayor, the Massachusetts general resigned in disgust.[20] In July, Thomas Conway of the Freedmen's Bureau appointed a special investigator to examine reports of police repression and corruption[21] and in September clashed with Governor Wells over the same issue.[22]

With the assistance of President Johnson, Wells managed to sideline the Freedmen's Bureau and Union Army and push ahead with his plans for state elections in November. At the end of May, the governor visited Washington to discuss his vision for the reconstruction of Louisiana. As James Hogue has suggested, this meeting may well have convinced Johnson of the need to reconcile with former Confederates in order to prevent Radical domination of the South: just four days after his conference with Wells, the president presented his Proclamation on Pardon and Amnesty. Some weeks later, under pressure from Wells and Kennedy, Johnson removed Conway from his leadership of the Freedmen's Bureau in Louisiana and replaced him with the more pliable Joseph Fullerton.[23] The field was now clear for Wells to press ahead with his electoral ambitions, and the results gave an overwhelming victory to the governor and his new allies among returning Confederates. Wells easily won election to continue as Louisiana's chief executive, and the new state government would feature such large majorities of Confederate veterans that it came to be known as the Rebel legislature.[24]

Almost immediately, the new Louisiana state government set out to codify in law what Mayor Hugh Kennedy had already attempted in practice: a sharp curtailment of the rights of former slaves. On 13 December, the Rebel legislature passed four bills that collectively became known as the Black Codes. This legislation aimed to restrict the mobility and bargaining power of black agricultural workers. The first of these mandated binding, yearlong contracts for plantation hands, and insisted that employers had the right to demand service from the whole black family so contracted, including women and children. The second and third bills attempted to restrict the competition between employers by setting out punishments for anyone who attempted to "entice away" a properly contracted laborer. The final of the four bills provided for the "apprenticing" of young African Americans to white employers. Taken together, the four Black Code acts gave local courts and police juries enormous power to regulate the lives and labors of Louisiana freedpeople.[25] And they immediately provoked a strong reaction from local federal authorities. General Absalom Baird, who had assumed control of the Freedmen's Bureau in Louisiana after the brief tenure of Joseph Fullerton, wrote to Governor Wells, urging him to forego signing the new laws because they undermined the authority of the Bureau and noting that the Bureau could enforce them "only in so far as they as they are in accordance with the orders by which I am governed."[26]

Resistance

The newly ascendant white supremacist bloc would not go unchallenged, however. The working people of New Orleans had lived through four years of war, occupation, social disorder, and revolutionary change. These had been tremendously radicalizing experiences, and expectations among the popular classes remained high as the military struggle gave way to a fragile peace. Just as important, the war years had seen a significant increase in the size of the urban black population. The stage was set for a showdown between urban working people and the Rebel legislature.

The weeks and months following the cessation of hostilities witnessed a significant increase in the size and proportional weight of the urban black population. Although precise figures for the years immediately following the war are not available, the number of African Americans living in New Orleans rose from 24,000 in 1860 to over 50,000 in 1870, and from less than 15 percent to more than 25 percent of the total population.[27] These new black urbanites clearly saw the city as home to greater freedom and economic opportunity than the countryside. In July 1865, a white resident of Lafourche Parish wrote to the Freedmen's Bureau to describe "a large and increasing travel on the Railroad to N[ew] Orleans, of colored people," including many young African American women assumed by the writer to be heading to the city to earn "pocket money" as prostitutes.[28] In November, the local Freedmen's Bureau agent for Jefferson Parish reported that rural freedpeople had a tendency to "become dissatisfied and leave the plantations and go to the city to work on the levee, on the steamboats, or at anything else where they can obtain higher wages and receive pay more frequently."[29]

The presence of black soldiers and recently demobilized black veterans added a potent disorderly element to this expanded African American urban population. Whether they remained stationed at military installations or had been demobilized and returned to their communities, some black soldiers and veterans demonstrated little respect for private property. In the late summer of 1865, for example, a group of white planters complained that African American troops stationed at Fort Banks, just outside New Orleans, were "making a thoroughfare through our places, and coming thereon without our permission, and against our will."[30] Likewise, in October 1866, a white resident of Jefferson Parish complained that African American troops were "in the habit of stealing from the residents in that vicinity," and would sometimes "tear off the pickets from enclosures and enter the gardens and orchards and take therefrom whatever they may fancy."[31] As we have already seen, Freedmen's Bureau agent William Dougherty thought that black troops played a role in convincing other freedpeople to refuse to sign labor contracts.[32]

The expanded black population of New Orleans, and particularly the large numbers of recently demobilized black veterans, provided the rank-and-file for an emerging political movement centered on the radical black-owned newspaper the *New Orleans Tribune*. This newspaper had begun life as the French-language *L'Union*, publishing its first issue in September 1862. Under the editorial control of Afro-Creole intellectual Paul Trévigne, *L'Union* took a clear stand against slavery from its very first issue and situated itself in the Republican political tradition of the French and Haitian revolutions.[33] The newspaper moved in an even more radical direction in 1863 when its owners hired Jean-Charles Houzeau as editor. Houzeau, a native of Belgium, had participated in the European revolutions of 1848 before migrating to Texas and becoming part of the antislavery underground there. A talented journalist, pioneering astronomer, and socialist activist, Houzeau brought a new coalitional approach to *L'Union*. He encouraged the Afro-Creole intellectuals around the newspaper to expand the audience of the journal by publishing in English as well as French, and in the fall of 1864, the *New Orleans Tribune* began publication with Houzeau as chief editor.[34]

The *Tribune* gave voice to an extraordinary group of black and white male Radicals, the most prominent of whom were probably Thomas J. Durant and Oscar J. Dunn. A Pennsylvania-born white lawyer, Durant had lived in New Orleans since the 1830s and had been active in the Democratic Party before the war. He had also become an ardent admirer of Frenchman Charles Fourier's utopian socialism and a follower of Fourier's American disciple Albert Brisbane.[35] During the wartime federal occupation of New Orleans, Durant had risen to prominence as the leader of the radical Unionist faction in city politics.[36] Dunn's background was very different. His parents were English-speaking free people of color from New Orleans: his father, a carpenter, worked for the businessman James Caldwell, and his mother operated a boardinghouse.[37] Before the war, Oscar Dunn had worked as a music teacher and a barber in New Orleans, and he quickly became one of the most prominent black leaders of the Reconstruction period. Houzeau of the *New Orleans Tribune* called him the leader of "the English-speaking free element."[38]

Thomas Durant invited *Tribune* readers to attend a strategy session in New Orleans on the night of 10 June 1865. This became the inaugural meeting of a new organization called the Friends of Universal Suffrage, dedicated to fighting for the voting rights of all black men. Attendees voted to create a Central Executive Committee with six representatives from each of the city's four municipal districts. A week later, the Friends unanimously approved a slate of twenty-four names for the committee, with Durant as president, and voted that the organization begin "a voluntary registration of Citizens not recognized as voters."[39] The executive committee began to create an organizational structure capable of registering potential black and white voters in New Orleans, appointing commissioners and clerks from among the supporters of the CEC.[40] Finally, in August, the committee called on all registered supporters of the group to head to the polls on 16 September and elect delegates to a special convention of the Friends of Universal Suffrage, to be held on 25 September.[41]

The Friends of Universal Suffrage's "territorial convention" in September 1865 represented the leadership of the Radical movement in the early post-war years. More than three thousand black and white male residents of New Orleans voted on 16 September, electing 111 delegates to the convention on 25 September. Roughly half of the delegates were black men, representing a selection of businessmen, professionals, and prosperous artisans, the great majority of whom had been free before the war.[42] They included newcomers to New Orleans such as Virginia-born Robert Cromwell, who had been an abolitionist and successful physician in antebellum Wisconsin, and scions of the black Creole establishment such as Bernard Soulié, a wealthy commission merchant.[43] Three of the delegates representing the English-speaking black community—W. H. Pearne, Robert McCary Jr., and Lewis Banks—were preachers.[44] Oscar Dunn, who had been one of the seven founding members of the Friends of Universal Suffrage, chaired the CEC's platform committee in the summer of 1865.[45]

The Radical movement in New Orleans was characterized by an unusually close alliance between the freedpeople and freeborn men of color. For one thing, the two groups had served side-by-side in the Native Guard units of the Union Army. Unlike black regiments that mustered later in the war, the Louisiana Native Guards had black officers, the great majority of whom came from New Orleans's free black community. Some, like wealthy merchant Francis Dumas, had their origins in the upper echelons of the local free black elite. But most of the Native Guards' line officers—the captains and lieutenants who had most contact with the rank-and-file troops—came from what James Hollandsworth calls "the ranks of the city's working elite." They were artisans like Captain Andre Cailloux of the First Native Guards, who had worked as a cigar maker, or Lieutenant Emile Detiege of the same regiment, who was a bricklayer.[46] The political culture of the New Orleans free men of color further encouraged them to seek unity with the former slaves. Jean-Charles Houzeau and other contributors to the *New Orleans Tribune* shared a social-romantic vision of human progress, one that imagined the unity of Radical intellectuals, urban workers, and the rural masses in a movement for full democracy and equality.[47] Houzeau had, from the very beginning, quite consciously steered the *Tribune* in a direction that would facilitate an alliance between the men of color of New Orleans and the freedpeople of the Louisiana countryside.[48] When the Louisiana Equal Rights League met in January 1865, therefore, the *Tribune* urged the group to send "a black man" as an emissary to Washington. "We want him to be thoroughly identified with the working of slavery," the paper stated.[49]

Black and white delegates to the Friends of Universal Suffrage territorial convention consciously set out to mold their movement into a new political party. They first debated the possibility of merging with the national Republican Party. White Radicals Thomas J. Durant and Benjamin Flanders spoke strongly in favor of the merger, but other speakers dissented. African American delegate Robert H. Isabelle pointed out that the national Republicans had not yet taken a position in favor of black suffrage. Despite these concerns, Durant's resolutions won a majority, and the delegates reconvened as the founding convention of the Republican Party of Louisiana.[50] The debate then shifted to the new party's position on the correct course for Reconstruction. Henry Clay Warmoth, a young white Union officer from Illinois, proposed that Louisiana Republicans should draft a new constitution for the state and submit it to Congress for approval. But many delegates spoke against Warmoth's plan and in favor of a prolonged federal oversight of Louisiana so that unrepentant white supremacists could learn to accept black equality. Ultimately, the convention decided to organize an election for a territorial delegate, so that Louisiana Radicals would have a representative in Washington. The meeting unanimously chose Henry Clay Warmoth as its nominee, and adjourned.[51]

New Orleans Radicals felt that the first priority for their movement should be to secure the right to vote for black men and decided to make the territorial election a testing ground for their theories.[52] In a provocative move, the CEC—now the Central Executive Committee of the Republican Party of Louisiana—called the election for 6 November, the same day as the state elections. Of necessity, most of the organizing for the election took place in New Orleans, its suburbs, and rural hinterland. But the CEC managed to send emissaries into the plantation districts, too. In places like Terrebonne Parish, the sugar district to the southwest of New Orleans, and in the area surrounding Baton Rouge, activists registered black voters and held political meetings for the freedpeople.[53] The results were impressive: with almost nineteen thousand votes cast in his favor, Warmoth had won almost as much electoral support as James Madison Wells, the Conservative candidate for governor in the official election of the same day. And although more than half of the votes came from New Orleans and its environs, thousands of rural freedpeople went to the polls in Terrebonne, East Baton Rouge, and other rural parishes.[54]

The New Orleans Radicals planned to push the revolutionary process well beyond the struggle for the vote, however. Land reform and the confiscation of plantations formed a crucial part of the program of the *New Orleans Tribune* and the most militant leaders of the CEC. As early as November 1864, the *Tribune* had argued that real equality could not exist unless the plantation system came to an end.[55] In order to facilitate land redistribution, the *Tribune* proposed a system of self-help banks. Using the small deposits of black working people, these banks would buy land and rent it to "voluntary associations of workers."[56] The first such experiment took place in February 1865, when Durant, Dunn, and others founded the Freedman Aid Association. As Gilles Vandal notes, the explicit aim of the association was to "create labor communes on plantations."[57] Members of the organization met with representatives of the plantation hands from the surrounding countryside, and seem to have met with a positive response. Within a month, the association had helped to create at least four such communes and had plans for many more.[58]

Beginning in the spring of 1865, the New Orleans Radicals attempted to bring the idea of labor communes into the city itself. They hoped to create worker-run cooperatives in which the employees bought shares and divided the profits among themselves. The first concrete attempt to implement this plan was the Louisiana Association of Workingmen in November 1865. Better known in New Orleans as the People's Bakery, the plan required two thousand working people to purchase shares at five dollars each, with the money going to purchase a lot and outfit a bakery. Membership in the association was open to all, regardless of race or gender. The Radicals hoped that, if the People's Bakery could succeed in selling bread at low rates, the project could cause an expansion of the workers' cooperative movement. The bakery opened in April 1866, but struggled financially and faded within the year. Nevertheless, the project signaled that New Orleans Radicals would not let free-labor ideology proscribe the limits of their revolutionary vision.[59]

Labor unrest among white workingmen also contributed to the radical climate of late 1865. Political changes since the end of the war had left white workingmen facing a contradictory situation. On the one hand, as we have already seen, returning Confederates used the summer and fall of 1865 to strengthen their hold over the Louisiana state government, undoing the reforms carried out under the Union occupation in the name of restoring white supremacy. On the other hand, however, the neo-Confederate brand of racial politics did not always redound to the benefit of white working men. The neo-Confederate mayor of New Orleans, Hugh Kennedy, used his powers to cut the wages of public employees, for example. In May 1865, white workingmen rallied outside city hall to demand Kennedy's resignation and petitioned Union Army commander Nathaniel Banks to remove Conservative municipal officials. That fall, the white labor movement stepped up its pressure on the neo-Confederate state government when it began a petition campaign demanding legislative action to reduce the hours of labor.[60]

The most dramatic expression of the new labor unrest came with a prolonged series of strikes on the New Orleans waterfront in December 1865. As Eric Arnesen has shown, these strikes revealed the complex interaction of race and class among Crescent City waterfront workers. The action began when white cotton screwmen struck for higher wages and shorter hours on 20 December. These skilled white workers had been the strongest element of the city's labor movement in the 1850s, but in the new conditions of postwar New Orleans, the actions of a whites-only craft union could have a much broader resonance on the waterfront. The strike quickly spread to other sections of the levee workforce. On 21 December, black longshoremen joined a procession of striking workers that, according to Arnesen, "effectively halted most work on docked steamships." Other groups of African American waterfront workers struck on 24 and 27 December, using physical coercion to prevent other longshoremen from working during the protests. The strikers were so successful in stopping work on the levee that steamship masters repeatedly called on the Union Army to protect those laborers who wanted to work. While the nonunionized black workers eventually returned to work with their demands unmet, the skilled and organized white screwmen won their wage increase when just after the New Year, their employers capitulated.[61]

By late 1865, the labor unrest in the streets and on the wharves of New Orleans had begun to spread beyond the boundaries of the city and find an echo in the surrounding countryside. The *New Orleans Tribune* probably played a role in this process: as David Rankin has noted, "It claimed to have an audience among 'the most active' freedmen in rural Louisiana" and became an organizing tool for the local branches of the National Equal Rights League.[62] In January 1866, the Freedmen's Bureau agent in Jefferson Parish reported that rural freedpeople were "delaying to make a permanent contract" unless they could get fifty cents an hour, an idea that the official believed "originated probably among the freedmen working on the levee in the city who have recently been 'striking' for the aforesaid amount."[63] A month later, the same agent reported evidence of an even more direct connection between urban radicalism and rural unrest: black plantation hands in Jefferson Parish were "very doubtful about the propriety" of signing yearlong labor contracts. Their reluctance was reportedly due to "the advice and action" of the "'Central Executive Association" [*sic*], under [whose] auspices . . . the freedmen of these parishes are directed and in a measure controlled in regard to labor." Plantation hands had flatly informed the Bureau that they would only go to work "if the 'Committee' agree to it."[64] The agent's concerns suggest that the CEC of the Republican Party functioned like an embryonic trade union for rural freedpeople and testifies to the ability of urban Radicals to exert an influence on the countryside surrounding New Orleans.

The culmination of the radicalization of late 1865 came during the Christmas Day insurrection panic of that year. As early as the summer of 1865, rumors began to circulate connecting the Christmas and New Year holidays with some profound transformation of Southern society.[65] In July, a Freedmen's Bureau agent in rural Clinton, Louisiana, alleged that "some evil disposed persons about here have informed the negroes that unless they run away and leave their former masters 'before the first of next January' they 'will be slaves for life.'"[66] In September, one agent in the Louisiana countryside reported that rural freedpeople were refusing to sign labor contracts "in Expectation of having land assigned them by the Government," while white residents in Monroe, Louisiana, blamed black troops for spreading the rumor.[67] By this time, fears that the freedpeople would seize the plantations by force were so widespread that Oliver Howard, the commissioner of the Freedmen's Bureau, exchanged letters on the subject with Thomas Conway, his subordinate in Louisiana. Although Conway claimed that there were "no grounds whatever from [*sic*] any fears on that score," Howard was forced to issue a circular letter dispelling rumors of confiscation less than two months later.[68]

There is no direct evidence to suggest that the activism of New Orleans

Radicals encouraged the rumors of confiscation in late 1865. The Radicals did, as we have seen, exert an influence on at least those rural freedpeople who lived in the immediate vicinity of the city. Furthermore, as Steven Hahn has suggested, the massive migration between town and country in 1865 may well have facilitated the transfer of political news and gossip from cities like New Orleans to the plantation districts of Louisiana, thus opening up a channel between urban Radicals and freedpeople in the countryside.[69] At the very least, we can say for certain that the events of late 1865 highlighted the extent to which, on the issue of land reform at least, the CEC was capable of articulating a Radical program with tremendous appeal for rural freedpeople.

The New Orleans Massacre

The mass radicalization and mobilization of urban working people ran head-on into the reactionary expectations of returning Confederates, leading to a wave of racial violence that culminated in the New Orleans Massacre of July 1866. From the beginning, white supremacist forces targeted the fragile infrastructure of black community institutions. Churches and schools in particular came under repeated attack. In mid-July, Thomas Conway complained to Mayor Kennedy that "the Police of the City are breaking up Religious meetings of Colored people."[70] Kennedy's police singled out the Frenchman Street church of John Lewis, an African American preacher who would in September serve as a delegate to the founding convention of the Republican Party.[71] A group of black men complained to Conway that, at the end of the service at the African Methodist Episcopal church, "the Police made their appearance armed with Clubs and holding their watches in their hands and ordering people to disperse."[72] During the summer of 1866, white terrorists carried out a series of arson attacks against black schools, burning down four churches so that their premises could not be used for the education of African American children.[73]

In this context, Governor Wells began to have second thoughts about his relationship with the Confederate veterans who now dominated the Louisiana state government. He felt, for example, that the Black Codes went too far in restricting the right of former slaves and would only serve to bring federal power down upon the state once again. After the Black Codes passed the state legislature, Wells wrote to Absalom Baird of the Freedmen's Bureau and explained that he had "already determined in my own mind" that the new laws were "not only impracticable, but unnecessary."[74] Reluctantly, the governor signed three of the bills into law but vetoed the fourth, claiming that it violated the Thirteenth Amendment. In the early weeks of 1866, Wells again found himself at loggerheads with the white Conservatives he had escorted to their positions of power, first over economic issues and then over the question of whether to hold new municipal elections in New Orleans. When the Rebel legislature overrode Wells's veto on the latter issue and forced new local elections for March, a clear break developed between the conservative Unionist governor and the former Confederates.[75]

Wells abandoned his erstwhile allies with breathtaking speed. In March, he approached the Radical faction led by Durant and Dunn and announced his intention to commence political war with white conservatives. Wells declared himself ready to reopen the constitutional convention of 1864 and unite with the Radicals in order to disenfranchise former Confederates and put the vote in the hands of black men. Although the serving president of that body, Judge Durrell, refused to recall it on legal grounds, his departure from New Orleans in May altered the political terrain. A minority caucus of convention delegates voted in a new president—the more sympathetic Judge Howell—and their nominee initiated proceedings to recall the convention. For their part, the Radicals attempted to mobilize grassroots support in defense of the convention. On Friday, 27 July, just three days before the convention was due to open, Radical white dentist A. P. Dostie addressed a mass meeting of several thousand black and white Republicans, defending the convention, calling for black suffrage, and urging the freedpeople to prepare for armed self-defense.[76]

Alarmed by the militant mood among the Radicals, local authorities prepared to repress the convention. The white supremacist state government petitioned President Johnson and vowed that local courts would declare the convention illegal and issue injunctions to prevent its reopening.[77] Mayor John Monroe wrote to Major General Baird on 25 July stating his intention to arrest any anyone involved in efforts to reopen the convention. "It is my intention to disperse this unlawful assembly," Monroe told the Union officer.[78] The stage was set for a violent confrontation.

On the morning of Monday, 30 July, a crowd of several hundred black and white protesters gathered outside the Mechanic's Institute and rallied to demand the suffrage for black men. The demonstrators were ignoring a proclamation from Mayor Monroe, printed in all of the city's newspapers, which declared the convention an illegal assembly. Several hundred white policemen and "special deputies" surrounded the convention building. When a column of two hundred black veterans, some of them armed, marched up to the Mechanic's Institute from the French Quarter, scuffles broke out and quickly escalated into a general street battle. White policemen and civilians beat, stabbed, and shot the outnumbered African American veterans, killing many, and then turned their attention to the convention hall. Inside, a small number of black men braved volleys of pistol fire in order to barricade the door but proved unable to keep out the white attackers. Police burst into the convention hall and set about the fleeing delegates, killing and injuring several. The violence only abated when General Baird finally mustered his troops and brought them to the Mechanic's Institute at three o'clock that afternoon.

If Monroe and his allies had intended to decapitate the local Radical leadership, they could not have asked for more from the New Orleans Massacre. Although estimates vary, we can say for certain that white rioters killed between forty and fifty people and wounded as many as three hundred. The vast majority of those killed and injured were African American men, but they also included A. P. Dostie, the Radical white dentist who had played such an important role in the development of the revolutionary movement. Dostie died in a hail of half-a-dozen bullets and was also stabbed with a sword. Michael Hahn, the former governor and moderate Unionist who had recently thrown in his lot with the Radicals, was badly beaten and crippled for life. Thomas J. Durant, probably the single most important white Radical leader, heard the sounds of the massacre from his office two blocks away; he snuck out a back entrance, took a closed carriage to the waterfront, and left New Orleans on a steamboat, never to return.[79]

The events of 30 July in New Orleans, along with similar outbreaks in Charleston and Memphis, are widely regarded as a turning point in the coming of Radical Reconstruction. Rioting erupted in Memphis in early May 1866 after black veterans confronted local police over the arrest of an African American man. In the violence that followed, white mobs torched and looted black neighborhoods, leaving forty-six African Americans dead.[80] Black veterans were also centrally involved in several days of unrest in Charleston at the end of June.[81] But the New Orleans Massacre probably eclipsed both of these incidents in terms of its impact on national politics. Donald Reynolds argues that the massacre "convinced a majority of Northerners that the South was determined . . . to keep the Negro in a state of semi-slavery."[82] In a similar vein, Gilles Vandal notes "the role it played in the congressional elections of 1866, and . . . the impetus it gave to the passage of the Reconstruction Acts of March 1867."[83] In other words, the grassroots radicalization of late 1865 and early 1866 provoked the white supremacist authorities of New Orleans to bloodily repress the constitutional convention of 30 July 1866, and this violence in turn stimulated the desire of many Northerners to intervene more forcefully in the postwar South.

Nevertheless, the decapitation of the Radical leadership in the New Orleans Massacre would have profound consequences for the development of Reconstruction politics. The destruction of the Radical faction around the *New Orleans Tribune* put paid to any hopes of a political alliance between the black movement and the white working people of New Orleans. As Eric Arnesen and Caryn Cossé Bell have shown, Thomas Durant and the *Tribune* leadership had been the only forces to seriously advocate such an alliance, and even they did so tepidly. As early as 1863, Durant had "pressed the issue of free black voting rights" at a meeting of the white Workingmen's National Union league and received a surprisingly warm reception from the craftsmen and professionals in attendance.[84] The *Tribune,* meanwhile, expressed support for the eight-hour movement among white workingmen and hoped that an interracial labor coalition might undermine the basis of white supremacy in New Orleans.[85] Even if the Radical leadership had remained intact, however, it is far from clear that white working people in New Orleans would have supported Radical Reconstruction. Many white workingmen remained tied to white supremacy through the political hegemony of the Democratic Party. As Eric Arnesen has noted, "the Democratic Party succeeded in winning most whites—workers included—to its banner in opposition to the black Republicans."[86]

The Radical Coalition

The clash between former Confederates and freedpeople in New Orleans played a major role in prompting greater federal involvement in the South. As early as April 1866, Radical and moderate Republicans had banded together in Congress to pass the Civil Rights Act. Intended to negate the Black Codes, this law granted citizenship to the former slaves, and the Republicans proved willing to override President Johnson's veto in order to pass it. In the summer of 1866, moderate Republicans also spearheaded the effort to enshrine civil rights in the Constitution through the Fourteenth Amendment. The New Orleans Massacre, along with the riot in Memphis, pushed moderate Republicans even further to the left and strengthened their alliance with congressional Radicals. The fall elections both discredited Johnson and delivered a resounding mandate to the Republicans. In March 1867, the new Fortieth Congress passed the Military Reconstruction Acts, which imposed the rule of federal officers on the South and provided for black suffrage.[87]

The Reconstruction Acts had an immediate impact in New Orleans. General Philip Sheridan, who became the military governor of Louisiana and Texas in the new Fifth District, used his new authority to sideline the neo-Confederates. On March 27, the Northern commander removed from office Mayor John Monroe, Attorney General Andrew Herron, and Judge Edmund Abell, all of whom he blamed for the racial violence of the previous summer. The following day, Sheridan called an immediate halt to all local elections and began to explore the possibility of registering a new electorate himself. Despite a lack of advice from further up the chain of command, Sheridan began registration of voters for the fall elections in New Orleans on 12 April and across the state on 21 April. Sheridan's officials registered both black and white voters but excluded hundreds of former Confederate officeholders from the rolls. When the New Orleans police tried to interfere with black registration, Sheridan removed Chief of Police Boylan from office.[88]

The sudden shift in local power dynamics gave new strength and confidence to African American activists in New Orleans. Immediately following the passage of the Reconstructions Acts, black Radicals inaugurated a new campaign against the city's segregated streetcars. Free people of color had resented the system since the antebellum period and had protested it as early as 1833.[89] During the war years, black officers in the Native Guards had demanded the right to use the same cars as their white comrades. But the campaign of April and May 1867 was far more explosive. The *New Orleans Tribune* commenced agitation on the subject in early April, calling on people of color "to show their hands" if they hated segregation.[90] On 28 April, an African American man forced his way onto a white streetcar with the intention of being arrested and testing the issue in court. Although the charges were dismissed, others followed his lead. The campaign came to a head on the weekend of 4 and 5 May. On the Saturday morning, a crowd of young black men gathered on Love Street and began harassing the passing streetcars. One man of color boarded a car, seized the reins from the white driver after a short scuffle, and took off down the street with the police in hot pursuit.[91] Clashes between armed black men and the police continued throughout Saturday and into Sunday. As the weekend drew to a close, a huge crowd of black men and women gathered in Congo Square and threatened or commandeered the passing cars. Fearing that the use of military force was inexpedient, the Republican mayor of New Orleans Edward Heath addressed the crowds himself and convinced them to disperse. The next day, railroad representatives agreed to end the practice of segregation.[92]

Not much more than a week later, black protesters again took to the streets.

This time, the demonstrators were African American longshoremen, and they were angry about the behavior of labor contractors on the waterfront. Trouble between black laborers and the "stevedores," or contractors, was a common occurrence on the waterfront. On 16 May, a crowd of several hundred black men gathered on the levee and claimed that African American contractors were cheating them out of their wages. The strikers managed to blockade and stop work on two steamers, mobbed a particularly unpopular black contractor, and fought with the police. Once again, Mayor Heath came out in public to placate African American protesters, but this time only the threat of military intervention halted the demonstrations. Strikers came out again the following day and successfully stopped work along much of the levee. Finally, on 18 May, federal authorities made a public statement condemning the use of contract labor on the levee and calling on shipmasters to pay their hands themselves. The employers soon fell into line: militant action had brought yet another victory to the black working people of New Orleans.[93]

African American men went to the polls for the first time in September to choose delegates for the constitutional convention. A majority of white Louisianans had either been disenfranchised under Military Reconstruction or decided to boycott the election altogether. Black men made up fifty of the ninety-nine delegates to the constitutional convention when it convened at the end of November. Together with Radical whites, they adopted laws enforcing the desegregation of public accommodations and the creation of an integrated public school system. All future state officials would be required to accept the notion of racial equality. The convention did not, however, agree on a radical measure calling for the redistribution of plantation lands, and neither did it undertake a dramatic disenfranchisement of former rebels.[94]

The state elections of April 1868 showed, once again, the potentially explosive interaction of political conflict and extraparliamentary agitation. Black and white men voted on whether to approve the constitution and elected the state government. In March, violence erupted once more between waterfront workers and contractors in Algiers. When sixty-four black and white laborers threatened their employers, Archer Hinton and John Chase, police took the two contractors into custody "to save them from being mobbed."[95] While the ongoing electoral campaign may well have given confidence to these and other black workers, their employers were more than capable of striking back. In April, a Freedmen's Bureau agent reported that "a great many business men" in Algiers, including the owners of the dry docks and railroad, had fired their black employees "for no other reason than they did not vote according to their employers' wishes at the late election."[96] Similar incidents were taking place across the state. In April, as John Rodrigue has noted, black plantation hands in St. Mary's Parish organized a strike that demonstrated "the unity that freedmen achieved through their political clubs."[97] Understating the case somewhat, one Bureau agent noted that the "heretofore comparatively harmonious actions of the parties seem to have been somewhat disturbed by party spirit in the late elections."[98]

The confluence of electioneering and labor struggles in the spring of 1868 demonstrated the power and volatility of the Radical coalition. It was an alliance based on popular mobilization as well as the ballot box. Caryn Cossé Bell has called Louisiana's 1868 constitution "arguably the Reconstruction South's most radical blueprint for change."[99] While Bell is certainly right to note the influence of Francophone black radicalism on the new state constitution, we must also see the document as the crystallization of the grassroots struggle of the years immediately following the Civil War. This period offers a very concrete view of how an alliance came to be forged between the national Republican Party and black working people in a key urban setting in the former slave South. Partly because of the particular strength and political confidence of urban working people, New Orleans became a crucible of this process. The expanded African American population of the postwar period provided a radicalized and mobilized base for the Central Executive Committee of the Friends of Universal Suffrage; white attempts to contain the upsurge of 1865 led to the New Orleans Massacre, and despite their intentions, to Radical Reconstruction. And the intervention of the national government in turn gave working people the confidence to make yet more demands.

Notes

1. William Dougherty, *Inspection Report for Jefferson Parish*, January 1866, Assistant Inspector General's Consolidated Reports of Conditions of Freedmen on the Plantations, Office of the Assistant Commissioner for Louisiana, BRFAL-LA, RG 105 (M1027).

2. See, for example, Wade, *Slavery in the Cities*; Fields, *Slavery and Freedom on the Middle Ground*; Takagi, *"Rearing Wolves to Our Own Destruction."* On tensions between the Southern elite and white urban workingmen, see Towers, *Urban South*.

3. Hahn, *A Nation under Our Feet*, 119–20.

4. Peter Rachleff, *Black Labor in Richmond*.

5. Buchanan, *Black Life on the Mississippi*; Cecelski, *Waterman's Song*.

6. Fitzgerald, *Urban Emancipation*, 9–10.

7. Hunter, *To 'Joy My Freedom*.

8. Butler, *Butler's Book*, 324.

9. On the changes in the conditions of slaves and masters in occupied Louisiana, see

Ripley, *Slaves and Freedmen* and Gerteis, *From Contraband to Freedman*. On the enlistment of black troops, see Hollandsworth Jr., *Louisiana Native Guards*. For a less complimentary assessment of federal policy in southern Louisiana, see Messner, *Freedmen and the Ideology of Free Labor*.

10. On the emergence of Lincoln's loyalist state government, see McCrary, *Abraham Lincoln and Reconstruction*; Taylor, *Louisiana Reconstructed*; and Capers, *Occupied City*.

11. See Abraham Lincoln to Michael Hahn, 13 March 1864, in Lincoln, *Collected Works*, 7: 243, and Lincoln, "Last Public Address," 11 April 1865, *Collected Works*, 8: 404.

12. Foner, *Reconstruction*, 179–81.

13. Shugg, *Origins of Class Struggle*, 199–200.

14. McCrary, *Abraham Lincoln and Reconstruction*, 219.

15. *New Orleans Bee*, 6 March 1865.

16. Reed, *Life of A. P. Dostie*, 181.

17. J. Burke to T. W. Conway, 10 August 1865, Registered Letters Received, 1865: A-B, Office of the Assistant Commissioner for Louisiana, BRFAL-LA, RG 105 (M1027).

18. Capt. Andrew Morse to John Mitchell, 15 August 1865, Office of the Assistant Commissioner for Louisiana, Provost Marshal General of Freedmen, Letters and Endorsements Sent, vol. 128, p. 2, Ser. 1365, BRFAL-LA, RG 105 [FSSP A-8500].

19. James Emery to T. W. Conway, 17 July 1865, Registered Letters Received, 1865: C-F, Office of the Assistant Commissioner for Louisiana, BRFAL-LA, RG 105 (M1027); Col. Frisbie to Capt. Hennessey, 31 July 1865, Registered Letters Received, 1865: A-B, Office of the Assistant Commissioner for Louisiana, BRFAL-LA, RG 105 (M1027).

20. Dawson, *Army Generals and Reconstruction*, 22–23.

21. Thomas Conway to E. W. Dewees, 19 July 1865, Office of the Assistant Commissioner for Louisiana, Letters Sent, vol. 15, Ser. 1297, BRFAL-LA, RG 105 [FSSP A-8635].

22. J. Madison Wells to T. W. Conway, 24 September 1865, Registered Letters Received, 1865: L-Mc, Office of the Assistant Commissioner for Louisiana, BRFAL-LA, RG 105 (M1027).

23. Hogue, *Uncivil War*, 21.

24. Dawson, *Army Generals and Reconstruction*, 31–32.

25. *New Orleans Bee*, 15 December 1865.

26. Maj. Gen. Absalom Baird to James M. Wells, 18 December, and Baird to O. O. Howard, 20 December 1865, both in Letters Sent, Office of the Assistant Commissioner for Louisiana, BRFAL-LA, RG 105 (M1027).

27. Somers, "Black and White in New Orleans," 21.

28. W. Fisk to T. W. Conway, 29 July 1865, Registered Letters Received, 1865: C-F, Office of the Assistant Commissioner for Louisiana, BRFAL-LA, RG 105 (M1027).

29. Lt. W. Dougherty to Lt. D. G. Fenno, 7 November 1865, Registered Letters Received, 1865: C-F, Office of the Assistant Commissioner for Louisiana, BRFAL-LA, RG 105 (M1027).

30. E. Trefagnier et al. to Lt. William Dougherty, 24 August 1865, L-142, 1865, Letters Received, Ser. 1757, Department of the Gulf, USACC, RG 393 [FSSP C-649]. From the

same record group see also Lt. W. Dougherty to Capt. L. E. Granger, 27 August 1865 and Capt. G. A. Spink to Capt. B. B. Campbell, 3 September 1865.

31. T. J. Beck to Bvt. Lt. Col. G. Lee, 15 October 1866, B-64, 1866, Letters Received, Ser. 1756, Department of the Gulf, USACC, RG 393, pt. 1 [FSSP C-585].

32. William Dougherty, *Inspection Report for Jefferson Parish*, January 1866, Assistant Inspector General's Consolidated Reports of Conditions of Freedmen on the Plantations, Office of the Assistant Commissioner for Louisiana, BRFAL-LA, RG 105 (M1027).

33. *L'Union*, 27 September 1862; Bell, *Afro-Creole Protest Tradition*, 223–25.

34. Houzeau, *My Passage*, 1–24.

35. Tregle Jr., "Thomas J. Durant," 490.

36. Ibid., 494–512. See also, for example, Thomas J. Durant to Stanislas Wrotnowski, 14 December 1863, Thomas Jefferson Durant Papers, New York Historical Society Library.

37. Foner, *Freedom's Lawmakers*, 67.

38. Houzeau, *My Passage*, 75.

39. State of Louisiana Republican Party, *Proceedings of the Convention*, 1–2.

40. Ibid., 5–8.

41. Ibid., 8–9.

42. Ibid., 11; Rankin, "Origins of Black Leadership," 436–40.

43. Rankin, "Origins of Black Leadership," 426, 431–32.

44. State of Louisiana Republican Party, *Proceedings of the Convention*, 11.

45. Ibid., 1–5.

46. Joseph Wilson, *Black Phalanx*, 169; Hollandsworth, *Louisiana Native Guards*, 26–27.

47. See David Owen Evans, *Social Romanticism*.

48. Houzeau, *My Passage*, 79–83.

49. *New Orleans Tribune*, 26 May and 1 June 1865.

50. State of Louisiana Republican Party, *Proceedings of the Convention*, 13–17.

51. Ibid., 21–31.

52. Ibid., 26.

53. Hahn, *A Nation under Our Feet*, 124–25.

54. State of Louisiana Republican Party, *Proceedings of the Convention*, 33.

55. *New Orleans Tribune*, 29 November 1864, and 6 May 1865.

56. Vandal, "Black Utopia," 443.

57. Ibid.

58. Ripley, *Slaves and Freedmen*, 79–83.

59. Vandal, "Black Utopia," 444–52.

60. Arnesen, *Waterfront Workers*, 7–9.

61. Ibid., 21–24. On the waterfront strikes, see also Maj. A. M. Jackson to Lt. Z. K. Wood, 21 December 1865, vol. 353/847 DG, p. 59, Letters Sent by the Provost Marshal, Ser. 1491, Provost Marshal of Orleans Parish, Provost Marshal Field Orgs, USACC, RG 393 pt. 4 [FSSP C-663]. And Maj. Gen. Canby to Nathaniel Burbank, 23 December 1865; Mayor H. Kennedy to John Burke, chief of police, 25 December 1865; Burke to Kennedy, 26 December 1865; and Kennedy to Gov. J. Madison Wells, 29 December 1865, all filed in

P-243, 1865, Letters Received, Ser. 1757, Department of Louisiana, USACC, RG 393 pt. 1 [FSSP C-663].

62. Rankin, introduction to *My Passage*, by Houzeau, 39.

63. William Dougherty, *Inspection Report for Jefferson Parish*, January 1866, Assistant Inspector General's Consolidated Reports of Conditions of Freedmen on the Plantations, Office of the Assistant Commissioner for Louisiana, BRFAL-LA, RG 105 (M1027).

64. Monthly Report of W. E. Dougherty for Jefferson Parish, February 1866, Inspection Reports of Plantations from Subordinate Officers, Office of the Assistant Commissioner for Louisiana, BRFAL-LA, RG 105 (M1027).

65. Such fears were nearly universal across the South in late 1865. See, for example, Litwack, *Been in the Storm So Long*, 425–30 and Hahn, "'Extravagant Expectations' of Freedom."

66. G. W. Bridges to Lt. D. G. Fenno, 29 July 1865, Registered Letters Received, 1865: A-B, Office of the Assistant Commissioner for Louisiana, BRFAL-LA, RG 105 (M1027).

67. C. W. Hawes to T. W. Conway, 25 September 1865, Registered Letters Received, 1865: G-K, Office of the Assistant Commissioner for Louisiana, BRFAL-LA, RG 105 (M1027); R. W. Jamison et al. to Gov. James Madison Welles, 13 October 1865, Registered Letters Received, 1865: L-Mc, Office of the Assistant Commissioner for Louisiana, BRFAL-LA, RG 105 (M1027).

68. T. W. Conway to Maj. Gen. O. O. Howard, 23 September 1865, Letters Sent, vol. 1., June 1865–April 1869, Office of the Assistant Commissioner for Louisiana, BRFAL-LA, RG 105 (M1027); Maj. Gen. O. O. Howard, Circular Letter, 11 November 1865, Registered Letters Received, 1865: R-S, Office of the Assistant Commissioner for Louisiana, BRFAL-LA, RG 105 (M1027).

69. Hahn, *A Nation under Our Feet*, 142–43.

70. Thomas Conway to Mayor Hugh Kennedy, 17 July 1865, Office of the Assistant Commissioner for Louisiana, Letters Sent, vol. 15, p. 161, Ser. 1297, BRFAL-LA, RG 105 [FSSP A-8635].

71. Thomas Conway to Mayor Hugh Kennedy, 22 July 1865, Office of the Assistant Commissioner for Louisiana Letters Sent, vol. 15, p. 185, Ser. 1297, BRFAL-LA, RG 105 [FSSP A-8635].

72. George Washington et al. to Thomas Conway, 1 August 1865, Registered Letters Received, 1865: T-Z and 1866: Y-Z, Office of the Assistant Commissioner for Louisiana, BRFAL-LA, RG 105 (M1027).

73. Annual Narrative Report of Operations and Conditions for 1866, Monthly and Annual Reports of Operations, Office of the Assistant Commissioner for Louisiana, BRFAL-LA, RG 105 (M1027).

74. James M. Wells to Maj. Gen. A. Baird, 18 December 1865, Registered Letters Received, 1865: L-Mc, Office of the Assistant Commissioner for Louisiana, BRFAL-LA, RG 105 (M1027). And in the same record group see also, Maj. Gen. A. Baird to O. O. Howard, 20 December 1865, Letters Sent.

75. Hogue, *Uncivil War*, 31–33.

76. Reed, *Life of A. P. Dostie*, 289–98; *New-Orleans Riot*, 1.

77. *New-Orleans Riot*, 1–2.

78. Mayor John T. Monroe to Gen. Baird, 25 July 1866, N-67. 1866, Letters Received, Ser. 1757, Department of Louisiana, USACC, RG 393, pt. 1 [FSSP C-679].

79. Tregle, Jr., "Thomas J. Durant," 485.

80. Ryan, "The Memphis Riots" and Waller, "Community, Class, and Race." For a short discussion of the political and social context for these outbreaks, see Litwack, *Been in the Storm So Long*, 280–82.

81. *Charleston Daily News*, 25 and 27 June 1866. See also, Robert N. Rosen, *Charleston*, 124.

82. Reynolds, "New Orleans Riot," 5.

83. Vandal, "Origins of the New Orleans Riot," 135.

84. Bell, *Afro-Creole Protest Tradition*, 249–50.

85. Arnesen, *Waterfront Workers*, 24.

86. Ibid., 31.

87. Foner, *Reconstruction*, 243–80.

88. Dawson, *Army Generals and Reconstruction*, 46–49.

89. Bell, *Afro-Creole Protest Tradition*, 82.

90. *New Orleans Tribune*, 9 and 21 April 1867.

91. Ibid., 5 May 1867.

92. Fischer, "A Pioneer Protest," 223–28.

93. *New Orleans Tribune*, 18, 19, and 20 May 1867; Arnesen, *Waterfront Workers*, 29–31.

94. Bell, *Afro-Creole Protest Tradition*, 272–73; Shugg, *Origins of Class Struggle*, 221–23.

95. Trimonthly Report for Parish of Orleans, Left Bank, 31 March 1867, Monthly and Trimonthly Reports, New Orleans Field Office, BRFAL-LA, RG 105 (M1483).

96. R. Folles to Capt. Sterling, 30 April 1867, Letters Sent, Agent and Assistant Sub-Assistant Commissioner for Algiers, Louisiana, BRFAL-LA, RG 105 (M1905).

97. Rodrigue, *Reconstruction in the Cane Fields*, 97–98.

98. Monthly Report for Parish of Orleans, Left Bank, 1 June 1867, Monthly and Trimonthly Reports, New Orleans Field Office, BRFAL-LA, RG 105 (M1483).

99. Bell, *Afro-Creole Protest Tradition*, 1.

3

"Surrounded on All Sides by an Armed and Brutal Mob"

Newspapers, Politics, and Law in the Ogeechee Insurrection, 1868–1869

JONATHAN M. BRYANT

On 29 December 1868, the *Savannah Republican* ran an editorial presenting the advantages of annexing the Republic of Santo Domingo. There would be no international outcry, argued the editor, and the people of Santo Domingo would welcome American control. "The negroes' . . . rule," explained the newspaper, "has been marked in every stage by the grossest misgovernment and atrocities at which humanity shudders." The free blacks of Santo Domingo were by their nature "cruel and debased," and would only benefit from American rule. The black people of Santo Domingo, who had lived in idleness since 1821, could be made productive again under American management. Most readers probably nodded their heads in agreement. Reconstruction was a time of grave uncertainty, but if there was one thing elite white Savannahians could agree on, it was the propensity of former slaves to indolence and violence.[1]

Turning the page, those same readers would have found another article entitled, "Armed Negroes on the Ogeechee Road." The *Republican* reported that armed blacks were guarding the road some seven miles south of the city and continued, "evidence accumulates from day to day showing that there are armed and organized bodies of negroes on every road leading into the city." This in itself was disturbing news, but that same day events along the Ogeechee would inspire a frenzy of fear in Savannah. By early January 1869, readers of many papers across the United States, including the *New York Times*, the *Quincy Whig* (Illinois), the *Philadelphia Daily Evening Bulletin*, the *Maine Farmer*, and even the *London Times* read of a massive insurrection by freedpeople along the Ogeechee River, the burning of plantation houses, and the plight of frightened refugees pouring into the besieged city of Savannah. There, brave citizens organized a several hundred man defense force until the city was finally saved by the arrival of hundreds of federal troops. It was an exciting tale that caught the interest of readers across the county. The only problem was, there was no insurrection on the Ogeechee.[2]

The Ogeechee insurrection is more than a story of criminal acts by disaffected workers in the Ogeechee rice district and an overreaction by threatened white elites in Savannah. The conflict connects the political and economic rights of laborers and highlights the freedpeople's desire to control the land upon which they worked. It raises questions about the influence of newspapers and the role of the legal system in the reconstruction of Georgia. Finally, it illustrates a central lesson often found in Reconstruction stories. Thirty years ago David Brion Davis showed us that the existence of slavery in Western culture fueled the creation of concepts of free labor and universal human rights. This story, however, shows us how fragile those rights are in the face of elite legal stratagems, media manipulation, and state power.[3]

In antebellum America the belief that enslaved Africans would only work under compulsion was common. So too were fears that slaves might rise in violent insurrection. Thus, the slave regime created a system of overseers and patrols to monitor the work and the activities of the enslaved. Of course, the newspaper's mention of Santo Domingo would have raised images of the most fearsome slave revolt of all, the revolution that created Haiti in 1804. The specter of large-scale slave insurrection and the massacre of whites haunted slaveholding Americans, and this menace was reemphasized by John Brown's 1859 raid. During the Civil War the fear of revolt continued enhanced by rumors of numerous slave conspiracies, by the ongoing disintegration of the slave regime, and by the appearance of armed African American soldiers in the Union Army.[4]

Such fears did not magically vanish with emancipation. Newspapers across Georgia expected both sloth and violence from the newly freed slaves. The Thomasville *Southern Enterprise* asked, "Will the Free Negro Labor?" Joseph Addison Turner's *Countryman* answered that "Negroes will not work unless they are forced to do so, and they can not be forced to do so unless they are slaves." The editor of the *Albany Patriot* agreed, arguing, "A great majority of the freedmen will not work unless compelled to. And the sooner they are forced to earn their bread by the sweat of their brow, the sooner affairs will resume their customary channels." During the last half of 1865 the *Savannah Daily Herald* ran dozens of stories about "negro outrages," printing tales from correspondent newspapers across the country of freedmen attacking whites, raping white women, or refusing to work. In December 1865 an article entitled "More Negro Disturbances" called for action. The law was of no use in dealing with the problems of black indigence and violence, argued the *Daily Herald*, and so white Georgians should turn to other means. "The recent manifestations, in different parts of the State, of insubordination and violence by evil (*sic*) disposed freedmen clearly demonstrate the necessity for an immediate organization of volunteer companies . . . to suppress violence and preserve order." While the "Negro Disturbances" complained of in the article occurred on rice plantations along the Savannah River, the whites of Savannah were also disturbed by rumors of a planned Christmas uprising by freedpeople across the South. While nothing came of these rumors, they reflected the atmosphere of fear that followed emancipation.[5]

Readers of the *Savannah Morning News* surely shared this feeling of crisis. The leading newspaper in the city, its offices were on East Bay Street next to the customs house in the commercial center of Savannah. The telegraphic connections to the Associated Press wire were located in the newspaper's building, and so the *Morning News* mediated most news sent to the larger world. Through 1866 and 1867 the paper's reports had presented a city battered by unnecessary political conflict, struggling against unconstitutional oppression, and threatened by bestial enemies. The core problem was the freedmen. By August 1868 the paper argued "The negroes are daily provoking the whites—by their acts saying 'we defy you.' It is time their insolence should be checked, and when it is done, let it be done in such a manner that . . . it will strike terror to the heart of each member of the race so long as it is in existence." Over the next several months the paper continued with similar threatening observations as it ridiculed Republican Governor Rufus Bullock's administration, reported on armed black militias drilling in the plantation districts, and argued that the freedmen presented a threat to a legitimate presidential election in November.

When Governor Bullock suspended poll taxes for the coming election, the *Morning News* suggested this would allow every "lazy negro" to vote. They reported with outrage the "insulting" statements made at Republican political meetings. They worried over the details of voting procedures established for the November 3rd general election. They discussed the disposition of federal troops across the state for Election Day. The editors of the *Morning News* made it clear that Republican plots and the bestial nature of the Freedmen meant disaster for the city of Savannah.[6]

On Election Day, 3 November 1868, perhaps a thousand freedmen lined up before dawn at the Chatham County courthouse to vote. Soon after voting began a qualifications committee began turning away most black voters, citing their inability to prove they had paid the poll tax. Hundreds of disappointed black men gathered in the square in front of the courthouse as hundreds more waited patiently in line to vote. Suddenly, a large group of policemen pushed the line of freedmen away from the doorway of the courthouse so that a group of white railroad workers could go in to vote. The freedmen pushed back, and violence erupted. Policemen opened fire on the crowd, killing three freedmen. At least seventeen more freedmen were wounded, and black voters were driven from the polls. Two policemen died in the fray as well. Assembling at a church about an hour later, black leaders concluded it was too dangerous to vote and warned freedmen not to return to the polls. Thus, the Democratic presidential candidates won a resounding majority in Savannah.[7]

That evening a white posse rode out from Savannah to search for "black radicals," and found them. There followed a gun battle on the Ogeechee Road that resulted in the death of the son of a prominent white Savannahian. Nor was the battle finished, warned the *Morning News*. Armed gangs of freedmen, the paper reported, influenced by black politician Aaron Bradley and the Loyal League, roamed the countryside around Savannah. Over the next several weeks, shots were often exchanged between freedmen and posses of whites. These skirmishes resulted in the deaths of two German immigrants, who were on patrol, and an unknown number of freedmen. By late December the isolation and siege of Savannah that had been predicted and feared by the editors of the *Morning News* seemed finally in place.[8]

The siege began in earnest, according to the newspaper, when freed workers on the Ogeechee plantations rose in rebellion. These plantations, between the Little Ogeechee and Ogeechee rivers south of Savannah, made up Georgia's richest rice plantation district before the Civil War. The newspaper reported that on Monday, December 21, freedmen had fired on the night watchmen at Southfield and Prairie plantations, wounding both, before stealing thousands of pounds of rice. "The negroes have become emboldened" declared the newspaper, "and threaten to drive out the whites." Two days later, J. Motte Middleton, who rented two Ogeechee plantations and managed a third, swore out warrants against seventeen of his workers for theft and attempted murder. On 24 December 1868, the *Savannah Morning News* warned that "on all the Ogeechee plantations the negroes appear to be banded together, thoroughly organized, and armed."[9]

On the morning of 29 December 1868, Chatham County Sheriff James Dooner and two deputies, Julius Kaufmann and Emanuel Mendel, took the seven o'clock train to Miller's Station in the Ogeechee district. There, they spent the day serving warrants for the attacks at Southfield and Prairie plantations. In later sworn testimony the sheriff characterized his actions as very circumspect, reasonable, and even cautious. He allowed four of the men arrested to go to their homes to pick up clothes and tobacco to take with them to jail. The fifth man arrested, Solomon Farley, was thought to be the president of the local Loyal League. Keeping Farley under arrest, the sheriff and his deputies returned to the train station at about three in the afternoon. There they waited for the other four men to surrender themselves. To their surprise, instead of the four freedmen, a large body of men they said were armed with muskets and bayonets and formed in military order emerged from the woods. This was entirely unexpected by the sheriff and his men. Terrified, they abandoned their prisoner and ran from the open train platform to take refuge in William Miller's house a few hundred yards away.[10]

According to the *Savannah Morning News*, the freedmen surrounded Miller's house. According to the sheriff, a group of freedwomen armed with sticks joined the crowd and began beating the sticks on the ground rhythmically and calling on the men to kill the whites. Freedmen shouted, "Come out, you white sons of bitches, sons of rebels." Confused and disoriented by the unexpected response of the freedpeople, the sheriff and his deputies surrendered but still tried to exercise authority over the freedpeople. The sheriff explained that he was there to serve warrants, but a freedman cut him off, saying "We have our own law here." The freedmen manhandled the sheriff and his deputies, taking their pistols and papers. Then, one man said, "Now clear out, you white sons of bitches." The sheriff and his deputies hurried down the road that paralleled the railroad toward Savannah. Sometime later a freight train picked them up and took them to the city.[11]

Many whites in Savannah were terrified or outraged by these events. While Savannah's population was approximately half white and half black, whites in the city knew they were an island surrounded by a sea of freedpeople living in the plantation districts around the city. The 1870 census counted more than 4,200 black people in the Ogeechee plantation district and only 411 whites. Nearby Bryan County was almost 60 percent African American, while neighboring Liberty County was more than 70 percent black. This demographic reality only increased the fears of whites in Savannah.[12]

Sensational reports in the *Morning News* of attacks on whites, of entire families fleeing the Ogeechee, of the violence spreading to other areas, increased the anger and panic in a city under siege by black rebels. Thanks to the magic of telegraphy and the correspondent relationships between newspapers, readers across the United States were able to follow the story. The *New York Times* printed the telegraphic summaries of events until copies of Savannah papers arrived by sea. On January 4 the *New York Times* printed verbatim accounts from the *Savannah Morning News* and from the *Savannah Republican* of the freedpeople assaulting the sheriff and rejecting the warrants. Newspapers across the political spectrum, such as the *Philadelphia Daily Evening Bulletin*, the *Reading Eagle* (Pennsylvania), and the *Daily Quincy Herald* (Illinois), printed the story as well.[13]

On December 30 more than one hundred men volunteered to support the sheriff's return to the Ogeechee. The next day, Thursday, the sheriff and this posse set out in a special train. As they neared Miller's Station, members of the posse opened fire on every black person in sight, reportedly killing a fourteen year old boy, wounding others, and causing people gathered at the train station to flee. Some of the posse yahooed and whooped, giving "rebel yells" as if they were in battle. Unable to control the posse and having lost the element of surprise, Sheriff Dooner ordered the train to return to Savannah. The *Morning News* argued that the posse's failure revealed the increasingly dire situation facing Savannah, claiming, "The negroes are receiving reinforcements from Bryan and Liberty Counties . . . and have all the roads . . . strongly guarded."[14]

In Savannah, Henry Rootes Jackson thrust himself forward as the leader who could save the city. A former U.S. Attorney, Minister to Austria, and a published poet, during the Civil War Jackson rose to the rank of brigadier general in the Confederate Army. After the posse's retreat, General Jackson spoke to a large crowd gathered at the courthouse square. "What becomes of the City of Savannah," Jackson asked, "surrounded on all sides by an armed and brutal mob?" Savannah would be destroyed, commerce would wither, and blacks would rule. The only hope for survival was to "meet organization with organization, force with force." After this speech, a "Committee of Public Safety" headed by Jackson organized a posse comitatus to march on the Ogeechee district. Colonel Arthur Williams, the United States Army officer commanding at the barracks in Savannah, reported that General Jackson "organized four (4) battalions of citizens with complete military organization commanded by Generals and Colonels to go down and fight the negroes on the Ogeechee." Made up of "former rebels," Williams reported the militia numbered six to eight hundred men.[15]

In fact, Colonel Williams harbored significant questions about the Ogeechee insurrection, as the *Morning News* had dubbed events. On 1 January

1869, he telegraphed General Caleb Sibley in Atlanta that he thought the newspaper reports of violence and insurrection were exaggerated, that he was investigating events, and to await a fuller report. Meanwhile, General Sibley ordered four companies of the Sixteenth Infantry to Savannah to suppress the insurrection. Even as the first companies boarded trains in Atlanta on January 3rd, a hurried telegram arrived from Colonel Williams reporting he had matters in hand and there was no reason to send troops. He asked General Sibley to wait for his full report because "Newspaper accounts are not correct."[16]

Colonel Williams's full report arrived later that day. It stood in remarkable contrast to the newspaper accounts of events along the Ogeechee. Williams, accompanied only by his aide Major Perkins, went to the Ogeechee plantation district on the night of 2 January 1869. There, after much searching, he found a group of about fifty frightened freedmen. The only arms he saw were three guns and a bayonet on a stick. There were no fortifications, no organized militia units, no hostile demonstrations. The men named in the warrants were willing to surrender to the military but not to the sheriff. In fact, on January 4th these seventeen men came to Savannah and surrendered. Williams saw nothing to suggest that the events along the Ogeechee were anything more than a bitter labor conflict between plantation managers and workers.[17]

On the night of Sunday, January 3rd, the first two companies of U. S. infantry arrived in Savannah. Two more companies arrived the next day. The army ordered the posse comitatus dissolved, and began planning the U.S. Army's expedition into the Ogeechee district. Complicating matters was the revelation that over thirteen hundred warrants had been issued by local Justice Philip M. Russell Jr. for the arrest of virtually every black man living in the Ogeechee district. All were charged in the warrants with insurrection against the State of Georgia, a capital crime.[18]

On Wednesday, January 6th, the Ogeechee expedition left by train for Miller's Station. Sheriff Dooner and eight deputies, no doubt weighed down by warrants, accompanied the soldiers. The soldiers reported "all quiet along the Ogeechee." Rice had been stolen from barns, and the great houses on Southfield and Prairie plantations had been ransacked, but not burned as had been reported in the *Morning News*. Other plantation houses were untouched. The troops found no sign of armed militia or resistance to U. S. authority. The military expedition confirmed Colonel Williams's earlier reports. General Sibley's report to General George Meade on the expedition suggested that Sheriff Dooner and his deputies were cowards who had run from imaginary threats. Having restored order, the army protected Sheriff Dooner and his deputies as they performed their civil duties. That first day the sheriff arrested sixty-eight men. These were sent back to Savannah by the army and kept at the Oglethorpe Barracks under military guard. Eventually, 143 freedmen from the Ogeechee district would be arrested by Dooner. All were charged with insurrection.[19]

The court of inquiry dealing with these suspects would normally have been a small affair, reported on briefly in the local affairs columns of the newspaper. The scale of the arrests and the reporting of the *Savannah Morning News*, however, had transformed the importance of the proceeding dramatically. Then, on 10 January 1869, the U.S. Army's reports on the Ogeechee insurrection became public. These reports vindicated Colonel Williams's report. There had been no insurrection along the Ogeechee; instead this was a labor conflict poorly managed by incompetent local officials. The editor of the *Morning News* expressed shock. These reports maligned the sheriff, his deputies, and Savannah's best men with lies and errors. Characterizing Republicans as a "fanatical Junta," the *Morning News* then argued that the military reports intended "to excite the unjust prejudice and provoke the vindictive legislation of Congress against our people." Governor Bullock and other Republicans, argued the paper, had organized and directed the insurrection in order to influence the current national conflict over reimposing military reconstruction in Georgia. "When the secret history of the Ogeechee Insurrection is fully developed," wrote one correspondent, "it will be established . . . it was but . . . a vile party plot. In a word, that it was intended to be another Camilla affair, to be used in Washington to influence the actions of Congress."[20]

Suddenly the court of inquiry seemed even more important. It would provide a forum where sworn testimony could establish what really happened on the Ogeechee and perhaps reveal that "secret history." The hearing would vindicate the reporting of the *Morning News* and the actions of Savannah's white leaders, while revealing the U.S. Army's complicity with the Radical Republicans. In other words, rather than using the newspaper and public opinion to influence a trial, conservatives in Savannah hoped to use the court proceedings and the newspaper reports, passed through the *Savannah Morning News* and the Associated Press, to shape public opinion nationally.[21]

That opinion, meanwhile, was increasingly not good. The response of some national newspapers to contradictory reports about the Ogeechee insurrection had been worrisome to the editors of the *Morning News*. Even in Savannah, the reporting of the other leading paper, the *Republican* had been more cautious about the Ogeechee troubles. As early as December 31, the *Savannah Republican* printed affidavits about the events along the Ogeechee, arguing that while the situation was bad, reports of some outrages, "like many other sensation (*sic*) reports which obtained circulation, proved to be without any foundation in fact." The *Republican* did not control the AP wire, so it took the arrival of actual copies of the newspaper by sea for those in other cities to read the more cautious reporting. Once this occurred, controlling the Ogeechee story grew more difficult. On January 5th, the *Philadelphia Daily Evening Bulletin* reported that military dispatches from Washington suggested "a different version . . . from that heretofore published coming from rebel sources through the Associated Press." The *Quincy Whig* stated simply "Rebel Reports Much Exaggerated." These and other dismissive newspaper reports meant there was a need to give the nation convincing evidence of what happened on the Ogeechee, argued the *Morning News*. The commitment hearing would provide that opportunity.[22]

Savannah's legal elite all wanted a part of this important and much publicized hearing. Instead of just one justice, a board of all four magistrate judges assembled; an unprecedented occurrence. George Wilfong, a reporter for the *Morning News*, was asked to act as court reporter. In fact, Wilfong's daily proceedings were published within hours in the *Morning News* and the next day in the *Savannah Daily Advertiser*. Daily summaries composed by the *Morning News* were sent out over the Associated Press wire. Spectacular legal teams also assembled for this minor hearing. The Georgia Solicitor General, Alfred B. Smith, was present, but the state's lead prosecutor was former Confederate General Henry Rootes Jackson. The defense team consisted of Amherst W. Stone, a Vermont-born former U.S. Attorney and Republican politician, and James Johnson, the former provisional governor of the state of Georgia. The defense was joined by the current U.S. Attorney, Henry Fitch, who had been ordered by federal authorities to assist the defense only against the charge of insurrection. As the *Morning News* correctly observed, "It is a remarkable proceeding . . . for an officer of the United States Government to be sent to defend persons charged with insurrection against State Authority."[23]

At nine o'clock on 15 January 1869, the Chatham County courthouse filled with spectators. Blacks packed the gallery and the hallways, while whites occupied the seats in the courtroom and crowded into the doorways. This was not a trial, so witnesses were allowed to sit in open court, to hear the testimony of other witnesses, and to read the testimony printed daily in the newspaper. Twenty-five freedmen charged with insurrection were brought into the courtroom, and Justice Philip Russell Jr., who had taken the position of presiding magistrate, asked if the defense would allow all twenty-five cases to be heard at the same time. James Johnson answered for the defense that each case should be taken separately. General Jackson agreed, and the magistrates called the case of Captain Green.[24]

This court of inquiry was merely a commitment hearing, similar to an arraignment, intended to protect defendants' habeas corpus rights by having a magistrate determine if sufficient evidence existed to support the charges against a defendant. Such hearings rarely took more than a few minutes. Even full-blown felony trials before Georgia's Superior Courts in the mid-nineteenth century rarely took more than half a day. The commitment hearing for Captain Green, however, would last two weeks. As the case proceeded it became clear that the defendant was merely incidental to the attorneys' purposes. Prosecutor Henry R. Jackson portrayed Captain Green as part of a large and frightening conspiracy to resist the laws of Georgia, an insurrection that revealed both the threat posed by unrestrained freedmen and the need for the State to provide civil order by strict control of the freedmen. Jackson also presented the "insurgents" as tools used by the Radical Republicans to discredit civil authority in Georgia, even as the U.S. House Reconstruction Committee in Washington debated re-imposing military reconstruction.[25]

In contrast, U.S. Attorney Henry Fitch intended to show there had been no insurrection along the Ogeechee. This conflict, he argued, had grown out of disagreements over employment contracts on the Ogeechee plantations. The freedpeople were not insurrectionaries; they were strikers. In fact, Fitch argued, the case demonstrated that Georgia's civil authorities were not capable of managing their own affairs, for they could not even deal with simple labor conflicts between employers and workers. Thus, they had called in the military. As the hearing went forward, Fitch showed little interest in the actual defendant, and only Stone and Johnson demonstrated any concern about the plight of the prisoners.[26]

The State's case began well. Sheriff Dooner along with Deputies Kaufmann and Mendel, recounted the events of December 29, when armed freedmen rescued Solomon Farley at Miller's Station and disarmed, robbed, and humiliated the law officers. Captain Green was identified as the man who took Deputy Kaufmann's pistol. Sheriff Dooner described an organized military unit of about two hundred men. Deputy Mendel testified that there were at least 350 armed men. Despite sharp cross-examination by Fitch, the stories held up. Fitch pressured the witnesses so roughly that at one point Deputy Kaufmann burst out "I can not explain what I mean . . . in English. I can explain it in German." By the end of the fourth day the State seemed to have made a strong case that was virtually identical to the reporting in the *Morning News*.[27]

On the fifth day, however, the first cracks appeared. Two state witnesses explained that the entire affair was really part of a conflict over the possession of the land and labor contracts. Testifying for the prosecution, George Houston, a black manager at Prairie Plantation, explained that there was no military organization among the freedpeople. Then, Reddin Baxley, an experienced white overseer on Southfield Plantation, insisted, he'd seen "no military organization there . . . never have heard of or seen any drilling among the negroes there." On the sixth day the state encountered more problems with its witnesses. George Berrien, a freedman, was called. He told of meeting several freedmen who had been on their way to work when the sheriff's large posse arrived by train at Miller's Station and opened fire. He saw one black man shot through the arm. More important, when asked, he testified that there were no militia units or military units of any kind on the Ogeechee.[28]

His testimony surprised the prosecution, and an outraged General Jackson shouted for the magistrates to charge the freedman with perjury and strike his testimony from the record. Henry Fitch calmly pointed out that the state could not impeach its own witness. General Jackson was livid, for the core of his case was predicated upon the idea that militia units were prohibited by the federal authorities in Georgia, and thus any military organization or militia among the blacks would be prima facie evidence of insurrection. The irony of a former Confederate general insisting that military force outside the control of the federal government was evidence of a capital crime apparently occurred to no one.[29]

Over the next eight days the defense presented its witnesses. All denied the existence of any organized military unit and attributed the conflict to contract difficulties on the plantations. A few discussed the issues of land ownership, but defense attorneys generally led witnesses away from such matters. The thrust of the defense presentation was to minimize the nature of the conflict along the Ogeechee and emphasize the failures of state officials in dealing with the problem. On the final day U.S. Attorney Fitch gave an astounding closing argument for the defense. Captain Green, he explained, was "an ignorant and primitive negro," one whose execution for insurrection "might not be a serious loss to society, but as a precedent, it was a serious matter." State authorities had overreacted to reports made by cowardly law enforcement officers covering their failures. Fitch even quipped that Deputy Kaufmann was the "Flying Dutchman," for running away so readily. There was no insurrection; there were merely thieving and lazy blacks who sought "a life of indolence and ease." The freedmen should be punished for theft, perhaps punished for resisting arrest, "but to arraign this prisoner for insurrection was the most tempestuous tempest in the most infinitesimal teapot" that he had ever seen."[30]

General Jackson erupted with rage: "A tempest in a teapot, where a whole region of the country had been ravaged!" He pointed to testimony that there were muskets, bayonets, even new Enfield rifles seen in the hands of the freedmen. Military organizations had been proved, he argued, and once the conflict assumed the character of a military movement it then became an insurrection. The threat was real, and the people of Georgia were powerless to defend themselves thanks to the policies of the federal government. Captain Green was guilty of insurrection beyond any doubt, as were all the others, and the Republican Party and the state government shared their guilt.[31]

The court of inquiry ruled in the case of Captain Green on 29 January 1869. Reflecting the grandiosity of the entire event, the decision was laid out like a Supreme Court opinion. As Justice Russell read it aloud in the courtroom, the lawyers must have realized how much politics had caused them to lose sight of the true nature of the proceeding. As Justice Russell explained, "The simple question to be determined is whether the testimony [supports] suspicion of the guilt of the accused." In other words, the magistrates simply decided if the evidence gave sufficient reason to charge the defendant. If so, then the magistrates were duty bound to commit the defendant to trial. That, and nothing else, was the nature of the hearing. Given the evidence, Russell ruled that Captain Green should be committed to trial.[32]

As the lawyers wrangled and dragged the case out over half a month, the attitude of many whites in Savannah began to change. The hearing was no public relations coup and instead produced a story that was messy and ambiguous. The convoluted and contradictory evidence, the clear political agendas of the attorneys, and concerns about the costs of the proceedings, all began to dominate public discussion of the event. Public jesting outside the courtroom about the Flying Dutchman nearly resulted in a fistfight between Deputy Kaufmann and a reporter. Even the *Savannah Morning News* began to refer to the "long and tedious investigation of the Ogeechee Insurrection." "The darkies have had their fun out of the affair," wrote the editor, as if this extended hearing was the choice of the freedmen involved or some absurd game to be expected of ignorant ex-slaves. Then the paper lamented that "the white people will now have to pay the piper." This from the paper that only a month before had presented Savannah as a city under siege and had welcomed the hearing as a source of truth about the Ogeechee insurrection.[33]

Meanwhile, though the *New York Times* continued dutifully to print the

AP dispatches about the hearing, they appeared under "Brief Notes" or as filler after other articles about the South. Other newspapers, including the *Philadelphia Daily Evening Bulletin*, the *Daily Quincy Herald*, the *Quincy Whig*, the *Reading Eagle*, the *Lancaster Intelligencer* (Pennsylvania), and even the *Maine Farmer* dropped the story and turned to other matters. As the *New York Tribune's* correspondent, reporting from Savannah, explained, "the newspapers caught up the big item, and in blazing headlines made of it a first-class sensation." Then, reliable information came from the military, and "pricked thus, the whole bubble burst."[34]

The commitment proceedings for the remainder of the prisoners went forward quickly and were recorded only in the docket. Forty-three freedmen were committed to trial, thirty-one discharged by the magistrates, and the remainder released by the Solicitor General. These men languished in jail for five months until the May term Superior Court. At that time the Grand Jury returned true bills against only six of the Ogeechee prisoners, including Captain Green, charging them with robbery and assault. As to the charge of insurrection, the Grand Jury returned no bill. At trial, the focus was upon the robbery of the sheriff and his deputies at Miller's Station. Captain Green and the five others were convicted of stealing Kaufmann's pistol and money. They were sentenced to five years at hard labor. These events were only briefly noted in the local columns of the *Morning News*. As debate over the reimposition of military reconstruction continued, the newspaper's editors probably thought it best to avoid mention of the Ogeechee insurrection. A year later, in July 1870, Governor Rufus Bullock pardoned all six freedmen.[35]

So, what had happened on the Ogeechee? Thankfully, there are rich sources in the Freedmen's Bureau records and in the records of the American Missionary Association that shed some light on Ogeechee troubles and the nature of the "insurrection." In the winter of 1866, Dr. John R. Cheves returned to his Grove Point plantation of about 2,000 acres on the Ogeechee neck to resume operation of what had been a very successful rice plantation before the Civil War. Soon after arriving, Cheves contracted with one hundred of his former slaves for a year's labor on the plantation. Then things began to go wrong. Perhaps the most difficult work on the rice plantations was maintenance of the irrigation system. The heavy labor involved in ditching, dyking, and keeping the waterways clear of vegetation was exhausting, and the freedpeople refused to do the work because it was not specifically included in the contract. "They did not prepare the lands according to custom but in the rudest and most slovenly manner," complained Cheves, who evidently thought the ditching was implicit in the contract. When Cheves tried to assert his authority both as the landowner and employer under the contract, the freedpeople ignored him. "For a year past," he explained, "[they had] been indoctrinated in the wildest theories of freedom and personal rights." This experience, he explained, made the freedpeople unwilling to work as they had under slavery.[36]

Dr. Cheves asked the Freedmen's Bureau for help in enforcing the contract, and the local officers complied. Their efforts, however, were ineffectual. Part of the problem, Cheves realized, was the lingering impact of General William T. Sherman's Special Field Order, No. 15, of January 1865, which had allowed freedmen to obtain "possessory title" to land along the coast from Charleston to the St. John's River. While these titles had been subsequently revoked by President Andrew Johnson, many freedpeople nevertheless felt entitled to the land. On Grove Hill plantation bordering Grove Point, fifty freed families had obtained title to 641 of the 1,100 acres. On Cheves's own Grove Point, thirty families had received possessory title to 245 acres. As Cheves marveled, "These freedmen, in actual possession [of the land], declared they 'would work for no man.'" Cheves, unable to believe that the workers would not eventually recognize his mastery, continued his efforts to direct work on the plantation. Finally, the workers made their position crystal clear, even to their former master. "They assembled as a Landsturm," wrote their astonished employer, "surrounded my house and drowning my voice with violent, insolent, and contemptuous denunciations declared that there was no master on the plantation." In September 1866, Cheves abandoned his efforts to direct affairs on Grove Point.[37]

If Cheves, a successful planter before the Civil War, faced such problems and failed, how could others expect to do better? J. Motte Middleton, who swore out the first warrants that set off the "insurrection," had previously had trouble with his workers. In February 1868, Middleton had dismissed numerous workers on Southfield, Grove Point, and Prairie plantations, which he rented or managed for absentee investors. When the fired workers would not leave the land, Middleton convinced the Freedmen's Bureau to send troops and remove the unwanted freedpeople. The core conflict was the freedmen refused to accept the contracts Middleton offered them, which only gave the freedmen a one-third share of the crop instead of the half share they thought they deserved. As Joseph Haskell, an employee of Middleton explained, "Difficulties between overseers and laboring men were frequent. . . . The chief origin of disputes [was the] difference as to the amount of work done and the manner in which it was done." In other words, the same problems Dr. Cheves had encountered two years before. In December 1868, freedpeople, feeling cheated of their labor, began to steal rice in order to make up what they considered their rightful wages.[38]

In 1865 when freedpeople occupied land along the Ogeechee under Special Field Order, No. 15, they had organized a local militia they named the Ogeechee Home Guard. This unit, however, was disbanded in 1866 under orders from the Freedmen's Bureau. As freedmen began to participate in politics, however, whites interpreted the usual political demonstrations of the time—marches, music, drumming, and parades—as signs of military organization. In their conflict with Middleton, perhaps the freedmen resurrected the idea of the Ogeechee Home Guard? They certainly threatened the sheriff and his deputies, and there were surely Union veterans and arms among these freedpeople. Someone had fired on the night watchmen. No matter how militant the rhetoric of the freedmen, the U.S. Army reports from January 1869 showed there was no organized military insurrection among the freedmen of the Ogeechee district. That lack of an organized defense meant that the quick arrival of the army probably saved lives along the Ogeechee. As the wild and indiscriminate firing by the sheriff's first posse suggested, the army created by Henry Rootes Jackson may have engaged in massacre along the Ogeechee had it not been quickly disbanded by federal troops.[39]

This story may seem a defeat for the white conservative elite of Savannah. The truth came out, the army intervened, and Reconstruction could continue. That reconstruction, however, changed little for the freedpeople along the Ogeechee. Already dispossessed of land they had thought theirs, their labor complaints were left unresolved. They remained dependent upon white employers and exploitative contracts. Demands for just contracts went unheard, and their attempts through demonstrations to force change had been crushed. While the arrival of the U.S. Army may have saved lives, it also reestablished civil authorities, reinforcing the powers of the landowners and their managers. Freedpeople injured or killed in this conflict had no legal recourse, and the legal actions taken resulted in the imprisonment of more than 140 freedmen for almost a month, and more than forty men for more than five months, probably causing significant economic distress. This conflict showed that freedpeople had no control over the legal system, no voice in the media, and no influence over state actions.

Shut out of politics, harassed and humiliated by the legal system, with no voice in the newspapers, the freedpeople of Georgia's coast turned in the only direction they could: inward. Freed families increasingly built peasant-like existences, separate from and outside the mainstream of regional development. Where whites saw pine barrens, good only for timber and turpentine, blacks saw potential homesteads. White landowners, struggling with the capital losses of emancipation and costly repairs to the hydraulic systems of the rice fields, gladly sold small parcels of sandy uplands to freedmen to raise money. In other cases, freed families simply squatted on a few acres of marginal land and stayed there, ignored. By the late nineteenth century, freedpeople in the Ogeechee neck had built lives centered around their small farmsteads, making a living through fishing, oystering, and truck farming for the city of Savannah. Occasional wage-work on the rice plantations contributed some cash to these otherwise economically independent lives. Over time the community of Burroughs developed on the Ogeechee neck, where black families maintained a rough independence well into the mid-twentieth century. By that time, the once so wealthy rice kingdom was dead.[40]

There is a final irony. In *The Death of Reconstruction*, Heather Cox Richardson argued that northern understandings of Reconstruction underwent a crucial transformation when Southern conflicts seemed no longer focused on citizenship and "rights" for the former slaves, but instead spilled over into struggles over labor and contracting. Story after story of labor difficulties, strikes, and violence involving former slaves eroded Northern support for the freedpeople's goals. The Republican Party, built around the free labor ideal, strove to support the demands of freedpeople for rights, but hesitated in lending support to freedpeople who appeared engaged in class conflict. "The conflict," Richardson explained, "between the idea of a harmonious economic world based on free labor and the idea of class struggle pervaded late nineteenth-century politics and directly affected the question of African Americans' role in American life." Even as Johnson, Stone, and Fitch fought the charges of insurrection, their very arguments about the intractability of labor conflict and the character of the laborers potentially undermined national support for Reconstruction. The truth was that without land, the freedpeople could never participate fully in the idealized world of free labor envisioned by the Republicans.[41]

Notes

1. *Savannah Republican,* 29 December 1868. For the story of attempts to annex Santo Domingo, the modern Dominican Republic, see McFeely, *Grant,* 336–55.

2. *Savannah Republican,* 29 December 1868; *New York Times,* 31 December 1869; *Quincy Whig* (Ill.), 1 January 1869; *Philadelphia Daily Evening Bulletin,* 5 January 1869; *Maine Farmer,* 9 January 1869; *London Times,* 2 January 1869.

3. David Brion Davis, *Slavery and Human Progress.*

4. There is a vast literature on the control of slaves and on slave insurrections and fears of insurrection. Important studies include Aptheker, *American Negro Slave Revolts*; Hadden, *Slave Patrols*; Mohr, *On the Threshold of Freedom*; Clavin, *Toussaint Louverture and the American Civil War*; Jordan, *Tumult and Silence at Second Creek*; Behrend, "Rebellious Talk and Conspiratorial Plots"; and Donald E. Reynolds, *Texas Terror.*

5. *Thomasville Southern Enterprise*, 12 July 1865; *Turnwold Countryman*, 13 June 1865; *Albany Patriot*, 8 January 1866; *Savannah Daily Herald*, 14, 16, and 18 December 1865; Rable, *But There Was No Peace*, 16–32; "Specters of Insurrection," in Hahn, et al., *Freedom*, 796–908; Summers, *A Dangerous Stir*, 49–68.

6. *Savannah Daily News and Herald*, 31 August 1868. *Savannah Daily Herald*, 11 January 1865; *Savannah Morning News*, 28 September 1868; Jacqueline Jones, *Saving Savannah*, 318–26. The *Savannah Daily Herald* began publication using the old *Morning News* office and equipment on 11 January 1865, soon after Union forces captured the city. Originally Unionist in tone, the prewar editors who had vociferously supported secession eventually regained control of the paper. On 28 September 1868, the Savannah *Daily News and Herald* changed its name to the *Savannah Morning News*, a local redemption of sorts.

7. *Savannah Morning News*, 4 and 5 November 1868; J. Murray Hoag to Col. J. R. Lewis, Savannah, 9 November 1868, in Tift, *Condition of Affairs in Georgia*, 55–56; Bryant, "We Defy You!" forthcoming in Daina Ramey Berry and Leslie Harris, eds., *Slavery and Freedom in Savannah* (Athens: University of Georgia Press: 2013).

8. *Savannah Morning News*, 4, 5, and 6 November and 7, 10, and 24 December 1868.

9. Ibid., 24 December 1868; Smith, *Slavery and Rice Culture*, 123–28; *Savannah Daily Advertiser*, 15 January 1869; Cimbala, *Under the Guardianship of the Nation*, 166–92, provides an excellent account of the labor conflicts that plagued coastal Georgia from 1865 to 1868; Bell, "The Ogeechee Troubles," 375–97, deals with the land tenure conflicts that precipitated these events.

10. *Savannah Morning News*, 30 December 1868; 17 and 18 January 1869.

11. Ibid., 17, 18, and 19 January 1869.

12. United States, Bureau of the Census, *Compendium of the Ninth U.S. Census*, 139.

13. *Savannah Morning News*, 31 December 1868; *New York Times*, 1, 3, and 4 January 1869; *Philadelphia Daily Evening Bulletin*, 4 January 1869; *Reading Eagle* (Pa.), 4 January 1869; *Daily Quincy Herald* (Ill.), 3 January 1869; Tift, *Condition of Affairs in Georgia*, 1–6. The *Savannah Republican* was not a Republican Party newspaper; it had been founded to support the Jeffersonians early in the century.

14. *Savannah Morning News*, 1, 2, and 29 January 1869; Gen. C. C. Sibley to Maj. Gen. George G. Meade, 4 January 1869, quoted in *Savannah Morning News*, 11 January 1869.

15. Ibid., 1 January 1869; Coleman and Gurr, *Dictionary of Georgia Biography*, 513–14; Col. Barstow to Gen. Meade, 2 January 1869, No. 12, USACC, RG 393, vol. 1 [E-5742], NA.

16. Col. Barstow to Maj. Gen. Meade, 2 January 1869, No. 12, No. 20, No. 412; Col. Barstow to Maj. Gen. Meade, 3 January 1869, No. 188, No. 199; Gen. Meade to Col. Barstow, 2 January 1869; Gen. Meade to Col. Barstow, 3 January 1869. All in USACC, RG 393, vol. 1 [E-5742], NA.

17. Gen. C. C. Sibley to Gen. George Meade, 4 January 1869, quoted in *Savannah Morning News*, 11 January 1869; *Savannah Morning News*, 5 January 1869.

18. Ibid., 4 and 5 January 1869; *Macon Telegraph*, 6 January 1869.

19. *Savannah Morning News*, 6, 7, 8, and 9 January 1869; C. C. Sibley to Gen. Meade, 8 January 1869, USACC, RG 393, vol. 1 [E-5742], NA.

20. *Savannah Morning News*, 5, 10, and 11 January 1869. The Camilla affair was a massacre of freedmen in southwest Georgia in the fall of 1868 (see Formwalt, "Camilla Massacre of 1868").

21. See Summers, *Press Gang*, for a wonderful account of the first clumsy attempts to use newspapers for focused propaganda.

22. *Savannah Republican*, 31 December 1868; *Philadelphia Daily Evening Bulletin*, 5 January 1869; *Quincy Whig* (Ill.), 7 January 1869.

23. *Savannah Morning News*, 11, 15, and 16 January 1869; Population Schedule, 1870 Manuscript Census Returns, Chatham County, Georgia, GDAH; "Amherst Willoughby Stone" vertical file, Savannah, Georgia, GHS; "James Johnson," in the *New Georgia Encyclopedia*, accessed 14 February 2010, http://www.georgiaencyclopedia.org/nge/Article.jsp?id=h-2814; "Henry Rootes Jackson," in the *New Georgia Encyclopedia*, accessed 14 February 2010, http://www.georgiaencyclopedia.org/nge/Article.jsp?id=h-865&hl=y. The accounts in the *Morning News* and in the *Savannah Daily Advertiser* are apparently the only surviving records of these hearings.

24. *Savannah Morning News*, 16 and 17 January 1869.

25. Ibid., 16–31 January.

26. Ibid., 11 and 16–31 January; 1 February 1869.

27. Ibid., 16, 18, and 19 January 1869.

28. Ibid., 21 and 22 January 1869.

29. Ibid.; "Proclamation by the Governor," printed in *Savannah Morning News*, 12 September 1868; see also Irwin, ed., *Code of the State of Georgia, 1867*, sec. 4249.

30. *Savannah Morning News*, 23–29 January 1869. The closing arguments are found in the *Morning News*, 29 January 1869.

31. Ibid., 29 January 1869.

32. Ibid., 30 January 1869. *Savannah Morning News*, 21 and 22 January 1869; Irwin, ed., *Code of the State of Georgia, 1867*, sec. 4249; *Savannah Morning News*, 23–30 January 1869.

33. *Savannah Morning News*, 1 February 1869.

34. *New York Times*, 15, 18, 25, 30, and 31 January and 1, 6, and 14 February 1869; *New York Tribune*, 8 January 1869. See the runs for January and February 1869 of the *Philadelphia Daily Evening Bulletin*, the *Daily Quincy Herald* (Ill.), the *Quincy Whig* (Ill.), the *Reading Eagle* (Pa.), the *Lancaster Intelligencer* (Pa.), and the *Maine Farmer*.

35. *Savannah Morning News*, 12, 13, and 14 May 1869; State v. Captain Green et al., Chatham County Superior Court Minutes, 1869; "Pardon of Captain Green, Ned Edwards, Dandy McNeil, Jack Cuthbert, Thomas Benedict, and Nick Bailing," 7 July 1870, Executive Minutes, Roll 15, GDAH; Conway, *Reconstruction of Georgia*, 186.

36. J. R. Cheves to D. Tillson, 14 September 1866, BRFAL-GA, RG 105 (M798); Cimbala, *Under the Guardianship of the Nation*, 184–85.

37. J. R. Cheves to D. Tillson, 14 September 1866, BRFAL-GA, RG 105 (M798); Bell, "Ogeechee Troubles," 379–81.

38. *Savannah Morning News*, 18, 19, and 20 January 1869; J. Murray Hoag to Caleb Sibley, 21 March 1868, BRFAL-GA, RG 105 (M798); Jacqueline Jones, *Saving Savannah*, 305.

39. Cimbala, *Under the Guardianship of the Nation*, 169–72, 191; *Savannah Morning News*, 3 and 4 November 1868.

40. Jacqueline Jones, *Saving Savannah*, 400–401; Clifton, "Twilight Comes to the Rice Kingdom," 146–54; Armstrong, "From Task Labor to Free Labor"; Strickland, "Traditional Culture and Moral Economy"; Lichtenstein, "Was the Emancipated Slave a Proletarian?." Coclanis, in *Shadow of a Dream*, does a marvelous job explaining the complicated factors behind the collapse of rice production; and labor problems played a crucial role.

41. Heather Cox Richardson, *Death of Reconstruction*, xiii and xiv.

4

"It Looks Much Like Abandoned Land"

Property and the Politics of Loyalty in Reconstruction Mississippi

ERIK MATHISEN

In the spring of 1866, a writer in a Vicksburg newspaper directed readers to what he thought was a new phrase in American politics. It was, he claimed, "a word that we never heard or saw used . . . until this late war of the 'so-called' rebellion," a phrase better suited to the "bloody purposes of court-martials and military commissions" than the politics of a republic. The new phrase was "loyalty," and what concerned the writer and many Mississippians in the immediate aftermath of the Civil War was that an individual's loyalty to the Union had become the key to membership in a postwar body politic.[1]

Editorials revealed little that whites in Mississippi were not aware of already. During the Civil War, oaths and pledges of loyalty had become a fact of life: a language of rights used by Mississippians in their day-to-day interactions with both Union and Confederate states. In the immediate postwar period, however, loyalty quickly came to define something more: not only individual civic rights but also the act of legitimating claims to property. Loyalty—the measuring of an individual's faithful allegiance to government—became something of a political currency, used by whites to secure the property of those who had lost their land or possessions during the war. And in countless local battles over property, white Mississippians attempted to minimize their past transgressions as former Confederates and claim a renewed spirit of Unionism, often with checkered results.

This essay looks at this process, focusing particular attention on how Mississippians fused political loyalty with rights to property, in a manner that had a lasting impact on Reconstruction.[2] Understanding this process is crucial, if only because it focuses attention on how whites and blacks alike practiced a complex politics of loyalty in a bid for property. Freedpeople had spent much of the war attempting to secure a close, meaningful relationship between themselves and the Union. Their efforts had not always been successful, but one of the outcomes of civil war and emancipation was that African Americans learned how to make use of their new relationship with the federal state, leveraging their loyalty in return for federal protection and civic rights. Claiming their loyalty to the Union as both more profound and all the more trustworthy when compared to that of former Confederates, African Americans deployed the politics of loyalty to make a bid for citizenship and possessions they believed were rightfully theirs.

The relationship between citizens and the American state has long been difficult to define. From the founding of the nation onward, the ties that bound citizens to the nation were clear: they were formed from the ideological materials that undergirded the American nation. But if being American meant preserving the liberties and freedoms associated with the Revolution, nineteenth-century Americans found it harder to identify their relation to the national state. Local struggles over property in occupied portions of the South immediately following the war, however, forced individuals (white and black) to confront the ambiguities of this relationship head on.[3] At a point during the earliest months of Reconstruction, former Confederates and former slaves in Mississippi clashed not only over who owned what but also over what citizenship in a postwar United States would entail.

Conflicts over loyalty and property also point to an unexplained aspect of Reconstruction history. While scholars have made much of the efforts by the federal government to craft a meaningful peace in the former slave South, this work has, with some justification, focused on what was lacking in the federal response. Presidential Reconstruction, according to the prevailing literature, was the prelude to a much wider conflict.[4] But by focusing more attention not on what Washington failed to do in this period, and instead on what Mississippians hoped Washington would do in the months that followed Confederate surrender, a picture emerges of a rural people whose demands for property became the basis of their relationship with an elusive federal government.[5]

By the winter of 1863, the line of occupation that divided Confederate Mississippi from Union-controlled territory forced those living along that line to constantly clarify their allegiances to one state or another. One of those caught on that border was R. Phelps, who addressed a high-ranking official in Mississippi's state militia, asking that he be pardoned for taking an oath of allegiance to the Union. Like most of the letters of this sort written in the midst of the war, Phelps's decision to swear an oath to one state or another often reflected the reality of living in a war zone. With property being seized by both states, from the loyal and the disloyal, declaring one's allegiance was often the only way in which many white families could sustain themselves.

For his part, Phelps had offered his allegiance to the Union to support his family and secure his property. But it was not a sure thing and when it became clear that his oath amounted to little, Phelps asked to be brought back into the Confederate fold. He claimed that he had only sworn an oath to the Union out of necessity and that his heart had never really been with the Union cause. Phelps threw himself on the mercy of the state government, claiming that both he and his friends who had taken the Union oath had learned the error of their ways. Determined to regain their status as loyal citizens of the Confederacy once more, Phelps wrote: "I know I regret taking the oath to the U.S. as much as is possible."[6] The stakes could not have been higher. By 1863, those deemed disloyal knew that their failure to make their professions of loyalty convincing would mean the loss of whatever property they had.

The pledges of Phelps and so many others reflected one of the many problems of political allegiance in wartime Mississippi. Desperate for help and facing ruin, many white Mississippians declared their loyalty as a means of keeping body and soul together. That they declared their loyalty at all was in large part a result of Union policies that had, by 1863, divided the occupied South into loyal Unionist and disloyal Confederate regions. Union officials particularly in the Mississippi Valley developed a policy of "total war" on the disloyal white inhabitants, who they blamed for their part in precipitating the breakup of the nation.[7]

Though the language of loyalty was born in part out of a Union desire to take command of an almost impossible social upheaval, defining what a pledge of loyalty meant to Mississippians drew on a much older set of ideas. Allegiance, whether to individuals, families, or fictive kin, informed not only how Mississippians understood their political choices before the war but also made up the foundation of local politics itself. Embedded in pledges of allegiance was an implicit declaration of supplication. Reflecting the same mixture of lowly deference and elite noblesse oblige that had propped up the slave system, many white Mississippians used a familiar antebellum language of debt and obligation to express wartime loyalty in return for protection. Bending this political language to suit difficult wartime circumstances, pledging allegiance was a canny political strategy. It was an act of political imagination that drew on an older world of political meaning, which helped to make sense of a moment of profound change.[8]

However, the act of declaring one's loyalty created manifold problems, and Union officials became aware of them from the moment their army began to occupy Confederate territory. Given the political culture of counties, where ties of loyalty connected neighbors to one another and not a central government, how could a policy of oath-taking and loyalty work? Union officials, who did not know the individuals who pledged their loyalty any better than white Mississippians knew the men to whom they were pledging, lacked the social context within which political loyalty and allegiance could be judged. Taken together, the nagging doubts among Union officials about whether a pledge made today could be trusted tomorrow made separating the loyal from the disloyal difficult but vital. Writing from DeSoto County, Union Brigadier General Quinby reported that whites were crossing the border from Union Tennessee into Confederate Mississippi on wagons driven by people "acknowledging themselves to be disloyal," filled with goods purchased in Union territory. "This thing is so manifestly wrong," wrote Quinby to Ulysses S. Grant, "that I have taken the responsibility of stopping and sending back all cotton in the hands of the original owners who cannot produce more satisfactory proofs of loyalty."[9] For soldiers like Quinby, policies meant to delineate between loyal and disloyal whites were not up to the challenge.

Quinby's frustration was understandable. From an early stage in the war, Union occupation policies made loyalty the foundation of any claim to property, creating a connection between claims and things that proved difficult to disentangle. For the Abraham Lincoln administration, the confiscation of property was a key weapon in their attempt to bring the war to the doorstep of the Southern slaveholding class. The 1862 Confiscation Act strengthened policies that were already being enforced, making loyalty to the Confederacy a treasonable offense. The act also directed the coercive powers of the Union State directly at the property of Confederates, with "the seizure of all the estate and property, money, stocks, credits, and effects of the persons," serving as the price of disloyalty. All property seized would serve to support the army of the United States.[10]

The legislation left the ultimate powers of enforcement in the hands of the executive branch, though Lincoln left it up to his military commanders to use the powers of the Confiscation Act at their own discretion. The law placed slaveholders and their property at the mercy of Union regiments, who could destroy plantations, impress all manner of goods and livestock, leaving white Southern families destitute, all without breaking any code of military conduct. In reality, the property of all whites was vulnerable unless safeguarded by claims of loyalty, and much like decisions about who was loyal and who was not, the veracity of an individual pledge of allegiance was ultimately decided by soldiers in the heat of the moment. While the complexities of wartime loyalty tied some Union officers in knots, others saw simple solutions. Calling on his superiors to rectify the problem of runaway rents in occupied Vicksburg in the winter of 1865, Assistant Adjutant General T. L. Bowers offered his own opinion on the thorny subject: "Loyal persons, including those who have been disloyal but who have availed themselves of the benefit of the President's Amnesty Proclamation . . . should be permitted the same privileges in the rental of their property as if they resided in the Loyal States of the North," wrote Bowers, "while the property of the disloyal persons should be taken possession of and used or rented to the highest bidder for the benefit of Government."[11]

By turns, Confederate confiscation policy was a more informal but no less destructive expansion of state power. The early passage of the Sequestration Act in August 1861 effectively put Confederate courts and military policy squarely behind a law that made all Unionist property within Confederate territory subject to seizure. The law also made loyal citizens of the Confederacy bound to disclose information about suspected Unionist property, with that information given to a new bureaucracy of court officers, or receivers, who would ensure that cases were brought before courts against those with Unionist sympathies.[12] What both Union and Confederate policies brought about was complete chaos for most communities in the Mississippi Valley. For many in the region, confiscation by both Union and Confederacy slowly erased the distinctions between the states. For those who had property, and even those who did not, both Union regiments and bands of Confederates who both seized property at gunpoint became part of the same scourge. As one official remarked to Governor Charles Clark, armed bands of Confederates were fast becoming "far more dangerous and destructive than are the Yankees in their frequent raids."[13]

The seizure of property, coupled with the slow emancipation of slaves, altered not only definitions of ownership but the political meanings of property itself. It was in this environment of complete upheaval that the sight of former slaves seizing property of their own proved the most profoundly jarring signal of an overturning of power. By the winter of 1864, Isaac Shoemaker had traveled to occupied Mississippi to lease a plantation seized by Union forces in Adams County. Writing in his diary from Vicksburg, he remarked on the arrival of some five thousand black men, women, and children, who had been marched into town from around the surrounding countryside, under guard. According to Shoemaker, they arrived in town "in all sorts of Vehicals" and on all sorts of animals, the "remnants of Massa's property."[14] For Shoemaker and so many others who were witness to emancipation, the sight of former slaves with property represented perhaps the most profound image of the war. The act of freedpeople seizing property from their former owners, however, was an inherently political act, and both Shoemaker and slaves saw it as such.

As early as the fall of 1863, letters sent to the Union Adjutant General's office disclosed persistent talk among freedpeople that with freedom and their continued loyalty to the Union, rights to land and property would follow. "Some [blacks] it is true have a false idea of their freedom and its responsibilities," wrote Julian E. Bryant, "thinking that it releases them from all restraint, and are consequently roving the country stealing and committing depredations on property." While Bryant was convinced that a firm Union hand would disabuse former slaves of their misguided expectations, he missed a key component of wartime black politics. Political loyalty, which the Union would come to require and many black men and women would eagerly offer, would come at a price for both parties. Black Mississippians had seen that loyalty protected property. As Union forces increasingly depended upon freedpeople to cement Unionism in the postwar South, former slaves pressed their case that loyalty could claim property and political power as well.[15]

With the surrender of Confederate forces in the spring of 1865, pledges of loyalty as claims to property took on a whole new urgency. Particularly as the Andrew Johnson administration turned oaths of wartime loyalty into oaths of postwar amnesty, the ties between personal claims of loyalty and property quickly became the benchmarks for political membership in the postwar United States. But what constituted a rightful declaration of loyalty—and by extension what constituted an appropriate claim to property—remained ambiguous. The 29 May 1865 Amnesty Proclamation, which extended amnesty and restored property rights to those who were "participants" in the Confederate "rebellion," as well as pardons at the president's discretion for high-ranking Confederate officials, wealthy landowners, and twelve other classes of white Southern citizenry, required oaths of loyalty and written support for emancipation. Without a clear definition of whether whites should be counted as rebellious Americans or defeated Confederate citizens, loyalty had to be defined by the Johnson administration, and it would be a definition that did not include African Americans. Designed as it was to "induce all persons to return to their loyalty," the proclamation implied that the act of amnesty was perforce a political declaration that brought wayward white Southerners back into the Union. The proclamation set to one side the thorny question of whether slaves could declare their loyalty not only by denying them citizenship but also defining them as prepolitical persons. Though they had acted during the war in a manner that made a mockery of Johnson's Amnesty Proclamation, the political straitjacket of Presidential Reconstruction forced freedpeople to make declarations of loyalty in other ways.[16]

Opening the door to amnesty opened the floodgates to a torrent of letters from white Mississippians. In letters sent to officials of the Freedmen's Bureau, Union military commanders, and members of the newly installed state government in Jackson, writers mixed resignation with a sense of purpose. Many expressed an acceptance of Confederate defeat and a determination to rejoin the Union. Others papered over the complexities of having been citizens of an enemy nation. "Now . . . that our arms have proved unsuccessful," wrote one petitioner in June 1865, "I feel it my duty to return my allegiance to the U.S. Government . . . I thought, and so expressed . . . that the institution of slavery was Staked upon the outset of the war. We have played and lost, and I, for one, am willing to surrender the stake." Like poker players whose luck had run out, many white Mississippians hoped that by returning to the Union they could cash in their chips.[17]

It was one of the ideas at the heart of Presidential Reconstruction that Southerners could become citizens of the United States again. As Johnson's proclamation reasoned, the war had not severed the connection between individuals and the Union but had instead frozen the rights of white Southerners in amber.[18] No matter how hard Union officials tried, however, former Confederates renewing their pledges of loyalty remained suspect. Measuring these pledges ultimately became a shaky basis for citizenship, and it exposed an age-old problem in the American republic. If the nation was constituted by "the people," what need was there for oaths and pledges at all?

This question echoed in Mississippi's state legislature, which met in Jackson during the summer of 1865. Convened quickly and composed largely of former Whigs loyal to Governor William Sharkey, the loyalty question surfaced as one of the primary issues in that body's deliberations. "I cannot regard it as lawful," declared George L. Potter of Hinds County, "that our Senators and Representatives shall be first required to take a special oath contained in the acts of Congress—a sort of test oath of loyalty—the sum and substance of which may be stated in this way: that no man can present himself there, as a Representative of a State, who has even smelled the recent rebellion."[19] For those in Jackson, loyalty to the state smacked of forced fealty to the Republican Party. It was the partisan agenda that many saw between the lines of the proclamation, which showed the true intention of Johnson's plans.

While members of the constitutional convention passed off the problem of loyalty in postwar Mississippi as a political ploy, the letters and petitions sent from around the state muddied the water significantly. Divided loyalties and divided communities were eroding whatever social and political order remained in counties throughout the state. Petitioners writing to Mississippi's provisional governor disclosed political squabbles and pitched battles between Union and Confederate sympathizers. Letters detailed efforts by loyal Confederates to organize the takeover of local government, while others charged that secession and war had laid waste to the entire state. To raise a militia in Tippah County, H. E. Moore wrote of an attempt by Confederate loyalists to discredit him in the county as little more than an appendage of Unionist occupation. "[T]he northern part of the County is Composed mostly of Union men (I mean loyal men)," wrote Moore, in the new political language of the moment, "and many of them too are men who have served their time out in this War in the U.S. Service. And these Very men who are saying the most against the Company are the Very men who are Saying that 'there is not any *Union* and that all union men and men who served in the U.S. army shall leave this Country, leave their homes, land &c.'"[20]

Requests for amnesty and declarations of renewed allegiance often resulted in intricate personal histories. With counties in disarray, those whites who attempted to make their own claims to Unionist loyalty, in a desperate effort to stave off ruin, could do little but offer tortured letters of regret. These letters provide insight into the political imaginations of their writers. By recounting their history of loyalty to the Union, these stories manufactured a kind of hierarchy of allegiance. Each one was designed to stake a claim to true fealty, in contrast to Confederate sympathizers who were often their own neighbors.

For example, J.W.C. Watson was a member of Mississippi's Union Convention in 1851, the political organization formed to block the secession of the state in the wake of the Compromise of 1850. Though, a decade later, he claimed to have been "politically opposed to Mr. Lincoln," he had stood in opposition to secession, an act of bravery which, Watson hoped, would sway skeptical Union officials. When it became apparent that secession would become a reality, however, Watson acquiesced in favor of the Confederacy. He accepted positions of government office and later would serve the state as a senator in the Confederate Congress. Despite his active involvement at the highest levels of its government, Watson claimed in his plea for amnesty that he was never truly loyal to the Confederacy. He wrote that he was "conscientiously prepared to take the amnesty oath and to assume the duties and responsibilities of a good, true, and loyal citizen of the United States. . . . No one could have been more opposed to disunion than I was, and no one, to the extent of his abilities, labored more earnestly to avert it." By minimizing his influence over a seeming historical inevitability like secession, Watson could deemphasize his role as a leader in the Confederate government.[21]

This claim of secession's inevitability pervaded the pardons and pleas of white Mississippians. They reveal a good deal not only about what had occurred over more than four years of secession and Civil War but also about the mechanisms of Confederate loyalty itself. Many writers emptied their letters of intention, particularly on their role in the formation of the Confederate government. "My record will show that I offered opposition until secession was consummated and before us," wrote one man from Ripley, in north-central Mississippi. "Out of it came a government. Within its limits, was my home. I would not leave it, but resolved to do all in my power to defend it." For some, the clever manipulation of language and the suggestion that the act of having been citizens of another state changed little, gave former Confederates and their amnesties added weight.[22]

In contrast, black Mississippians who had no prior claim to citizenship used pledges of loyalty to claim property because theirs was a history of allegiance to the Union that was seemingly beyond reproach. In a case brought before the Freedmen's Bureau in July 1865, the black members of the Wall St. Baptist Church in Natchez petitioned the Bureau to address an injustice of religious and political importance. The petitioners stated that while they had observed services before the war as lesser participants of the congregation, emancipation had caused a conflict within the church. White members had closed the church entirely rather than allow newly freed black congregants through its doors. In reaction, black petitioners demanded that the Bureau open the church once more. To support their claim, they detailed a political history of the white members' disloyalty and, by extension, a history of their own allegiance. Describing white congregants as lukewarm Unionists and recent citizens of the Confederate States of America, the petitioners argued that in contrast to a white loyalty that could not be trusted, black support for the Union had never wavered:

> We need not say to you, that at the breaking out of the rebellion, the white members, officers & all went with it. . . . But you may not know that the house was closed some two years before our forces came into Natchez, to take possession, open a Head Quarters here, during which time we had to do the best we could. After our forces came to this city, the Chaplains opened the said Wall St. House, partly to preach to the soldiers, & partly to gather in the white inhabitance. But our Citizens

> had so much of old man Jeff in them, they would rather hear the Devil Preach than a Yankee, so they would not go, & soldiers finding no body there but themselves, they soon Stoped going.

When white congregants refused to observe services during the Union's occupation, the black members of Wall St. Baptist argued that their church "has been abandoned by trators," and as the "humble servants" of the Union cause, they should be given ownership of the building. A few weeks later, the black deacons of the church sent an additional petition, further cementing their community's claim. While they allowed that some of the white members of the church had taken the amnesty oath, black members of the church needed no such declaration to prove their loyalty. We "have never been disloyal neither to the government nor Church," they wrote, "we are the rightful owners of the property, as it looks much like abandoned land."[23]

The black congregants of Wall St. possessed a canny understanding of just how politics worked in the months that followed the Civil War. Their battle to secure ownership over their church through their claims of loyalty echoed in other parts of Mississippi, as declarations of competing loyalties were used to claim black ownership over all manner of possessions. By defining their church as abandoned and those who would oppose their membership in it as traitors, the black congregants claimed ownership by wrapping their demands in their own declarations of loyalty to the Union and all that it stood for.

Understanding the opportunities and the limits of black loyalty requires a different interpretive lens from white ones. In the first place, black pledges were not as readily documented in letters and petitions. Rather than tortured written pleas for pardons, the professions of freedpeople were often more public and articulated at the point of conflict between laborers and landowners, or in conflicts with white sheriffs. Like white pledges and pleas, black efforts centered on expectations, but what distinguished them was what black communities understood their loyalty to the Union to entail. Freedpeople understood the war and its aftermath as a turning point of profound importance. But African Americans also understood the day of jubilee as just one part of a relationship between their community and the state that had a hand in securing their freedom. It was a state whose soldiers freedpeople could see but whose intentions were not always clear. Throughout Presidential Reconstruction, black pledges of allegiance took shape in an environment of contest and violence—and without the rights and privileges of citizenship. Indeed,

African Americans in Mississippi placed their trust in a Union that did not always serve their interests. But like the black congregants of Wall St. Baptist, the pledges of freedpeople conjured an imagined state that, they hoped, would act as a bulwark to protect fledgling free black communities, even if that state did not always meet their expectations.

The pledges of loyalty freedpeople made as part of their claims to property also took on an added importance, given that what so many African Americans sought was not only a claim to possessions but also Union protections for their families. For many freedpeople, the opportunities to prove their loyalty came about as part of their efforts as parents to claim children as their own. When a Works Progress Administration interviewer asked Anna Baker in the 1930s about what she remembered of her moment of freedom, the former Monroe County slave recounted a scene involving her former master, a mother she did not know, and the papers her mother received from a Union state official. "After de war was over my ma got some papers from de Progro Marshall and come to de place and tell de marster she wants her children," remembered Baker. "He say she can have all cepten me but she say she want me too and dat I was hern and she was gwineter get me. She went back and got some more papers and come show dem to Marse Morgan, and he say, 'G***D***, take em all!'" Baker remembered that her reaction to seeing her mother for the first time was one of trepidation: "She came out of de house to get us and at fust I was scared of her case I didden know who she was. But she put me in her lap and loved me and I knowed den I love her too. She most nigh cried when she look at de back of my head. Dere was awful sores whar de lice had been and I had scratched dem."[24]

Baker's remembrances were recounted in similar scenes all over the South in the months following the war. Together, they make some of the most heartrending stories of Reconstruction, as African Americans attempted to reconstitute families torn to pieces by slavery and the slave trade. Typically, historians have interpreted these stories as part of the emancipation process, as former slaves attempted to achieve some measure of social stability over their communities and families. For mothers and fathers, however, protecting their children from remaining the property of whites was not just a claim to liberty. It was also a battle over property rights in people. The specter of reenslavement and the threats made on the sanctity of freed families were constant, as white Mississippians attempted to find new ways to maintain control over their former human possessions. Moreover, Union policies intended to jump-start the Southern cotton economy placed added strain on an already tenuous black freedom. As one historian has remarked, emancipation brought about a "revolution in property." But in the months after the war, the issue of whether whites in the post-emancipation South would continue to count people as property remained an open question.[25]

The legal basis for the continued enslavement of black children was created out of a bundle of policy directives that dealt with the wartime care of African American women and children. By the middle stages of the war, the Union Army and charity organizations like the American Missionary Association had taken on the care of thousands of freedpeople in camps along the Mississippi River and in the conquered northern portion of the state. It was a system that fell under the aegis of the Freedmen's Bureau, but at the war's end, local courts and local law enforcement took up apprenticeship as part of an effort to keep black families bound to their former owners. By the end of 1865, the apprenticeship of young freedpeople amounted to little more than bondage with a contract. By April 1866, Freedmen's Bureau officials received complaints from freedpeople, attesting to the outright enslavement of their children, who were bonded into labor (often by their former owners) until the children reached adulthood.[26] "By Binding out children . . . in direct opposition to the wishes of either Parent or child" one sub-assistant commissioner revealed state judges were apprenticing children in his district, removing them from families who easily satisfied the basic requirements of the child's welfare.[27] As part of the reaction to the relatively lax policies of presidential amnesty, white Mississippians had reconstituted a base of power in state and local governments that increasingly sought to legislate freedpeople back into slavery in all but name.[28]

The effect of apprenticeship policies shocked members of the congressional committee convened to discuss the problems of emancipation and Reconstruction in the former Confederacy. Called before the Joint Committee on Reconstruction to give his testimony, Major General Clinton B. Fisk disclosed the contents of a letter he received from a former slaveholder living in DeSoto County, who staunchly refused to recognize the emancipation of a girl to her mother. "He declined to give up the girl, and wrote me a long letter in relation to it, which closed up by saying: 'As to recognizing the rights of freedmen to their children, I will say there is not one man or woman in all the south who believes they are free, but we consider them as stolen property—stolen by the bayonets of the damnable United States government.'"[29] As a political issue, the apprenticeship of children quickly contributed to a growing will in Congress to dissolve white Southern claims to freedpeople. Freedmen's Bureau officials and Unionists alike offered pessimistic assessments of the likelihood of emancipation and Reconstruction succeeding at all. "I find the general opinion is that the Bureau will soon be over in Miss. & the day of jubilee will come for the former slave owners," wrote James Livingston at the end of 1865. "[T]hey are now as rapidly as possible binding out all children old enough to work, whether they have parents or not, leaving the young and helpless for some body else."[30]

By the end of 1865, incidents of black children being apprenticed by whites were commonplace. Nelson Gill, a sub-commissioner of the Freedmen's Bureau in Holly Springs, wrote his superiors to inform them of a case involving a freedwoman whose former master had bonded her daughter until the young child reached adulthood. According to Gill's report, the former slaveholder had predicated his claim to the girl on her mother's inability to care for her. Fearing retrenchment, Gill believed that if the Bureau did not step in and stop former masters, cases such as this would multiply throughout the state: "If this is allowed they will have every Negro between the ages of 12 and 18 bound no matter what the circumstances."

Another case involving two freedwomen revolved around an even more brazen white claim to black children. Jane Fitzgerald and "Mary" had both been slaves to a man named Archie Fitzgerald, who offered contracts to both women to work in his home at the beginning of 1866. When the women refused to sign, Fitzgerald claimed sole rights to Jane and Mary's children, until they reached the age of twenty-one, backing up his threat to both women with local law enforcement. When Mary and Jane refused to relent, both women were placed in prison, with their former slaveholder threatening to sell both women.[31]

Union officials worried at length about these abuses taking place throughout the state. Threats to the children of freedpeople struck a chord with Northern audiences reared on affective antislavery literature and harrowing tales of families torn apart. Attending these moral concerns were political ones as well. By the end of 1865, it had become clear to many Republicans that the success of Reconstruction depended upon protecting the rights of freedpeople. The problem reached a critical point as rumors of both black insurrection and the widespread seizure of property took shape in the summer and fall of 1865. Initially, reports described armed bands of freedpeople acting in localities independent of one another. By the end of that year, talk of blacks operating in concert and with the help of the Union state across Mississippi spread throughout the region.

What lay at the heart of the white rumors of black actions (real or imagined) was not only fears of an outright war over property rights. In truth, struggles over property had been raging for several years. Rather, what signaled a turning point in Presidential Reconstruction was that the black frustration that loyalty to the Union had not brought about a stable claim to either their families or citizenship, mixed with white worries about the very idea of black Unionism, gave struggles over property in late 1865 a deeper and more ominous meaning. As early as October, letters sent to officials suggested that unless black troops were removed from the state, they would set a "universal Massacre" in motion that would turn "this fair land into another Haiti," while other reports from Freedmen's Bureau field offices recounted stories of armed whites seizing black property with impunity. Newspapers also fanned the flames. An article in the *Natchez Daily Courier* in October dismissed the talk of property seizure as idle and vicious rumor, while it printed the accounts from other reports all the same. Southern newspapers began to carry these rumors as fact, whipping whites into a frenzy about the prospect of a potentially violent overthrow of the status quo.

Though officials in the Freedmen's Bureau attempted to correct it, the logic at the heart of the presumed Christmas Day insurrection scare of 1865 was the determination of freedpeople that their loyalty should guide the division of Southern property. "The freedmen are generally unwilling to enter into any contract that extends longer than Christmas," wrote R. S. Donaldson to his superiors, "as some of them have the erroneous idea that their former master's lands and stock are to be divided among them at that time. I have used every available means in my power to disabuse their minds of this idea, and at the places where I have been able to send agents of the Bureau, I think that they have given up the false hope that they had at one time of having property given to them by the Government."[32]

Though Donaldson was dismissive of black expectations about property, whites took part in the same game.[33] Hayden Leavel, of Yazoo County, wrote the state's governor in September to have him confirm rumors he had heard about reparations for former white slaveholders who had lost their fortunes. Relating things he had heard from reliable sources in South Carolina, Leavel pressed Sharkey to confirm that the federal government was planning on paying reparations for "the value of all property (negroes included) that had been taken by the U.S. Government, previous to a certain time—and said property—not being within their lines, could be recovered."[34] Open talk of reparations coming at the same time as freedpeople were pressing for land, speaks to the problems inherent in the fusion of personal loyalty and property together.

By the end of October, letters from around the state reported the broad expectations of freedpeople that the redistribution of land was just around the corner. Marion Shields, a Noxubee County planter, wrote a letter to President Andrew Johnson detailing the rumors among blacks in his county, who hoped that the federal government would reward its loyal constituency with property, homes, mules, and horses. "[T]hey even believe that they will own all & we will have to emigrate else where. The most of them will not work. They Seem to be entirely out of their element . . . waiting [for] their supposed joyful day of Christmas, when they will be blessed with the fat of the land. They seem to think all will come by & from you they will not believ any thing else."[35] Governor Sharkey felt compelled to write a letter that month, asking the Freedmen's Bureau to send agents around the state to make sure freedpeople understood that freedom did not entail the property of former owners. In his letter, Sharkey painted a grim picture of what would happen if the federal government did not act. "It is very certain that the negroes are expecting a distribution of property this winter," wrote Sharkey, "and it is also certain that we have many reasons to believe that a general revolt is contemplated unless the property is divided. . . . Most of the Negroes in the country have arms, procured from soldiers or officers, which it is supposed they are producing for the purpose of carrying out their diabolical scheme."[36]

Sharkey's worry about the rumors of a coming battle between white landowners and black laborers did not materialize. In reality, the fear of insurrection created opportunities for state and local governments to bolster their control over black populations. The confiscation of weapons and provisions from the homes of freedpeople indicated that not only would Reconstruction not bring about the dramatic division of land but also that with the use of force it would be black, not white property, which was under threat.[37] What these attacks amounted to was not just an attempt to diminish the claims of freedpeople to defend themselves; it was a political statement by whites, who intended to show freedpeople just what their loyalty to the Union amounted to. Local governments and local law enforcement, disregarding black rights to property, served as a stinging rebuke of the federal state in the Reconstruction South. By showing what whites could do, regardless of federal law, freedpeople were made to appreciate the limits of their loyalty.

Yet, the seizure of property only cemented something that had been merely inchoate a few months before. By the end of 1865, the ownership of property had become symbolic of a relationship to the Union state. It was a relationship that did not treat former slaves and former Confederates on equal terms. Whites had to prove their loyalty. African Americans did not. Even before the state government called for the raising of white militia companies to protect communities throughout the region, freedmen expressed pessimism about the future for African Americans in Mississippi. "The more intelligent freedman . . . seemed to be very much discouraged indeed at their future prospects in this state, and some of them having means were preparing to emigrate to some more favored locality where they would be protected in their rights of person and property." According to many whites in the state, the sentiment was an accurate reflection of what lay ahead.

By January 1866, testimony in a complaint made by a Pike County freedman about his being beaten by a gang of whites for his two horses, clarified the new parameters of loyalty and property. When the freedman presented a bill of sale for the horses, the self-styled lieutenant of the armed band informed him that "Negroes were not allowed any property larger than a Chicken." The Bureau official who issued a report about the occurrence claimed that most of the witnesses to the event perjured themselves, rather than give testimony against the assault. "All or nearly all, have subscribed to the Amnesty Oath, and have sworn to refrain from the very acts, they are performing . . . while at the same time it should be remembered that this same . . . country is continually reporting negro insurrections being on foot, a perfect 'Hot-bed' for originating insurrection canards."[38]

Reports of unreconstructed former Confederates vying for control of local and state government and an intensifying battle between President Johnson and the Republican Congress over the scope of Reconstruction itself left little doubt in the minds of legislators in Washington that Mississippi's future in the Union would depend upon the continued loyalty of former slaves. The relationship between state and constituency was anything but perfect. Radical Republicans believed that dependent slaves, lacking the most rudimentary tools necessary to becoming good citizens, would have to learn the value of frugality, respectability, and rugged independence. But a political relationship between African Americans and the Union state, which had developed during the war, now opened the door to freedpeople to create their own political structures, vie for their own place in state and local government, and make a bid for citizenship in a postwar United States as among the most loyal of Americans.

At the first session of the Fortieth Congress, held in the spring of 1867, Thaddeus Stevens presented a bill on the floor of the Senate, proposing changes to the Confiscation Act of 1862, which placed African American loyalty front and center. The bill, entitled "Claims to Loyalists for Damages," stipulated that as punishment for the disloyal who cast their lot with the Confederacy, all public lands "belonging to the ten States that formed the government of the so-called 'confederate states of America' shall be forfeited by said States and become forthwith vested in the United States." The land would be distributed to freedpeople in much the same way that General Sherman had allotted lowcountry Georgia land to former slaves in the war's final months: forty acres to each male or widowed female head of the household. "The punishment of traitors has been wholly ignored by a treacherous Executive and by a sluggish Congress," declared Stevens, and a bill intended to place loyal African Americans on a social and economic footing as independent producers would do more than any other measure would to ensuring the stability of a postwar South. "Nothing is so likely to make a man a good citizen," argued Stevens, "as to make him a freeholder."[39] Though it would never become law, the boldness of Stevens's bill lay in the planned revolution of property that the legislation portended and in the clearly worded assumption that lay behind the project. By 1867, "loyalty" in a state like Mississippi had become synonymous with freedpeople and the small but significant pockets of white Unionists who made a lie of white opposition to Radical Reconstruction.[40] Black political allegiance and black loyalty would form the skeleton of a postwar political culture of former slaves turned freeholders, creating a political bulwark to the disloyalty of former Confederates who were left on the periphery.

In the spring of 1868, a report printed in the *Vicksburg Herald* took stock of the state of political allegiance, black loyalty to the Union, and the power of the federal government in Mississippi. With tongue planted firmly in cheek, the report disclosed a gruesome altercation in a county that had been a hotbed of white insurrection against the Confederacy during the war. "In the days of the Confederacy, the county of Jones . . . acquired a wide notoriety for the 'loilty' of its people, many of whom never could be persuaded to be good Confederates." But now that military rule over the state had been imposed and loyalty to the Union now amounted to letting "negroes do any sort of devilment without retribution in kind," whites in Jones were in an uproar. A white woman had allegedly been raped by a black man in the county, and the aggrieved husband "instead of leaving the pursuit of the 'citizen' who had wronged him to the officers of the law, and his punishment to the courts, ventured upon the dangerous ground of taking vengeance in his own hands." A posse was formed, and the alleged black rapist was chased by dogs, captured, and skinned alive.[41]

The editorial writer was at pains to point out the impartiality of the account, "in narrating this atrocity committed by *white* men on a negro for merely ravishing a white woman and leaving her tied fast in the woods."[42] But the incident revealed some important changes in how the politics of loyalty had changed. The suspected black attacker, figured by the writer as a "citizen," was beaten by those who saw themselves as dispossessed from the federal government. If Reconstruction was a battle over labor and land, it was also a battle for access to state power, and by 1868, it was loyalty that mattered above all.

The politics of loyalty that emerged during and immediately following the Civil War had a profound impact on the political system that followed. While the connections between citizens and the American state would not be completely resolved, Presidential Reconstruction marked a turning point in that relationship. In their efforts to proclaim their loyalty and secure their rights over their property or their personhood, black and white Mississippians sought to narrow the distance between themselves and a federal government. Whether in their attempts to secure land, or in the problems African Americans faced in trying to sustain and strengthen their status as freedpeople after the Civil War had ended, both white and black Mississippians could not ignore that the future of both groups had become tied up with their relationship to a powerful, centralized state.

Notes

1. *Weekly Panola Star* (quoted from *Vicksburg Herald*), 12 May 1866.

2. Battles over property as one of the key points of conflict during Reconstruction has been a focus of study in Ransom and Sutch, *One Kind of Freedom*, 81–105; Magdol, *A Right to the Land*; Foner, *Reconstruction*, 124–75, 346–411; Schweninger, *Black Property Owners in the South*, 143–84; Saville, *Work of Reconstruction*, 5–31; and Penningroth, *Claims of Kinfolk*, 131–62. Much less has been written, however, on the problems that claims of loyalty posed for Southerners and the federal government during Reconstruction. Perhaps the best remains McKitrick, *Andrew Johnson and Reconstruction*, 120–52.

3. Any discussion of nationalism and the connections between citizens and the nation leans heavily on Anderson, *Imagined Communities*. Linda Kerber's work on the relationship between citizens and states has laid out a research agenda of which this paper is a part. See Kerber's *No Constitutional Right to Be Ladies* and "The Stateless as the Citizen's Other."

4. The best work on Presidential Reconstruction includes Du Bois, *Black Reconstruction*, 248–323; McKitrick, *Andrew Johnson and Reconstruction*; Harris, *Presidential Reconstruction in Mississippi*; Sefton, *United States Army and Reconstruction*; Perman, *Reunion without Compromise*; Carter, *When the War Was Over*; Foner, *Reconstruction*, 176–227; Hahn, *Nation under Our Feet*, 116–59; and Summers, *A Dangerous Stir*.

5. A work that focuses more on the expectations among freedpeople during Presidential Reconstruction is Hahn, "'Extravagant Expectations' of Freedom." My intention in this essay is to push this line of analysis further by focusing on white and black expecta-

tions during this period, and in particular the expectations of both groups for what they hoped would be a lasting relationship with the federal state.

6. R. Phelps to Gen. Adams, Jackson, Miss., 21 February 1863, Folder 3, Box 394, Ser. 608, Correspondence of Various Mississippi Officers and Military Staff Members, 1861–1865, Misc. Civil War Documents, MDAH.

7. Grimsley, *Hard Hand of War*, 151–70.

8. A process examined in more detail in my dissertation, "Pledges of Allegiance."

9. Brig. Gen. I. F. Quinby to Maj. Gen. U. S. Grant, Crossing of the Pigeon Roost and M. & C. Railroad (DeSoto Co., Miss.), 6 January 1862, in OR 1:17:2, 542.

10. U.S. Congress, *Statutes at Large*, 12: 589–92 (quote on 590). See also Syrett, *Civil War Confiscation Acts*.

11. Asst. Adjut. Gen. T. L. Bowers to Maj. Gen. Dana, City Point, Va., 5 February 1865, Entry 2433, Letters Received, Box 1, USACC, RG 393, NA.

12. On Confederate sequestration policy, see Hamilton, "Confederate Sequestration Act," 380–82.

13. S. J. Gholson to Gov. Clark, Tupelo, Miss., 16 April 1864, Folder 5, Box 949, Ser. 768: Governor Charles Clark, Correspondence and Papers, 1863–1865, MDAH.

14. Entry for 3 March 1864, Isaac Shoemaker Diary, DUSC.

15. Report of Maj. Julian E. Bryant to the Adjut. Gen., Goodrich's Landing, La., 10 October 1863, Box 2, Ser. 363: Letters Received by Adjutant General L. Thomas, 1863–1865, Colored Troops Division, 1863–1889, AGO, RG 94, NA.

16. Foner, *Reconstruction*, 183–84. For the text of the Amnesty Proclamation itself, see James D. Richardson, ed. and comp., *Compilation of the Messages and Papers of the Presidents*, 6: 310–12.

17. O. David to Gov. Sharkey, Ripley, Miss., 28 June 1865, Folder 4, Box 954, Ser. 771: Letters and Petitions, 1865, MDAH.

18. A point made best by McKitrick, *Andrew Johnson and Reconstruction*, 93–152.

19. State of Mississippi, *Journal of the Proceedings and Debates in the Constitutional Convention . . . August 1865*, 56–57.

20. H. E. Moore to Gov. Sharkey, Tippah Co., Miss., 23 September 1865, Folder 11, Box 956, Ser. 771: Letters and Petitions, MDAH.

21. J.W.C. Watson to Gov. Sharkey, Holly Springs, Miss., 17 June 1865, Folder 1, Box 960, Ser. 776: Governor William Lewis Sharkey, Correspondence and Papers, 1865, MDAH.

22. O. David to Gov. Sharkey, Ripley, Miss., 28 June 1865, Folder 4, Box 954, Ser. 771: Letters and Petitions, MDAH.

23. Congregants of the Wall St. Baptist Church to Col. Samuel Thomas, Natchez, Miss., 1 July 1865; Deacons of the Wall St. Baptist Church to Col. Samuel Thomas, Natchez, Miss., 26 July 1865. Both in Roll 8, Letters Received, BRFAL-MS, RG 105 (M826).

24. Narrative of Anna Baker, Monroe Co., Miss., in Rawick, ed., *American Slave*, vol. 6, pt. 1, 90–101 (quote on 94–95).

25. Penningroth, *Claims of Kinfolk*, 133. The historiography surrounding postwar apprenticeship is well known and has been fruitfully mined in case studies of North Caro-

lina, Maryland, and other regions of the Reconstruction South. In this work, apprenticeship of African American children has served a larger argument about either the problems of labor control or the difficulties freedpeople faced in rebuilding their families after slavery. Its place in this essay serves as a way into understanding more about the political ideas that evolved out of this conflict. For the literature on apprenticeship, see Fields, *Slavery and Freedom on the Middle Ground*, 131–66 (esp. 142–43); Edwards, *Gendered Strife and Confusion*, 24–65; and Harris, *Presidential Reconstruction*, 121–40. For the efforts by freedwomen to protect their rights as parents to their children, see Farmer-Kaiser, *Freedwomen and the Freedmen's Bureau*, 96–140.

26. As an example of an indenture contract, see Indenture of Rosanna Charles, Canton, Miss., 1 October 1865, Canton Field Office, Roll 12, Miscellaneous Records, vol. 102, Sub-Assistant Commissioner Field Office Records, BRFAL-MS, RG 105 (M1907).

27. Bvt. Maj. Jonothan J. Knox to Capt. E. Bamburger, Meridian, Miss., 28 January 1866, Meridian Field Office, Roll 30, Letters Sent, vol. 197, Sub-Assistant Commissioner Field Office Records, BRFAL-MS, RG 105 (M1907).

28. Capt. W. H. Hunter to Bvt. Lt. Col. M. P. Bestow, Headquarters, Department of Mississippi (Vicksburg), 18 April 1866, Folder 1, Box 963, Ser. 779, Governor Benjamin Humphries, Correspondence and Papers, 1865–1868 and Undated, MDAH. The literature on the Black Codes, particularly in Mississippi, includes Wharton, *Negro in Mississippi, 1865–1890*, 80–124; Harris, *Presidential Reconstruction*, 121–40; Rabinowitz, *Race Relations in the Urban South*, 4–124; Wiener, *Social Origins of the New South*, 35–73; Bardaglio, *Reconstructing the Household*, 115–36; and Waldrep, *Roots of Disorder*, 84–119.

29. U.S. Congress, *Report of the Joint Committee on Reconstruction*, H.R. Rep. No. 30, 39th Cong., 1st Sess., pt. 3, 31.

30. James Livingston to "The Agent of the Freedmen's Bureau," Richmond, Miss., 26 December 1865, Roll 15, Letters Received, BRFAL-MS, RG 105 (M826).

31. Nelson G. Gill to Lt. Bernberger, Holly Springs, Miss., 20 December 1865, Roll 10, and Chap. Thomas Smith to Capt. E. Barnberger, Jackson, Miss., 11 January 1866, Roll 13, Letters Received, BRFAL-MS, RG 105 (M826). See also Capt. Henry E. Rainals to Maj. George D. Reynolds, Meadville, Miss. (Franklin Co.), 13 February 1866, Roll 16, Letters Received, and Lt. Samuel Eldridge to Maj. Gen. Thomas J. Wood, 3 February 1866, Roll 1, Letters Sent, both also in BRFAL-MS, RG 105 (M826).

32. E. B. Baker to Misters Irby, Ellis, and Moseby, Panola Co., Miss., 22 October 1865, encl. in Gov. Humphries to Maj. Gen. M. F. Force, Jackson, Miss., 3 November 1865, Entry 2433, Letters Received, December 1864–August 1868, Box 1, H-77, USACC, RG 393, NA; Lt. John L. Critchfield to Lt. Col. R. S. Donaldson, Canton, Miss., 14 October 1865, Canton Field Office, Roll 12, Letters Received, Sub-Assistant Commissioner Field Office Records, BRFAL-MS, RG 105 (M1907); *Natchez Daily Courier*, 6 October 1865; Lt. Col. R. S. Donaldson to Capt. J. H. Weber, Jackson, Miss., 6 November 1865, Roll 9, Letters Received, BRFAL-MS, RG 105 (M826).

33. A tension best examined by Carter, "Anatomy of Fear" and Hahn, "'Extravagant Expectations' of Freedom."

34. Hayen L. Leavel to Gov. Sharkey, Yazoo Co., Miss., September 1865, Folder 1, Box 956, Ser. 771, Letters and Petitions, MDAH.

35. F. Marion Shields to President Andrew Johnson, Noxubee Co., Miss., 25 October 1865, Roll 11, Letters Received, BRFAL-MS, RG 105 (M826).

36. Gov. Sharkey to Maj. Gen. O. O. Howard, Jackson, Miss., 10 October 1865, Roll 11, Letters Received, BRFAL-MS, RG 105 (M826).

37. Maj. Wood to Governor Humphries, Vicksburg, Miss., 8 January 1866, Folder 10, Box 962, Ser. 779: Governor Humphries Correspondence, MDAH.

38. Lt. Col. R. S. Donaldson to Lt. Stuart Eldridge, Jackson, Miss., 18 December 1865, Roll 9, Letters Received; Capt. J. H. Mathews to Eldridge, Pike Co., Miss., 12 January 1866, Roll 15, Letters Received. Both in BRFAL-MS, RG 105 (M826).

39. Cong. Globe, 40th Cong., 1st Sess., 38, 203–8.

40. A point made by Bynum, *Long Shadow of the Civil War*, 19–36; 101–16.

41. For a study of Jones County and its unique history, see Bynum, *Free State of Jones*.

42. *Vicksburg Daily Herald* (reprinted from the *Meridian Mercury*), 17 April 1868.

5

Anarchy at the Circumference

Statelessness and the Reconstruction of Authority in Emancipation North Carolina

GREGORY P. DOWNS

In 1867, a North Carolina freedman named Peter Price walked fifteen miles to a Freedmen's Bureau office in a Piedmont North Carolina town with a complaint: he was being cheated out of his share of the previous year's crop. The man Price had come to see, Hugo Hillebrandt, the face of the national state in this section of North Carolina, was someone who seemed well placed to aid him. By 1867, Hillebrandt was on his third revolution, having fought for Lajos Kossuth in his native Hungary, for Giuseppe Garibaldi in Italy, and for the Union cause in the American Civil War, and he was willing, even eager, to battle for democracy and racial equality. But when Price handed Hillebrandt's order to his landlord, the man threw the paper on the ground and stomped on it, telling the freedman that the landlord would see "Hilly Brand further in Hell than a Jay Bird could fly before we should have the crop. . . . you might send ten thousand Yankees there and he did not intend to be governed by no such laws."[1]

As a judge of the actual relationship between state and society, the landlord was prophetic. Earlier, Hillebrandt had told his superiors that he could not effectively administer the region around his office because of a lack of manpower. Beyond the limits of town whites ignored his orders, and, in the most-vivid proof of Hillebrandt's weakness, the agent had been unable to retrieve the corpse of a murdered Union soldier left rotting in the road. His title and his office did not convey authority over his district; nor could his honest intentions protect the rights of the freedpeople. Up to this point, our understanding of Price's interaction was mediated, as many were, by the agents who issued the reports. Then, however, Price, "almost upon starvation," looked for help up the Bureau's ladder, writing in his own hand first to a larger office in Greensboro and then in an intensely personal appeal to the new state military commander, whom he addressed as "Mr Freedmans Bureau" and begged to "take pity on me."[2]

Price's story illustrates the necessary but unreliable relationship between freedpeople and the Freedmen's Bureau in the relative statelessness of Reconstruction. Like Price, thousands of freedpeople in North Carolina had frustrating, even baffling, experiences trying to obtain aid from Bureau agents and Union soldiers. Often, their frustration, like Price's, had less to do with lack of sympathy than with a lack of effective tools at their disposal. Historians surely understand, in often-painful detail, that the American state failed the freedpeople, but it is not clear that we understand why federal power failed them so badly. Price's story, and dozens more like it, confounds common explanations that focus upon a failure of intentionalities rooted in racism or free-labor ideology. Like many more Bureau agents than the literature has recognized, Hillebrandt possessed the will to assist the freedpeople. What he lacked was the power.

By foregrounding capacity, scholars can see anew the central role of state institutions in shaping the experience of Reconstruction and the extent and limits of emancipation. Freedpeople's extraordinary mobilization, first through kinship and labor groups and then through Union and Loyal Leagues and the Republican Party, grew within, not in isolation from, engagement with government institutions and often for the purpose of gaining direct assistance from state actors.[3] Grounding freedpeople's actions not just in community building or ideological expression but in practical access to particular state functions helps remind us of the ways that emancipation was not solely a labor struggle or an ideological crucible. This view directs us to questions about the meaning of rights, the mystery of authority, and the salience of the state. The rights freedpeople sought to defend had little meaning absent their attachment to state apparatuses powerful enough to make them felt. Therefore, looking at efficacy directs our attention not just to what freedpeople wanted to be emancipated from but what they wanted to be emancipated into. Understood on its own terms, not as a beacon for future generations, freedpeople's politics were, like many people's politics, deeply practical. In a mutual dependence too little appreciated in the literature, freedpeople were frequently most assertive in asking for help from above; their claims—and the claims of many other relatively powerless people—were not isolated from but deeply intertwined with the need for support from government actors. Instead of operating in opposition, freedpeople's agency and state action were often mutually constructing.

Foregrounding efficacy also directs attention to one of the fundamental problems of Reconstruction: the inability of the federal government to make itself felt. Why, exactly, did the federal government that Peter Price called upon find itself so powerless? How could private actors have toppled government authority so quickly in large regions of the South? Thinking about government authority in these terms means untangling government's capacity from its form. While the historical literature has detailed the extraordinary growth of democracy in the Reconstruction South, the distinct question of government capacity to defend rights had a different timeline and trajectory. Even as the democratic promise of 1867–1868 opened up access to officeholders and legislatures and constructed a foundation for decades of political involvement, the evaporation of reliable force undercut those gains. What does the North's lack of control tell us about how legitimacy and authority were constructed in the nineteenth century? Most practically, if Hugo Hillebrandt needed a dozen mounted men to regulate his twenty-five-mile-wide district, why did he have only four?

Together these questions push us beyond the established explanations for Reconstruction's failure that emphasize the limits of Northern free-labor capitalist ideology, of Northerners' efforts to recreate cash-crop plantations in the South, of Northern racism, or of President Andrew Johnson's single-handed sabotage. They also lead us past presumptions by recent political economy scholars that resistance to taxation alone explained Reconstruction's limitations.[4] And they go beyond an emphasis upon the violence of Southern resistance—which surely was robust—and toward an explanation of the Northern weakness that made Southern resistance efficacious. While Hillebrandt was an exceptional case, many Freedmen's Bureau agents were committed and courageous. Even after Andrew Johnson replaced some Bureau leaders, many agents found themselves limited not only by their own ideologies but also by the tools at their disposal, and many of the most dedicated agents—like Hillebrandt—lasted until the Bureau itself dissolved.

So why were freedpeople's interactions so disappointing? Here, the answer lies in part in a basic institutional problem of Reconstruction that has eluded attention not because it was too well hidden but because it was obvious—the very reason why Hillebrandt could not enforce his order: a catastrophic lack of manpower. From the beginning, the Freedmen's Bureau was drastically understaffed, and its most rigorous agents found themselves hopelessly overwhelmed. This lack of manpower undermined Bureau agents' efforts to reconstruct a civil society dependent upon bodily safety and reliable authority.

Thinking about Reconstruction in terms of the problems that Northern officers faced is to ponder the dilemmas of occupation. Scholars like Edward Ayers and Bertram Wyatt-Brown have explored Reconstruction in the light of financially, morally, and humanly draining occupations in Iraq and Afghanistan. Pointing to the power of local resistance and to the weakened case for occupation's effectiveness or virtues, Ayers and Wyatt-Brown have raised provocative questions about the easy valorization of a process in the South that scholars find troublesome elsewhere. At the same time, the near ubiquity of local, violent resistance to occupiers makes the white Southern response unremarkable, even predictable. But this aspect of the analogy only touches upon its potential utility. The ongoing occupations have not just produced new moral discourses about occupation; they have also produced a great deal of analysis.

Studies of occupations both illuminate and make mysterious the nature of authority. Embedded deeply and often opaquely in local associations, authority can rarely be imposed from above but must be painstakingly constructed by engagement with competing factions of local actors. This, in turn, demands a significant, enduring, strategic use of manpower, which itself places significant financial burdens upon the occupying nation. This, in turn, produces inherent crises within democratic occupiers, as the popular cry to cut taxes and bring the soldiers home constrains the world of possibilities for elected officials. Even a nascent effort to think through the analysis of occupations, rather than their relative morality, suggests a great many areas of overlap, where explanations developed by journalists, Iraqis and Afghanis, international agencies, and increasingly sophisticated military scholars of counterinsurgency may help cast new light on American Reconstruction.[5]

There are good reasons, however, to be skeptical. The thousand contextual differences between the 1860s South and the 2000s Afghanistan and Iraq rightly brake any inclination to draw too-facile connections that explain too much. More problematically, the seemingly profound moral distinctions between American Reconstruction, which virtually every scholar supports, and the occupations of Iraq and Afghanistan, which most scholars, including myself, oppose or have doubts about, seem to raise an insuperable hurdle. The very discomfort the analogies provoke, however, may speak not to their lack of utility but to their usefully disruptive potential. Turning Reconstruction toward occupation opens up the possibility of seeing the moment in dramatically new light, a prospect both threatening and exciting.

Thinking through Reconstruction as occupation may also help historians place the moment more clearly within powerful new work on the nineteenth-century American state has opened many important questions but has, for peculiar reasons, largely bypassed Reconstruction. Without understanding the peculiar formation of the postwar state, we cannot understand why Northern occupation was so ineffective. If we do not comprehend Northern lack of efficacy, then explanations of white Southern resistance or freedpeople's assertiveness lose their analytic force. Those portrayals describe actors upon a stage without describing the stage itself. What framed the behavior of everyone in the postwar South was the collapse of civil authority, and what explained that collapse, in large part, was the contours of Northern occupation.[6]

In the rest of this essay, I avoid direct analogy and illustrate the many ways that the problems of occupation are visible in the way white and black North Carolinians wrote about their experiences during Military Reconstruction. The dilemmas occupation points to are among the very challenges of statelessness that the historical actors wrestled with. "The sudden collapse of the rebellion . . . was like an earthquake," the national Freedmen's Bureau director Oliver O. Howard wrote. "It shook and shattered the whole [Southern] social system. It broke up the old industries and threatened a reign of anarchy." North Carolina's Bureau director encountered scenes of "much confusion" upon his June 1865 arrival in Raleigh as displaced whites and blacks clustered around Bureau offices for food, and everyone watched for portents of the social order that would replace the slave South.

As Freedmen's Bureau agents worked to create order, they found themselves up against the most intransigent and influential problem of postwar Reconstruction: a basic lack of manpower. In his first year, at least two-fifths of North Carolina's Bureau offices were vacant at all times; at the worst moments, only fifteen agents covered a state of roughly one million people spanning almost five hundred miles from the Atlantic Ocean to the Smoky Mountains. Across the former Confederate states, the Bureau was never able to maintain more than nine hundred agents at any one time to protect 3.5 million ex-slaves and large numbers of white loyalists and refugees spread over more than three-quarters of a million square miles.[7]

Founded by an 1865 congressional act, the Freedmen's Bureau was meant to take freedpeople "by the hand in their passage from the house of bondage to the house of freedom," by "protecting them in the enjoyment of their rights, promoting their welfare, and securing to them and their posterity the blessings of liberty." In the words of Senator Charles Sumner, "The power of the Government must be to them a shield." A defender of the bill in the House of Representatives called it an effort to "organize them into society; we are to guide them, as the guardian guides his ward for a brief period, until they can acquire habits and become confident and capable of self-control;

we are to watch over them. . . . If we do not, we will doom them to vagrancy and pauperism." The bill created a bureaucracy in each ex-Confederate state to manage the needs of freedpeople, defend their rights, rent out abandoned and public lands, readjust unfair contracts, adjudicate disputes, and provide rations to both freedpeople and to destitute whites. In keeping with the paternalistic metaphors and mindful of Republican qualms about taking on ceaseless financial obligations, the Freedmen's Bureau was meant to be a merely "temporary expedient." But the act left it to the president to furnish "the military and other support needful to carry this act into effect."[8]

Putting the Freedmen's Bureau into practice raised significant problems because of limited resources, the challenge of creating a new bureaucracy overnight, the extremely dire situation of many freedpeople, and many Bureau agents' own internal conflicts about freedpeople's status in society. The first person to try to impose order on this chaos was North Carolina Freedmen's Bureau assistant commissioner Eliphalet Whittlesey. When Whittlesey arrived in Raleigh in June 1865 to administer the Bureau, he found "much confusion. Hundreds of white refugees and thousands of blacks were collected about this and other towns occupying every hovel and shanty." Immediately, Whittlesey plunged into the task of creating a functioning system of governance. In many ways Whittlesey was ideally suited to the task. A Connecticut Yankee, "as tough and dry as his name," Whittlesey was "intense almost to the point of being comic." He had grown up around the military and the government, the son of a state legislator and the grandson, great-grandson, and great-great-grandson of American soldiers. A former schoolteacher, pastor, and Bowdoin professor, Whittlesey joined the Union Army during the Civil War and served General Oliver O. Howard first in combat and then in the Bureau. After his time in North Carolina, Whittlesey returned to Washington as the national Freedmen's Bureau's adjutant-general, where he helped oversee the founding of Howard University and developed a vast system of clerks and requisition vouchers. Later, he served for eighteen years as secretary of the federal Board of Indian Commissioners.[9]

The Freedmen's Bureau set up shop in anarchic regions left without continuity of law as the Union removed Confederate governments, including not just imprisoned governors but also, in some states, every magistrate and justice of the peace. Washington, D.C., and its provisional governments did not staff their replacements quickly or adequately. In nearly ungoverned regions away from Union barracks, white Confederates sought to restore as much of slavery as they possibly could. In August 1865, after an agent rode forty miles with a guard of six men to arrest a planter who beat, kicked, whipped, chained, overworked, and threatened to shoot his former slaves, the agent despaired of all the undiscovered wrongdoing that happened in the wide swathes of territory "far from garrisons and northern influences." Wrongs to the freedpeople "increase just in proportion to their distance from United States authorities," he reported. A Northerner traveling through the South in September described an "overworked" and "disheartened" officer in Greensboro who supervised seven counties with only one additional officer and no garrison. "A Negro who seeks redress for a real or imaginary injury must travel perhaps ten, perhaps fifty, miles." With no effective occupying force to pacify a society turned upside down, the first years of Reconstruction were chaotic, anarchic, and intensely violent. Soon, almost every report from Freedmen's Bureau officers included long lists of assaults and murders and rapes: some intended to intimidate laborers, some to quell political resistance, some a furious response to the overturned racial and labor order.[10]

Whittlesey tried to impose order upon the confusion. At once he fought vigorously to defend freedpeople and also acted high-handedly in the presumption that he knew their interests better than they did. This duality, a duality embedded deep within free-labor ideology, was embodied in his first guideline to his agents: "To aid the destitute, yet in such a way as not to encourage dependence." Characteristically, he started by divvying his state and his problems into measurable pieces. For the state, he created twenty-seven sub-districts and then went about trying to hire "a large number of efficient officers" to "investigate the conditions" and "minister to the wants of the destitute." Quickly he clarified the ration system, cutting food supplies to any "able bodied man or woman" who was not "utterly destitute." By "constant inquiry and effort the throng of beggars was gradually removed," and he slashed statewide rations by more than a third in two months. By May 1866, only 200 out of 1,500 freedpeople at the large contraband camp on Roanoke Island received rations, and Whittlesey's primary goal seemed to be moving those freedpeople off the land and out of sight. By early 1866 only 5,000 of the state's freedpeople received any relief at all, and many rations went to families of dead Confederate soldiers.

Even when help was available, the Bureau distributed it in "indiscriminate" ways, an agent complained, and the lack of "systematic manner" left the "really suffering . . . too weak to avail themselves of the opportunity to receive assistance." Even more egregiously, but like other Bureau agents, Whittlesey intermixed his business and professional responsibilities, sharing ownership of a plantation with several partners including wartime freedmen's superintendent Horace James. Despite his limitations, Whittlesey was in other areas a fierce warrior against the "wrongs" committed against freedpeople. In the first six months, the Freedmen's Bureau certified contracts for more than 5,300 freedpeople, helped establish eighty-six schools for 8,500 freedpeople, moved fifty criminal cases to trial, heard at least 5,000 complaints, oversaw several thousand sick people in hospitals, apprenticed 400 orphans, and rented out large tracts of abandoned lands to freedpeople.[11]

Despite deep ideological tensions, the primary problem facing the Freedmen's Bureau was the practical question of how to improvise order without force. A new agent in Charlotte in June 1865 took over an office "without any rules, Laws or regulations where by to be governed." He found something like chaos. "The whole population of Blacks were completely wild," he wrote. "The Whites not being willing to yield their former right of Slavery used the lash quite freely." With "no instructions or authority as to this matter, I am at a loss to know what to do." Two weeks later, he was still stumped. "My District is a very large one and my labors are arduous And unless I have something to be Governed by I know not what to do." In desperation he turned to Whittlesey for help, but Whittlesey offered something less than reassurance. Although he sent orders and circulars, Whittlesey warned him that "in many things your own good judgment will be your only guide." The agent's judgment, and his close observation of the people he was supposed to govern, led him to a personal vision of power. Soon, he reported, "I am often challenged as to my rights and Authority in adjusting difficulties between the former Master and Servant. I have referred such persons to Maj Genl Howard or the President."[12]

Despite Whittlesey's efforts to create order, many freedpeople saw the Freedmen's Bureau as less systematic than idiosyncratic. Primarily this was due to the extraordinarily thin nature of Bureau coverage. The problem of enforcing law far away from the "influence of troops and where the military power of the Government has been little felt" plagued Whittlesey and his successors' efforts to impose order upon the land. Although he planned for thirty-three military agents to govern the state, the largest number he had on hand in his first few months was twenty. As the Union discharged soldiers in the months after Appomattox, Whittlesey lost agents (many of whom were on loan from the military) in three more waves of musters. By the time he wrote to the Bureau director Howard in the fall of 1865, he was down to fifteen. "Thus more than half the State is still without an office or representative of the Bureau," he complained. In December 1865, Whittlesey explained the relationship between force and authority. "With an efficient office in each Sub District it would be possible I think to 'control all affairs relating to freedmen,'" he wrote. "The Bureau is hated as a representative of Federal rule, but it is respected as a representative of Federal power." Without an increase in federal troops, however, equal enforcement proved a chimera. Instead of an ideal, abstracted state, the federal government created pockets of control that were surrounded by chaos. In February 1866, Whittlesey was still struggling with the same problem. "At points distant from any military force some gross outrages have been committed, by outlaws and desperadoes," he wrote to Howard.[13]

Ex-Confederates poured into the breach left by the lack of manpower and by President Andrew Johnson's weak policies by launching a campaign for violent, exploitative control over their ex-slave laborers. "In many counties slavery still exists as a fact even if abolished as a name," Sidney Andrews wrote in a postwar travel memoir. In November 1865 state elections in North Carolina, ex-Confederates turned out in force, especially in the eastern plantation belt, to defeat provisional governor William Holden and install former Confederate state treasurer Jonathan Worth. Two months later, the new state legislature passed a Black Code that increased punishments for black criminals, banned them from testifying against whites or serving on juries, and gave ex-masters preference in forcibly apprenticing black children. Vagrancy laws criminalized unemployment, nudged freedpeople into exploitative labor contracts, and prevented them from renegotiating or seeking new jobs. In coastal Elizabeth City, ex-Confederates celebrated with "the swaggering air, the insolent look, the defiant manner and the reckless conduct." In wanton "acts of violence," whites assaulted black men on the street, shot a black woman in her house, and beat a black former sergeant with a gun. "Instead of reciprocating the magnanimous trust of the President, they take advantage of the governor's loose construction of the law to exemplify their patriotism in abusing 'the inferior race' and in acts of insult to any and all who labor to elevate and improve them," a local lawyer complained. A Bureau agent said that political success encouraged Confederates to believe they would receive their rights, and "What they mean by rights is their power."[14]

Although African Americans quickly mobilized for self-defense, the only reliable safeguard against this overwhelming force lay in the Freedmen's Bureau and the remaining units of the army. If the army withdrew, one lieutenant testified, former owners spoke openly of their plans to "make it worse" for freedpeople than before emancipation, "that is, to make their freedom of no avail to them." The superintendent of the western district claimed that "under the advice and authority of the Bureau" perhaps "two thirds of the Whites are willing to do well by their former slaves," but "there are not one hundred men that I know of in this District who would deal out what I call justice to the Blacks, unless for the Bureau." In the fall and winter of 1865, anxiety about congressional reauthorization of the Freedmen's Bureau fueled desperate cries for the continuance of the Bureau from freedpeople and Unionists and agents. A freedman told the *Philadelphia Inquirer* that freedpeople did "well enough in town" but had "mighty hard times" in the countryside, where whites felt free to beat them for the "least little thing." In May 1866, to "cries from all parts of the house," a Wilmington freedman told a visiting panel of generals that the Bureau was their only protection. "Remove this refuge, and you will see that we have lost our protection. We might just as well be in the open field, and the hail beating down as big as hen's eggs on our heads." Another speaker stated that if the Bureau were abolished, "in less than two weeks you will have to allay a riot in Wilmington." Freedpeople would be "at the mercy of those who hate" them. Famously, three decades later, white vigilantes in that same city would launch a notorious and bloody coup, driving the city administration out of power and many African Americans into the woods.[15]

After a nine-month recess through most of 1865, Congress in December took up the problem of Reconstruction in a world that looked decidedly different than it had in the months before Appomattox. Appalled by the steady drip of reports of continual, everyday violence, Republicans returned to Washington ready to expand the scope of Reconstruction. Quickly they reauthorized the Freedmen's Bureau and expanded its jurisdiction over court cases involving freedpeople. Additionally Republicans in Congress passed the Civil Rights Act that invalidated discriminatory laws and made it possible to remove cases from state to federal courts. To the shock and dismay of moderate Republicans, President Johnson vetoed both bills, calling the Freedmen's Bureau a bloated patronage machine that unfairly aided blacks over "our own people" and the civil rights bill a "Stride towards centralization." Outraged Republicans overrode the President's vetoes and moved to pass the Fourteenth Amendment, incorporating much of the civil rights bill into the Constitution.

During the summer of 1866, bloody massacres at Memphis and New Orleans convinced many moderate Republicans that Southern violence was both widespread and partisan in nature. Then, emboldened by victories in the 1866 midterms, Republicans returned to Congress in December 1866 with a plan to take control of Reconstruction. They refused to seat congressmen from the Southern states, carving the South into military districts governed by commanding generals with broad authority, disfranchising former Confederates, and requiring states to include black voting rights before readmission into the Union. From the Black Codes, North Carolina and other states would move to black suffrage. It was a sweeping, even staggering transformation, as a quiescent Reconstruction policy suddenly grew teeth.

Although black voting rights changed Southern politics dramatically, in the short run much of the promise of the military division of the South was lost in the absence of troops to enforce it. Military rule was limited in the absence of a sufficient army to implement it. By the autumn of 1866, there were fewer than 18,000 soldiers left in the entire South, and almost one-third of them were stationed in far-away Texas. In all of North Carolina there were 1,226—almost 45 percent fewer than there had been at the beginning of the year. Although the Reconstruction act gave more power to federal courts, blocked the retrograde efforts of Southern legislatures to recreate slavery, and prevented Southern congressmen hijacking Congress, by the winter of 1866–1867 much of the potential for Reconstruction on the ground had already vanished, even as the potential for democratic inclusion was only being born.[16]

If Republican intentions were so powerful, why exactly was the government they controlled so weak? At the root of Reconstruction's politics lay a little-examined but defining aspect of the era: the federal government's massive and nearly immediate demobilization. Absent a force on the ground large enough to make itself felt, later efforts to remake the South would be frustrated by an inability to create order. Historians frequently emphasize 1866 and 1867 fights among Democrats, Moderates, and Radicals about the future of Reconstruction, but by that time politicians debated a policy whose fate had largely been determined. Earlier, a series of uncontroversial, commonsensical—but ultimately foolish—decisions made the U.S. Army too small to govern the South. Even those politicians who had castigated Southern traitors during the war quickly celebrated the disbanding of the army after the war. Although ideological limitations and racism constrained Reconstruction, in many respects Reconstruction was just as handcuffed by a common victor's blindness to the problems that follow victory.

Union leaders almost universally failed to understand the need for a large occupying force to subdue the South. Looking back, their confusion is so puzzling as to suggest that they did not in fact wish to subdue the South. In fact, however, some of the most strident critics of the South were the most certain that they could subdue it without significant force. Many simply could not get past the traditional American resistance to large standing armies. Others—including some of the sharpest critics of slavery—believed so strongly in slavery's maleficent impact upon institutions that they paradoxically were convinced that removing slavery excised the problems it created. Therefore, without the nefarious impact of slavery, white Southerners would become, simply, Northerners. Others shared a common nineteenth-century belief in the power of democracy. Rather than separating democracy from other state institutions that create stability, they naturalized the interplay between democracy and stability. Still others placed too much faith in the power of legal rights, presuming that white Southerners would in the end obey the law. This constellation of assumptions helped establish the idea that subduing the South might be done from Washington.

Even many Radicals did not anticipate the need for widespread occupation. In the face of financial and political forces, a consensual, uncontroversial plan for massive demobilization took hold over the winter of 1864–1865 with consequences that stretched for decades. It is likely that demobilization was actually not a decision at all, but an assumption set in place early in the war and never re-examined. By January 1865, three months before General Robert E. Lee's surrender at Appomattox, President Lincoln was already at work scaling back war expenses. When the U.S. Navy took Fort Fisher near Wilmington, Lincoln immediately ordered the Secretary of the Navy to cancel orders and cut costs. As generals Ulysses S. Grant and William T. Sherman faced off against Lee and Joseph E. Johnston in the fields of Virginia and North Carolina, the navy had already eliminated half its squadrons, and, by the end of 1865, 442 of 471 vessels. Two days after Johnston surrendered in North Carolina, the War Department issued general orders "reducing expenses of the military establishment" through an "immediate reduction of the forces in the field." By August 22nd, some 640,000 of the Union's one million soldiers had been discharged; by November 22 the number was 800,000, and Sherman's army had disappeared completely; by October 1866, there were only 17,679 troops left in the southeastern states. In North Carolina the numbers were especially stark. In June 1865, there were almost 44,000 federal troops in the state, but by September more than 35,000 were gone. It was, Lincoln's secretaries wrote, the "quick and noiseless dispersion of the enormous host when the war was done. . . . The orders came as a mere matter of course, and were executed with a thoroughness and rapidity which then seemed also a matter of course." In his poem "Armies at the Peace," Herman Melville celebrated the speed of this demobilization by comparing it to the way stars fade into night. "What power disbands the Northern Lights / After their Steely play?" he asked at the beginning of the poem, then concluded with an image of the disappearance of the "The million blades that glowed, / The muster and disbanding—/ Midnight and Morn."[17]

Although this demobilization profoundly influenced the course of Reconstruction, it was not an effort at sabotage. Instead, Union decisions during the key months before and after Appomattox were determined almost exclusively by financial considerations and an impoverished understanding of authority rooted in a belief that democratic self-government inherently produced stability. Fears of deficits and war fatigue created, as they often do, a seemingly nonpolitical momentum for decisions that would have grave political consequences. By the winter of 1864–1865, many politicians, newspaper editors, and generals were concerned that the burden of taxation and federal debt payments would sink the Republican Party or even the nation's credit. To fund a million-man army in a two-front war, the Union budget had grown from $63 million in 1860 to nearly $1.3 billion in 1865.

In part the Union met this gap by decoupling the currency from the gold standard and introducing a wide range of new excise and consumption taxes, including the nation's first indirect income tax, measures that were accepted for wartime purposes but were expected to be unsustainable in peace. The great bulk of the cost was covered by $2.4 billion in interest-bearing bonds. This debt not only saddled the nation with decades-long payments but also with a newly empowered class of finance capitalists in New York City who had a vested interest in government debt collection. In the winter of 1864–1865, as General Grant boasted that the Confederacy was a "hollow shell," the centrality of the debt took center stage.

When the debt approached two-and-a-half billion dollars, the Secretary of the Treasury warned that if it reached three billion, the Union might have to give up the fight or face default and collapse. Over the winter of 1864–1865, the *New York Times* warned frequently of the "calamity" of "National bankruptcy" and the "destruction of the public credit," which was "improbable" but "within the limits of things that can happen." Because the debt could not be readjusted, the only answer was to cut spending and the only place for savings lay—even in December 1864—in "compacter armies." Months before Appomattox, Lincoln warned government finance expert David Ames Wells that "great difficulties were yet to be encountered through the possible unwillingness or inability of the nation to pay the war debt, or the great increase in taxation which the war had made necessary." By the time of Lincoln's assassination, he was associated strongly with the idea of retrenchment, a word that combined the discharge of the army and the leavening of financial burdens.[18]

Over time the Union's effort to contract the currency and establish the gold standard would become a vibrant, even bitter, political issue, but in the key moments of 1865 and 1866, many politicians and generals seem not to have considered any option other than a massive, cost-saving demobilization. The U.S. Army did indeed demobilize white troops first, both because of political demands and because more of their terms were set to expire over the summer and fall. After moving African American units in to replace them, in some states the army responded to political pressure by sending black units away from cities and toward the coasts and relatively isolated forts. It is easy, however, to attribute too much importance to these decisions. In some states African American units continued to man highly populous areas; other states continued to be regulated by white troops. Even if every one of those racially based decisions had been made differently, it would have had little effect. Demobilization was taking place at such a massive scale that placement decisions were but tinkering around the edges by the spring and summer of 1866.

As soon as the war neared its close, "strict retrenchment" was visible everywhere, in the shuttering of military hospitals, armories, and naval yards, in the sale of ships and supplies, and in the steady homeward march of Union soldiers, all at a savings estimated at a million dollars a day. At the end of 1865, the Department of War, which spent $516 million in that fiscal year, cut its request to $33 million, the U.S. Navy from $116 million to $23 million. In December, the Secretary of the Treasury's call for decreased spending and lower taxes passed the Congress by a vote of 144 to 6. Soon, the Senate and House established a Joint Committee on Retrenchment, dedicated to reducing military expenses, cutting taxes, and, eventually, enacting civil service reform. Additionally, after surrender, these fiscal fears meshed with soldiers' demands to return home now that—in their view—the war was over. Quickly, they worked the levers of power to make sure their regiments were on the list for speedy demobilization. With powerful political and economic pressures, and without a clear rationale for maintaining the army's size (even among people who expected some military rule in the South), the forces speeding toward the great muster out were too large and widespread to resist.[19]

This profound demobilization structured the actions of everyone, Northern and Southern, white and black, in postwar North Carolina. Far from Raleigh and Washington, in lonely offices in hostile towns across the state, freedpeople and Freedmen's Bureau agents experienced this stateless society in frightening and personal terms. There, the pockets of order seemed smaller and smaller, and the anarchy of society even more apparent. In Kinston and Greensboro, Hugo Hillebrandt worried that he managed not the birth of a new state but simply an isolated garrison in the wilds. Hillebrandt had reason to think broadly. While the roots of his ideological commitments are vague, the Civil War was his third revolution, and his experiences with governments from monarchies to republics were as broad as anyone's. Born in southeastern Hungary in 1832, Hillebrandt as a young man joined Lajos Kossuth's nationalist revolution, displaying "military genius and cool courage." From there he'd traveled to Turkey and the United States. Upon hearing of Garibaldi's uprising, he left his job at the U.S. Coast Survey to fight in Italy, returning to the United States in 1860, and volunteering for the Union Army a year later. Wounded at Gettysburg and weakened by disease after the sleet and rain of the Mine Run campaign, Hillebrandt was mustered out in December 1863 and served in the Veterans Reserve Corps in Washington, D.C., for the remainder of the war. In 1866, he joined the Freedmen's Bureau and was stationed in North Carolina in the Kinston and Greensboro offices until the end of 1868. Later, President Grant appointed him U.S. Consul to Crete.[20]

A hardened, determined and courageous man, Hillebrandt nevertheless found himself frequently powerless. Without adequate support, no amount of personal valor mattered. In May 1866, a freedwoman ran into his office in Kinston to deliver the awful news that a Union soldier had been murdered nineteen miles away. Hillebrandt, a man who had fought in three wars on two continents, could do nothing but wait while his soldier's body rotted in the road. Hillebrandt wanted to rush immediately to get the body, but was horrified when he "was advised by the citizens not to go without ample force." When Hillebrandt asked these locals to come with him, "none of them was willing to offer his services." They "state that there is an organized band of horse thieves well armed ready to offer resistance." From a distance, the Bureau not only failed to protect freedpeople; it could not even protect its own officers, nor retrieve their dead bodies.

A month later, Hillebrandt complained again about "horses and mules . . . mostly stolen from freedmen by white citizens." The "general impression is that a negro should not, and has no right to own property" in the "upper part of the county." There, "they are determined to carry out their purposes, the civil authorities and citizens do not act upon such cases the horse thieves are well known to them, but some are affraid to arrest or even report them for fear their life and property would be endangered." At his office Hillebrandt had four enlisted men and no rations. To "scour the country a little" and arrest the horse thieves, he needed twelve soldiers and horses. Trying to cover a twenty-four-mile range without them was impossible, he argued, as "The rascals are all mounted we might meet with strong opposition or they run away."[21]

Many others echoed Hillebrandt's judgment. To a Massachusetts man touring the state in January 1866, the Freedmen's Bureau was full of good intentions and "good and energetic" agents but not good effect, because it lacked the "strong hand of power." To create order and safety and "subdue and protect the country," a "simple force of 25 men would be entirely adequate," the Northern traveler wrote. "The rebels are frightened at the very sight or name of Yankee. But they need to be kept in awe." Instead of awe, however, the Bureau inspired at best wariness, at worst contempt. One agent warned Whittlesey that no matter how "vigilant an officer may be at a central point he cannot make his influence felt as it ought to" at the "circumference." Another despaired of all the undiscovered wrongdoing that happened in wide regions of territory "far from garrisons and northern influences." With no effective occupying force to pacify a society turned upside down, the first years of Reconstruction were chaotic, anarchic, and intensely violent.[22]

The narrow spatial limits of Bureau power confirmed freedpeople's suspicion that rights could not be relied upon generally but needed to be invested in particular guardians who might be able to make them felt within particular regions. This judgment of the world produced a politics of territoriality: a sense that politics and policies could only be judged based upon their impact upon the world immediately in front of them. Made suspicious of analogy and of programs by the weakness of the federal government, freedpeople—and, to different ends, other Southerners—practiced a politics that both claimed control over their immediate area and also sought protection from patrons above.[23]

At the same time, interactions with the Freedmen's Bureau helped foster a politics rooted in claims of friendship and personal attachment among freedpeople, who sought not just parchment guarantees but the backing of particular patrons felt in specific, bounded regions. Over and over freedpeople like Lucy Council called upon the Bureau as a friend to offer protection since "We have not got any friends near around us please your honor to help us if you can." In Lexington, 106 freedpeople claimed on a petition that they did have a friend in the person of their agent, Colonel W. F. Henderson. Calling him "our protector," the petitioners begged the Bureau not to reassign him elsewhere. "Being in the midst of enemies to our race," they would "certainly have to suffer" without him. In a fascinating cover letter, a local white man named H. Adams presented the petition, "gotten up by themselves in their own style, handwriting + the contents." The freedpeople had asked him to "transcribe the whole and put it in a more businesslike manner," but after contemplation,

Adams "prefered sending it in its original style and let you draw your own inferences." Adams hoped their raw style would show "these people not only speak their own sentiments + feelings, but they speak for other counties of the District."

Although Adams recognized the existence of other ways of talking about rights, he chose to maintain the letter's intimate, personal appeal because it accurately conveyed the needs of the people. More than a defense of abstract rights, these freedpeople needed recognition. Over the next decades the judgment that power depended upon patrons would reconfigure African American political organizing, forcing Southerners into alliances with local powerbrokers who could protect them in ways that legal codes could not. Rather than eliminating the old practice of paternalism, emancipation and Reconstruction shifted the sources of patronage from masters to politicians.[24]

The complexity of freedpeople's interaction with the Freedmen's Bureau was illustrated powerfully in petitions from the former contraband camp at Trent River, near New Bern. Even bad engagements with weak or malevolent agents served to confirm the necessary, if inadequate, role of the Bureau. In 1868, 501 freedpeople from Trent River turned to Howard, the Freedmen's Bureau director, for help against an agent that an investigator had called "arbitrary and despotic." Calling themselves "poor creatures left out door exposed to the cold," they promised the common pledge of the weak, God's favor, in exchange for Howard's assistance. "God will bless the United States fore her aid and support to the poor and will enable her to conquor all Governments upon the surface of the earth by showing love and charity to the poor."

Along with oaths of loyalty and love, the freedmen also treated assistance as a loan to be repaid and a covenant to be recompensed with "the performance of every honorable duty characteristic of good citizenship." But this covenant depended upon mutuality; in terms that were daring, even dangerous, the freedpeople said that the government "should not expect our support in any form" until it "guarantees to use every right privilege secured to other citizen." At once, the freedmen of Trent River put themselves forward as loyal and weak subjects, as trustworthy loan recipients, as alienated victims, and as proud citizens who would defend their rights with their lives. If the letter reads as a potluck of aspirations, it reflects the complex interactions with the Freedmen's Bureau and the contradictory anxieties these encounters with the government fostered.

The response to their letter would only confirm this judgment. The sub-assistant commissioner assigned to investigate was incensed that the freedmen had undercut him and declared that there was no destitution in the settlement at all. Absent any other way to gain anyone's attention, the freedpeople in desperation apologized to the agent, but to no avail. A short while later the Freedmen's Bureau disbanded all but its hospital operations in Trent River. While Howard pointed with pride to the Bureau's lists of accomplishments, agents like Hillebrandt and freedpeople like Price wondered how to fill the power vacuum left behind. While some state Republican governments, including Holden's in post–1868 North Carolina, tried to build upon Bureau efforts to create authority, their efforts continued to be hamstrung by weak revenues, a thin legitimacy, and intense opposition from many ex-Confederates.[25]

What emerges from this portrayal of Reconstruction is a nearly hopelessly muddled storyline: where freedpeople expressed themselves assertively, but often by asking for state actors to intervene and save them; where white Southerners used sadistic violence, but often to subdue already anarchic regions; where white Northerners proclaimed their intention to help freedpeople, but then provided very little of what was needed. Together these storylines suggest the importance of not isolating any group's actions from the surrounding context; freedpeople were not solely seeking self-assertion but also allies. White ex-Confederates responded not primarily to race-based psychosis but to opportunities presented to them. White Northern Republicans folded their hands not from a desire to surrender but from confusion over whether victory was still possible.

This portrayal lacks the neat coherence of sophisticated but ultimately reductive emphases upon ideology or labor struggle. If the muddle threatens our ability to connect the pieces, we might look for inspiration to one of those Northern occupiers in North Carolina during this period—carpetbagger, novelist, and activist Albion Tourgée. In his 1879 blockbuster *A Fool's Errand,* Tourgée explored the limitations of Northern commitment in a scene in which a white North Carolina Unionist delivers a private eulogy at the grave of carpetbagger Comfort Servosse, the aforementioned Fool. Servosse had the "grand idee" to "make this a free country accordin' to Northern notions," the Unionist tells his son, "but there wa'n't material enough to build of." Reconstruction collapsed not because of Southern white resistance or the corruption of carpetbag governments but because of the faulty planning of "the master workmen at the North, who would insist on the tale of bricks without furnishin' any straw." In October 1880, when Tourgée published his follow-up to his earlier novel, *Bricks without Straw,* he returned to the image of bricks without straw for the title and governing metaphor of his new book, just republished by Duke University Press. At the beginning of his novel, Tourgée extended the Exodus story, in which Pharaoh punished the Israelites for failing to meet their quota of bricks, even as he denied them the necessary materials. In Tourgée's version, Pharaoh's jester imagines these "ill-made" bricks laid in a slipshod palace that "will fall upon him and all his people that dwell therein."[26]

The image of bricks without straw captured not only Tourgée's imagination but a great deal of his view of who and what was to blame for the limitations of Reconstruction. Put baldly, Reconstruction faltered because Northern Republicans, especially Radicals, issued high-sounding orders without providing the necessary materials. The problem lay not in their ideology or their racism but in their governance. They were not quite hypocrites; they were fools. In the process they made fools of those carpetbaggers and scalawags and freedpeople who took their words seriously and seers of those—especially Southern white resisters—who ignored their words entirely. Tourgée arrived at a clear, compelling, and oversimplified explanation for Reconstruction's limitations: the folly of the North. Unable to understand Southern distinctiveness or Southern resistance, well-intentioned Northerners failed to comprehend what would be required of them. They wanted reconstruction on the cheap, bought with air and words, not blood and treasure.

At the same time, Tourgée's emphasis upon the failure of Northern planning also suggested a complex reading of freedpeople's agency. On the one hand, Tourgée meticulously portrayed freedpeople's actions, exploring the manifold ways people built a thriving economy, developed powerful religious and educational institutions, and resisted white terrorism. Tourgée's account, on the other hand, is also replete with warnings not to mistake freedpeople's actions for their wishes: what they wanted and expected, he suggests, was for the federal government to establish their rights firmly. Their very actions in trying to defend themselves were proof both of their agency and of its limits; not only did their self-defense often fail, but the very fact that they had to expend so much energy and, eventually, blood, demonstrated the confines they worked within.

A powerful defender of African Americans, a political candidate who organized their votes, and a carpetbagger vilified by Southern whites, Tourgée hardly seems likely to cast cold water on the aspirations of freedpeople. But he was a skeptic of the idea that enfranchisement was quite as important as Northern Republicans (and many modern scholars) seem to think it was. Voting was important, but the real struggles, for Tourgée, lay elsewhere, not in politics but in governance. The goal of Reconstruction, in his view, was not better politics but better use of power to destroy the structural differences between Southern and Northern society. Here, the North consistently disappointed him: it "would not . . . perform the duty laid upon it as a conqueror," he writes in *A Fool's Errand*.[27]

In this light, everything that appeals to modern sensibilities—legal rights, enfranchisement, and rhetoric about equality—was to him at best irrelevant, at worst distracting. Absent effective governance, rights meant nothing. Not to understand this was not to understand his conception of the relationship between democracy and government authority; democratic participation did not create but depended upon state power.[28] Tourgée conveys this lesson deftly, through a series of epiphanies where characters realize the futility—or, in Tourgée's favorite term, foolishness—of placing faith in rights. Over and over, the characters in *Bricks without Straw* come to the realization that a "*right* ter vote, an' hold meetin's an' be like white folks" was of limited use since "de right ter du a ting an' de doin' on't is two mighty diff'rent tings." When a white Yankee schoolteacher comes to understand that "naked privileges had been conferred, but the right to enforce their recognition had been abandoned," this "revelation of her own thought to herself" stuns her. Thinking bitterly on the rollback of Reconstruction, she dismisses many common explanations, including free labor capitalism, racism, and Southern violence. If freedpeople and Southern whites both behaved in understandable ways, the surprise of Reconstruction lay in the quick retreat of the white North.[29]

Having established that Northern weakness might be the key to unlocking the mystery of the postwar South, Tourgée for much of *Bricks without Straw* ducks the broader question of why the North had proved so weak. But near the end, Tourgée turns at last to the novel's missing characters, the Northerners who stayed in the North, who spoke eloquently but did too little, who, finally, averted their gaze. In a stilted scene between a white Southern scalawag and a Radical congressman, the scalawag realizes that the very success of the Northern way of life—its freedom and its prosperity—blinded Northerners to the true nature of the South. The flourishing structures of Northern society, in Tourgée's view, kept Northerners from realizing that they were, in fact, structures, not naturally occurring conditions and that they have to be planted, nurtured, and guarded. In Tourgée's terms, Reconstruction is a story of the arrogance of victory, the inability to imagine the demands of occupation, and the unwillingness to either pay the price of success or admit to defeat. These are failures, but human ones, ones that require a close examination not just of ideology and racism but also of Tourgée's favorite subject, folly.

Tourgée's work raises a broad question about the absence of folly—and of tragedy, properly understood—in our accounts of Reconstruction, or of most historical moments. While almost all scholars follow W.E.B. Du Bois in considering Reconstruction tragic in a certain use of the word, as a crushing disappointment, few actually fully portray it as tragedy. Chastened by the use of tragedy in Dunning School accounts, and alert to the forces that brought down Reconstruction, modern portrayals tend toward horror. The magnitude of Reconstruction's disappointments seems to demand villains worthy of the blame, whether in the form of violent Southern whites or capitalistic, racist Northerners. What Tourgée found, however, was something more disturbing, more difficult to portray, and, perhaps, even more dispiriting. Reconstruction ground to a close because of dull, commonplace sins: the disconnect between high-minded rhetoric and the steady accumulation of daily actions that would have constituted effective federal governance; the challenge of reining in a victorious arrogance; and the coercive and ever-present force of past habits upon daily actions. Freedpeople's heroism might tell us something of our own capacities; so, too, unfortunately, do the blind spots of Northern Radicals, and, even, the violent outrage of Southern whites.[30]

Satisfying as the standing story of Reconstruction is, I cannot help but wonder if we are nearing the end of its utility, if we have learned what we are capable of learning from it, and if it is past time to move on to new stories. These new stories, more engaged with both folly and tragedy, might perhaps send us wrestling again with the ever-present challenge of maintaining public (and even scholarly) interest in functioning institutions, with the blindness produced by self-satisfaction, with the gap between support for policies and support for paying for them, with narratives that force us from the reassuring conclusion that the failure of Reconstruction lies in some external *them* and back into the dispiriting, terrifying, but useful engagement with the idea that its failure may lie in a more recognizable *us*.

Notes

1. Peter Price to Mr. Freedman's Bureau, 17 March 1868, encl. in Peter Price to Gen. Nelson A. Miles, 25 March 1868, Roll 14, Records of the Assistant Commissioner of the State of North Carolina, BRFAL-NC, RG 105 (M843).

2. Ibid.

3. Hahn, *Nation under Our Feet*; Fitzgerald, *Union League Movement*, 265–317.

4. On the power of taxation in creating opposition to Reconstruction, see, especially, Franklin, *Reconstruction after the Civil War*, 139–41. For the best political economy explanations that flirt with overdetermined explanations of Reconstruction's demise, see Bensel, *Yankee Leviathan*; Beckert, *Monied Metropolis.*

5. In answer to a different set of questions about what Reconstruction might teach us about Iraq, rather than what Iraq might lead us to ask about Reconstruction, Edward

Ayers and Bertram Wyatt-Brown have explored the analogy in Ayers, "First Occupation," 20–21, and "Exporting Reconstruction," 145–66; Wyatt-Brown, "Honor, Shame and Iraq" and "Changing Faces of Honor." Historical accounts that emphasize Reconstruction as military occupation include Bradley, *Bluecoats and Tar Heels*; Sefton, *United States Army and Reconstruction*. For studies of other occupations, see Donald P. Wright, et al., *A Different Kind of War*; Filkins, *Forever War*; Rashid, *Descent into Chaos*; Bessel, *Germany 1945*; Hitchcock, *Bitter Road to Freedom*; Renda, *Taking Haiti*; Kramer, *Blood of Government*.

6. On the literature on the nineteenth-century American state, see, especially, Novak, "Myth of the 'Weak' American State" and *People's Welfare*; Balogh, *Government out of Sight*; Einhorn, *Property Rules*; John, "Ruling Passions"; John, *Spreading the News*.

7. United States, War Department, *Report of Brevet Major General O. O. Howard*, 6; U.S. Congress, *Report of the Joint Committee on Reconstruction*, 187–88; Miller, introduction to *The Freedmen's Bureau and Reconstruction*, xxix.

8. Cong. Globe, 38th Cong., 2nd Sess., 1 (1865), 688, 693, 768, 960–61. After stinging criticism of Bureau tyranny by early pro-Southern scholars and equally stinging denunciation of Bureau racism and paternalism by 1960s and 1970s revisionists like William S. McFeely, historians—perhaps most prominently Paul A. Cimbala—have recaptured the good intentions and even heroic efforts of some agents and administrators. McFeely, *Yankee Stepfather*; Cimbala, *Under the Guardianship of the Nation*; Foner, *Reconstruction*, 124–75; Bardaglio, *Reconstructing the Household*, 98–104, 124–32, 145–46; Edwards, *Gendered Strife and Confusion*, 1–15, 42–51, 97–104; Faulkner, *Women's Radical Reconstruction*.

9. Gates, *Men of Mark*, vol. 2, 394–96; McFeely, *Yankee Stepfather*, 78–83; Oliver Otis Howard, *Autobiography*, 298, 352; Alexander, *North Carolina Faces the Freedmen*, 50, 99; Click, *Time Full of Trial*, 148; E. Whittlesey to O. O. Howard, n.d., Quarterly Report Fall 1865, vol. 7, Records of the Assistant Commissioner of the State of North Carolina, Ser. 2446, BRFAL-NC, RG 105 [FSSP A-747].

10. Fitzgerald, "Emancipation and Military Pacification"; Rable, *But There Was No Peace*; Fellman, *Inside War*; Hahn, *Nation under Our Feet*; E. Whittlesey to O. O. Howard, n.d., Quarterly Report Fall 1865, vol. 7, Records of the Assistant Commissioner of the State of North Carolina, Ser. 2446, BRFAL-NC, RG 105 [FSSP A-747].

11. Click, *Time Full of Trial*, 148, 164, 184, 193–93; Alexander, *North Carolina Faces the Freedmen*, 50, 99, 101; McFeely, *Yankee Stepfather*, 78–83, 250–54; Schmidt, *Free to Work*; Oliver Otis Howard, *Autobiography*, 298, 352; Gates, *Men of Mark*, vol. 2, 394–96; J. R. Fleming to Lt. Col. Stephen Moore, 17 January 1868, Roll 11, Records of the Assistant Commissioner of the State of North Carolina, BRFAL-NC, RG 105 (M843).

12. John C. Barnett to Whittlesey, 29 June, 12 July, Quarterly Report, Box 1, 1865, Letters Received, Records of the Assistant Commissioner of the State of North Carolina, Ser. 2446, BRFAL-NC, RG 105 [FSSP A-506, 507 508]; Whittlesey to Barnett, 13 July 1865, vol. 1, p. 4, Letters Sent, Records of the Assistant Commissioner of the State of North Carolina, Ser. 2446, BRFAL-NC, RG 105 [FSSP A-506].

13. E. Whittlesey to O. O. Howard, n.d., Quarterly Report Fall 1865, vol. 7, Records of the Assistant Commissioner of the State of North Carolina, Ser. 2446, BRFAL-NC, RG

105 [FSSP A-747]; Whittlesey to Howard, 8 December 1865, N-53 1865, Letters Received, Ser. 15, Washington Headquarters, BRFAL-NC, RG 105 [FSSP A-712]; E. Whittlesey to O. Howard, 15 February 1866 and n.d., Roll 1, Records of the Assistant Commissioner of the State of North Carolina, BRFAL-NC, RG 105 (M843); McFeely, *Yankee Stepfather*, 78, 83, 245–53; Oliver Otis Howard, *Autobiography*, 279–80; Simpson, "Ulysses S. Grant and the Freedmen's Bureau," 12.

14. Dennett, *South As It Is*, 110–11; Andrews, *South since the War*, 188; U.S. Congress, *Report of the Joint Committee on Reconstruction*, 175–76, 182, 187–88, 199–202, 270.

15. U.S. Congress, *Report of the Joint Committee on Reconstruction*, 175–76, 182, 187–88, 270; Alexander, *North Carolina Faces the Freedmen*, 102–3, 134–35; Berlin, Reidy, and Rowland, *Black Military Experience*, 801–2.

16. Foner, Reconstruction, 242–75, McKitrick, *Andrew Johnson*, 253–325.

17. Melville, *Battle-Pieces*, 88–89; United States, Navy Department, *Report of the Secretary of the Navy*, iii, iv, ix, x, xxxii, xxxiv; Nicolay and Hay, *Abraham Lincoln*, 10: 336–37; Sefton, *United States Army and Reconstruction*, 261; OR 3:5:495–520.

18. Bensel, *Yankee Leviathan*, 14, 237; Skowronek, *Building a New American State*, 50–51; Robert P. Sharkey, *Money, Class, and Party*; Hormats, *Price of Liberty*, 79–86; Dewey, *Financial History*, 299, 329; Sefton, *United States Army and Reconstruction*, 65, 207–8; McKitrick, *Andrew Johnson*, 369–70; Mark R. Wilson, *Business of Civil War*, 202–3; Ferleger, *David A. Wells*, 6; P. S. Evans, *Funeral Elegy*, 5; Dean, *Eulogy*, 9; Simpson, *Ulysses S. Grant, Triumph over Adversity*, 391; Sherman, *Memoirs*, 2: 252; Wells, *Theory and Practice of Taxation*, 18–39 and *Our Burden and Our Strength*; *New York Times* (19 March 1864, 6; 5 December 1864, 4; 28 April 1865, 4; 7 January 1865, 4).

19. OR 1:47:3:243, 302 and 3:4:1280; 3:5:1, 65, 509–17; *New York Times* (28 April 1865, 4; 7 January 1865, 4; 30 April 1865, 4); *Philadelphia Inquirer*, 14 April 1865, 4; U.S. Congress, *Report of the Joint Committee on Reconstruction*, viii.

20. *New York Times*, 7 April 1896, 5.

21. Hugo Hillebrandt to E. Whittlesey, 13 May 1866, Roll 7; Hillebrandt to Clinton A. Cilley, 29 June 1866, Letters Received, Roll 7; Hillebrandt to William H. Wiegel, 25 June 1866, Roll 7. All in Records of the Assistant Commissioner of the State of North Carolina, BRFAL-NC, RG 105 (M843).

22. James Thurston to H. Wilson, 10 January 1866, Roll 9,; William B. Bowe to Col. E. Whittlesey, 27 January 1866, Roll 16,; Allan Rutherford, Report of Cases of Outrages upon Union Men in North Carolina, June 1866, Roll 7. All in Records of the Assistant Commissioner of the State of North Carolina, BRFAL-NC, RG 105 (M843). And see Fitzgerald, "Emancipation and Military Pacification"; Rable, *But There Was No Peace*; Dennett, *South As It Is*, 109–10; Click, *Time Full of Trial*, 164, 184; Alexander, *North Carolina Faces the Freedmen*, 101; McFeely, *Yankee Stepfather*, 81; E. Whittlesey to O. O. Howard, n.d., Quarterly Report Fall 1865, vol. 7, Records of the Assistant Commissioner of the State of North Carolina, Ser. 2446, BRFAL-NC, RG 105 [FSSP A-747].

23. Sefton, *United States Army and Reconstruction*, 261. On territoriality, see Guha, *Elementary Aspects*, 6–8, 12–13, 170–71, 333–34; and Ludden, *Agrarian History*. I develop the relationship between the Civil War and postbellum states, a political of personalistic

friendship, and imaginative territorialism in Downs, *Declarations of Dependence.* See also, Kaye, *Joining Places.*

24. Lucy Council to Col. J. V Bomford, 22 August 1867, encl. in Isaac Porter to Col. Chur, 29 August 1867, Roll 10, Records of the Assistant Commissioner of the State of North Carolina, BRFAL-NC, RG105 (M843); Berlin, Reidy, and Rowland, *Black Military Experience,* 805–6; L. A. Owens et al. to O. Howard, 12 December 1867, encl. in H. Adams to Howard, 17 December 1867, Roll 10, Records of the Assistant Commissioner of the State of North Carolina, BRFAL-NC, RG 105 (M843); Simon Handy et al. to Col. Moore, 6 September 1867, Letters Received, Records of the North Carolina Superintendent for the Eastern District, Ser. 2755, BRFAL-NC, RG 105 [FSSP A-889]. On personalistic politics, see Downs, *Declarations of Dependence,* esp. 1–14; Kaye, *Joining Places;* and Morgan, *Inventing the People.*

25. United States, Department of State, *Executive Documents Published by the Order of the House of Representatives during the First Session of the Thirty-Ninth Congress 1865–66,* 60, 68, 71; A. Blunt to Howard, 30 January 1868, encl. in Jas. G. Haniford to Howard, 31 January 1868, Roll 13, Records of the Assistant Commissioner of the State of North Carolina, BRFAL-NC, RG 105 (M843); Mobley, *James City,* 62–84.

26. Tourgée, *Fool's Errand,* 403–4 and *Bricks without Straw,* 81–83.

27. Tourgée, *Fool's Errand,* 171.

28. On this point, see Emberton, "Reconstructing Loyalty."

29. Tourgée, *Bricks without Straw,* 159, 230–31, 259–60, 292, 351–52.

30. Ibid., 432.

6

"The Negroes Are No Longer Slaves"

Free Black Families, Free Labor, and Racial Violence in Post-Emancipation Kentucky

J. MICHAEL RHYNE

In the summer of 1866, Jennie Addison, age twelve and, along with her mother, employed by the wife of James C. Ford as domestic help, testified to an agent of the Freedmen's Bureau, Louisville Sub-district, that Mrs. Ford had on several occasions ordered a male employee to beat her. During the worst of these beatings, the "man struck her 7 or 8 times with his fist saying that he was authorized by [Ford's wife] to inflict the punishment." The Freedmen's Bureau, on which the federal government placed responsibility for helping Kentucky's approximately 200,000 former slaves adjust to their new status, struggled to mitigate racial violence in the workplace and elsewhere. In this case, head of the household James C. Ford was ordered to appear before the Bureau to answer charges and cautioned to remember that "Negroes are no longer slaves and the law does not permit them to be beaten and abused in this manner either by the persons hiring them or by any person who they may also have employed."[1]

Their violent nature notwithstanding, such cases of abuse typically did not constitute a sufficiently serious offense for federal prosecution in the overburdened U.S. District Court in Louisville. In the months after the Thirteenth Amendment formally ended slavery in the Commonwealth of Kentucky, this often proved to be the court of last resort for Kentucky's former slaves in their efforts to get a modicum of justice. Attempting to prosecute such cases in local or state courts was normally not an option, as most Kentucky judges strictly adhered to state law and thus deemed black testimony against white defendants inadmissible. The Freedmen's Bureau, operating in the commonwealth from late 1865 through 1868, tried to intervene where possible, investigating reports of murder, violent intimidation, and more, including cases that did not result in long-term or fatal injuries to the victims. Bureau superintendents, understanding the limits of legal recourse for freedpeople, established a system of fines to punish white perpetrators in cases such as Jennie Addison's. Despite such penalties, the transition to free labor that the Freedmen's Bureau hoped to facilitate would face violent opposition from former slaveholders and stubborn white employers who, along with self-styled vigilantes, acted out their deep-seated notions of white supremacy with little reason to fear prosecution at local, state, or even federal levels.[2]

Former slaves in Kentucky, who made up a fifth of the state's population, had little ability to assert their hard-won liberty in the first months and years after emancipation became law. Self-proclaimed "Negro Regulators" and other white supremacist bands imposed reigns of terror in many counties. In particular, families—sometimes with male heads of household, sometimes not—faced significant hurdles as they sought to establish autonomous lives. Regulators pillaged their homes, stole any valuables they had, often burned them out, and sometimes violently abused them. Men reported being dragged out of their homes, beaten, and on occasion stripped naked and whipped. A few reported being bound and forced to watch as Regulators raped a wife or daughter. Enough freedmen were murdered—sometimes merely shot in the head, other times tortured to death—to send a clear message that attempts by freedmen to resist these bands of Regulators likely would prove fatal.[3]

With at least tacit community support, bands of white supremacists sought to enact their agenda by attempting to demonstrate the inferiority of freedpeople. Certainly these assaults represented denial on the part of white men of the manhood that many black men publicly demonstrated during and after the Civil War and, thus, they represented a form of symbolic emasculation. At the same time, violence against black men and their families helped restore a sense of manhood to some white men who had lost status, that is to say, white men who felt emasculated as a result of either the defeat of the Confederacy or abolition of slavery, or both.[4] Furthermore, violence against freedwomen and girls illustrated the extent to which many white Kentuckians regarded freedwomen as undeserving of the same basic courtesies and the same level of respect and protection accorded to white women in both public and private settings. As a result, free black women fell victim not only to white men who dealt them insults and beatings but also to perpetrators of rape. As Herbert Gutman phrased it, "Ex-slave husbands and fathers found it difficult to protect their wives and daughters from the conventional sexual insult and even abuse that remained after . . . emancipation."[5]

A range of other developments aimed to restrict the effects of emancipation as much as possible. Many masters proved reluctant to release their slaves, openly and violently defying federal policy regarding emancipation. Freedpeople expressed massive frustration with the commonwealth's disruptive, racially biased, and abuse-ridden apprenticeship system. Free black women working in white households and urban settings complained of the unfair, often vicious treatment they received at the hands of employers and other white Kentuckians. Taken altogether, these attempts to limit emancipation, powerfully reinforced by organized violence, constitute a concerted effort to maintain black subordination, thereby denying former slaves the free and potentially equal status they desired, expected, and demanded. The stories of Kentucky's freedwomen and children, told through the documents generated as they or their families attempted to gain redress for abuses committed against them by white employers and assailants, bring to light the unique challenges they faced.[6]

Unlike the former Confederate states, Kentucky as a whole had never seceded, and a clear majority of white Kentuckians had either enthusiastically or reluctantly supported the Union in the first years of the war. However, as the war progressed, many of the commonwealth's white residents exhibited growing bitterness concerning federal policy, especially regarding slavery, and at war's end some of them simply refused to recognize that the peculiar institution was in its death throes. Those who, either overtly or covertly, had sided with the Confederacy had experienced military defeat and witnessed the destruction of slavery, and thus they were bitter both toward the federal government and toward former slaves. Those who had remained loyal to the Union in hopes of preserving slavery were intensely bitter over uncompensated emancipation. Now all these men, along with their families, faced the prospect of black equality, and so some of them predictably engaged in violent resistance.[7]

Despite ample evidence of such defiance, and despite Kentucky's refusal to ratify the Thirteenth Amendment, President Andrew Johnson ordered an end to martial law on 12 October 1865. In contrast to the president's apparent lack of concern for the Commonwealth of Kentucky's former slaves, Major General Oliver O. Howard, commissioner of the Freedmen's Bureau, contacted Major General Clinton B. Fisk, assistant commissioner for the Tennessee District, and instructed him also to take charge of Bureau operations in Kentucky. Fisk immediately began building an organization and made ready to conduct a thorough inspection of the state at year's end, after the Thirteenth Amendment had become law.[8]

In February and March 1866 Commissioner Fisk filed reports to his superiors chronicling the extent to which white assailants were terrorizing freedpeople in the commonwealth. Bands of white supremacists frequently targeted community leaders, especially returning veterans, ministers, and freedmen who owned or rented their own land. Many black veterans were robbed, with one perpetrator going so far as to demand that the soldier disrobe and give him his blue uniform. Some veterans, like Peter Branford of Mercer County, were shot and killed "without cause or provocation." Others received beatings, whippings, or had their lives threatened simply for attempting to locate and reconstitute their families. Veterans frequently purchased their rifles as they mustered out, no doubt with forethought toward protection of households and communities. However, possession of firearms placed them at odds with Kentucky state laws prohibiting black men from bearing arms. Local law enforcement officers routinely seized arms from returning veterans near train stations or in other public spaces, sometimes ruthlessly enforcing the law by shooting any freedman who did not immediately disarm. Vigilante groups took it upon themselves to raid black communities in search of illegal weapons, as well, with the end result that families and communities had limited ability to defend themselves from heavily armed bands of Regulators.[9]

Military and civilian inspectors logged cases of women and girls being beaten or raped, freedmen being assaulted and sometimes shot or lynched, and particularly of free black households being violated and families being forced to flee for their lives. Further, emancipation had become law in early winter, and throughout Kentucky freedpeople suffered from the elements, as well as hunger and disease, with woefully inadequate resources available to mitigate their suffering. As one group of Bluegrass freedmen lamented, "our houses [are] pulled down on us & [we are] turned out of dores in the Cold & we have no portection from the whites of this naborhood." The unusually cold winter of that year and of several to follow would take a horrific toll on impoverished former slaves, particularly refugees fleeing racial violence.[10]

In the face of this onslaught against Kentucky's freedpeople, Fisk quickly recruited locals to work for the Freedmen's Bureau, noting that he chose such men on the basis of their loyalty to the federal government and "upon the recommendation of the best men I could consult." Thus the men directly responsible for implementing Bureau policy in most cases were Kentuckians themselves and members of the communities in which they operated. Nonetheless, agents found themselves at odds with those who resented what they deemed federal interference in local and state affairs. William Cassius Goodloe, nephew of the irascible Cassius M. Clay, summarized eloquently what Bureau agents in the Bluegrass were up against on a daily basis. After taking charge of Freedmen's Bureau operations in Boyle, Lincoln, and Mercer counties, he concluded:

> The Country is infested with Guerrilla bands and the outrages most generally are committed on Colored persons who are precluded from testimony against them. I am powerless to accomplish anything without Soldiers. . . . The people are generally well enough disposed so far as taking a proper view of the labor question is concerned, but are misled by politicians and seem to think the object of the establishment of the Bureau in Kentucky was to oppress them. . . . I found a great deal of vagrancy here but by the aid of many Loyal Citizens and the efforts of the leaders of the Colored population have to a great extent caused it to disappear. . . . You are quite aware that I have had to grope my way in the dark, the manual promised will be hailed as an Angel of light.[11]

By all appearances, Clinton Fisk simply failed to understand the extent to which many white residents of post-emancipation Kentucky not only condoned but viewed as necessary and legitimate such violent acts as were required to restore order as they defined it. Like many former Confederates, Kentucky's white supremacists attempted to construct a postwar society based on the idea that, because black people were inferior to white people, the two races could not peacefully coexist unless white people exercised rigid control over black people and kept them in a subservient status. If that status could not be maintained after emancipation, then freedpeople had to be driven out of the community. Furthermore, white supporters of even a modicum of black equality had to be taught the error of their ways by whatever means these self-styled vigilantes deemed necessary.[12]

For their part, freedpeople struggled mightily to reconstitute families, meeting tenacious resistance at every turn. Many slaveholders simply refused to release women and children to their parents or other family members, regardless of their legal status. In these cases, freedpeople appealed to the Freedmen's Bureau for help in liberating their children and grandchildren. On 26 December 1865, E. D. Kennedy, the Bureau's Louisville superintendent, wrote to Robert Carruthers, a Jefferson County farmer, demanding he "at once liberate" the daughter and two grandchildren of George Patton. The daughter, Harriet, was the wife of a soldier serving in the United States Colored Troops: technically, therefore, she and her children had been free since March. A few days later, he wrote to Mrs. Collins of the same county, stating that a complaint had been lodged against her concerning treatment of a black female child she had managed "to detain and misuse." In early January, Kennedy demanded that Walter Ayres of Woodford County liberate two freedwomen being held "against their will."[13]

As Freedmen's Bureau official John S. Graham reported in the summer of 1866, in Boone and other rural Bluegrass counties "there are many cases in which Negroes are still held as slaves." He and other agents proved unable to intervene "on account of the intense hostility to the Bureau on the part of the citizens who being a lawless class do not hesitate at any means to rid themselves of [our] presence." Without direct intervention against this "lawless class," freedpeople faced violent opposition as they attempted to build new lives, and local authorities simply refused to intervene. J. W. Read, the Bureau superintendent in Cynthiana, revealed the extent to which local authorities were frequently part of the problem, noting that he could not "see much chance for the Negroes to get any Protection from Civil authority here as they are shure to put Returned Rebel Soldiers in to fill all the County Offices this next election with but few exceptions." Similarly, Superintendent C. J. True of Maysville reported that the civil authorities in Mason County "have never made any attempts to punish or even arrest the guilty parties, so far as my knowledge is concerned. The consequence is that they (the Freedmen) have no protection except through the officers of this Bureau."[14]

Emily Churchill's March 1866 complaint reveals the extraordinary risks parents took when trying to claim children from bondage. Her former owner, Harrison Arterburn of Jefferson County, had refused to liberate her two sons, one age ten, the other just four years old and blind. Churchill determined to take matters into her own hands, so she waited until Arterburn left his house and then went in to get her sons. She successfully retrieved the boys, along with a chair she claimed to own, and started toward Louisville. Her luck ran out, however, when a buggy containing Arterburn came down the road toward her. He hopped out and bade the driver go on without him, after which he accosted his former slave and accused her of stealing. When she told him that her only intent was to claim her children and her chair, he grew angry and pulled out a pocketknife, which he used to threaten the ten-year-old. The boy smartly fled from him, running away down the road toward Louisville, but then the white man vented his anger on Churchill and her four-year-old, hitting the woman in the head, knocking her down, and then hitting her blind son twice with his fist. Finally, according to Churchill, he "threatened to cut my throat." At that point, "she begged him for her life and appealed to him in behalf of her children, her blind one particularly." Having spent his anger,

Arterburn responded favorably to her pleas, but then he had the audacity to ask her if she would consider returning to stay with him. She refused and proceeded toward the city with her sons "without further molestation."[15]

The Churchill incident illustrates the extremes to which some former slaveholders went in their efforts to retain former slaves, and yet Arterburn's actions indicate how little he seemed to value the lives and well-being of the two children. Rather, he appears to have been using them to control their mother. In anger he had threatened to kill her, but he appears to have needed her, as in the end he asked her to return to his house and stay with him. His plea thus provides clues as to the frustration and, indeed, panic many slaveholders experienced when faced with the reality of life after slavery. Kentucky resident Betty Howard, for example, lamented in her diary that she and her children now were forced to perform daily work, such as milking and meal preparation "in the absence of a servant to do it." She was "resolved" to pay a "servant" to take on these chores.

In antebellum Kentucky, many white families had either purchased slaves or hired enslaved women and children to do these tasks. Now they faced the prospect of either having to do these chores themselves or, if they had the means to hire a servant, having to negotiate directly with former slaves regarding labor contracts. Further complicating these new economic relationships, domestic servants openly demonstrated their status as free laborers both by changing jobs and by challenging white employers to live up to contractual obligations. Underlying all of these negotiations was the fact that many former slaveholders simply could not accept the reality that their former slaves, once freed, wanted to leave their households and build new lives for themselves elsewhere.[16]

Even as Churchill and other parents struggled to reclaim their children from former masters, other free black mothers and fathers throughout Kentucky had to contend with disruption of families wrought by a legal apprenticeship system. Supporters argued that apprenticeship was a reasonable practice by which to ease children through the transition from slave to free laborer. However, the policy of giving former owners priority when assigning black children for apprenticeship led to much consternation on the part of the Freedmen's Bureau and the commonwealth's black population. Additionally, masters of black apprentices could simply make a one-time payment to the child and absolve themselves of all responsibility for educating them. The most frequent complaints about this system came from black mothers whose children had been removed from their homes, sometimes without their consent, and apprenticed to their former owners. While some mothers who lost their children in this manner were in fact destitute, others were quite capable of caring for their own children. Among the reported abuses to apprentices were failure to teach a trade—which undermined the basic rationale for apprenticeship—and physical abuse, including not only frequent whippings but also battery resulting in serious injury to the apprentice.[17]

The experience of Hannah Neille and her son clearly illustrates the perils of this apprenticeship system. Her son was apprenticed to Mrs. Olden of Louisville in the summer of 1866, but in December his mother took him home to care for him, as he was suffering from wounds inflicted when Mr. Olden beat him with a broomstick. After a few days, she took the boy back to the Olden house, only to have Mr. Olden tell her that he did not want him "because of being accused of beating the child." Neille testified that she had bound the boy out for food and clothing, apparently being unable to support him herself. During the whole time he was with the Oldens, he only received a pair of worn pants that Mrs. Olden had cut off to fit him. Neille asked the Freedmen's Bureau to help her collect "a reasonable hire for the boy for the time he worked." He had worked about eleven weeks, and Neille deemed a reasonable sum to be fifty cents a week. Likewise, Harriet Sutherland's son, Alfred, had been severely whipped by his master, Augustus Ryan. Alfred "left him and came home" to live with his mother, who wrote the Bureau to ask what might be done to force Ryan to pay Alfred for the four weeks he had already worked.[18]

The Freedmen's Bureau sought to mediate in these cases, though as was the case with the negotiation of labor contracts, they often took action that diverged from the hopes and wishes of their free black clients. Indeed, as historian Laura Edwards has argued, Bureau agents attempted to impose white middle-class notions of marriage, family, and work on former slaves, while embracing the basic assumption "that African-American parents did not have legitimate households or legitimate rights to their children." Kentucky's system of apprenticeship led to much frustration, particularly among freedwomen who not only bore the brunt of racial violence but also the separation of children from mothers. Additionally, these mothers were denied whatever labor around their own households apprenticed children might have provided.[19]

Women who hired out themselves and their children as domestic help suffered equally demeaning treatment. In November 1867 Josaphine Beadford reported to the Freedmen's Bureau "that the man where I have been living for the last twelve months . . . will not pay me anything for my work." Beadford noted that she was "a smart healthy woman" living in the home of Collin

Eggin of Taylorsville, Spencer County. She inquired as to whether "there is any protection by the government for us poor colored people," particularly women such as herself and children such as her "daughter hired to Eli Snider who has abused her very much." When confronted by the Bureau, white employers typically rationalized nonpayment and downplayed the severity of alleged abuse, frequently saying they had only given their employee a switching, rather than the beating described by the employee. For example, Lavina Newland described in detail an altercation in which her twelve-year-old son was beaten by Shelton Scott, the man for whom she worked. Scott "picked up a stick and struck him with it 3 or 4 times and struck him with his fist." After the boy was on the ground, the man "put his foot on him and beat him with the stick." When Newland tried to intervene, Scott assaulted her, first throwing a rock that "hit her on the forehead" and then beating her with the stick. The Freedmen's Bureau confronted Scott, but in his statement, the "stick" became a "switch" with which he had merely "switched the boy." When "the mother interfered," he "struck her on the forehead with the switch," and when she then attacked him, he "threw her down and gave her several cuts upon the back with what was left of the switch."[20]

White Kentuckians exhibited a conspicuous fondness for using the switch, the stick, the fist, and the cowhide on their black apprentices and hired help. While the Freedmen's Bureau dutifully recorded affidavits, it did little more than impose the occasional fine in its attempts to discourage such abuse, and, in many cases, took no action, as agents lacked what they regarded sufficient evidence in that they did not have third-party testimony. Additionally, the Bureau appears to have viewed apprenticeship and domestic servitude in white Victorian middle-class households as having the potential to affect a positive influence on former slaves. The Freedmen's Bureau proved reluctant to intervene in all but the most serious cases of abuse, even cooperating fully with the removal via apprenticeship of children from mothers they deemed unfit. Reflecting Bureau policy across the former Confederacy, in Kentucky any desire to aid the efforts of freedpeople in their attempts to reconstruct and sustain families appears to have been subordinate to the Bureau's determination to limit the number of children dependent on its aid—even when that meant shoring up the apprenticeship system. Further, the Bureau had to combat longstanding practices of slave hiring and use of slave children as domestic help. Faced with the possibility of having to hire an immigrant girl or having to perform menial household tasks oneself, white residents of the commonwealth embraced the apprenticeship or hire of free black women and children as the preferred option. In as much as they condoned and even supported such practices, Bureau agents often seemed oblivious to the maelstrom of abuse, terror, and poverty in which former slaves—particularly women and children—were caught.[21]

H. C. Howard of the Lexington Sub-district revealed such bias when he reported that freedpeople in his jurisdiction were "not . . . inclined to enter into contracts by the year, and are too much disposed to seek the small Towns, too much idling and demoralization among them in regard to the Obligations of Virtue and Chastity." "The increase of children by indiscriminate intercourse," he fretted, "is producing poverty and degradation requiring protection and attention from the Bureau." Its agents felt compelled to push freedpeople toward economic self-sufficiency with all due haste, supporting both apprenticeship and stronger antivagrancy laws in the process. As Mary J. Farmer has observed, agents frequently used the threat of prosecution in their efforts to force able-bodied freedmen "who could not find employment to move to areas where work was more plentiful." Likewise, the Freedmen's Bureau regarded unemployed freedwomen, even the able-bodied, as "dependents on the government" and, in order to reduce their numbers, worked less to secure for them gainful employment than to "assist black women in holding black men accountable for their responsibilities as husbands and fathers."[22]

Far from drifting into town to live an idle life filled with "indiscriminate intercourse" and other licentious activities, freedpeople fled to Kentucky's urban centers to escape unchecked Regulator violence and work conditions reminiscent of slavery. A report from John J. Evans, Freedmen's Bureau agent in Mount Sterling, is illustrative. Working in a county that had been plagued by guerrillas during the war, and noting that he himself was in great danger, Evans asked for troops to counter "a gang of whites who as I understand call themselves Regulators." This band, against which civil authorities in Montgomery County would take no action, intended that "No Negro or White Man shall stay or live in that Section of Country unless he be of their class (a Rebel)." As evidence of this Regulator policy, Evans noted that a white man in Owingsville had taken the life of a black man. Federal troops had been stationed in Mount Sterling earlier, but Evans had sent them back to Lexington, thinking the situation improved. As soon as the soldiers moved out of the area, the Regulators resurfaced.[23] Given that the Freedmen's Bureau in Kentucky never had sufficient troops to establish garrisons everywhere the situation demanded them, this frustrating cycle characterized the experience of most field agents.

Regulators not only murdered numerous Unionists and freedpeople but also used a wide variety of other tools in imposing local reigns of terror. Armed bands of white men disarmed, robbed, and whipped freedmen, particularly former soldiers, and they did not spare their families equally rough treatment. Attacks on households, particularly those that included veterans of the United States Colored Troops (USCT), provide clues as to the role of violence in maintaining a white supremacist social hierarchy. With combat training and, at least in some cases, firearms, these men represented the most direct physical threat to white supremacy when they came home to the commonwealth. Other black men became targets because, like former soldiers, they represented black autonomy. For example, Regulators beat and robbed a black preacher and then made him watch as they raped his wife. Finally, they shot him in the head, killing him. Another band kicked and stomped to death a freedman because he owned his own land.[24]

Like the few freedmen who owned their own land, the many freedmen who rented land also represented a challenge to white supremacy. By controlling even to a degree their own means of subsistence and production, these freedmen competed with poor whites for clientage with wealthy patrons, and as such they and their households became targets for racial violence. In Bath County a gang of five white men robbed a returned soldier who had rented a piece of land and had the means to employ another freedman, also a former soldier, as his laborer. The white men came to his house at night and opened fire on him, grazing his head with two balls. His wounds, literally very close shaves, proved minor, and apparently the assailants did not necessarily mean to kill him, as they easily could have done so after wounding him. Instead, they robbed him of "meat clothes and money to the amount of thirteen dollars in silver."[25] Likewise, Stephen Jeffers reported to W. R. Bourne, the Freedmen's Bureau agent in Danville, that four white men came to his house, threatened his life if he did not let them in, and proceeded to rob him of a feather bed, eight dresses, dishes, and "such other goods as they could carry on their horses." Jeffers and his family had hired ten acres of land south of Danville, paying two years' rent in advance, but they had to abandon it or risk a more deadly return visit.

This pattern of violence against community leaders and economically independent freedmen and their families is consistent with the pattern of Ku Klux Klan violence in the former Confederate states, as well as racial violence in other border states, including Maryland. Indeed, historian Barbara Jeanne Fields noted that such "attacks on black people were frequently gratuitous and arbitrary; but they were not random, nor did they represent the caprice of deranged or especially malignant individuals. They had a clear logic, which most white people understood perfectly and accepted with little question."[26]

Additionally, Regulators used Kentucky law to full advantage, sometimes going so far as to pose as legitimate authorities in their efforts to disarm freedmen. One group "visited the houses occupied by freedmen at Yellmanville, near Lexington, and demanded admission claiming they were ordered from Louisville" to search the houses and seize any firearms found within. Among other weapons, they confiscated an Enfield rifle from a veteran of the USCT and broke it into pieces. At one point they opened fire on two freedmen, wounding one in the ear. At least one free black resident of Yellmanville identified several members of the band of Regulators as men from the Lexington area, and the Freedmen's Bureau quickly determined that these men had no official permission to conduct such a search and seizure operation. The investigating Bureau agent concluded that the men simply "desired to have the Negroes defenceless in case they should attempt further outrages upon them."[27]

Refugees quickly inundated Ohio River cities such as Louisville, Covington, and Maysville, with Frankfort, Lexington, Paris, and most Bluegrass county seat towns being equally flooded. In these cities and towns, as in Atlanta and other southern urban centers, free black women and girls typically had little alternative to accepting jobs in white households in order to support themselves and their families. At the same time, as historian Tera Hunter has argued, they asserted "their rights to enjoy the fruits of their labor and to reconstitute their lives as autonomous human beings." However, the supply of wage laborers quickly outstripped demand in urban centers, and so former masters and white employers, beneficiaries of this refugee crisis, attempted to insure the subservience of this black female labor pool, utilizing both civil authority and physical violence to achieve this goal. The flood of new residents brought hardship to towns and cities, but also provided opportunities for landholders, carpenters, and others to profit from this demographic shift by developing new, almost exclusively black, neighborhoods or "suburbs" separated from the older residential areas. That these communities, sometimes little more than shantytowns built for mostly impoverished residents, lay on the least hospitable, and therefore least valuable, parcels of land almost goes without saying. Typically, urban-dwelling freedmen worked as draymen, factory workers, laborers, or field hands on nearby farms, while freedwomen worked as domestic servants, cooks, or washerwomen.[28]

In the face of old prejudices and increasing racial segregation, black working women frequently struggled simply to defend their rights as free women on city streets. Hannah Jones, a resident of greater Louisville's Portland community, who worked as a laundress for a steamboat, drew the ire of a white man when he staggered from a saloon and fell against her as she carried clothes back to the crew. He spat upon her and the clean clothes, and as she moved away, he grabbed "a barroom chair" and threw it at her, "striking her on the arm and side hurting her so much as to prevent her from continuing her work on the boat." She quickly located a policeman for whom she had worked and asked him for help. He replied that he "could do nothing for her as the colored people had no law here." Discouraged and hurting, Jones started home, but the man who had hit her with the chair followed her. She ducked into a neighbor's house, but he forced his way in and assaulted her, at one point kicking her "in the eye with his boot." When two white men came to the door to see what was going on, her assailant left, but he sent word back later that if she reported him "to any body he would blow her head off." A black schoolteacher in Portland who had visited the badly beaten Jones noted "that there is a class of men in Portland who are very troublesome to the colored people there and the civil authorities cannot be got to do any thing to stop it."[29]

Many white men and women in Kentucky—including some Freedmen's Bureau agents—simply did not believe in black equality and continued therefore to treat freedwomen as perpetual children rather than the free wage laborers, wives, and mothers they were struggling to become. In so doing, they came into conflict with these women, who were developing and acting upon clear ideas about free black womanhood. Given the demands of establishing a life for themselves and their children, black women sometimes made practical decisions at odds with the dominant ideals of Northern white society, living single lives as female heads of households and sometimes even resorting to prostitution to provide for their families. Such actions, needless to say, went against Bureau expectations.[30]

When freedwomen, faced with little alternative, turned to sex work for survival, the Freedmen's Bureau intervened with a heavy hand. Actively participating in Victorian America's campaign against prostitution, agents tried to break up brothels in which freedwomen worked, and they readily removed children from mothers who could demonstrate no viable means of support other than sex work. Still, Bureau agents were confronted with the reality that some white men sought out black women for their sexual enjoyment, as well as for displays of white power and male dominance, sexual or otherwise. Both consensual interracial liaisons and intraracial extramarital sexual relationships violated Bureau ideals, and so were discouraged. And yet the Freedmen's Bureau appears to have been no more effective at protecting black women from unwanted sexual advances and sexual assault than it was at attempting to regulate consensual sexual behavior. One reason for this was that Bureau agents had internalized the nineteenth-century stereotype of the promiscuous black female and thus did not take seriously reports of sexual assault. Moreover, not all federal soldiers and officers were "model Victorian gentlemen," and certainly many white male civilians failed to live up to that ideal.[31]

Confounding the stereotype, freedwomen frequently found themselves in danger of being raped or sexually imposed upon in an uneven power relationship with a white man or men. D. F. Bligh testified in May 1866 that three white men had robbed Stephen Scott and "four other negroes." After robbing the men, the assailants strung one of them up "until he was nearly dead," then assaulted and attempted to rape a black woman who was present. Tellingly, these men were arrested and charged in connection with their involvement in this and other robberies, but not because of the attempted rape. Black women who tried to speak out against unwanted sexual advances frequently stood accused of lying. Emma Gwinn, a domestic servant living in the home of Mrs. James Prather, reported that Prather's son made unsolicited sexual advances toward her one night as she lay in bed. She got up and left him there, and on the advice of another servant, went straight to his mother to tell her what had happened. The next morning the young Prather accosted her, beating her with a poker as he yelled, "Damn you you went and told my mother a Damned lie on me and if you don't go out of the yard I will shoot you." She fled immediately and contacted the Freedmen's Bureau, beseeching them to force the man to answer for his actions.[32]

Freedmen in Kentucky certainly received unwanted attention in the form of violent challenges to their efforts to enact free black manhood. On the night of 12 June 1867, for example, a band of armed, mounted, disguised white men staged a raid on a free black community in northern Lincoln County. The gang moved from house to house, kicking in doors and taking men out of the homes at gunpoint. Joseph Swope stated that his assailants hoisted him in the air by means of a rope around his neck until he passed out. They then let him down until he came to his senses, at which time the disguised men forced him to take down his pants and whipped him with a pistol belt—about thirty lashes. Swope testified that his acquaintances Henry Helm and Anderson Gilbert received similar treatment.[33]

Although Swope, Helm, and Gilbert apparently sustained no serious injuries, they doubtless found the experience deeply humiliating and degrading—and perhaps reminiscent of their treatment under slavery. Punishment by whipping represented denial on the part of whites of equal status for African Americans and may even be viewed as an act of symbolic emasculation of black men.[34] For their part, Swope, Helm, and Gilbert uniformly declared that they had been attacked as punishment for holding a "social neighborhood party." While not indicating any biracial neighborhood activities, they claimed such parties to be a common practice by both black and white families in the area. The freedmen further stated their belief that any attempt to resist the Regulators would have gotten them killed. Regulators, as indicated by this incident and the well-documented attacks on Camp Nelson, sought to exercise rigid control over African American communities and the social activities that bound them together, even as slaveholders had exercised such control prior to emancipation. As a Freedmen's Bureau agent noted, "the Negro, though free in theory, is practically held in a state of slavery by the acts of these men."[35]

Upon conducting a thorough inspection of his district, Freedmen's Bureau agent A. Benson Brown eloquently spoke to this "unhappy state of affairs" in central Kentucky. The Bureau had begun circulating petitions in the area regarding extension of the franchise to black men, a move that predictably had been met with white supremacist violence. Of Boyle County, he wrote that in a white population of about 2,500 "Danville has about 50 Union White Men who are not only anxious to aid the Freedman in his present desperate struggle for liberty, and life, but are already in the means of quietly rendering their material assistance, and advice. But this force is insufficient for any general movement to influence a change in the local procedure bearing upon the Freedmen." This "procedure" involved "unjust laws, and inhuman prejudices existing and continually felt by them on account of the Rebel element, a large majority of these people not having been whipped in the late War."[36]

Brown's district also included Mercer, Lincoln, and Rockcastle counties. Lincoln County, he concluded, is "the grand center around which revolves and from which emanates the flying embers which have fired this Section into demonic Rebel fury." The recent burning of two "colored School houses" had intimidated the freedpeople from trying to acquire property on which to build others. Small schools could and did operate, but attempts to organize large ones had been met with violent resistance. Finally, Brown commented on "the most wicked murder" of local Unionist James H. Bridgewater and identified the community of Crab Orchard as headquarters of area Regulators. "Here they hold high carnival," he wrote, "and now here they pounce upon their unsuspecting Union victims wherever certain they can strike them in the back."[37]

A Baptist minister preaching in Lincoln County in 1867 confirmed Brown's assessment, observing that in the southern Bluegrass "the waves of passion that had been raised so high by the winds of war, had not yet subsided." Elder W. H. Stewart, raised a Quaker in Ohio, had converted to the Baptist persuasion and become something of an itinerate preacher and school teacher, traveling through Kentucky, Arkansas, Virginia, and elsewhere before finding himself in Louisiana in the midst of the war over slavery. He set out to visit old friends in the commonwealth in 1866, hoping the situation farther south would improve by the time he returned. But the situation he encountered in Lincoln and surrounding counties left him almost speechless: "What malice! What deep-seated rancor! What hatred of each other! I will not attempt to describe it, for language would fail me. It can never be described." And yet he continued to try: "The fire that had been nursed within, was ready to be fanned into a flame, and to burst out like a volcano, destroying every thing within its reach. I saw the danger, and trembled at the consequences." Sadly, too few of his listeners appear to have understood the dangers, nor did they appear to tremble at the consequences of the outrages carried out by militant white supremacists in their midst. Whatever their motivations or their psychological predispositions, the actions of Regulators, Judge Lynch's men, and other so-called vigilantes wrought havoc on their communities and begat a legacy of racial violence and political assassination that Kentucky struggles with to this day.[38]

In fear and frustration over post-emancipation violence and lack of economic opportunity, thousands of freedpeople appear to have fled the commonwealth in the first years after the end of the Civil War. Kentucky counted approximately 236,000 persons of color in 1860, but only about 222,000 in 1870. Still, those numbers indicate the large population of freedpeople who remained and thus had to endure the years in which, as George C. Wright has convincingly argued, Kentucky experienced its zenith of racial violence: 1868 to 1871. In the early 1870s, black men received the franchise and, at long last, Kentucky judges were forced to admit black testimony in cases involving white assailants. Still, the Democratic Party dominated state politics, in large measure due to the ability of leading newspaper editors to mobilize its base via the rhetoric of white supremacy.[39]

The contents of affidavits, complaints, and reports collected by the Freedmen's Bureau clearly reveal the extreme hostility many white Kentuckians, including many who had fought for the Union in the Civil War, held toward freedpeople and their federal allies in the months and years following ratification of the Thirteenth Amendment. This hostility at times spilled over into violence against white political opponents or Freedmen's Bureau agents. In such an environment, it is little wonder that so many former slaves reported being beaten and abused. If one could rationalize Regulator violence and even political assassination as unpleasant but necessary, of what consequence were reports of servants being whipped? Men and women who condoned or engaged in whipping and other abuse of black laborers and apprentices could not forcefully criticize more violent acts—even rape and murder—committed by individuals who claimed to be operating in the best interests of their communities. Their embrace of violence as a legitimate means of establishing and maintaining white supremacy cumulatively served to disrupt free black households and quash the aspirations of many former slaves, particularly women and children. Though in theory they had been granted equal rights and equal protection under the law, in reality free black families in the Commonwealth of Kentucky fell far short of attaining the levels of autonomy, prosperity, and security they hoped for when first they were freed.

Notes

1. C. H. Frederick to James C. Ford, 3 July 1866, Affidavits and Records Relating to Complaints, Louisville Superintendent and Sub-Assistant Commissioner's Office (hereinafter cited as ARRCLS & SCO), Entry 1218, Kentucky District, BRFAL-KY, RG 105, NA. This essay contains content from and reiterates arguments I have made in two previously published articles: "'Conduct . . . Inexcusable and Unjustifiable,'" and "'We Are Mobed and Beat.'"

2. Lucas, "Kentucky Blacks," 410–12; Victor B. Howard, *Black Liberation in Kentucky*, 130–40. On post-emancipation racial violence, see George C. Wright, *Racial Violence in Kentucky*, 19–60.

3. See Rhyne, "'We Are Mobed and Beat'" for more detail on Regulator violence.

4. Regarding reports of physical emasculation, see for example, Sidney Burbank to Oliver O. Howard, 13 January 1868, Roll 53, Registers and Letters Received by the Commissioner, BRFAL-KY, RG 105 (M752). On black manhood, see Cullen, "'I's a Man Now,'" 76–91. On white manhood, see Kimmel, *Manhood in America*, 94–96.

5. Gutman, *Black Family in Slavery and Freedom*, 396–402; Clinton B. Fisk to O. O. Howard, 8 June 1866, Roll 33, Registers and Letters Received by the Commissioner, BRFAL-KY, RG 105 (M752). See Hannah Rosen, "'Not That Sort of Women,'" 268, 285, for analysis of rape in a post-emancipation community. One major difference between the situation in Memphis and that in Kentucky is that the women in Memphis had the opportunity to testify and to declare before the court that they were virtuous ladies, not the wanton creatures of white male fantasy, while the women in the Bluegrass region could only submit their affidavits to a clerk for recording, a much less public forum. See

Edwards, *Gendered Strife and Confusion*, chapter 5, for a discussion of rape in the context of the post-emancipation struggle over meanings of manhood and womanhood. See also Bardaglio, *Reconstructing the Household*, 194–96.

6. For a detailed examination of the transition from slave to wage laborer and its often problematic relationship to free-labor ideology in a former Confederate state, see Saville, *Work of Reconstruction*. See Jacqueline Jones, *Labor of Love, Labor of Sorrow*, 3–10, for discussion of the unique social and cultural space occupied by black working women. In the years since publication of *Labor of Love, Labor of Sorrow*, numerous scholars have turned their attention to the study of free black families and particularly female wage laborers in post-emancipation societies. In particular, Schwalm's *Hard Fight for We*, focusing on black women in the Lowcountry, Hunter's *To 'Joy My Freedom*, chronicling the lives of Atlanta's black workingwomen, and Frankel's *Freedom's Women*, were case studies that revealed much about the lives, struggles, ambitions, and setbacks of black women and families during Reconstruction. Edwards's *Gendered Strife and Confusion*, comparing and contrasting black and white Reconstruction households in north-central North Carolina, and Bercaw's *Gendered Freedoms*, comparing and contrasting white and black households during the Civil War and Reconstruction in the Mississippi Delta, served to complicate, and indeed blur, previous distinctions made between black and white, elite and common, public and private, social and political. A new generation of scholarship, exemplified by O'Donovan's gendered narrative of slavery and freedom in southwest Georgia, *Becoming Free in the Cotton South*, is providing further rich detail on black women's struggles during Reconstruction, particularly concerning their all-too-frequent failure to realize personal visions of freedom—especially dreams of building independent lives.

7. For in-depth analysis of Kentucky's Civil War experience, particularly bitterness toward federal policy and especially emancipation, see Astor, *Rebels on the Border*.

8. Coulter, *Civil War and Readjustment in Kentucky*, 288; Berlin, Reidy, and Rowland, *Freedom*, 515–18; McFeely, *Yankee Stepfather*, 67.

9. J. M. Nolan to John M. Palmer, 2 February 1866, Letters Received, Department of Kentucky, Entry 2173, USACC, RG393, NA; Clinton B. Fisk to O. O. Howard, 14 February 1866, Roll 21, Registers and Letters Received by the Commissioner, BRFAL-KY, RG 105 (M752); Fisk to Howard, 29 March 1866, Roll 28, Registers and Letters Received by the Commissioner, BRFAL-KY, RG 105 (M752).

10. Wyiat Lewis and Others to John Ely, 16 February 1866, Unregistered Letters Received, Lexington Chief Superintendent and Chief Sub-Assistant Commissioner's Office, Entry 1186, BRFAL-KY, RG 105, NA (quote); Fisk to Howard, 14 February 1866, Roll 21, Registers and Letters Received, BRFAL-KY, RG 105 (M752); and Fisk to Howard, 12 March 1866, Roll 28, Registers and Letters Received, BRFAL-KY, RG 105 (M752). The two reports from Fisk are closely related, in that the former is a summary of outrages, while the latter contains over one hundred pages of detailed documentation on these outrages. See Lucas, *History of Blacks in Kentucky*, 178–209, for discussion of the role of racial violence in the displacement of freedpeople in Kentucky in the first years after emancipation, particularly the disruption of the agricultural economy, as well as a thorough discussion of the hardships faced by black refugees, exacerbated by harsh winters.

11. Fisk to Howard, 14 February 1866, Roll 21, Registers and Letters Received, BRFAL-KY, RG 105 (M752); William Cassius Goodloe to Clinton B. Fisk, 22 January 1866, Roll 10, Registers and Letters Received by the Assistant Commissioner, Registers and Letters Received, BRFAL-KY, RG 105 (M999), reprinted in Sears, *Camp Nelson, Kentucky*, 317.

12. Waldrep, *Many Faces of Judge Lynch*, 67–68, 75–84; Rhyne, "A 'Murderous Affair in Lincoln County,'" 337–59; Hodes, *White Women, Black Men*, 147–52.

13. Edwards, *Gendered Strife and Confusion*, 51; E. D. Kennedy to Robert Carruthers, 26 December 1865, Kennedy to Mrs. Collins, 29 December 1865, Kennedy to Walter Ayres, 2 January 1866, all in Press Copies of Letters Sent, Louisville Superintendent and Sub-Assistant Commissioner's Office, Entry 1201, BRFAL-KY, RG 105, NA; Fields, *Slavery and Freedom on the Middle Ground*, 133.

14. George C. Wright, *Racial Violence in Kentucky*, 185–87; James H. Rice to R. E. Johnston, 15 July 1866, J. W. Read to R. E. Johnston, 26 July 1866, C. J. True to R. E. Johnston, 30 September 1866, all in Unregistered Letters Received, Louisville Sub-Assistant Commissioner's Office, Entry 1186, BRFAL-KY, RG 105, NA.

15. Jacqueline Jones, *Labor of Love, Labor of Sorrow*, 72; Affidavit of Emily Churchill, 20 March 1866, Affidavits and Records Relating to Complaints, Louisville Superintendent and Sub-Assistant Commissioner's Office, Entry 1218, BRFAL-KY, RG 105, NA.

16. Betty Howard, Diary, 1865–1866, FHS; Barton, "'Good Cooks and Washers,'" 436–60. See Edwards, *Gendered Strife and Confusion*, 116–17, for discussion of the "plight" of white women who now had to do their own domestic chores.

17. Fields, *Slavery and Freedom on the Middle Ground*, 139; Lucas, *History of Blacks in Kentucky*,, 272–73. For similar issues in North Carolina relating to black apprenticeship, see Edwards, *Gendered Strife and Confusion*, 39–54. See also Rebecca Scott, "Battle over the Child," 101–13. Regarding contractual obligations, see for example, Indenture of Apprenticeship, 14 June 1866, between Saul Lewis and L. H. Martin, Monthly Reports of Operations, Lexington Chief Superintendent and Chief Sub-Assistant Commissioner's Office, Entry 1190, BRFAL-KY, RG 105, NA.

18. Affidavit of Hannah Neille, 24 December 1866, and Affidavit of Harriet Sutherland, 28 June 1867, both in Affidavits and Records Relating to Complaints, Louisville Superintendent and Sub-Assistant Commissioner's Office, Entry 1218, BRFAL-KY, RG 105, NA.

19. Edwards, *Gendered Strife and Confusion*, 39. See Schwalm, *Hard Fight for We*, 249–54, on the importance of black child labor to the household economies of lowcountry black families.

20. Josaphine Beadford to Freedmen's Bureau, 24 November 1867, Unregistered Letters Received, Louisville Sub-Assistant Commissioner's Office, Entry 1209, BRFAL-KY, RG 105, NA; Affidavits of Lavina Newland, 3 September 1867, and Shelton Scott, 11 September 1867, encl. in Isaac. S. Catlin to Sidney Burbank, 14 September 1867, Letters Received, Louisville Superintendent and Sub-Assistant Commissioner's Office, Entry 1208, BRFAL-KY, RG 105, NA.

21. Finley, *From Slavery to Uncertain Freedom*, 36; Schwalm, *Hard Fight for We*, 254.

22. H. C. Howard to R. E. Johnston, 25 February 1868, Unregistered Letters Received, Lexington Chief Superintendent and Chief Sub-Assistant Commissioner's Of-

fice, Entry 1186, BRFAL-KY, RG 105, NA; Farmer, "'Because They Are Women,'" 161–92; Schwalm, *Hard Fight for We*, 250. In her citations, Farmer notes that Clinton B. Fisk had strong views on black female dependency, writing pamphlets instructing black men to be responsible husbands and fathers, while encouraging black women to support their husbands' efforts to earn a living wage. Unfortunately, some freedmen exercised their free black manhood by using violence and threat of violence to subordinate freedwomen and children. For example, see the affidavits of Melinda Greathouse, 1 October 1866, and Rev. Willis L. Muir, 3 October 1866, Affidavits and Records Relating to Complaints, Louisville Superintendent and Sub-Assistant Commissioner's Office, Entry 1218, BRFAL-KY, RG 105, NA. Melinda Greathouse, a black woman from Louisville, testified that she had seen her neighbor, a black man named John Lisker, tie up and whip with a rope a twelve-year-old orphaned girl who lived with him and his wife. The commotion of the whipping drew the attention of several neighbors, who witnessed the end of it. Afterward, Lisker left the house and some black neighbors tried to intervene on behalf of the girl, untying her and taking her across the street. Lisker's wife later persuaded the neighbors to let her take the girl back home. Upon his return, she told her husband all about the neighbors, and he angrily called out threats to them, stating in particular "that he would cut Mrs. Willis throat if she meddled with his business." Willis's husband Jonathan took exception, and in the ensuing shouting match Lisker made clear his intention to "cut Mrs. Willis's or any other Niggers throat that interfered with his business."

23. John J. Evans to R. E. Johnston, 2 October 1866, Unregistered Letters Received, Lexington Chief Superintendent and Chief Sub-Assistant Commissioner's Office, Entry 1186, BRFAL-KY, RG 105, NA (emphasis in original).

24. Fisk to Howard, 14 February 1866, Roll 21, Registers and Letters Received by the Commissioner, BRFAL-KY, RG 105 (M752).

25. J. E. Rice to Clinton B. Fisk, 19 February 1866, Unregistered Letters Received, Lexington Chief Superintendent and Chief Sub-Assistant Commissioner's Office, Entry 1186, BRFAL-KY, RG 105, NA.

26. W. R. Bourne to James H. Rice, 22 May 1866, Unregistered Letters Received, Lexington Chief Superintendent and Chief Sub-Assistant Commissioner's Office, Entry 1186, BRFAL-KY, RG 105, NA; Hodes, *White Women, Black Men*, 152–53; Fields, *Slavery and Freedom on the Middle Ground*, 143 (second quote).

27. James H. Rice to R. E. Johnston, 13 June 1866, Unregistered Letters Received, Lexington Chief Superintendent and Chief Sub-Assistant Commissioner's Office, Entry 1186, BRFAL-KY, RG 105, NA.

28. Hunter, *To 'Joy My Freedom*, 21–22; Lucas, *History of Blacks in Kentucky*, 181–209; Thomas, "Victims of Circumstances." See Ged M. Layson, from near Millersburg, Ky., to Joel T. Hart, 24 September 1868, Joel Tanner Hart Papers, FHS, regarding white perceptions of these new free black communities. Layson, a resident of Bourbon County, attempted to describe the Bluegrass region's post-emancipation urban landscape to his friend Hart, who had gone to Italy to hone his skills as a sculptor. Of freedpeople, he observed, "It seams to be a part of their nature as is the case with the wild dog to go to town

or to live in town or towns." He lamented that "the Suburbs of all our Towns are more or less built up with . . . huts. I believe about half of the population of Paris & Lexington both are blacks." He noted the building of "two towns that are exclusively negro in the Suburbs of Paris." Citing the poor condition of these black urban-dwellers, Layson concluded, "the very large majority of them would be better off if they were Slaves with there old masters." Finally, he echoed the widely held belief that the destitute "could get work at fair wages if they would work," but that "so many of them prefer to be idle."

29. Affidavits of Hannah Jones, 13 August 1867 and George Griffith, 10 August 1867, both encl. in Isaac S. Catlin to Sidney Burbank, 15 August 1867, Letters Received, Louisville Superintendent and Sub-Assistant Commissioner's Office, Entry 1208, BRFAL-KY, RG 105, NA.

30. Edwards, *Gendered Strife and Confusion*, 153, 55–56, respectively.

31. Finley, *From Slavery to Uncertain Freedom*, 38–44; Gutman, *Black Family in Slavery and Freedom*, 385–89.

32. Affidavit of D. F. Bligh, 24 May 1866, Letters Received, Louisville Superintendent and Sub-Assistant Commissioner's Office, Entry 1208, BRFAL-KY, RG 105, NA; Affidavit of Emma Gwinn, 5 July 1867, Affidavits and Records Relating to Complaints, Louisville Superintendent and Sub-Assistant Commissioner's Office, Entry 1218, BRFAL-KY, RG 105, NA.

33. Affidavits of Joseph Swope, Henry Helm, and Anderson Gilbert, all encl. in Benjamin P. Runkle to John Ely, 20 June 1867, Roll 47, Registers and Letters Received by the Commissioner, BRFAL-KY, RG 105 (M752).

34. R. E. Johnston to T. N. Finnell, 24 September 1866, Unregistered Letters Received, Lexington Chief Superintendent and Chief Sub-Assistant Commissioner's Office, Entry 1186, BRFAL-KY, RG 105, NA; Foner, *Reconstruction*, 428–29.

35. Runkle to Ely, 20 June 1867, Registers and Letters Received by the Commissioner, Roll 47 (including enclosures), BRFAL-KY, RG 105 (M752) (Runkle's emphasis).

36. A. Benson Brown to R. E. Johnston, 10 October 1867, Unregistered Letters Received, Lexington Chief Superintendent and Chief Sub-Assistant Commissioner's Office, Entry 1186, BRFAL-KY, RG 105, NA.

37. Ibid.; Rhyne, "A 'Murderous Affair in Lincoln County,'" 347–54.

38. Stewart, *Reminiscence of Elder W. H. Stewart*, 30.

39. George C. Wright, *Racial Violence in Kentucky*, 307–11; 1870 county-level census data for Kentucky obtained online from the *Historical United States Census Data Browser*, using data from the Ninth Census of the United States: 1870, compiled by the Inter-university Consortium for Political and Social Research, Ann Arbor, Mich., accessed 10 July 2005, http://www.fisher.lib.virginia.edu/census/.

7

Ex-Slaveholders and the Ku Klux Klan

Exploring the Motivations of Terrorist Violence

MICHAEL W. FITZGERALD

The Ku Klux Klan is one of the best-known organizations in American history: the most recognizable group expression of militant white supremacy. The general public may not make fine distinctions regarding the era and circumstance, or distinguish between the myriad kindred groups, but it is a universally understood image. Hooded figures populate television and the cinema with frequency, and one can enter any bookstore and encounter works on the Klan. Since the events of 11 September 2001, this interest has intersected with the wider issue of terrorism. There are terminological issues regarding the use of this emotion-laden word, but by any sensible definition, the Ku Klux Klan of the Reconstruction era qualifies. The Klan is rightly viewed as America's most important terrorist movement, an assessment that enhances its contemporary resonance.[1]

Historians have responded to the obvious importance of this topic, producing a sea of scholarship. Hefty bibliographic volumes have appeared devoted to the Ku Klux Klan alone, and even if one limits the literature to the Reconstruction era, it is daunting.[2] Despite this outpouring, the movement's pattern of participation has received sparse attention. Steven Hahn recently referred to "interpretive disagreements" over the Klan's social composition and leadership, among other things.[3] This makes sense: it is difficult to define the membership of a shadowy criminal conspiracy undertaking acts of violence in disguise. Nor is it easy to distinguish between the nebulous Klan and bodies of ad hoc nightriders. Furthermore, uncovering the social basis of the movement has long involved laborious census research. For these reasons, perhaps, there are only a relative handful of local studies of Ku Klux Klan participation during the Reconstruction era—fewer than one might expect given the significance. Still, most scholars affirm that nightriders were mostly younger Confederate veterans, but the analysis seldom extends much further into the antebellum era. Allen Trelease, in his *White Terror*, articulates what is still the prevailing emphasis: "the Klan was drawn from every rank and class of white society."[4]

The composition of the Ku Klux Klan intersects with important issues, especially the crucial one of its social intent. Historiographically, the place to start is with Eric Foner's *Reconstruction: America's Unfinished Revolution*, the standout work in the modern literature. Foner's book argues that the Reconstruction political struggles grew out of the conflict over the future of the plantation regime. He too sees the Klan as a cross-class social movement, but he emphasizes that the agenda was substantially directed toward elite ends. In his view, "the Klan was a military force serving the interests of the Democratic Party, the planter class, and all those who desired the restoration of white supremacy." And he insisted that freedmen had "good reason" to blame the South's aristocratic classes for the violence. The explicit goal was generally political repression, but for Foner the wider impulse was to restore white supremacy in all the ways it had been threatened.[5] Other prominent scholars of Reconstruction have come to similar conclusions about the Klan's motivation.

The composition and intention of the Ku Klux Klan remain indistinct. One way to address these issues is through examination of a single state: an endeavor small enough to be manageable but large enough in scope to gain meaningful insight. The subject of this study is Alabama, which is a plausible choice for several reasons. Alabama suffered a long and well-documented outbreak, with hundreds of indictments under federal anti-Klan legislation and congressional testimony on the subject filling three full volumes. The Ku Klux Klan first spread outside Tennessee here, and Alabama was about the last place in which the movement continued to operate. Beyond this unfortunate profusion of evidence, the state has fair claim of being typical of the Deep South, at least. Cotton was the dominant crop, and Alabama had no huge and atypical urban concentrations. No obvious reason exists why the experience here should be unrepresentative of events elsewhere.

Racist vigilantism in Alabama was hardly limited to the Ku Klux Klan; it included groups like the Knights of the White Camelia and numerous variants and also local clusters who utilized similar techniques. The intent of this essay is to assess the confusion of contending motivations in view of what can be determined about the perpetrators. Some years ago, for a study published in *Agricultural History*, I compiled a list of individuals accused of participation in Klan-style groups. These were mostly composed of men indicted under the federal anti-Klan legislation of 1871, or publicly named in congressional testimony, both from late in the Klan period. About four hundred white Alabamians were named in these sources, of which some ninety unique matches could be found in the postwar census with some degree of certainty. The striking thing about these alleged participants was their poverty. They were predominantly young men without property; the median real wealth of their households being precisely zero; and about 60 percent being landless. What sparse property they did own, according to the agricultural census, they disproportionately held in hogs and livestock. Drawing upon Steven Hahn's insight into the centrality of free-ranging stock for self-sufficient yeoman farmers, the article contended that petty theft has to be taken seriously in assembling a popular constituency for violence. The image that emerged was of an evolving movement increasingly responsive to the racial grievances of poorer white farmers—one less amenable to outside political direction over time.[6]

In recent years it has become much easier to undertake such research, and for the current project it was possible to identify a larger body of accused participants. Of these 530 names, 164 could be found in one or more decennial years.[7] Thus, 31 percent of the names were located, a significantly larger proportion of the whole. This seems substantial given that they were members of a clandestine movement, often fugitives when federal census takers came around. Research into the social origins of Klan-style nightriders ought to be more effective today, given the available technology.[8] One heartening aspect of the new findings—for this practicing scholar, at least—is that it confirms the findings of the previous study. In 1870, the median real wealth of accused Klansmen is still zero; fifty-three of ninety-six located owned no land at all. Median personal wealth is still modest, two hundred dollars. Average total wealth is a bit higher, but if one uses $1,000 as the upper limit of a "lower-middle-class" household, as Carl Moneyhon's modern study of Arkansas does, we still find the average below that figure, under eight hundred dollars. Fully nineteen were described as farm laborers, day laborers and the like, low-status occupations by any standard. These men may not be quite as destitute as the previous findings suggested, but they look impoverished enough.[9]

Upon reflection, the earlier findings may be correct but perhaps not so meaningful. These are young men, with a median age of twenty-four, concentrated around age twenty. It is likely true, but not very revealing to say that as they formed their own households, they held little property. It would be surprising if young men starting out had assembled vast sums in the five troubled years after the war. But if one examines these suspects' antebellum origins, their postwar poverty takes on a darker tinge. These individuals might have been children or adolescents before the war, but their parents' wealth suggests much about them, and one quickly forms a different impression of their circumstances.

In examining the prewar backgrounds of those reported or indicted as Klansmen, the bulk look anything but poor. Of the ninety-four whose family or parents' property is reported in 1860, either in the same household or occasionally with apparent parents residing nearby, the pattern seems clear.[10] The average household wealth is quite substantial, nearly $17,000, though this figure is inflated by a handful of high-income families. More revealing is the median wealth of $4,920. In round numbers, about half surpassed a benchmark of modest affluence of $5,000, some forty-five individuals. Another ten were adults who had assembled that much wealth in their own households before the war, and they likely had access to further family resources. Thus, the substantial majority of those located in 1860 look tolerably well-situated. Men of at least middling background predominate.[11]

One could define a wealthy family in the antebellum South in numerous ways. Contemporaries certainly did, and historians still have no universally accepted yardstick. One might arbitrarily choose a $10,000 threshold for prosperity. If one adopts this measure, thirty-five of the suspects' families surpassed it in 1860, well over a third of those located. President Andrew Johnson himself provided another gauge in his initial effort to punish the secessionist oligarchs that had led the South to ruin. Johnson exempted those with more than $20,000 in wealth from his general amnesty, insisting that these individuals petition for individual pardon. By the president's definition of the treason-tainted oligarchy, fully nineteen came from such families.[12] Whatever definition one might choose, the suspects located met that standard in substantial numbers.

Slaveholding presents the crucial criterion, the bright red social demarcation, given the issues that inspired the Civil War. Owning slaves represents full investment in the society and politics of the Old South, and in the Confederate legacy. Of the entire number of suspects located, the families (or fathers) of some fifty-five appear as owners in the 1860 slave schedules, with a median slaveholding of seven slaves. Two more families appear in the previous census, for a total of fifty-seven. Even this probably understates the reality, because several other families report enough wealth that they likely were overlooked in the slave schedules. Also, some suspects had relatives living nearby with large numbers of slaves, while holding several in their own names.[13] The point is that most suspects who can be located came from slaveholding backgrounds, a substantial majority in fact. If this evidence is remotely representative, it suggests widespread ownership of human property among the families of those later identified as suspected or indicted terrorists. They presumably held substantially more than the 35 percent slaveholding reported among free Alabama families as a whole.[14]

Still, if planter standing is the ultimate determinant of high status in the Old South, this group mostly did not reach it.[15] Only one family owned more than fifty slaves. The traditional definition of a planter is someone who owns twenty slaves, and only nine of the suspects reached this apex of Southern society. However, if one adopts a more lax standard of ten slaves as the standard for a small planter, then a significantly greater twenty-two suspects' families achieved it. Several more individuals were either overseers or raised in overseers' families. The image that emerges is of a substantial number of men from well-off families, but few who were scions of great privilege. One possible explanation for this lack of elite participation reflects longstanding partisan divisions. Before the war, Whigs were notoriously the party of the great planters of the central cotton belt, and they long were inclined toward sectional moderation; their Democratic opponents tended more to states' rights fundamentalism and a confrontational approach toward the North. This ideological legacy may have colored how postwar Whiggish "conservatives" viewed extralegal violence as a tactic; the elite commonly resented extremist politicians for whipping up the thoughtless masses and provoking a ruinous war. Additionally, rich planters tended to live in areas with large black majorities, a reality which may have sobered potential vigilantes.

Political divisions at the top notwithstanding, all slaveholding families would have had much of their wealth invested in slaves. The suspects had considerable direct stake in slavery, and they were shaped by the system of racial control it spawned. The evidence suggests a substantial cohort of young terrorists of prosperous background, presumably embittered and impoverished by the war. The data is accumulated from disparate sources, everything from federal indictments and congressional hearings to local trials and newspaper accounts, from private complaints to partisan accounts for public consumption. Viewed one way this diversity might provide some confidence in the evidence, but it poses interpretive issues. The sample is weighted toward the end of the period, after the federal government began prosecutions under the Ku Klux act of 1871. To better gauge the pattern as it unfolded over time, one promising method is to identify one earlier source and follow it throughout. Allen Trelease's *White Terror*, still the best overall study of the Klan, suggests few Southern governors retained their correspondence. Fortunately for the purposes of this study, "much the fullest and most valuable files were those of Governor William H. Smith of Alabama."[16] Republican Governor Smith held office from July 1868 until November 1870, a period mostly bracketing the early years of the terrorist outbreak. Governor Smith's unique body of records facilitates various avenues of inquiry, by providing a consistent vehicle for examining the movement's evolution.

Smith's correspondence contains numerous allegations of collective violence. There can no way to know what is or is not a real or spurious Ku Klux Klan operation, but if the topic is the wider phenomenon it barely matters. We can define terrorist participation in one of several ways. The main definition is being named as a participant in Klan-style violence involving three or more white perpetrators, generally in disguise, targeting freedmen or other Republicans. Another category is anyone who participated in a lynching, in places of terrorist activity. Finally, a number of individuals confessed, were named by another participant, or were shot in the act of nightriding, which might be taken as conclusive proof. Eyewitness mail contains allegations rather than indictments, but then again, these letters were not meant for public consumption. The victims stated what they did and did not know about their assailants with surprising precision. Informants risked death if their identities were revealed, which presumably inhibited loose accusations. Furthermore, nowhere in his correspondence does Governor Smith suggest any doubt that the episodes described had actually occurred. He seldom did much about them, but he never questioned the reports.[17]

If one adds to this number a handful named as terrorists in the press during the Smith administration, mostly under indictment, we arrive at 131 names, spanning the first years of the Klan outbreak, the period of its expansion throughout most of northern and much of western Alabama. Of these, it was possible to locate some fifty-one names in the census, a relatively large proportion that is perhaps explained by the unlikelihood of state prosecution. While sharing much the same age distribution of the larger sample, this subset of early participants look better off. None of the individuals located in 1860 came from families without property, while 74 percent came from families that owned slaves. Fully 21 percent come from families holding over twenty slaves, sons of the planter class.[18] By any standard, those reported to Governor Smith as nightriders had been far more invested in slavery than the average white Alabamian, or even the average slaveowner.[19]

One might expect such men to fare ill during the Civil War, but the pattern that emerges is striking nonetheless. Median household wealth for suspects declined from about $13,000 in 1860 to $1,000 in 1870, that is to say, a decline of over 90 percent. Creation of new households by these young men accounts for some of this drastic decline. Still, the declines are large if one looks only at the households who could be located in both censuses. Even in 1870, these men remained slightly more prosperous than the average white Alabamian, but that is not the issue in terms of how their lives felt. These accused terrorists seem downwardly mobile on a vast, even catastrophic scale, to a far greater extent than historians generally acknowledge.

Patterns of participation changed over time. If one examines the year in which the violent episodes took place, the median age of alleged perpetrators declined from 33 in 1868, to 26.5 in 1869, to 24 in 1870. That is to say, the age of participants plummeted as the years went by. Median wealth evolved in tandem, declining from $2,050 in 1868, to $975 in 1869, to $365 in 1870. Those named in Smith's correspondence increasingly resembled the impoverished social profile of those indicted in the federal prosecutions in the early 1870s. The implication is that those who participated in the early stages were better established than those who came later. Ku Klux Klan apologists, and the turn-of-the-century Dunning School thereafter, often contended that the early terrorist groups were elite-initiated and led, but they fell into the hands of poorer elements, more inclined toward unrestrained violence and brigandage. Walter L. Fleming observed with unusual precision that "By 1869 the order had fallen under control of a low class of men who used it to further their own personal aims."[20] E. Merton Coulter, one of the last historians writing in the Dunning vein, similarly contended that as "originally promoted" the Klan received the support of the "best element" in the South.[21] Whatever the political motivation of these arguments, and the evident class animus, the evidence suggests they had some substance.

Foner, in his *Reconstruction*, highlighted the role of elite leadership in the terrorist movements of the era, though for quite different purposes than the Dunning School.[22] The record in Alabama certainly supports Foner's notion of substantial participation by the former slaveholders. Still, this underscores the urgency of explaining what the intentions of these crucial actors were. One suspects that there was something of a social permission process at work: that violence expanded through the countryside as it became clear that the Democratic leadership largely sanctioned it and that a significant number of planters were involved. There is some evidence that the leaders of terrorist bands were older and better off than the average participants.[23] If we understand the motives of the slaveholders' sons who appear so strongly represented in the early movement, we come closer to understanding the motivations that created it.

The place to start is with the ruinous impact of the war and emancipation for slaveholders and their sons. The Ku Klux Klan arrived first and was most pervasive in and around the Tennessee valley at the northern edge of the state. Here the Klan most resembled a mass movement, with hundreds parading in disguise on several occasions.[24] This plantation area had a distinctively harsh experience of Civil War, by comparison to the rest of Alabama at least. It had been the first region invaded, undergoing years of intermittent Union occupation starting in the spring of 1862. Both armies stripped the area bare, repeatedly, to prevent the enemy from gaining access to resources. Furthermore, men of the planter class had been heavily involved in partisan warfare behind Union lines. One such guerilla leader, Samuel Moore of Limestone County, was later convicted for his Klan activities along with several neighboring planters. The region became a cauldron of political violence, exacerbated by the in-migration of draft-evaders and Union sympathizers as well as the ebb and flow of invasion and reprisal. Thus the postwar antiblack violence dovetailed with the class-tinged guerrilla war waged against Unionists, a conflict that continued at significant levels into the postwar period—in venues from church rivalries to the jury box. Rampant Ku Klux Klan terrorism throughout northern Alabama owed much to this legacy.

Then there is the financial impact of emancipation itself, which was of course concentrated in slaveholding families and particularly among the most wealthy. For some suspects, the financial loss reported in the census looks mind-boggling. Take William Halloway of Sumter County; in 1860, his family was worth over $100,000, but a decade later he reported $100 in real estate at age twenty-six. Columbus Avery of Conecuh County lived in 1860 with his mother, who was reportedly worth over $90,000; a decade later he appears to have become a landless railroad carpenter with $500 in personal property.[25] D. B. "Brown" Bozeman of Coosa County went from his father's home worth $121,000 to his own family worth $3,400 in 1870. Young Bozeman's situation was perhaps tolerable, but it appears his father, now propertyless, was living with another son in Texas, and farming. Such evocative family dramas recurred frequently, even if on a less biblical scale. If postwar losses were anything like the 90 percent reduction in median wealth suggested, that might well disorient formerly prosperous young men, pushing them toward confrontational racial politics.

Combined with this loss is the resentment of the emancipated slaves, a global preoccupation among Alabama's ex-Confederate population. Fury at assertions of black equality was widespread across all classes. Still, it is certainly true that former slaveholders were the most shaped by the customs of the peculiar institution, and they were the most immediately affected by its loss. They faced the necessity of trying to make good their losses after the war. They confronted the changes in behavior among the formerly enslaved population, and they faced the task of rebuilding the plantation system on an utterly transformed basis. Ex-slaveholders had to haggle over pay disputes, which were legion, and negotiate annual contracts with people they had recently owned. In the desperate postwar years, their complaints over the work behavior of black men and women were heartfelt and earnest. By 1868, the worst of their transition was over, as plantation cotton production finally began to be profitable under free labor, ironically just as the Ku Klux Klan spread across the South.[26] But by this point, ex-slaveholders had experienced years of frustration in trying to get the freedpeople to work and behave to their satisfaction. Their resort to violence reflected the cumulative effect.

These social grievances were pressing, and they help explain the locally significant terrorist groups that developed even before the spread of the Ku Klux Klan. Still, the tangible grievance was political: the advent of Congressional Reconstruction. Resentment was likely sharper for those of slaveholding background than for anyone else, and younger members of this class might be counted on to respond to unfavorable political developments with the most vigor. Their education and expectation of exercising power would engage them in wider political events. And these national developments were drastic by any standard, bearing upon their future lives directly. Formerly prosperous Southerners received the advent of black suffrage with shock, a reaction most intensely felt in the plantation areas, and rising partisan agitation portended racial conflict.

The political changes were indeed unprecedented. The Military Reconstruction acts of the spring of 1867 essentially abolished ten Southern state governments that slaveholders had long dominated. The pending Fourteenth Amendment would bar from office those who had once held public positions and then supported the rebellion. In Alabama, the Republican constitution extended these provisions into the basic suffrage law of the state, disfranchising such individuals. These measures bore disproportionately on those at the upper end of the social scale and were perceived as punitive. And in June 1868, the U.S. Congress declared the Alabama constitution in effect, after it had been apparently defeated by a white boycott of the polls, thus delivering state and local government entirely into the hands of the unopposed Republican candidates. The modest origins of the new officeholders added a distinctive grievance for the expelled former leadership, steeped in the class expectations of the old regime.

An atmosphere of national crisis inflamed other social woes. Against the backdrop of President Johnson's impeachment in the spring of 1868 and the presidential election of that fall, partisan anger intensified. One way to conceptualize the emergence of widespread terrorism is that a broad social constituency, the restive sons of middling slaveholders, linked up with the displaced political establishment. Outgoing officeholders certainly had plenty to obsess about, especially the long-dominant Democrats. During the previous year, the military frequently removed ex-Confederate civil officeholders on grounds of obstructing Reconstruction. In Alabama, military orders established that freedpeople would serve on juries, something judges and lawyers felt directly. And newspapers confronted an order that those obstructing Reconstruction would lose government advertising, a matter of life and death for small-town editors. In the spring of 1868 came the suppression of newspapers for publicizing or encouraging the Ku Klux Klan itself. All three groups—lawyers, editors, and Democratic politicians—provided some of the more vocal Klan enthusiasts. In Tuscaloosa, the firebrand future legislator Ryland Randolph combined the latter two categories in one person, and others managed similar feats elsewhere on a less flamboyant scale.

All this brings us back to the original question: what was the motivation for a disparate collection of terrorists, and what precisely would substantial ex-slaveholder participation mean? The profusion of terrorist groups demonstrates a disparate assembly of actors, and scholars frequently analyze the goals in terms of varied motivations. These may be grouped into seven categories, though one could certainly reconfigure or add to the list. The legacy of slavery is one obvious one, encompassing the encouragement of brutality and the intolerance of dissent as well as the patrol system and other specific racial control practices. The Civil War itself is the second, with the desensitization to violence and shock of ex-Confederates at defeat and at having their world and personal finances abruptly upended. The third motive relates to African American social behavior: the sense whites shared of racial entitlement and their resentment of any assertion of real freedom. The fourth category would be economic motives illustrated by the efforts of planters to impose labor control or other actions by whites relating to the workforce and its behavior. The fifth would be the nightriders' much-touted crime suppression function, especially punishment of theft. The sixth would be perceived self-defense and the alarm that rising conflict could generate a race war. And the seventh grouping of motives are the explicit political grievances growing out of Radical Reconstruction and, most of all, black enfranchisement and its concomitants. All these motives overlap, and all are political in the broad sense of involving power relations. But for the purposes of this paper, political goals will be defined as narrowly partisan measures directed at the defeat of the Republican Party and the overthrow of Reconstruction.

In examining a social phenomenon of this scale, one approach would be to look for the motives that appealed across class lines—goals that unified participants rather than divided them. In thinking about the ex-slaveholders' role, parochial motives are presumably less crucial than those that are broadly felt. In the list of grievances outlined above, it seems clear that several of them were not widely shared, or rather, were felt in different ways. The direct financial loss of emancipation did not affect all whites; nor did the war's destruction devastate all sections equally. Contract disputes and labor control troubled planters, but not other whites, and nightriders could do nothing about one of the planters' major complaints, labor shortage. By the time of the Ku Klux Klan's expansion in 1868, sharecropping had begun to stabilize the plantation regime, and an improving cotton price promised planters real profits for the first time since the war. Planters had reason to rejoice, but in contrast, poorer tenants sometimes sought to drive the freedmen out of whole neighborhoods, to eliminate the competition. Economic motives could easily divide rural whites, however much racial animus they shared.

Increasing theft, particularly of swine and other livestock, was probably a more widespread grievance. I have argued elsewhere that emancipation meant that the ex-slaves gained access to guns and hunting dogs, which had negative effects on those who depended on pigs for their livelihood.[27] The eventual shift to decentralized tenant farming, and especially sharecropping, meant that the freedmen became responsible for providing their own provisions, while it simultaneously moved tenants out of the old slave quarters and away from employers' supervision. Large landowners obsessed about the subsequent losses, always blamed on the freedmen, and this encouraged vigilantism. The suddenly impoverished sons of slaveholders would feel livestock losses as strongly as other farmers, and they might equally well take their frustrations out on the freedpeople. Still, large landowners benefitted from the reemergence of cotton production as a paying concern, and they depended on black labor. Their less prosperous neighbors experienced all the inconveniences of the shift to sharecropping with few of the benefits from improved production. Small wonder that Klan activities tended to last longer and be more intense in areas where small farmers preferred to drive out freedpeople altogether. Resentment of small-scale theft unified a broad constituency, but "racial cleansing" as a remedy opened divisions over how far to pursue this issue.

Likewise, fear encouraged racist mobilization. The Old South's nightmares, of Haiti and Nat Turner and John Brown, only intensified after war and emancipation. Consider as well the recent scares over a mythical Christmastime 1865 insurrection, exacerbated by the demonization of Radical Republicans exercising power in Washington and the renewed discussion of Thaddeus Stevens's confiscation proposals. Discussion of race war ran through the press and in private correspondence; it is difficult to evaluate how seriously people took the talk, but it was pervasive. Given how restrained the freedmen's actions were, it may seem ludicrous, but ex-Confederates commonly perceived Klan participation as prudent caution, especially given their confidence that they would prevail in an armed showdown. One leader of the Knights of the White Camelia highlighted the self-defense function. Decades later, he recalled "its organization and discipline was as perfect as human ingenuity could have made it," and four hours would have been "ample time" to summon a thousand men.[28] Veterans spontaneously organized whenever trouble threatened, and these measures segued easily into aggressive action when undertaken by racists. There was a fear that campaign rallies could generate an armed confrontation, and given the possibility of a liquor-fueled exchange escalating into a riot, this wasn't altogether irrational. No one in the white community could prevent provocative behavior by their own, and such outbreaks happened a lot. Still, one suspects that these fears were probably more felt in the plantation belt and county towns than throughout the region. They were probably more pressing for ex-slaveholders than for the general population.

Two overarching grievances remain that were sharply experienced by ex-slaveholders yet broadly shared across the white population. One is the loss of the customs and behavior patterns of slavery and the resulting resentment that the freedmen were asserting equality across a broad spectrum of areas: on the plantations, in churches, in schools, in personal interactions with whites—just about everywhere in fact. Both contemporaries and historians agree that these complaints had some basis: the freedmen were distancing themselves from the legacy of slavery as thoroughly as human imagination could devise. Southern whites experienced black behavior after the war as an affront; it generated a widespread feeling of insecurity, even anarchy. Given the behavior patterns of slavery, a longing existed to place the unsupervised ex-slaves under control and to get something like the old patrol system back again. There was enthusiasm for re-creating the old state militia for this purpose, and when the army prevented this, local groups anticipating the Klan popped up all over the countryside. Most whites just could not imagine a future in which someone was not responsible for monitoring black behavior, and this enabled the resort to racial terrorism.

But to explain the timing and the emergence of the Ku Klux Klan as a region-wide movement, one returns to Congressional Reconstruction and the political desire to reverse it in whatever way possible. The timing of the early phases of Klan operations provides one demonstration of this. If one plots the 264 individual Klan-style terrorist acts reported to Governor Smith, one sees a suggestive pattern month by month.[29] Episodes initially follow electoral events more than, say, the agricultural calendar. Attacks spike before the November 1868 national election and decline sharply afterward to near zero. They then rise even higher than before the August 1869 congressional elections and again drop off to near zero for months afterward. By 1870, though, the pattern becomes less intelligible in terms of either politics or labor demands. Increasing randomness suggests that the partisan motivation of the violence was strong initially but became less evident over time. The implication is that this parallels decreasing upper-class sanction, as the movement became more problematic before the national press and public. The Democratic triumph in the November 1870 state elections and the likelihood of federal anti-Klan legislation encouraged savvy participants to desist. But terrorist activities continued well thereafter. One might conceptualize this as moving from racial politics narrowly defined to broadly defined, but it bore less relation to electoral demands or upper-class priorities.

Overturning Republican rule and black suffrage were the tangible goals that galvanized popular resistance. Resentment at congressional intervention was nearly universal among all but the beleaguered Unionist minority of the white population. This political grievance united broad segments of the public, which is why the movement grew to the dimensions it achieved. Reconstruction centrally featured "Paramilitary Politics," in Steven Hahn's apt phrase.[30] Historians, of course, from Allen Trelease to Eric Foner himself have noted this; it will come as no surprise that however tangled the Ku Klux Klan's motivation, partisan goals belong at the top of any list.

There is a different, concluding, point about the centrality of politics in this era. The evidence highlights the fissure lines among opponents of Reconstruction. Some decades ago, William Barney depicted the secession movement in Alabama as a middle-class revolt spearheaded by young men concerned for their futures if slavery's spread was stopped. This represented the crucial constituency for Democratic states' rights extremism, and one can follow this logic into the postwar era. Michael Perman's *The Road to Redemption* highlighted the disunity among postwar white Southerners. Perman emphasized the tension between Democratic fundamentalists, prone toward force, and more cautious, legality-minded conservatives, thoroughly racist but leery of endless confrontation. His interpretation of white factionalism is compelling as a political narrative but less persuasive as social history. The record in Alabama, however, adds an additional dimension. If the findings of this paper are correct, who had more motivation for terrorist activity than the downwardly mobile sons of middling slaveholders? The war had wrecked their futures. They may not have been able to control the movement they helped create, and its political utility soon appeared dubious to many. Still, without their aid, the terrorist groundswell could not have achieved the regional scope that it did with fatal consequences for Reconstruction and the future destiny of the United States.[31]

Notes

1. The usage is at least not anachronistic. The terms "terrorist" or "terrorism" were commonly used in reference to the Ku Klux Klan. See, for example, the New York *Times*, 13 March 1869, 26 November 1869, and 20 July 1870.

2. See Davis and Sims-Wood, comps., *Ku Klux Klan*.

3. Hahn, *Nation under Our Feet*, 268.

4. Trelease, *White Terror*, 51.

5. Foner, *Reconstruction*, 425, 432.

6. Hahn, *Roots of Southern Populism*; Fitzgerald, "Ku Klux Klan."

7. The total number of suspects had increased primarily because of inclusion of those accused in the governors' correspondence (see below). The proportion of the sample located is larger than in the previous research. Still, it should be conceded that most could not be uniquely matched in the census, so that these findings are more suggestive than conclusive.

8. I am referring here to tools like http://www.ancestry.com, which permit sophisticated searches in the population and slave schedules of the federal census. This supersedes previous research techniques dependent on laborious scanning of microfilm.

9. Moneyhon, *Impact of the Civil War and Reconstruction on Arkansas*, 42.

10. In assessing this data, it should be borne in mind that misidentification of family members of suspects seems less likely than of the participants themselves. The census often contains so much material about ages and siblings and birthplaces that connecting men with their families is relatively certain.

11. The problem with all studies of this sort is that transients tend to be poorer than the general population, which suggests some upward bias in the sample located. For this study, one would expect census takers disproportionately to miss modest farmers and tenants—even before the war. Given how pronounced the findings are, the bias would

have to be large to alter the conclusion of pronounced downward mobility; the upward bias would also have to be improbably concentrated in the prewar censuses. Still, all of the rest of the 530 names without unique matches theoretically could have been destitute. Even in this unlikely event, some 11 percent, a significant number, must have had $5,000 in family resources before the war.

12. In his study of Arkansas, Carl Moneyhon chose $25,000 as his indication of membership in his "elite" category, and seventeen families met this standard. Moneyhon, *Impact of the Civil War and Reconstruction on Arkansas.*

13. At least four more had apparent slaveholder grandparents living in the immediate vicinity.

14. Calculated from http://www.fisher.lib.virginia.edu/collections/stats/histcensus/php/state.php. Here, too, there may be some overrepresentation of slaveholding because of census takers missing poorer nonslaveholders. But the bias would have to be very large to alter the basic pattern indicated.

15. Of the whole number, only one came from a family holding more than fifty slaves, one common definition of what constitutes a great planter. For one older source using this definition, see Sellers, *Slavery in Alabama.*

16. Trelease, *White Terror*, 527.

17. For this portion of the research, I would cheerfully acknowledge the assistance of a student co-author, Adam Lozeau of St. Olaf College. We presented our findings at the Alabama Historical Association in April 2008, under the title "The Social Profile of the Alabama Ku Klux Klan during Reconstruction: Terrorism and Motivation."

18. If one assumes that all the unmatched suspects had owned no slaves before the war, the identified slaveholders still must represent a substantial minority of the whole number, well over a fourth.

19. By my calculations, there were 96,603 free families in 1860. A reported 33,750 individuals owned slaves—or just over a third—and of them 6,032 owned over twenty slaves. This would suggest a dramatic overrepresentation of these suspects relative to the general population. Calculated from http://www.fisher.lib.virginia.edu/collections/stats/histcensus/php/state.php.

20. Fleming, *Civil War and Reconstruction in Alabama*, 668, 681, 690.

21. Coulter, *South during Reconstruction*, 171.

22. Foner, *Reconstruction*, 432. See also the footnote on page 434, which dismisses the notion of New Departure restraint on the Klan.

23. Fitzgerald, "Ku Klux Klan," 195–97.

24. Just before the presidential election, hundreds of Klansmen rode around a Republican rally being held in the county courthouse in Huntsville, provoking a riot as they departed.

25. He was the only Columbus Avery listed in the state in 1870, and he was born in Alabama and the right age. The family was not utterly ruined, however; there is an apparent brother still in Conecuh County with about a tenth of the family's prewar wealth left.

26. For the larger analysis of the interconnection between plantation agriculture and Reconstruction mass politics, see Fitzgerald, *Union League Movement in the Deep South.*

27. Fitzgerald, "Ku Klux Klan."

28. G.P.L. Reed to Walter L. Fleming, n.d., Walter Lynwood Fleming Papers, New York Public Library.

29. The definition qualifies as a single terrorist episode each action conducted in a separate location, even if several involving the same nightriders occurred the same evening. Events occurring at the same place and time were counted as a single episode.

30. Hahn, *Nation under Our Feet*.

31. Barney, *Secessionist Impulse*; Perman, *Road to Redemption*.

8

Drovers, Distillers, and Democrats

Economic and Political Change in Northern Greenville County, 1865–1878

BRUCE E. BAKER

Writing about the Republican Party in southern Appalachia after the Civil War, historian Gordon B. McKinney has observed that its "decentralized party structure" meant that the national party found itself unable to dictate positions to the Republican administrations in the southern states, who had to respond to challenging local situations in ways that might place them at variance with national priorities. Instead of ironclad national platforms, local groups and leaders at the community level were instrumental in shaping the party's fortunes in the mountain South. In the mountains of North Carolina, Unionists who formed the core of the Republican Party found themselves a minority amongst their secessionist neighbors, while at the same time they formed a minority within North Carolina's Republican organization and had little influence on its direction.[1] McKinney has nothing to say about mountain Republicans in South Carolina, presumably because the fringe of Appalachia that extends into the Palmetto State is so small that it could not support a Republican Party of any significance.[2] And yet, if we look at Greenville County, South Carolina, we can see that for a brief period after the war, there was a potential constituency for a white, mountain Republican Party. The mountainous part of the county, comprising the upper four townships and covering an area perhaps ten miles by twenty miles, lacked the commitment to slavery and secession of the rest of the state and experienced the dislocation and guerrilla activity that helped create a separate political identity for mountaineers in other parts of Appalachia—social disruption that provided material for the Republicans to work with.[3]

Some of the most important figures in Greenville County's Republican

Party during Reconstruction came from the mountains. However, by the time of South Carolina's dramatic 1876 election campaign, which involved the extensive mobilization of the Democratic Party and the ouster of the Republican administration in spring 1877, whites in northern Greenville County were firmly in the Democratic camp. At the six polling locations in northern Greenville County that year, the Republican candidate for governor received only between 5 and 30 percent of the vote.[4] This essay seeks to explain this political alignment and the evaporation of the possibility that mountain whites in South Carolina might provide a constituency for the Republican Party during the course of Reconstruction. This dramatic realignment was driven by important shifts in the economic structure of northern Greenville County, brought about partly by local Republican initiatives along with national party policies that worked against the interests of their potential supporters there.

Geography is critical to understanding what happened to northern Greenville County's white Republicans because it shaped both transportation possibilities and economic options. Greenville County sits in South Carolina's northwest corner, bordering North Carolina. It is approximately fifteen to twenty miles wide from east to west, but closer to fifty from its northern edge along the North Carolina state line to its southern extremity where it meets Laurens and Spartanburg counties. This narrow shape means that the county encompasses both the rolling hills of the Piedmont, eminently suitable to cotton cultivation, and rugged mountains of the Blue Ridge escarpment, rising to over three thousand feet. The Saluda River, festooned with shoals, divides Greenville County from Pickens and Anderson counties on the west. Many smaller creeks in the center of the county drain into the Reedy River, which flows south to Laurens County, and other waterways, especially the Tyger River, flow southeast into Spartanburg County. Three large mountains largely cut off from more extensive ranges—monadnocks—loom north of the town of Greenville: Paris Mountain, just a couple of miles out of town, and Glassy Mountain and Hogback Mountain, only a few miles south of the Blue Ridge.[5] Two important gaps in the Blue Ridge—Saluda Gap and Jones Gap—provide crossings into North Carolina. Greenville County's combination of mountains and Piedmont makes it unusual, though not quite unique, in the South. To the extent that topographical facts constrained economic possibilities, and economic activity provided at least a substantial part of the forces that drove political interest and affiliation, Greenville County was inherently a county divided, and we should not be surprised to see a level of internal conflict there greater than we might find in a county that did not straddle such a regional border.

Prior to the Civil War, the northern part of Greenville County was a zone of what Wilma Dunaway calls "peripheral capitalism."[6] It was certainly not integrated into the system of cotton production: its topography and lack of relevant infrastructure prevented that.[7] At the same time, it was not an area characterized by near universal land ownership and true subsistence.[8] Instead, the uneven land distribution created, in Dunaway's term, a "landless agrarian semiproletariat."[9] "Over their work lives," Dunaway argues, "agricultural laborers in peripheral areas accrue part of their income from subsistence farming, part from direct wages (in cash or in kind), part from sales of commodities or services on the market, and part from public subsidies or family gifts."[10] This description seems to fit northern Greenville County. Agricultural production was important, and it created some opportunities for waged work, but the area's proximity to Greenville offered other choices for making a living not available to those further in the mountains, such as coming in to trade on salesday. Once a month, on the Monday when the sheriff sold property on the courthouse steps, country folk came in and camped on the edge of Greenville, selling produce, buying supplies, swapping and racing horses, drinking some whiskey and doing some fighting.[11] Greenville's location meant that it served as an "intermediate inland distribution center" for an important part of southern Appalachia.[12] "From upland South Carolina, western North Carolina, East Tennessee and East Kentucky," Dunaway explains, "trade wagons and livestock drives aimed for Greenville, South Carolina, the major intermediate distribution center for re-export further south and to the coast."[13]

The droving trade tied local agricultural production to the transit and distribution of agricultural goods from elsewhere. Late in the eighteenth century, farmers in Appalachia began sending droves of animals, especially hogs, out of the region. By the late antebellum period, several hundred thousand hogs moved each year from East Tennessee and even Kentucky eastward through the French Broad River valley of Western North Carolina to Asheville and then south, to be distributed in South Carolina and Georgia. These hogs, along with cattle, horses, mules, and even turkeys, came down through the gaps at the northern edge of Greenville County on their way to and often through the town of Greenville itself.[14] Many of the hogs fed hungry slaves in the plantation districts of South Carolina who devoted less energy to food production and more to the production of staples for export.[15] A wagon road was completed in 1797 over Saluda Gap from Merrittsville on the North Fork of the Saluda River to Green River Cove in North Carolina. An improved road along the same route was completed in 1820.[16] In the 1850s, Solomon

Jones opened a new route over the mountains at Jones Gap to compete with the State Road.[17]

Geography and lack of good transport meant that the rapid expansion of cotton in the 1850s did not affect Greenville very much. We can see this by examining census reports on amounts of cotton grown, and contemporary observers back it up. Lacy K. Ford has calculated that in 1850, Greenville District's cotton production was second lowest in South Carolina's Upcountry (above Pickens), as was its cotton-corn ratio.[18] Good river transport was not available in Greenville County. Cotton planters in Anderson County to the west could boat their cotton down the Savannah River to Augusta, and those in Union County to the east followed the Broad River to Columbia, but Greenville County's rivers were too narrow, too shallow, and too beset by shoals to make this practical.[19] The Greenville and Columbia Railroad did finally arrive in 1853, but it provided only slow, haphazard service at a high cost.[20] The Civil War put even this poor service out of action until September 1866, and floods sometimes washed out bridges along the way.[21] Even in 1860, several years after the Greenville and Columbia Railroad opened, Greenville District still lagged behind other upcountry districts in cotton production, producing barely two hundred bales more than it had in 1850 and with a cotton-corn ratio that was still dramatically lower than any district besides Pickens.[22]

In northern Greenville County, the droving trade, unlike cotton, would have had a fairly significant effect on the local economy. Hogs could travel eight to ten miles per day, so stopping points known as "stands" were located every few miles to accommodate the traveling animals and the drovers who accompanied them. At first these had been crude campsites for teamsters, but as the droving trade increased taverns and stores sprang up.[23] The drovers' stands were located at several places along the way, and droves would have probably stopped at four of them as they made their way down Saluda Township. One hundred hogs would eat eight bushels of corn, so those 150,000 hogs would have put away 12,000 bushels of corn a year at each of these stands. In the late 1870s, keepers of these stands were paying local farmers fifty cents per bushel of corn, so that would mean about $6,000 a year that each stand was putting into the local economy of Saluda Township, or probably around $24,000 if we estimate droves stopped four times as they passed through the township. Drovers typically paid by IOU on the way down, stopping on their way back to settle accounts with the proceeds of their sales.[24] Adding in the wagon trade and the regular stage coaches that used the route, provisioning and serving these travelers gave the area around the mountain roads access to cash income not available to those living in more isolated regions.

At the same time, farmers in northern Greenville County were probably not in a position to earn significant amounts of money by selling actual animals to the drovers. Situated relatively close to the Greenville market, they would be more likely to sell their animals there themselves, and the drovers would have bought all the animals they needed by the time they got to South Carolina.[25] The droving trade would have provided an economic lifeline to farmers in northern Greenville County, a welcome source of cash to supplement agricultural subsistence and waged work, but probably not enough to provide real economic independence. This inability to support a family independently of opportunities granted by community leaders with greater resources would leave small farmers in a precarious position when it came to taking political sides. Had they been wealthier, they could have afforded to alienate the local Democratic power brokers, and had they been poor but more numerous, as was the case in parts of the state with a much greater population of ex-slaves or deeper in the mountains where the power of planters was much less substantial, they could also defy the will of planters. As it was, though, the white farmers in Greenville County's mountains had little room in which to maneuver, and however much appeal the Republicans might enjoy, that appeal would be limited by the hard facts of the position in which poor mountain whites found themselves.

Nonetheless, several white men influential in Greenville County's Republican organization lived along the drover routes. James M. Runion preached but also ran a farm within two miles of a crossroads at the southern edge of Saluda Township, where J. W. Garmany provided lodging for drovers.[26] William B. Johnson lived in Cleveland Township alongside the Gap Creek Road over the mountains. According to the agricultural census, in 1859 Johnson operated a small farm of seventy improved acres, with several horses and oxen, milk cows, and other livestock, probably marketing them to travelers coming past.[27] Absalom Blythe had left South Carolina for Florida and then Texas after the war before returning in 1869.[28] He moved from the Union Reform Party in 1871 (a fusion of Democrats and disgruntled Republicans) to the Republicans in 1872 and served as United States Commissioner and also Solicitor; his roots were in northwestern Cleveland Township, where his family ran a mill.[29] Solomon Jones, the road builder, was also connected with the Republicans in the first few years after the war.[30]

During the war and immediately afterward, the prospects for Republican recruitment among whites in northern Greenville County were good. The region had often found itself at odds with the fire-eating tradition of the Palmetto State. With the importance of transportation infrastructure to the local economy, it is not surprising that many in Greenville County supported the tariffs that touched off the Nullification Crisis of the early 1830s. The leading voice of Unionism at that time was a young newspaper editor, Benjamin F. Perry. When Greenville County registered its attitude to nullification in the election of October 1832, voters came out against it by over 70 percent, and when nullification passed anyway, Greenville County was outspoken in its opposition to the policy, denouncing the test oath and supporting Andrew Jackson against their own fellow upcountryman, John C. Calhoun.[31]

The divisions between Greenville County and the rest of the state took on even greater significance during the Civil War and divided the county itself between the prosperous plantations in the southern two thirds of the county, territory very committed to slavery and the Confederate cause, and the mountainous north, where discontent broke into outright armed opposition. Volunteering for Confederate service was always slow in the mountains of Greenville County, and after units raised there faced a difficult couple of years, desertion became a serious problem by the middle of 1863. Large bands of deserters essentially controlled parts of the mountains in north Greenville County, organizing mutual defense so they could raise their crops and fortifying a building in Gowensville to defend against Confederate conscription officers.[32] By the last year of the war, there were two companies of deserters numbering as many as 150 men.[33] Sometimes, bands of these deserters would raid plantations and grist mills in the lower parts of the county.[34] Throughout the war, Unionists and deserters in the mountains helped escaped Union prisoners of war make their way toward Union lines.[35]

The end of the war brought about a brief, but intense, period of even greater chaos to northern Greenville County. Union General George Stoneman raided from Tennessee into western North Carolina in April 1865, and his cavalry came south from Hendersonville on 29 April 1865 to pursue Jefferson Davis and intercept any unsurrendered bands of Confederate soldiers. A detachment moved south from Jones Gap and entered the town of Greenville on 2 May 1865, but when Stoneman's men moved on and the Confederate military had collapsed, there was essentially no check on violence until federal troops arrived to garrison Greenville in July 1865.[36] By May 1865, northern Greenville County was in "a general state of disorder," and "bands were robbing and doing other mischief." Many women without men moved into the city because outlying areas were unsafe.[37] Eventually, the warring parties "called a peace meeting at Tyger Church, and entered into a written agreement to stop these proceedings."[38] As Daniel Sutherland argues, these kinds of conflicts were not resolved neatly once the official war was over: "Revenge and retaliation remained important ingredients [of Reconstruction], too, with their roots often anchored in wartime collisions."[39]

The violence and chaos continued throughout Presidential Reconstruction in parts of Greenville County. A Freedmen's Bureau agent in neighboring Anderson County reported in October 1865 that five freedpeople had been murdered in Greenville County within two weeks.[40] A simple lack of adequate force was the root of the problem. As the officer explained: "A battalion of cavalry in addition to the present force is actually needed. We do all we can do with our present force but can not do all that can be done with an ample force of mounted men."[41] One man claimed to have killed twenty-eight freedmen in the first year after the war and "offered his services to kill others if there was any that were particularly offensive to the community." Quite a lot of the violence seems to have been connected to labor control: "Parties have been organized titled beat companies with Captains, Lieutenants, etc to go about and whip and drive back freedmen found employed away from their former owner, especially if the present employer was not formerly a slave owner."[42]

The balance of power shifted decisively after the Reconstruction Acts of 1867 were passed. With a newly energized federal commitment to effective military control of the region and the sudden displacement of ex-Confederate officials who would turn a blind eye—or lend a hand—to abuses of freedpeople or white Unionists, many whites in the region came to support the Republicans.[43] For the first time, the Union League began to organize in the county, attracting support from both blacks and whites. Reverend James M. Runion, a Baptist minister and farmer who had served as tax collector during the war, made an impassioned speech for the Union League in July 1867. Runion recognized the generosity of Congress's terms and argued that the Republican Party provided the surest route to restore peace and prosperity to "our distracted, devastated and desolated country." He accepted, if not necessarily enthusiastically, the prospect of sharing rights with African Americans, saying, "To my colored friends, I would say . . . We are Southern men born upon the same soil, live in the same country and our destiny is the same."[44] Union League members from the Dark Corner, in the mountains, sometimes came in to Greenville for meetings.[45]

After Greenville County experienced a fairly uneventful registration period in summer 1867 and an election on 19 and 20 November 1867, a convention was held in Charleston in January 1868 to write a new state constitution.[46] James M. Runion and William B. Johnson were both delegates from Greenville County.[47] The election held in April 1868 to approve the new state constitution was the occasion for more violence and intimidation. The Republican Party held a public meeting on 23 March 1868 to explain what the convention had accomplished and encourage voters to approve the proposed constitution. Benjamin F. Perry spoke at the meeting, opposing the adoption of the constitution but calling for the nomination of conservatives if it were passed, nearly provoking a riot.[48] A few days after the election in mid-April, several white men pistol-whipped and shot at two freedmen at Taylor's Mill on Mush Creek in northern Greenville County, their only motive being membership of the Republican Party.[49] The Ku Klux Klan, and possibly other "secret organizations of a diabolical character" became active in the weeks after the election, threatening and assaulting both whites and blacks who supported the Republicans. One freedman found a notice tacked to his door threatening reprisals since he had informed revenue agents about the location of certain illicit distilleries.[50] By the summer, recalcitrant whites had begun to organize a "white man's party" and brought serious economic pressure to bear against all who supported the Republicans, which proved an effective way of strangling the Union League. These tactics worked especially well against those who lacked the ability to be self-sufficient and were remote from the larger settlements and more dependent on one merchant for supplies.[51]

The result of this range of tactics—violence, intimidation, economic coercion—was to weaken the Republican Party at its very conception in Greenville County, meaning that it could not necessarily draw strength from the portion of the county that should have been its natural stronghold—the southern part of the county with the larger black population. In such a context, the importance to Republicans of gaining and keeping the loyalty of whites in the mountains who had no particular fondness for and, indeed, a good deal of historical antipathy to the county's aristocracy, was that much more important. This seemed quite possible at one time. As late as 1871, two men from the mountains told a traveler that there were more than eight hundred white Republican voters in northern Greenville County.[52]

But in this all-important task the Republicans failed, and they failed on a variety of levels from the very local to the national. From the inception of the party until the re-election of Franklin D. Roosevelt in 1936, the Republican Party at a national level felt it could take for granted the votes of black Southerners when they were able to cast them. During Reconstruction in areas such as the South Carolina Upcountry where blacks and whites were fairly evenly matched, the key political contest was for the loyalty of whites who lacked commitment and connection to the planters, whether they were landed yeomen or landless poor whites. But in the decisive 1876 campaign, Democrats appealed to the voters of northern Greenville County for several reasons.[53] The deepest reason for the Republican Party's inability to attract and hold a following in northern Greenville County was simply a failure to deliver what these potential voters wanted, especially economic change that would alter their lives in a meaningful way.

The key issue was land. Freedmen's Bureau agent John W. De Forest observed, "The idea of confiscation was received with more favor by this caste than by the Negroes."[54] Five Confederate veterans posed the question starkly in an 1869 letter to Land Commissioner C. P. Leslie. "In fighting the battles of the South," they wrote,

> we thought we were in the right path of duty, and as her sons were needed at the front, did not hesitate to place ourselves firmly in ranks. Consequently, we are now without an arm, a leg, or otherwise maimed for life, have our wives, little ones and widowed mothers to support in our feeble way, and us a Democratic, moneyless, landless set of men, we appeal to you to know if in the distribution of lands in this State, under your supervision, we are to be remembered.

Leslie replied, "I am ready to do the best I can for you and for all who are anxious to go upon a little farm, make it their home, and to labor and economize to pay for it. In seeking for such men I shall not be restricted by 'race, color, nativity or previous condition.'"[55] Nonetheless, the Land Commission seems to have had little effect in the mountains. In none of the four partly mountain counties of South Carolina (Oconee, Pickens, Greenville, and Spartanburg) did the Land Commission purchase more than two thousand acres of land for settlers. Greenville had only 1,766 acres available; enough for perhaps forty-five families if divided into farms just under forty acres in size.[56]

More seriously, perhaps, a number of the Republicans' policies at both the state and national level actively alienated whites in northern Greenville County. Probably most significant of these self-defeating policies was the high taxation of the 1870s. In studying Reconstruction, historians are often skeptical about whites' complaints over high taxes. There are, after all, many examples of the crocodile tears of rich planters resentful at being required to pay a reasonable rate of tax on land to support the expanded public services of the Reconstruction government. As J. Mills Thornton III has argued, however, in South Carolina and other states of the lower South, "Republican tax policy adversely affected the small white farmer," and in this case, voters in northern Greenville County had a fairly legitimate complaint.[57] One reason taxes were high was that two Republican county treasurers in the space of two years defaulted. The first, James M. Allen, a white stonecutter who came south after the war, served as state senator from 1868 to 1872 and then as county treasurer from 1872 to 1873, when he defaulted on approximately $40,000 of tax funds.[58] The other treasurer was Reverend James M. Runion, who had several years of experience in tax administration and was considered honest, even by his political opponents.[59] Runion's misfortune happened because the Board of County Commissioners refused to accept his bond on the grounds that his bondsmen lived outside the county lines. Runion's bond was finally approved, but one of his bondsmen was Hardy Soloman, a banker in Columbia. In return for the assistance, Runion deposited the county's funds in Soloman's bank, which went bust in dubious circumstances in July 1875, losing another $10,000 for Greenville County.[60] As an example of how bad Greenville County's finances were in the 1870s, a newspaper notice in 1877 gave the good news to the county's teachers that they would finally be paid for 1873.[61] The lack of ready cash also meant that when a June 1876 flood washed away most of the bridges in the county, they took a very long time to be replaced, making the northern townships' isolation from mills and markets all the worse.[62]

A substantial portion of the taxes paid in Greenville County in the 1870s went to pay the interest on bonds the county had issued for the Richmond and Atlanta Air Line Railroad. The Air Line was a project begun by railroad magnate Tom Scott in 1868 to connect Richmond and Atlanta with a railroad that hugged the edge of the Appalachian Mountains more closely than existing lines, making it easier to access and export the crops of the Piedmont region. Scott used elaborate ruses and front companies to hide the fact that it was his Pennsylvania Railroad that was behind the construction of the Air Line. The state of South Carolina supported the line's construction by selling its interest in the Spartanburg and Union Railroad and the Blue Ridge Railroad and allowing their consolidation—under Scott's control, as it turned out.[63] The General Assembly also authorized those counties through which the railroad would travel to pass local bonds.[64] Greenville County took advantage of this, approving the issue of $200,000 worth of bonds. When the vote to approve the bonds came, the city of Greenville provided 869 votes, more than half the total for the bonds, while the four townships of northern Greenville County cast only 45 votes in favor and 87 against.[65] The Air Line certainly jump-started growth in the town of Greenville once it opened in 1873, but it was costly for the entire county. Interest on the bonds began to fall due almost immediately. Greenville's Board of County Commissioners paid $1,750 on the first year's interest in January 1872, then $3,500 on another batch of bonds just six months later.[66] By the mid-1870s, a little over half the tax levied by Greenville County went to service Air Line debt, and this made up around a fifth of the combined burden of state and county taxes.[67]

Mountain residents were probably hard pressed to see how the railroad benefited them. It certainly added to the growth of Greenville, creating markets for any number of new merchants and facilitating the growth of manufacturing enterprises in the central and southern parts of the county. It boosted the production of cotton in the lowlands, but for farmers in the northern townships its main effect was the disruption of the droving trade that had been the region's economic mainstay and an important source of cash.

The exact extent and date of this decline is difficult to pinpoint. Retrospective accounts variously give 1870, 1880, and 1885 as ending dates.[68] One source specifically says that by 1885 "the railroads made them obsolete."[69] Newspapers sometimes noted the passage of drovers and their animals through town, but as this was an ordinary event we cannot be sure that their arrival would be noted each time. What is certain is that in the 1870 and 1871 seasons, the newspaper mentioned six droves coming through (half hogs, but also horses, mules, and even 350 turkeys), whereas the 1875 and 1876 seasons mention just a single drove of hogs, all purchased and slaughtered by a local merchant to feed Greenville's growing population.[70] It is likely that Greenville's growth made it increasingly impractical to have hundreds of hogs wandering down its main streets. A city ordinance forbidding residents to let their livestock roam freely was passed in May 1872, and this may have affected drovers, as the new street railway almost certainly did in 1877.[71]

The decline in the droving trade squeezed mountain residents at a particularly bad time. They might pay for the newspaper with chickens or buy dry goods with produce, and corn was sold and bought at many stores, but the tax collector insisted on cash. While farmers in the lower parts of the county found themselves with readier access to cash (and, of course, debt) as cotton cultivation increased and the railroad provided a marketing opportunity for other goods as well, and as city residents could work for wages in the many new mercantile and manufacturing establishments, and rural residents found employment at the sawmills set up in response to Greenville's insatiable demand for building materials, all these changes tended to work directly against the mountain farmers who for fifty years had found a way of getting their corn to market in the bellies of the thousands of hogs that flowed down the mountain roads.

Republican malfeasance and incompetence and local taxes created resentment among mountain voters, but federal action was almost certainly decisive in pushing them into the Democratic Party. Former provisional governor Benjamin F. Perry explained it best in a campaign speech at Glassy Mountain Church in August 1876:

> I will bring to your attention one act of this National Republican party. It is the tax on distillers, in favor of the rich and against the poor. You in the mountains, have all your lives been distillers of whiskey. It was almost the only means you had of converting corn into money. But, now, no one can carry on a lawful distillery unless he is rich and able to make his hundred or thousand gallons every day. He must have a host of officers, which none but a large establishment can maintain. If you poor men attempt to distil, you are hunted down like robbers, and sent to the penitentiary. I know many worthy men in these mountains, who, for making a few gallons of whiskey, have been dragged from their poor wives and children and sent to the penitentiary, their heads shaved, dressed in a striped suit like highwaymen and murderers, and condemned to hard labor whilst their wives and children were left to starve![72]

It was a fair criticism, and one Perry's listeners felt keenly. A heavier excise tax fell on liquor during the Civil War and remained after similar taxes were repealed.

As Wilbur R. Miller has argued, its enforcement became a key test of the newly expanded power of the national state during Reconstruction, and the frequent connections between moonshiners and the Ku Klux Klan led federal revenue agents to see both as common enemies of the nation and of the Republican Party.[73] In the early 1870s, the excise tax was enforced at the local level by a deputy collector stationed in Greenville. A. L. Cobb held the position, mostly making arrests in the city itself and in the surrounding parts of the county, focusing more on the distribution and consumption of illicit whiskey than on its production.[74] The local newspaper, strongly Democratic, praised Cobb's enforcement work. However, in May 1872, word came down that to save money the Revenue Department was discontinuing the position of local collector. Less than a week later, the new pattern for enforcement was revealed when a detachment of federal cavalry arrested four men in upper

Saluda Township, seizing five hundred gallons of contraband liquor, a wagon, and a team of mules.[75]

In the mid-1870s, as soldiers finished chasing Ku Kluxers and before they were shipped west en masse to fight Native Americans, they often found themselves called in to support revenue enforcement.[76] The pressure increased in summer 1875, when forty-seven soldiers with Company K of the 18th U.S. Infantry led a sweep through the upper part of the county, arresting dozens of revenue violators and chasing many others into the woods where they hid for several weeks until the annual August term of U.S. Court had passed.[77] Between July and December 1875, federal soldiers went on four raids supporting revenue enforcement, and in 1876 the pace increased, with four raids in February alone and a total of thirteen between January and August, at which time the detachment was reassigned to deal with unrest following the Hamburg Massacre.[78] In March 1876, a soldier shot a distiller who was resisting arrest, and a month later twenty-five prisoners were taken from Greenville jail to face trial in Charleston for revenue violations.[79] That year's annual term of U.S. District Court fell in August, just as the campaign to overthrow Republican rule in the state heated up, sending dozens of people—disproportionately from the mountainous end of the county—to jail for six months.[80] "This is the annual raid, which is made through our mountain section preparatory to the session of the United States Court, which sits in August," observed the local newspaper in July 1875. "In many cases the parties accused have taken to the woods, where they expect to remain until the approaching term of court is over."[81] For those who had resisted Confederate detachments scouring the countryside for deserters during the war and endured the chaos that followed its end, seeking refuge from federal troops in mountain coves more than a decade later must have seemed a bitter pill to swallow.

The Republican Party always had a tough row to hoe in the South. Democrats understood early on that if they could convince poorer whites, who had never really gained much from slavery, that the Democrats still better represented their interests than their adversaries did, they could fatally weaken the Republicans. We have long been accustomed to think of South Carolina as a sort of showcase for the Republican Party during Reconstruction. The rice and cotton plantations of the coastal plain and lower Piedmont produced black majorities in many districts of the state. This fact became politically salient with emancipation and the mobilization of freedpeople. As W.E.B. Du Bois pointed out in *Black Reconstruction*, "South Carolina has always been pointed to as the typical Reconstruction state."[82] Yet this natural interest in understanding how African Americans wielded political power when they had the opportunity has tended to obscure the process of Reconstruction in those other parts of the state where whites had a majority and used it ruthlessly to curtail the possibilities for freedpeople to transform their world. In these places, much more characteristic of the South as a whole, Republicans had to work harder to walk the fine line between giving enough to their black supporters but also not alienating the nonslaveholding whites who were the other half of their natural constituency.

In some states of the South, there was a critical mass of anti-Confederate white Southerners who could form the core of a durable Republican electorate. This was never the case in South Carolina, where the mountains that harbored Unionists who could become Republicans were but a fringe along the northern edge of the state and where no single county was dominated by mountain people. In these places, in a perfect world, the Republicans would have pursued policies that won the support of landless whites and small farmers in the mountains, wage workers and modernizers in the city, and freedpeople in the plantation districts. Instead, in Greenville County anyway, the Republican Party found itself too oriented on the town of Greenville, partly because of that town's rapid growth in the fifteen years after the war. The policies it pursued, while helpful to city dwellers, only reduced Republican support among mountain whites. A national policy on revenue enforcement served to further alienate would-be mountain Republicans and intensify intracounty factionalism within the party. As a result, the Republicans had little to offer whites in the mountains. And although these mountain people were never happy in a Democratic Party dominated by planters, they followed along as the path of least resistance, just like the creeks flowing down from their steep valleys into the slow-moving rivers of the plantation belt.

Notes

1. McKinney, *Southern Mountain Republicans*, 6, 44.

2. A recent study of scalawags in South Carolina says only that "White Republicans were more numerous there [in mountainous regions] than elsewhere, but white Democrats outnumbered them considerably" (Rubin, *South Carolina Scalawags*, 45).

3. In 1869, the counties of South Carolina were divided into administrative units of "townships" to facilitate local government. The area I am designating as "northern Greenville County" consists of the four northernmost townships: Cleveland, Saluda, Glassy Mountain, and Highland. For an explanation of the map, see *Greenville Southern Enterprise*, 17 March 1869. Furman University has a copy of the map, and it is available online at http://www.alpha.furman.edu/dept/history/CSPH/primary/1869Map/Mappage.htm.

4. *Greenville Enterprise and Mountaineer,* 25 October 1876 (poll locations and managers), 15 November 1876 (votes for each polling location).

5. Huff, *Greenville,* 1–2.

6. Dunaway, *First American Frontier,* 121.

7. Huff, *Greenville,* 63.

8. Dunaway, *First American Frontier,* 125–28.

9. Ibid., 87.

10. Ibid., 90.

11. Huff, *Greenville,* 99, 115–16; David, *Greenville of Old,* 10–16.

12. Dunaway, *First American Frontier,* 204.

13. Ibid., 205.

14. Ibid., 218, 206.

15. Nelson, *Iron Confederacies,* 117.

16. Huff, *Greenville,* 64, 87–88.

17. *Greenville Enterprise and Mountaineer,* 27 April 1870; De Forest, *Union Officer in the Reconstruction,* 172.

18. Ford, *Origins of Southern Radicalism,* 48.

19. Megginson, *African-American Life in South Carolina's Upper Piedmont,* 46–47; Ford, *Origins of Southern Radicalism,* 62; Nelson, *Iron Confederacies,* 116–17.

20. Huff, *Greenville,* 121; Ford, *Origins of Southern Radicalism,* 224–27.

21. Huff, *Greenville,* 181; Simkins and Woody, *South Carolina during Reconstruction,* 201.

22. United States, Bureau of the Census, *Agriculture of the United States in 1860,* 17.

23. Huff, *Greenville,* 65.

24. Burnett, "Hog Raising and Hog Driving," 102–3.

25. Ibid., 96–98.

26. Batson, *Upper Part of Greenville County,* 62; De Forest, *Union Officer in the Reconstruction,* 171.

27. United States, Bureau of the Census, 1860 Agricultural Census, South Carolina, Greenville Co., 588.

28. *Greenville Enterprise and Mountaineer,* 5 April 1876.

29. United States, Bureau of the Census, 1850 U.S. Census, South Carolina, Greenville Co., 16, 23; *Greenville Enterprise,* 4 January 1871, 5 June 1872, 26 June 1872, 13 November 1872.

30. Batson, *Upper Part of Greenville County,* 130; De Forest, *Union Officer in the Reconstruction,* 162, 172.

31. Huff, *Greenville,* 102–5.

32. Otten, "Disloyalty in the Upper Districts of South Carolina," 99–102.

33. *Greenville Enterprise and Mountaineer,* 5 April 1876.

34. Ibid., 14 February 1877.

35. Otten, "Disloyalty in the Upper Districts of South Carolina," 105–8; De Forest, *Union Officer in the Reconstruction,* 162.

36. Huff, *Greenville,* 143–44, 153.

37. De Forest, *Union Officer in the Reconstruction,* 142–43.

38. Testimony in a libel case brought in 1876 by one of Greenville County's leading white Republicans, William E. Earle, documented the guerrilla raids and bushwhacking that characterized the period between Lee's surrender in April 1865 and the establishment of the provisional government under B. F. Perry at the end of June 1865 (*Greenville Enterprise and Mountaineer*, 5 April 1876).

39. Sutherland, *Savage Conflict*, 277.

40. Lt. Col. C. S. Brown [Anderson] to Bvt. Brig. Gen. C. H. Howard, 23 October 1865, Roll 34, BRFAL-SC, RG 105 (M869); Abbott, *Freedmen's Bureau in South Carolina*, 124–25.

41. Lt. Col. C. S. Brown [Anderson] to Bvt. Brig. Gen. C. H. Howard, 23 October 1865, Roll 34, BRFAL-SC, RG 105 (M869).

42. Capt. W. E. Leighton [Greenville] to R. K. Scott, 5 March 1866, Roll 34, BRFAL-SC, RG 105 (M869).

43. Huff, *Greenville*, 142–44.

44. *Greenville Southern Enterprise*, 22 August 1867; Batson, *Upper Part of Greenville County*, 140.

45. De Forest, *Union Officer in the Reconstruction*, 141.

46. J. W. De Forest [Greenville] to Maj. Edward L. Deane, 31 August 1867, Roll 35, BRFAL, RG 105 (M869); John S. Reynolds, *Reconstruction in South Carolina*, 74.

47. State of South Carolina, *Proceedings of the Constitutional Convention of South Carolina*, 7.

48. W. F. DeKnight [Greenville] to Bvt. Maj. H. Neide, 31 March 1868, Roll 35, BRFAL, RG 105 (M869).

49. W. F. DeKnight [Greenville, Anderson] to Bvt. Maj. H Neide, 30 April 1868, Roll 35, BRFAL, RG 105 (M869).

50. W. F. DeKnight [Greenville] to Bvt. Maj. H. Neide, 31 May 1868, Roll 35, BRFAL, RG 105 (M869).

51. Carroll Neide [Greenville] to Bvt. Maj. H. Neide, 30 June 1868, Roll 36, BRFAL, RG 105 (M869).

52. *Greenville Enterprise*, 7 June 1871.

53. *Greenville Enterprise and Mountaineer*, 6 October 1876.

54. De Forest, *Union Officer in the Reconstruction*, 141.

55. *Greenville Enterprise*, 19 May 1869.

56. Bleser, *Promised Land*, 167.

57. Thornton, "Fiscal Policy and the Failure of Reconstruction," 391. The best overview of taxation during Reconstruction in South Carolina remains Simkins and Woody, *South Carolina during Reconstruction*, 147–85.

58. Huff, *Greenville*, 161–62; *Greenville Enterprise and Mountaineer*, 28 July 1875.

59. *Greenville Enterprise and Mountaineer*, 19 January 1876.

60. Ibid., 6 January 1875, 28 July 1875; Greenville County Board of County Commissioners Minute Book, 1873–1883, online at http://www.greenvillecounty.org, 37–41.

61. *Greenville Enterprise and Mountaineer*, 23 August 1876.

62. Ibid., 21 June 1876 and 28 June 1876; Greenville County Board of County Commissioners Minute Book, 1873–1883, online at http://www.greenvillecounty.org, 103.

63. Nelson, *Iron Confederacies*, 74–76, 79, 80–81.

64. State of South Carolina, *Acts and Joint Resolutions of the General Assembly*, 595 (No. 352); *Greenville Enterprise*, 18 February 1871.

65. *Greenville Enterprise*, 29 June 1870. Spartanburg County saw a similar intracounty conflict over taxation to support the construction of the Spartanburg and Union Railroad. Eelman, *Entrepreneurs in the Southern Upcountry*, 52–68.

66. *Greenville Enterprise*, 3 January 1872, 26 June 1872.

67. *Greenville Enterprise and Mountaineer*, 24 February 1875, 29 December 1875; Greenville County Board of County Commissioners Minute Book, 1873–1883, 34, 79, 119, 165.

68. Burnett, "Hog Raising and Hog Driving," 88; Huff, *Greenville*, 65.

69. Huff, *Greenville*, 65.

70. *Greenville Enterprise and Mountaineer*, 26 October 1870, 30 November 1870, 13 September 1871, 22 November 1871, 10 January 1872, 12 January 1876.

71. Ibid., 17 April 1872, 25 April 1877.

72. Ibid., 30 August 1876.

73. Wilbur R. Miller, *Revenuers and Moonshiners*, 1–6.

74. *Greenville Enterprise*, 3 May 1871, 17 January 1872.

75. Ibid., 5 June 1872.

76. Wilbur R. Miller, *Revenuers and Moonshiners*, 69–80.

77. *Greenville Enterprise and Mountaineer*, 14 July 1875.

78. Returns of Military Posts, 1800–1916, Roll 424, Greenville, S.C. (March 1866–September 1877), AGO, RG 94 (M617).

79. *Greenville Enterprise and Mountaineer*, 1 March 1876, 12 April 1876.

80. Ibid., 9 August 1876, 16 August 1876, 23 August 1876.

81. Ibid., 14 July 1875.

82. Du Bois, *Black Reconstruction*, 383.

9

Mapping Freedom's Terrain

The Political and Productive Landscapes of Wilmington, North Carolina

SUSAN EVA O'DONOVAN

On a chilly November morning in 1898, an army of rifle-toting businessmen, community leaders, recently returned veterans of the Spanish-American war, Red Shirts, and others interested in pinning their futures to an increasingly virulent racism, spilled into the streets of Wilmington, North Carolina, with mayhem and possibly murder on their minds. Having only days before seized back control at the polls from a four-year-old coalition of Populists and Republicans, the mob marched forward determined to secure their newly won grip on government by destroying or driving away what remained of their political opponents. From a white supremacist's perspective, their mission was nothing less than the last critical phase of a drawn-out and long-awaited counterrevolution.[1]

Their victims remembered something quite different. In their recollections, what unfolded on 10 November 1898, was one of the most concentrated moments of racial terror to take place on American soil. Before night fell, somewhere between nine and one hundred black citizens lost their lives, murdered by roving bands of thugs, victims of what one witness later recalled as "internecine street fighting." One of the nation's few black-owned and operated daily newspapers lay in ashes; its editor, Alex Manly, on the run. In following days, Wilmington's Democrats and their various allies would escort leading Republicans and Populists to the edge of town, forcibly evicting them with instructions that they never come back. Some were advised to leave the state. Thousands of the radical rank and file did not wait for their own invitations. Frightened by the violence that had swept the city and by the mobs that continued to patrol its streets, African Americans especially hurried to pack up their belongings and abandon Wilmington for new and hopefully safer homes.

It was an event and an exodus that dramatically remade the city's public and political face. Victorious white supremacists demanded and received the resignations of the mayor, his aldermen, the chief of police, the deputy sheriff, crack companies of black firemen, and the entire city police force—then swiftly replaced the latter with 250 "special policemen, chosen from the ranks of reputable white citizens." Approximately 80 percent of the city's barbershops and 90 percent of its eating establishments—businesses that had been owned and operated by black entrepreneurs—closed their doors virtually overnight, and working-class white men vied for what had previously been black men's jobs, soon discovering that most of their new bosses planned to pay them no more than a black man's wage. With their lives abruptly attenuated, those African Americans who chose or had no choice but to stay in the city sought safety in numbers. Closing ranks in the most literal way, they transformed the once booming and biracial midcity neighborhood of Brooklyn into a predominately black urban space. Jim Crow had come to roost in Wilmington, North Carolina.[2]

By nearly any measure, the Democrats' campaign to wrench control from their biracial and radical opponents was an unqualified success. Black voting turn-out plummeted, and with it black representation at all levels of local government. Public offices that had been occupied by a diverse mix of Populists, Republicans, and African Americans became the province of conservative white men. So too did a number of Wilmington's jobs, as employers hurried to replace black working men with white. But despite the velocity at which the final engagement unfolded, the Democrats' war had been a very long and drawn-out campaign. Indeed, North Carolina and New Hanover County's conservative loyalists had worked for more than thirty years—a generation—to reclaim political, economic, and civic authority. Attempts to dislodge Wilmington's robust black and white coalitions had been launched in the mid-1860s when Democrats and former Confederate officials—scarcely recovered from their wartime losses—mobilized once again, this time to turn back a rising Republican tide. Though beat back in 1868 by armed and angry ex-slaves who refused to relinquish any of freedom's gains, conservatives refused to give up. In following years, they would launch new and creative initiatives: artfully carving the heart of the city into three carefully designed electoral precincts, and later, hacking New Hanover County in half, hoping in each instance to dilute radical influence by reconfiguring the political landscape.[3]

But when a powerful Fusionist movement of Populists, Republicans, and laborers of both races won control of Wilmington and the state in 1894, North

Carolina's social and political conservatives plotted a much more malevolent coup, one that made up in bigotry what it lacked in legality. Pulling out all stops, and assisted by such New South luminaries as South Carolina's "Pitchfork" Ben Tillman, the state's Democratic leaders deployed every imaginable rhetorical tool to pry the attention of poor and wage-working white men away from the grinding problems of political economy and toward a carefully orchestrated "problem" of race. Leaving few opportunities unexploited, a rising generation of white supremacists articulated and then enacted a violently exclusionary civic and social vision. Filling the state's conservative press with savage cartoons that pilloried black people as little more than vicious animals, distorted their daily activities into base crime, and painted white women—and not incidentally, Lady Liberty—as innocent victims of a freedom gone terribly wrong. Good government, by which supporters meant white and middle-class government, became the Democrats' rallying cry. Bullets became the means of its achievement.[4]

Democrats and their allies had to work desperately hard to win back control of a city that, until the Confederate surrender, had been the stronghold of planters and slaveholders. This essay, and the larger project of which it is a piece, is an attempt to answer what is still an open question: what was it about Wilmington and its black citizens that made it such a difficult place to "redeem"? Why did it require years and years of craft, guile, deceit, and eventually outright violence on the part of white supremacists to accomplish what their counterparts elsewhere in the former Confederacy had done in much shorter periods of time? Numbers, which tend to be the fallback explanation for what little has been written on the genesis of the Wilmington riot, do not account for the whole of the story.[5]

To be sure, the black people of North Carolina's most prominent seaboard city had numbers in abundance, averaging a 60 percent majority up to the eve of the 1898 massacre.[6] But as countless black Southerners discovered in the years following full freedom, numerical advantage was no guarantor of social, political, or economic success. Take the case of black southwest Georgians, for example. Occupying a region characterized by high concentrations first of slaves and then of freedpeople, a place where black women and men approached or surpassed 70 percent of the population in some counties, radical Republicanism died an early and violent death. Hamstrung by the baneful and lingering effects of a late-blooming slavery on one of the nation's last antebellum cotton frontiers, their ability to mobilize effectively had been compromised from the first moment of freedom. Despite an overwhelming presence at the polls and in the fields surrounding those polls, black southwest Georgians' radical insurgency had passed its prime as early as the eve of the 1868 presidential election. It was a momentum they would not recover until the last third of the twentieth century.[7]

Nor does it appear that the black residents of Wilmington, the vast majority of whom made their living on the city's docks or in its naval stores sector, could claim the kind of industrial knowledge that transformed Louisiana's sugar parishes into one of the most robust radical strongholds of the post–Civil War era. There, where black people as slaves had developed an intimate knowledge of cane, about how to turn its juice into valuable sugar, and above all about how to leverage the plant's peculiar vulnerabilities to frost and rot, free workers not only squeezed thirty years of political ascendancy away from their old masters but also high monthly or quarterly cash wages. So successful were sugar's workers at tipping the balance of power toward black people's hands that they frightened more than a few of the region's ex-slaveholders into organizing overseas shopping expeditions, efforts that were aimed at recruiting a new and hopefully more biddable labor force. This was a freedom virtually unheard of among those hundreds of thousands across the plantation belt who would continue to grow cotton or tobacco on shares until well into the twentieth century. This was also a freedom that exposes the kind of power that can accrue to those familiar with all phases of an industrial process, including what happens to raw materials when allowed to lay overlong in a field.[8]

This type of strength was in exceedingly short supply in Wilmington, North Carolina, where most African Americans—and especially voting-aged men—made their living as unskilled laborers. Yet somehow the African American residents of Wilmington managed to hold ex-slaveholders and employers at bay for a generation, an astonishing achievement in the history of the post–Civil War nation. After all, this was an age characterized by intensifying assaults on the nation's workers, and especially on those who were of African descent, as conservative forces relentlessly if unevenly whittled away at laborers' political, civil, and social rights.[9] A close examination of the little-used records of the Freedman's Savings and Trust Company suggests, however, what it was about the black residents of the lower Cape Fear, and in particular their histories as slaves, that helps to explain why Wilmington's white landed and business classes had to work so terribly hard to win back what had once been their city. For if those clerks and the records they left can be believed, the black people of Wilmington exited bondage armed with an enviable array of social and institutional resources: attributes not shared by the vast majority of the nation's ex-slaves and attributes that could serve them as both shield and sword in a long-fought struggle over freedom's meanings.

Incorporated by an act of Congress in 1865 for the benefit of the nation's ex-slaves, the Freedman's Bank, as the Savings and Trust Company came to be known, opened and operated thirty-three branches before its untimely demise in 1874. Thirty of those banks were scattered throughout the former slaveholding states, and one of them was located in Wilmington, North Carolina. Although the bulk of the bank's records vanished after the institution failed, those that remain—the vast majority of which are the signature books—provide a useful vantage point from which to explore black people's lives in slavery and freedom. For when something on the order of 90,000 to 100,000 depositors opened their accounts, bank officials required them to provide a wealth of personal information, including their ages, complexions, places and dates of birth, and the names, locations, and occupations of close kin. Clerks also generally recorded the names of former owners as well as those of current employers, and some editions of the bank's signature books solicited information about the depositor's military service and the units they served in.

In many cases the bank's clerks and cashiers, a number of whom were themselves African American, also included additional and unsolicited information. Fleshing out in text the personal stories of the women and men who came before them, the bank's representatives developed what amounted to an extensive collection of mini-autobiographies for each new account holder. Clerks pinned to their pages the pasts of families that had been pulled apart and swept away by a massive antebellum migration. They recorded the horrors and heartaches of depositors who could not recall in freedom the names of mothers, fathers, sisters, and brothers last seen in slavery, and of slave owners who denied the rights of enslaved parents by renaming their children at the moment of purchase. Clerks often captured the physical when they augmented what were standard inquiries about age and complexion with detailed descriptions of infirmities, speech impediments, disfigurements, and rough amputations. A few, like the attentive clerk who kept the records at the Tallahassee, Florida, branch of the bank sometimes even jotted down descriptions of customers' clothes. The results, in many cases, open a window onto black people's lives unmatched in its scope, scale, and detail by any other extant source. (For an example of a register page, see figure 9.1.) Thanks to attentive and engaged clerks, we know now, for example, that in freedom at least, James Pearson combed his slightly grey hair up from his forehead; that Henry Hall, who had been born in Abbeville, South Carolina, was sold

100.
Record for Bateman Pinckney

No. of Application, 100
Date, May 24. 1867
~~Name of Master,~~ Always lived in Talla-
~~Name of Mistress,~~ hassee
~~Plantation,~~
~~Height~~ Age and Complexion, light brown
dead Father or Ellen Mother? Married?
Name of Children,
Regiment and Company,
Place of Birth, Tallahassee Fla
Residence, do
Occupation, goes to School
REMARKS, Father's name Jones — Bros & Sisters
Jo. Rachel — Cornelia & Lewis (dead)

Signature,

101.
Record for Jane Hunter

No. of Application, 101.
Date, May 24. 1867.
~~Name of Master,~~ Brought from Kentucky
~~Name of Mistress,~~ when a child
~~Plantation,~~ Lived in Bardstown Ky
~~Height~~ Age and Complexion, About 42 Dark Brown
dead Father or died Mother? Married? Charles Hunter
Name of Children, Catherine 25 yrs wife of John [illegible]
Regiment and Company, [illegible] 9 yrs. Davy about 14 yrs. Lucy 7 yrs
Place of Birth, Bardstown Ky
Residence, Near the Depot Tallahassee
Occupation, Washerwoman.
REMARKS, Father Charles [illegible] Mother
Rachel both died in Ky. Sister ~~Nancy~~ Sarah at Bardstown Ky
Has not heard from sister in 8 or 9 years
Bro. ~~Charles~~ George died young — Sisters Catherine & Margaret &
Elizabeth & Nancy & Louisa Maria — all dead —
Her sister **Catherine** has a son Charles — who is in
San Antonio Texas — Heard from him about a month
ago —
Signature, Jane his X mark Hunter
Daughter Catharine in Winchester Va.
other children at home
Her husband is a blacksmith at Depot.

102.
Record for Milly Hill

No. of Application, 102
Date, May 24. 1867
~~Name of Master,~~ Came from E Shore Md. 21 yrs.
~~Name of Mistress,~~ ago
~~Plantation,~~
~~Height~~ Age and Complexion, 24 yrs of age light Brown
dead Father or Harriet Hooper Mother? Married? Curtis Hill
Name of Children, Augustus 11 yrs old. Cornelius 9 yrs.
Regiment and Company,
Place of Birth, East Shore, Maryland,
Residence, on Main St near Depot Tallahassee Fla.
Occupation,
REMARKS, Daughter Ellen died in 1862 Margaret died
1867 — Father's name Edw Bridge — Sister Maria
Grice living — brothers Robt Robinson & Chas Hooper

Signature, Milly her X mark Hill

103.
Record for Alfred Lawrence

No. of Application, 103
Date, May 25th 1867
~~Name of Master,~~ Came from Cass Co Ga to
~~Name of Mistress,~~ Tallahassee in 16th Jan 186[illegible]
~~Plantation,~~
~~Height~~ Age and Complexion, About 20 yrs of age dark [illegible]
dead Father or dead Mother? ~~Married?~~
Name of Children,
Regiment and Company,
Place of Birth, Cass Co Ga.
Residence, near McClark's Tallahassee Fla.
Occupation, laborer for the City
REMARKS, father's name Wm Lawrence
went to Liberia about 12 yrs ago & supposed to be dead
Mother's Celia Millmer — brothers Aleck & Wm — dead
Spencer, Hannah & Emily —

Signature, Alfred his X mark Lawrence

Figure 9.1. Entries 100–103, Tallahassee, Fla., Freedman's Bank, Roll 5 (M816).

several times before coming to rest in Florida; and that planters' voracious appetite for enslaved labor had scattered Kate Bavis's family from Georgia to Texas.[10]

Seldom did the cashiers at the Wilmington branch of the bank provide similar details about those who came before them. Whether pressed for time (the bank's announced hours ran from 6:00 to 8:00 p.m. on Saturday nights) or simply not as compelled as were other clerks by the particularities of their customers' lives, B. C. Bryan, Jno. H. Smyth, and their colleagues generally resisted the temptation to expand their entries with unsolicited information. Most often, they kept their accounts to the bare minimum, recording only what was explicitly required: names, ages, addresses, occupations, and so forth, and only once in a while straying away from requisite just long enough to note the amount of a customer's deposit. Nevertheless, in committing to paper those parts of their clients' lives deemed most essential by the bank's managers, the information provided by the Wilmington clerks suggests something of what it was that made the black women and men of New Hanover County such a formidable social and political force.[11]

First and foremost, the information that can be extracted from the entries contained in the extant Wilmington signature books confirms what historians have already surmised: the black people of the lower Cape Fear and its city generally made their living as unskilled or underskilled workers. Of the 592 women and men who dictated a part of their life stories to one of the clerks, 112 or nearly 20 percent described themselves simply as "laborer[s]." Half that many (sixty-four women and two men) called themselves "housekeepers," twenty-five more (fifteen women and ten men) "work[ed]" or "work[ed] out," and two were by their own admission, "m[e]n of all work." Apparently seeing important distinctions between one kind of unskilled labor and another (differences historians ought likewise to take seriously), other applicants were more forthcoming about what it was they did to earn their daily subsistence. For instance, Dennis Wright, a twenty-year-old who opened an account on 10 June 1873, made a living as a "laborer at a saw mill." Edward Mears labored "in Guano." Seventy-year–old Harry Bernard, who opened an account in May 1873, wanted to be sure that the clerk understood that while he was a "laborer," he performed his chores "in [a] store."[12] Railroad employees Augustus Davis, Silas Brown, Rosser McIntosh, and Ephriam Smith also felt compelled to impress on the clerk that they were not simply jacks of undifferentiated trades but rather practitioners of specific, if low-skill, industries. In the case of these four men, that meant going to work every day at one of the three major railroads that terminated on the eastern shore of the Cape Fear River.[13]

Not all black depositors made their living performing menial work. Again, as historians of the city have acknowledged, the black women and men who deposited their money at the Wilmington branch of the Freedman's Bank figured into all sectors of the local economy. Although never a large part of the city's population (slightly more than 14 percent of the depositors claimed some kind of skill), they nevertheless performed services critical to the economic life of the city: fashioning the barrels in which manufacturers shipped turpentine and resin abroad, crafting wheels, building ships, making shoes, and constructing and reconstructing the wharves that ran the length of the city. Black women and men also baked breads and pastries, whipped together confections, styled hair, shined shoes, caught fish, laid bricks, sewed clothes, maintained machinery, and in at least one case, upholstered chairs. Samuel Gardner hoisted cargo on the wharf, a job that most likely required him and the men who earned their living as stevedores to have a practical knowledge of applied physics. Six depositors taught school. John W. Moore served as a post office clerk, the aforementioned and Virginia-born Jno. Smyth worked as one of the cashiers at the "F. S. and T. Co.," and twenty-two-year-old George Batson had already begun to learn the tinner's trade when he opened account number 1234 in September 1869.[14] Others operated their own businesses, inserting themselves into the heart of Wilmington's bustling commercial life as shopkeepers, merchants, barbers, grocers, hucksters, and drummers. Twenty-six-year-old Harriet Quince, for example, kept a stall at the town market, joining those who made their living selling ice cream, ground peas, and various "goods," and merchants Morris S. Robbins and W. B. Turlingland both operated their own stores.[15]

A number of the more highly skilled and entrepreneurial of Wilmington's black residents were able to translate their economic pursuits into civil and political power. Certainly that was the case with Alex Manly, who used the newspaper he owned and edited to advance a biracial vision of the post–Civil War nation, one that demanded that black women deserved the same kind of respect given to white women, and one that would eventually inflame North Carolina's white conservatives. James Lowery, who produced "carriages, buggies, wagons, carts, & drays" at his shop on the corner of Third and Princess streets, and who partnered with a Maryland carriage maker, used his business as a springboard into city government and onto the board of aldermen, offering an equally as public statement about the role of black people in national life.[16] So too did George W. Price Jr., who made his money selling "Farm[s] of Forty Acres"—language guaranteed to resonate with one of black Southerners' most deeply held dreams—and who served in numerous elective and appointed capacities, including the state senate and house of representatives in the early 1870s and as a customs official in the 1880s.[17]

But as historians have come in recent years to acknowledge, power resides in many locations, not all of them associated with the more conventional sites of civil and political life. Even in the grossly inequitable world of antebellum slavery, scholars now know that power could be found in the hands of those who were paraded across the nation's auction blocks, who delivered free people's babies, and the fugitives who bided their time in the dank interiors of the South's county jails.[18] Thus in a bustling seaport city like Wilmington, where trains from the interior clattered in on a "double daily" or more basis, where ships from abroad jockeyed for position along its crowded riverfront, and where resort beaches began in the last third of the century to attract inland vacationers seeking relief from summertime heat, power of varying degrees also accrued to those who occupied the lowest rungs on the region's social and economic ladders.[19] Indeed, as Henry Box Brown and others observed over and again in their antebellum narratives of bondage and freedom, even the least of the nation's people could strengthen their hand simply by keeping their eyes and ears open. It was in running his master's errands, Brown explained, that he had "acquire[d] some little knowledge of what was going on" in the world around him, information that he and men like Charles Ball would later deploy to enact their own liberation.[20] Such comings and goings, contacts and conversations, returned to black Southerners—in freedom as well as in slavery—precisely the kind of power that conservative white Southerners wanted desperately to deny them. As Donna Haraway noted of a later revolution in the technologies of knowledge, the discursive opportunities that opened up through travel and work had "serious potential for changing the rules of the game."[21] Nowhere was this more true than in post–Civil War Wilmington. Perched as it was between hinterland and sea, and where a continuous flow of products and people stitched the city into an Atlantic-sized space, just about any form of urban employment could conceivably tip the balance of power black people's way: so long, of course, as Jim Crow stayed away.[22]

As North Carolina's primary port, Wilmington had long been a commercial entrepôt. With the introduction of railroads, the first of which appeared in the 1840s, the town grew in size and importance, out-pacing its sister ports to the north, New Bern and Washington. Though rocked, like the entire Confederacy, by war and defeat, Wilmington quickly recovered. By the early 1870s, fertilizer plants had sprung up on the outskirts of town, crops of raw cotton sluiced down the Cape Fear River, and three major rail lines connected Wilmington to Georgia and Tennessee through South Carolina, to the mountains of west North Carolina, and northward to Richmond, Washington, D.C., and the rest of the nation. It was a vast traffic: until 1892, all north-south rail traffic passed through Wilmington.

Ships out of Old and New World ports routinely called at the docks. In 1880, for example, vessels from more than thirty-one nations entered the port at Wilmington. It was a flotilla that included eight ships from Brazil, seven from Belgium, fifty-four from Scotland, nine from Portugal, and twenty from the British West Indies. International traffic continued unabated. Five years later, foreign vessels accounted for more than 96 percent of the total tonnage registered by the Wilmington customs officials. Nor were they alone. Other ships served on the river, making regular trips as far inland as Fayetteville, or engaged in the coastwise trade, conveying cargoes to and from Baltimore, Savannah, New York, Philadelphia, and Boston.

Many of the city's industries cultivated connections with particular segments of these overseas and domestic markets. The Navassa Guano Company, which turned out vast quantities of sulphuric and muriatic acid at its plants in nearby Brunswick County, depended heavily, for instance, on regular shipments of phosphate from Navassa Island in the West Indies. The Champion Compress, next door to the Wilmington and Weldon Railroad yard, packed and loaded upward of 250,000 bales of cotton every year for the factories at "Liverpool, Bremen and Ghent." On the other side of town, the Kidder Lumber Company dressed and shipped tons of lumber for a South

Figure 9.2. Vessels loading cotton, 1875. Courtesy of the Dr. Robert M. Fales Collection, Slide No. 916, New Hanover County Public Library.

American market, doing a business that helped to net Wilmington almost $240,000,000 in lumber revenues alone in 1885. In the words of one observer, Wilmington's port often presented "a forest" of foreign and domestic masts.[23]

The black women and men of Wilmington played key roles in these lively processes of local and global exchange. The generally unskilled or slightly skilled who constituted the majority of the city's African American population constituted the majority of those employed by the turpentine, fertilizer, and lumber companies that made their headquarters along Front Street and whose plants jutted into the river to meet seagoing ships. In turn, these three industries were Wilmington's biggest employers in 1880, with cotton compresses coming in a close fourth. In all of these industries, black workers interfaced between the local and global: rolling hogsheads of turpentine onto the decks of seagoing sloops and shepherding logs from inland forests through the blades that hummed at Kidder's mill and into the holds of waiting ships.[24] Other African Americans serviced the city's industrial and Atlantic commerce as teamsters, draymen, and coachmen, filling the streets with the clutter of carriages, carts, wagons, and buggies that conveyed passengers and products from rail to wharf and back again. Black workers were especially visible along the docks and railroads. Constituting a significant proportion of those who opened accounts at the Freedman's Bank—those who worked on the wharves and rails outnumbered by a factor of two women who cooked and men who farmed—they inserted themselves directly into the global economy. They hoisted cargos from deck to dock; served on the water as deckhands, pilots, cooks, and firemen; and labored on the lines and in the yards of the three railway companies that served post–Civil War Wilmington. Many of them, including Benjamin Aman and John Allen Satathe, both seagoing watchmen who lived aboard ship, and James Davis, a railroad hand who claimed to live in three counties concurrently, conducted their lives in near perpetual motion.[25]

No less important were all those individuals who labored in Wilmington's shops, on its streets, and in private kitchens and liveries. Cogs of a different sort in what amounted to a massive transnational wheel, they fetched and carried, peddled soup, picked rags, scrubbed dirty linens, beat dust from rugs, nursed white people's babies, and otherwise attended to the myriad needs of both residents and visitors. While jobs of this order were not specific to Wilmington's transatlantic and coastwise economies, they nonetheless pushed the vast majority of the city's black residents out into the streets. The daughter of a Wilmington businessman, Julia Bowden, for instance, thought nothing of taking "Fanny, the colored girl, with me, to wait on me," when she joined an excursion up the Cape Fear River, or of dispatching a male house servant named Louis to the market to purchase a bouquet of flowers.[26] The aptly named Charles Wagoner who drove a baggage wagon—perhaps for one of Wilmington's several hotels—spent an even greater part of his time out and about on business, criss-crossing through town hauling for whoever needed his services.[27]

The black people of Wilmington worked hard in the years following the Civil War, but they rarely worked alone. Work places and public places were not empty places, nor were they silent places. Whether shifting goods from wagons to wharves to the decks of seagoing ships or dickering with a stranger over the price of a meal, Wilmington's black citizens were part and parcel of an always changing multicultural, multilingual, and multinational throng. It was a kaleidoscopic population that might include at any one time farmers in from the fields, out-of-town railroad hands, vacationers headed to the beach, delegates to locally held conventions, drummers out of Chicago, German and Jamaican immigrants, Algerian "wood choppers" such as a group who arrived via Trinidad, and ships' crews in port from Ireland, Uruguay, and French West Africa. Indeed so consistent was some of this traffic that the Portuguese-born and raised sailor, Frank Silva, opened his own account at the Freedman's Bank—never mind that he expected to continue to make his home "on the sea."[28]

Pre-1898 residential patterns only added to the polychromatic liquidity—and to the political possibilities inherent in such an environment. For until Jim Crow's violent arrival, Wilmington retained much of its pre–Civil War look, a period when as a matter of practice slaves lived intermixed with their masters and when racially based segregation was a thing of the future. Take for instance, the 313 blue-collar workers who opened accounts at the Wilmington branch of the Freedman's Bank. It seems from the residential coordinates that 133 of them provided the clerks that the city's unskilled laborers scattered their homes throughout the city. (See figure 9.3.) Most of Wilmington's industries, after all, hugged the bank of the river, while a rectangular business district lay sprawled across Market Street between Water and 4th. This meant that Edward Jones, who operated a ferry and who lived on Dock between 9th and 10th, had at the very least a nine-block commute between his place of residence and the closest possible place of employment. If he strode by the most direct route to the river (due west), it was a trip that would take him past the Catholic Church, a string of dry good and wholesale stores, the city ice house, cigar and liquor stores, a number of saloons (including the Acme, which advertised "everything first class"),

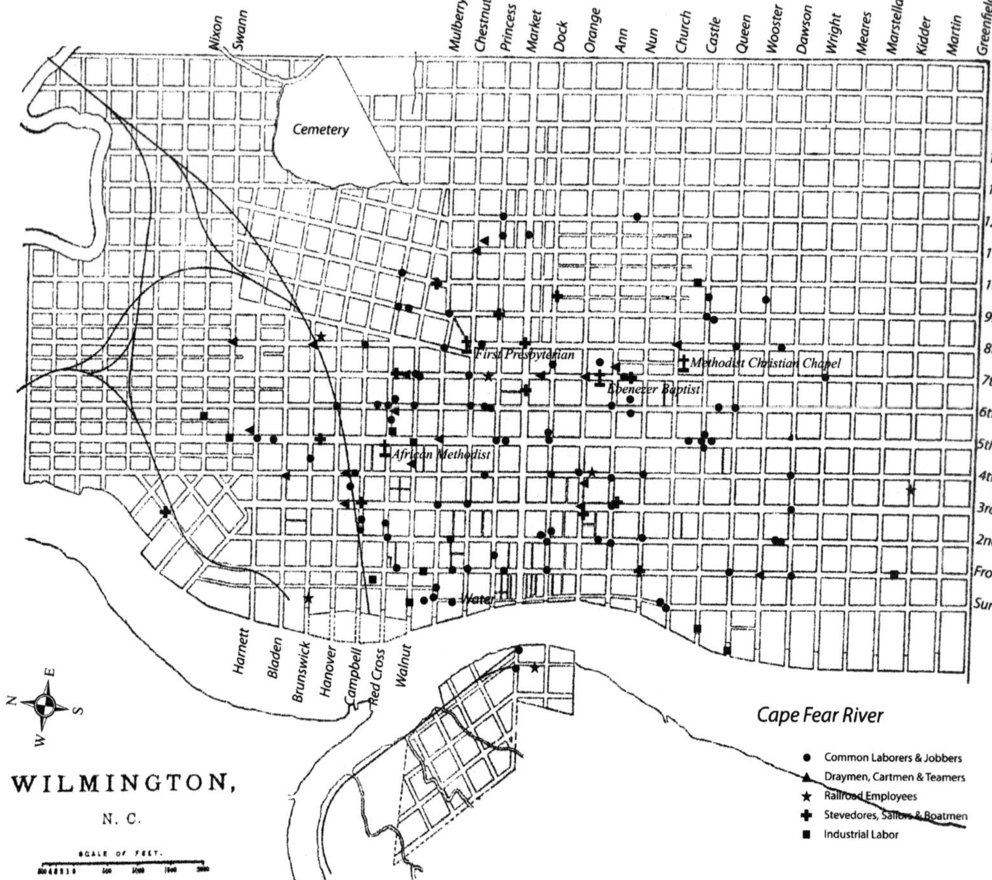

Figure 9.3. Map of residential patterns of Wilmington's blue collar workers.

the Colored Odd Fellows Hall, a "stove and cord wood dock," and a massive grist mill before coming to a stop at the river. He would even pass by the entrance to the Freedman's Bank building, which stood directly across the street from the Seaman's Home. It was hardly a trip that would be devoid of people.[29]

The residential patterns of Wilmington's common laborers, sailors, and turpentine hands were not out of the ordinary. Though teachers, preachers, and government officials had a tendency to cluster in the proximity of the black Methodist and Baptist churches, information gleaned from the Freedman's Bank signature books and augmented by business directories suggests that most of the city's black people located their homes throughout the city.[30] Thus like Edward Jones who had to steer his way through the city's industrial and commercial sectors in order to reach the river on which he made his living, James Caraway, co-owner of a barber shop located in the basement of Purcell House, a popular hotel located in the heart of the city's business district, lived three and a half blocks away on 2nd between Mulberry and Walnut. His partner, Charles E. Cleapor, lived further east on 7th, near Red Cross. It was a location that, depending on his choice of route, might take Cleapor past the Wilmington and Weldon Railroad freight yards, a flour and hominy mill, the back side of the "Mariner's Saloon," some abandoned tenement houses, at least two boarding homes, a number of groceries and dry good concerns, a billiards saloon, and the First National Bank of Wilmington. Lewis Green walked the opposite direction. A brakeman on one of the railway lines, Green lived on 4th near the corner with Orange. It was a location that required him to walk either due north, if he expected to meet the train at the passenger station at 8th and Brunswick, or northeast, if he routinely boarded at the rail yards on the river.[31]

All this public and industrial mixing had deeply political implications. For in sharing the city's streets, distilleries, mills, and docks—to say nothing of its saloons, brothels, and shops—with the polyglot population common to seaside and port cities, the black residents of Wilmington were embedded in and an embodiment of what Christopher Bayly calls "an information order": those systems of knowledge creation, collection, and diffusion that are themselves social and historical formations. More popularly known as grapevine telegraphs, such systems of informal contact, conversation, and exchange have long been used by oppressed and subordinate people to advance their own interests.[32] Charles Ball and Henry Box Brown surely did, when they turned words into routes out of bondage. So too did Wilmington's black women and men.

Indeed, Wilmington's black residents had long capitalized on the admittedly uneven, and often incomplete, dribbles of news that came their way via ocean, rail, or passing stranger. It was not by happenstance, for example, that several hundred copies of David Walker's fiery and subversive *Appeal* made landfall at Wilmington in late 1830, arriving in the possession of a sailor before materializing in the hands of a slave named Jacob who was subsequently sold out of state for having committed the "offense of distributing seditious" literature. Nor was it necessarily happenstance that a people who had been associated in slavery with the colorful Jonkonnu festivals—a West Indian ritual of social subversion—also organized one of the earliest chapters of the Union League to appear in the former Confederacy and in July 1865 provided a platform from which Wilmington's ex-slaves demanded equal representation on

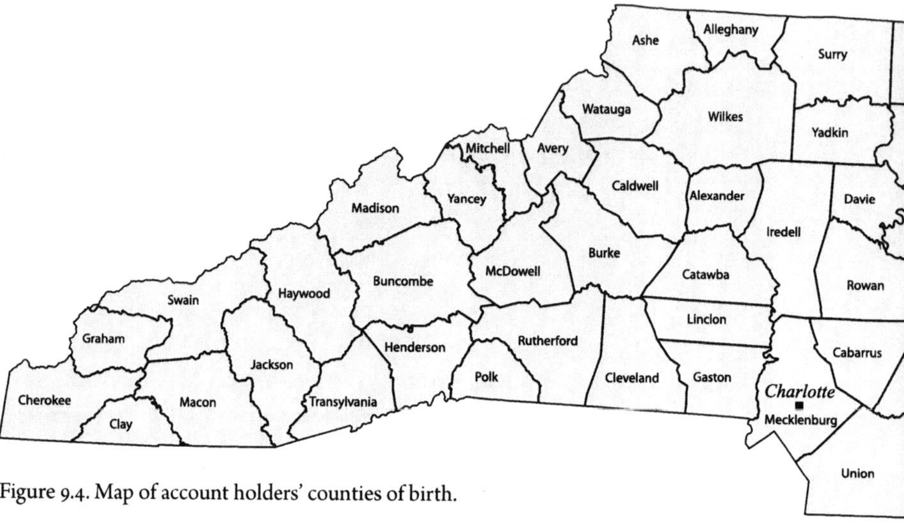

Figure 9.4. Map of account holders' counties of birth.

the local police force. Continuing in freedom to tap into and act on what Robert Darnton calls "public noises"—including those emanating out of the West Indies—the city's black citizens assembled themselves into all manner of clubs, benevolent societies, political organizations, protective associations, and in 1882, a railroad promotion and construction company. By 1886, labor unions, too, began to appear, the first of which was the work of female domestics who, tired of low pay and long days, attached themselves to the Knights of Labor, an organization that had entered the eastern half of North Carolina through Wilmington's harbor.[33]

Casual contacts and conversations with out-of-town visitors and strangers clearly mattered, arming the black people of Wilmington with invaluable alliances and ideas that they used initially to destabilize slaveholders' terrain and then later, to explore and expand freedom's potentials. But what one said or saw or surmised was not all that mattered. Friendships and families counted too, for who knew better than an ex-slave the political possibilities represented by close and trustworthy kin. As both Steven Hahn and Joseph C. Miller have recently observed, physical space had its place, but what mattered more as black people jockeyed for advantage in a dramatically inequitable world was often their conceptual location within generations, lineages, clans, and families. In fact, Hahn deems what Miller calls "relationally constructed place[s]" foundational not only to black Southerners' efforts to deflect the worst of slaveholders' impositions but also to their ability to advance as a people in freedom. Families especially, Hahn argues, constituted ex-slaves' "central weapons"—the sinews that gave structure and strength to their "earliest collective activities and formal organizations," their first line of defense.[34]

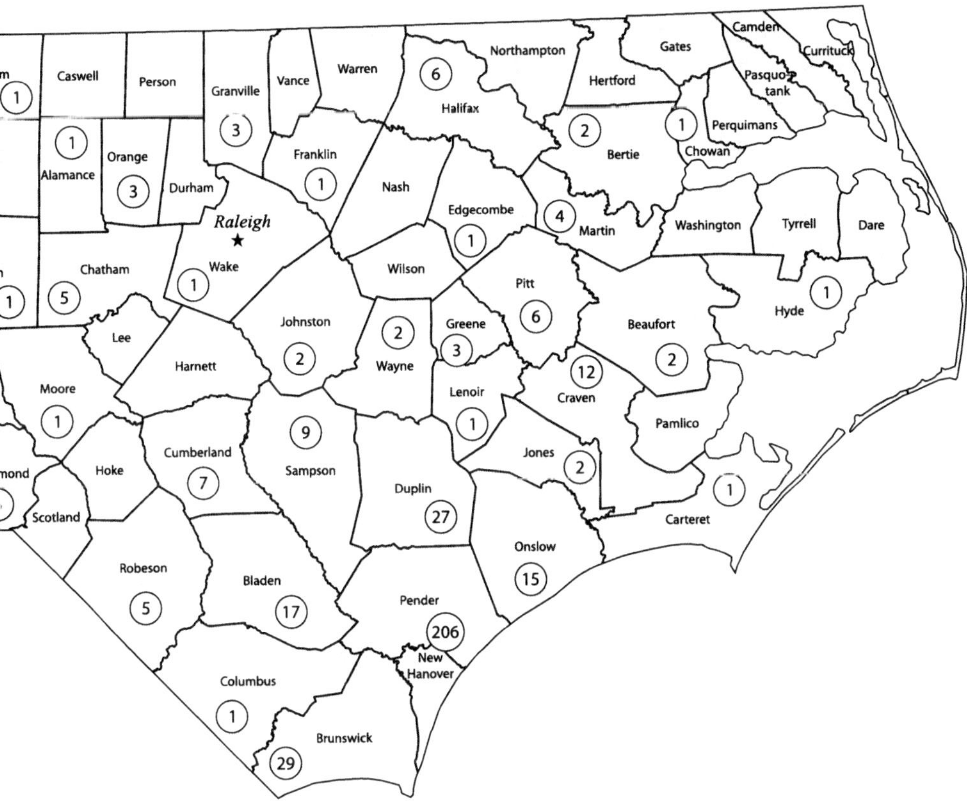

Families, it turns out from examining the Freedman's Bank records, were something that the black women and men of Wilmington had in surprising abundance. Indeed, those who opened accounts at the bank on Dock Street stand out in a world in which a violent national expansion had separated husbands from wives and orphaned hundreds of thousands of children. Located at neither end but rather off to the side of a massive forced migration that moved an estimated two million women and men across state lines and shifted the locus of American slavery from southern Virginia to western Georgia, the vast majority of black Wilmingtonians grew up and came of age in close proximity to their natal homes.[35] Unlike the former slaves who deposited their money at the Little Rock, Arkansas, branch of the Freedman's Bank—a population who traced their birth places back to no fewer than 17 states, 142 counties, and three foreign lands—500 of the 584 whose names appear in the Wilmington registers had been born and raised in North Carolina.[36] Of those who provided the places of birth, more than a third (206) had come into the world in New Hanover County. (See figure 9.4.) Another 20 percent had been born in the lower Cape Fear area, tracing their roots to the adjacent counties of Brunswick, Columbus, Bladen, Sampson, Duplin, and Onslow.[37] With the exception of Allen Calhoun who informed the clerk that he had been born somewhere near the mountains and near Tennessee, everyone else who claimed North Carolinian nativity had generally been born east of the piedmont.

Such intense localism meant that the black women and men of Wilmington and lower Cape Fear had been generally spared the arduous process of domestic reconstruction that consumed the resources of so many of the nation's ex-slaves. Rather than spending months or, as was more often the case, years reassembling families that had been torn asunder in slavery and then war, the overwhelming majority of those who opened accounts at the Wilmington branch of the Freedman's Bank not only knew the names and fates of their closest relatives: they knew where to find them.[38] Amanda Jones certainly did. In 1873, three generations of her family—all of them natives of Wilmington—lived together at the corner of Castle and 9th streets: Amanda, her sixty-three-year–old father Jupiter, her husband William, and their five young daughters—Mary, Fanny, Alice, Maggie, and Carrie.[39] Seventy-one-year-old wharf builder Joseph Jones likewise lived in the midst of an extended family. In fact, when he and his wife Polly opened an account in a city that Joseph had come to as a small child, the couple stipulated that whatever they managed to accumulate by the time they died should be held in trust by their son Emanuel for the benefit of their granddaughters, Margaret and Paulina.[40] The Tuckers were equally as well established. Henry Tucker Sr., a minister, had been born in Wilmington in 1819, and there he remained: growing up, marrying, and eventually raising a family, several of whom like their father would eventually open their own accounts at the Dock Street branch of the Freedman's Bank.[41]

The preexistence of such extensive domestic connections were more than a simple novelty. As Hahn and others have argued, bonds of marriage and birth greatly enhanced black people's ability to act collectively and to act in their own interests. Rather than have to engage in that uncertain and lengthy process of shaping strangers into friends, and friends into allies—a task that loomed especially large in those parts of the South where memories of wartime and antebellum migrations remained painfully fresh—the men and women of the Cape Fear region exited bondage with much of that work already accomplished. In Fanny's case, such ties were fortuitous, saving her wage and employment. "I have decided not to discharge [her,]" Julia Bowden observed to her diary of a girl she had hired on trial two months before. "[I]f we discharge her, we will have to discharge aunt Bella (her mother) and we don't want to, as she is a first-class cook."[42] As a traveling agent and eventually master workman of a "colored" assembly of the Knights of Labor, Ellen Williams also understood the advantages that accrued to those who could tap into existing systems of kin. After all, she presided over a chapter made up of at least six and probably eight overlapping families, a thickly knit community that understood itself as a cohesive entity within a much larger, international working-class movement. Indeed, so tightly woven was Local Assembly 10851, that nearly half of its families would later resurface in a single neighborhood in the northeast part of the state.[43] But perhaps most meaningful for Wilmington's Republican and later fusionist insurgency and for the challenges it posed fretful conservatives were the affective connections of one of the city's earliest black leaders. After all, it would be difficult to consider George W. Price's meteoric rise to entrepreneurial and political power without taking into account the weighty presence of his family, and especially that of his father: George Sr., a Methodist minister who in 1870 lived with his wife and four younger children two doors away from his ambitious son, and who like so many other black Wilmingtonians, had been born and raised close to, if not in, the city.[44]

Scratching the surface of post–Civil War Wilmington raises a number of new questions. Chief among them are who talked to whom, when, where, and about what. After all, as David Livingston and others have begun to argue, the production of knowledge is a dynamic process, and a contingent process. It is one that unfolds differently and to different effect depending on the time, space, and place. It is also a process intrinsic to the creation of communities, helping to shape their constituencies and to determine their purposes.[45] In the case of Wilmington, knowing more about the kinds of conversations and exchanges that took place as the city's black stevedores, preachers, seamstresses, and sailors went about their daily businesses will tell us more about how they managed to generate and then sustain a radical mobilization in what was an increasingly unradical time. Still, the information extracted from the records of the Freedmen's Savings and Trust Company reveals something about the kind of social and political resources that the black people of Wilmington had at their disposal in the years following emancipation. For even this very preliminary investigation suggests that one of the reasons that Wilmington's white Democrats had to work so hard to win back their city was because a good many of those who stood in their way had been spared the horrors of the domestic slave trade. Rather than having to rebuild in freedom the bedrock on which and from which they could begin to develop themselves as a free people—a task that loomed large for those whose families had been mangled by forced migrations—an overwhelming percentage of the city's black residents had exited bondage with those families and foundations intact. This was no small thing in a nation that had begun by the mid-1870s to turn its back on black workers.

Notes

1. While stories continue to circulate among Wilmington's citizens about the events of 1898, their origins, and their legacies—historical scholarship about the massacre has been surprisingly thin and is growing increasingly dated. For the most systematic explorations of the violence that returned power to white conservative hands, see Wooley, "Race and Politics"; McDuffie, "Politics in Wilmington and New Hanover County"; Prather, *We Have Taken a City*; and Cecelski and Tyson, *Democracy Betrayed*. More commonly, the Wilmington massacre is simply incorporated into larger discussions about the post–Civil War South; see, for example, Williamson, *Crucible of Race*, 195–201; Ayers, *Promise of the New South*, 301–4; Gilmore, *Gender and Jim Crow*; and more recently, Hild, *Greenbackers, Knights of Labor, and Populists*, 202, 216, 218, 221. Estimates vary regarding the size of the mob that trained its guns on Wilmington's black and white radicals, with Michael Honey weighing in on the low side and H. Leon Prather suggesting as many as 2,000 joined the ranks of the impromptu army. See Prather Sr., "We Have Taken a City," 32, and Michael Honey, "Race, Class, and Power in the New South," 176.

2. Prather, "We Have Taken a City," 15–41; Honey, "Race, Class, and Power in the New South," 163–84; Prather, *We Have Taken a City*, chaps. 4–5; McDuffie, "Politics in Wilmington and New Hanover County," 708–46; *Charlotte Daily Observer*, 11 November 1898.

3. Hahn, *A Nation under Our Feet*; William McKee Evans, *Ballots and Fence Rails*, 166–75, Prather, "We Have Taken a City," 55–75.

4. *Raleigh News and Observer*, 3 November 1898; *State* (Columbia, S.C.), 5 November 1898; *Baltimore Sun*, 14 November 1898.

5. See, for example, Honey, "Race, Class, and Power in the New South," 170–71.

6. Prather, *We Have Taken a City*, 31; *Historical Census Browser*, University of Virginia, Geospatial and Statistical Data Center, 20 August 2008, http://www.fisher.lib.virginia.edu/collections/stats/histcensus/index.html.

7. O'Donovan, *Becoming Free in the Cotton South*, chap. 5, 265–70.

8. Rodrigue, *Reconstruction in the Cane Fields*; Jung, *Coolies and Cane*; see also Rebecca Scott, *Degrees of Freedom*, chaps. 1–3.

9. As a lively debate has made abundantly clear, antidemocratic initiatives were hardly confined to the former slaveholding South. See, for example, Beckert, *Monied Metropolis*, 182–92, 228, 319–20; Foner, *Story of American Freedom*, chap. 6; McGerr, *Decline of Popular Politics*; O'Leary, *To Die For*; and Stanley, *From Bondage to Contract*, chap. 3.

10. Registers of Signatures of Depositors in Branches of the Freedman's Savings and Trust Company, 1865–1874, OCC, RG 101 (M816); Foner, *Reconstruction*, 531–32. For a his-

tory of the bank, see Osthaus, *Freedmen, Philanthropy, and Fraud*. Also see Entry of James Pearson, 31 August 1866, no. 11, Freedman's Bank, Roll 5; Entry of Henry Hall, 25 May 1867, no. 106, Freedman's Bank, Roll 5; Entry of Kate Bavis, 18 January 1870, no. 34, Freedman's Bank, Roll 6. All in OCC, RG 101 (M816).

11. Entry of Jno. H. Smyth, 23 December 1872, no. 5426, Freedman's Bank, Roll 18, OCC, RG 101 (M816); Haddock, *Haddock's Wilmington, N.C., Directory, and General Advertiser*, 65, 18.

12. Entry of Dennis Wright, 7 June 1873, no. 7012; Entry of Edward Mears, 16 August 1873, no. 7231; Entry of Harry Bernard, 17 May 1873, no. 6944. All in Roll 18, OCC, RG 101 (M816).

13. Entry of Augustus Davis, 13 June 1873, no. 7019; Entry of Silas Brown, 24 May 1873, no. 6962; Entry of Rosser McIntosh, 9 June 1873, no. 7003; and Entry of Ephraim Smith, 26 March 1873, no. 6802. All in Roll 18, OCC, RG 101 (M816).

14. Entry of John W. Moore, 1 August 1873, no. 7171; Entry of Jno. H. Smyth, 23 December 1872, no. 5426; Entry of George Batson, 14 September 1869, no. 1234. All in Roll 18, OCC, RG 101 (M816).

15. Entry of Harriet Quince, 10 June 1873, no. 7014; Entry of Morris S. Robbins, 18 February 1873, no. 6493; and Entry of W. B. Turlingland, 11 June 1873, no. 7017. All in Roll 18, OCC, RG 101 (M816).

16. Kenzer, "Black Businessman in the Postwar South," 61–87; Haddock, *Haddock's Wilmington, N.C., Directory, and General Advertiser*, 202, 227.

17. Haddock, *Haddock's Wilmington, N.C., Directory, and General Advertiser*, 113, 190; Foner, *Freedom's Lawmakers*, 173–74; 1880 U.S. Federal Census, schedule 1, Wilmington, New Hanover, N.C., district 145, p. 42, 25 August 2008, http://www.ancestry.com. In an advertisement published in T. M. Haddock's 1871 business directory, Price further encouraged potential customers by assuring them that "This is a rare chance to secure a farm and a home."

18. See, for instance, Johnson, *Soul by Soul*; Fett, *Working Cures*, chap. 5–7; O'Donovan, "Universities of Social and Political Change," 124–46.

19. *Macon Weekly Telegraph* (Ga.), 22 September 1893; *New Haven Register* (Conn.), 9 June 1882; *Charlotte News* (N.C.), 31 May 1892. While the debate about power and how to think about it and about what (and who) constitute the political continues to unfold, those who engage owe much to the intellectual and conceptual contributions made by James C. Scott (see *Weapons of the Weak* and *Domination and the Arts of Resistance*).

20. Henry Box Brown, *Narrative of the Life of Henry Box Brown*, 20–24; Ball, *Fifty Years in Chains*, 24; Heather Andrea Williams, *Self-Taught*, 7–29, 203–13.

21. Haraway, "A Manifesto for Cyborgs," 191.

22. Much has been written of late on the political and epistemological dimensions of the Atlantic world and of the special role played by mariners in fostering proletariat exchanges. See, for example, Bolster, *Black Jacks*; Cecelski, *Waterman's Song*; and Linebaugh and Rediker, *Many-Headed Hydra*.

23. U.S. Congress, House of Representatives, "Examination and Survey of Wilmington Harbor and Cape Fear River, North Carolina," *House Executive Documents*, 56th Cong.,

2nd sess., no. 180, serial set 4148; Switzler, *Report on the Internal Commerce of the United States*, 254–56; Wilmington Chamber of Commerce, *Wilmington, North Carolina*, 20–23; Isaacs, *Wilmington Up-To-Date*, 13, 24, 41, 53, 70–71; Haddock, *Haddock's Wilmington, N.C., Directory, and General Advertiser*, 95, 201; *Hillsboro Recorder* (N.C.), 3 September 1873, 21 January 1874; *State* (Columbia, S.C.), 18 April 1893; William McKee Evans, *Ballots and Fence Rails*, 183–93, 266; Duncan, "Wilmington, North Carolina," 441–51.

24. William McKee Evans, *Ballots and Fence Rails*, 282.

25. Entry of Benjamin Aman, 20 January 1873, no. 4405, ; Entry of John Allen Satathe, 1 February 1873, no. 5977; Entry of James Davis, 23 January 1873, no. 5524. All in Roll 18, OCC, RG 101 (M816).

26. Entries of 31 October 1879, 6 July 1880, *Julia Bowden Diary*, Lower Cape Fear Historical Society, Wilmington, N.C., 27 August 2008, http://www.latimerhouse.org/collections/text/bowden.shtml#1879.

27. Entry of Charles Waggoner, 11 October 1869, no. 1298, Roll 18, OCC RG 101 (M816); Haddock, *Haddock's Wilmington, N.C., Directory, and General Advertiser*, 57.

28. *Baltimore Sun*, 1 April 1887; *Macon Weekly Telegraph*, 28 April 1881; *Hillsborough Recorder* (N.C.), 31 March 1875, 25 April 1877; Switzler, *Report on the Internal Commerce of the United States*, 255; Entry of Frank Silva, 30 August 1869, no. 1275, Roll 18, OCC, RG 101 (M816); Duncan, "Wilmington, North Carolina," 441–51.

29. Entry of Edward Jones, 20 February 1873, no. 6501, Roll 18, OCC, RG 101 (M816); Haddock, *Haddock's Wilmington, N.C., Directory, and General Advertiser*, 85; Acme Saloon—Front and Dock Streets, Dr. Robert M. Fales Collection, Slide No. 350, New Hanover County Public Library, 27 August 2008, http://www.tmpapps.nhcgov.com/lib/history/fales/pages/slides/350.htm; Sanborn Map Company, *Digital Sanborn Maps, 1867–1970* (Ann Arbor, Mich., 2001), 28 August 2008, http://www.sanborn.umi.com.ezp-prod1.hul.harvard.edu/.

30. Maps representing the residential patterns of Wilmington's skilled workers, professionals and entrepreneurs, and female domestics are in the author's possession.

31. Haddock, *Haddock's Wilmington, N.C., Directory, and General Advertiser*, 26, 71, 76, 80, 187. Entry of James Caraway, 3 March 1873, no. 6538; Entry of Lewis Green, 7 September 1869, no. 1218. Both in Roll 18, OCC, RG 101 (M816). Sanborn Map Company, *Digital Sanborn Maps*, 28 August 2008, http://www.sanborn.umi.com.ezp-prod1.hul.harvard.edu/.

32. Bayly, *Empire and Information*, 3–5. Bayly is only one of many who explore the political dimensions of talk, particularly as deployed by the subordinate and enslaved. Among others, see Darnton, "An Early Information Society"; Edwards, "Enslaved Women and the Law"; Johnson, *Soul by Soul*, 63–77, 176–88.

33. Marshall Rachleff, "David Walker's Southern Agent," 100–103; Hinks, *To Awaken My Afflicted Brethren*, 137–39, 168–69; Darnton, "An Early Information Society," 1–35; McDuffie, "Politics in Wilmington and New Hanover County," 321; Berlin, et al., *Destruction of Slavery*, 675; William McKee Evans, *Ballots and Fence Rails*, 20; John Dawson et al. to His Excellency W. W. Holden, 12 July 1865, and Bvt. Brig. Gen. Saml. A. Duncan to Maj. C. A. Cilley, both in Hahn, et al., *Land and Labor, 1865*, 131–35; *Hillsborough Recorder*

(N.C.), 2 March 1870; Isaacs, *Wilmington Up-To-Date*, 71; Cecelski, *Waterman's Song*, 53, 194, and chap. 5; Fenn, "'A Perfect Equality Seemed to Reign,'" 127–53; Entry of 26 December 1879, Julia Bowden Diary; Hild, *Greenbackers, Knights of Labor, and Populists*, 94–98; *Worcester Daily Spy* (Massachusetts), 15 April 1882; *Philadelphia Inquirer*, 18 January 1883; *Charlotte Observer*, 21 January 1892. The groups that opened bank accounts provide a sense of the kind of associations and societies that sprouted in post-emancipation black Wilmington. See, for example, Entry of the "Oganic Society," 5 October 1869, no. 1285; Entry of "Sons & Daughters of Charity," 15 October 1869, no. 1305; Entry of "African Land & Building Association," 9 January 1873, no. 5474; Entry of "Cape Fear Fire Engine Company," 10 January 1873, no. 6620; Entry of "Wilmington [Monson] Club," 14 January 1873, no. 5479; Entry of "United Society of Solomon," 15 March 1873, no. 6575; Entry of "Sons of Tucker & Daughters of Zion," 23 June 1873, no. 6672; Entry of "Caucus Association of Wilmington" [4 April 1873], no. 6823; Entry of "Daughters of Wayman," 7 April 1873, no. 6838; Entry of "Mechanic Protection Institution" [19 Apr. 1873], no. 6868; Entry of "Daughters of Moses & Sons of Tucker," 18 July 1873, no. 7101; Entry of "Sons & Daughters of Jubilee," 21 July 1873, no. 7137; and Entry of "Independent Sons of America," 23 August 1873, no. 7258. All in Roll 18, OCC, RG 101 (M816).

34. Hahn, *A Nation under Our Feet*, 166–70, 172–73; Joseph C. Miller, "From Group Mobility to Individual Movement," 243–62.

35. That many, and perhaps more, slaves were exchanged in the intrastate trade. For a thoughtful discussion about both, see Deyle, *Carry Me Back*, 283–96. Furthermore, studies that attend only to the slave market deflect attention away from the hundreds of thousands of women and men who changed hands and homes by such nonmarket means as gift and inheritance or through hire arrangements, the latter of which may very well have outnumbered sales by a three to two margin. On the latter point, see Martin, *Divided Mastery*, 7–9.

36. Registers of Signatures of Depositors, Little Rock, Arkansas, Freedman's Bank, Roll 3, OCC, RG 101 (M816). Of the 84 depositors who gave out-of-state birthplaces, 56 hailed from South Carolina, 16 from Virginia, 6 from Georgia, and 1 each from Texas, Mississippi, Canada West, the West Indies, and Portugal.

37. Pender County was not created from New Hanover until 1875, two years after the last extant entry in the Wilmington signature books.

38. On the restoration of black families in freedom, see, for example, Saville, *Work of Reconstruction*, 102–10; Berlin and Rowland, *Families and Freedom*; O'Donovan, *Becoming Free in the Cotton South*, chaps. 1 and 3.

39. Entry of Amanda Jones, 10 May 1873, no. 6192, Roll 18, OCC, RG 101 (M816).

40. Ibid., Entry of Joseph Jones, 2 May 1873, no. 6648.

41. Ibid., Entry of Henry Tucker Jr., 8 February 1873, no. 6316; Entry of Benjamin Tucker, 29 March 1873, no. 6809; and Entry of Henry Tucker Sr., 22 April 1873, no. 6877.

42. Entries of 23 February 1880, 20 April 1880, 22 April 1880, Julia Bowden Diary.

43. Hilliard Braswell to [John W. Hayes], 10 March 1890; Ellen Williams to Jno. W. Hayes, 15 January 1891; Ellen Williams to [John W. Hayes], 23 February 1891; Jesse Artis, Robert Dawson, and Dora A. Artis, "Notice to the Journal," 1 June 1891; Robert Dawson

to Editor Journal, mid-Sept. 1891; Ellen Williams to John W. Hayes, 17 July 1893. All in Box 34, Folder 2, John W. Hayes Collection, Catholic University Archives, Washington D.C. See also 1930 U.S. Federal Census, Population Schedule, Indian Woods Township, Bertie County, N.C., district 85, pp. 53, 61; 1880 U.S. Federal Census, Population Schedule, Windsor Township, Bertie County, N.C., district 15, p. 297; 1900 U.S. Federal Census, Indian Woods Township, Bertie County, N.C., district 15, p. 43A; 1900 U.S. Federal Census, Snakebite Township, Bertie County, N.C., district 19, p. 128. All accessed on 31 August 2008, http://www.ancestry.com.

44. 1870 U.S. Federal Census, Population Schedule, City of Wilmington, New Hanover County, N.C., p. 313, accessed 31 August 2008, http://www.ancestry.com.

45. In addition to Livingston, *Putting Science in its Place,* see Latour, *Reassembling the Social*; Law, *After Method*.

10

Class, Factionalism, and the Radical Retreat

Black Laborers and the Republican Party in South Carolina, 1865–1900

BRIAN KELLY

Reflecting on the dramatic changes that had transpired over the previous quarter century, the prominent black North Carolina educator Charles N. Hunter wrote in 1902 that he felt "abundantly vindicated" for having counseled compromise and moderation among black South Carolinians caught in the vortex of the struggle over Reconstruction. His efforts to "influence his own race and party" during a visit to Charleston, South Carolina, in 1874 had met with boisterous hostility from the former slaves comprising the grassroots of the Republican Party. At a time when their hold on power seemed increasingly tenuous, freedmen rejected Hunter's appeals for conciliation with white conservatives and refused even to "accord [him] a decent hearing." But by the time he took pen in hand at the dawn of the new century, circumstances had conspired to shift political sentiment even among the formerly unyielding black South Carolinians, rendering them more amenable to moderation and gradualism. Relieved of the prospect of being hounded from the podium, Hunter felt exonerated by the transformation that had taken place, noting with satisfaction that "the mass of my people are now willing to hear me."[1]

In observing that the forceful, collective militancy animating black politics in the period before Redemption had been humbled over the course of a protracted retreat in the years afterward, Hunter's assessment seems to run counter to one of the principal trends in post–civil-rights-era historiography. In place of the bleak appraisal of an earlier generation of scholars who shared Rayford Logan's description of the same period as the "nadir" in African American history, the emphasis in recent scholarship on enduring black agency has generated a much more positive appraisal. Under adverse circumstances, recent studies emphasize, African Americans were able to sustain a vibrant community life, building institutions that allowed them to weather the storm of Jim Crow. Concentrating its energies on ambitious self-help schemes and espousing a strategy of racial uplift, an incipient black middle class successfully bridged the gap between themselves and African American urban and rural workers, some scholars contend, laying the basis for an impressive race solidarity that transcended class tensions. Far from being out of step with the plight of black Southerners, accommodationists like Hunter and—more prominently—Booker T. Washington appear in much of the recent literature as "radical and effective" advocates for "African American power." Their patient work behind the scenes, one historian suggests, "laid the groundwork for the militant confrontation of the Civil Rights Movement."[2]

Despite these recent trends, there are good reasons to take Hunter at his word when he suggests that the collapse of Reconstruction altered something fundamental in the internal life of the black community. This essay is an attempt to offer an explanation of those changes in a single southern state, South Carolina, between emancipation and the late nineteenth century. The dramatic deterioration in circumstances for black Southerners that accompanied the restoration of power to propertied whites affected all African Americans, of course; but I will argue that its effects were felt most acutely by the predominantly working-class constituency whose grassroots mobilization powered the Radical project in the early years after emancipation. The same pressures that marginalized black workers within the Republican Party and later re-subjugated them in the wider society, encouraged the ascent of a more conservative, cramped vision of "race progress" compatible with the new order. The carriers of this vision were drawn, disproportionately, from the ranks of those who had been free before the war and from a small but increasingly influential emerging black middle-class that included former slaves.[3]

As Thomas Holt noted in his pioneering study, *Black over White*, Reconstruction politics in South Carolina reflected from the outset an exceptional disparity in property-holding and prewar status among its black population—particularly along the coast. Elsewhere in the South only New Orleans could boast of an established free black community on a par with Charleston's,[4] and in the early period following emancipation many among the city's propertied, literate free black community seemed ambivalent about allying themselves with plantation field hands. The prominent Charlestonian J. H. Holloway's later attempt to distance himself from the "Crap Shooters" by whom, he suggested, the race was "now represent[ed]" was not completely untypical. In appealing to whites for support during his campaign for alderman in the period following Redemption, Holloway would stress his credentials as a member of the elite Brown Fellowship Society, his ownership of considerable property, and the fact that his "people" had been "tax-payers [for] three centuries." But in the immediate aftermath of emancipation, white hostility had been so pervasive that elite persons of color in Holloway's milieu felt the sting of exclusion acutely, and were compelled—when they were not so inclined anyway—to pursue an alliance with freedpeople.[5] For the most part, as Eric Foner observes, the "children of the Charleston elite cast their lot with the freedmen, bringing, as they saw it, modern culture to the former slaves" in an "encounter that was not without its tensions."[6]

In the arena of formal politics the Republican Party's ambiguous record on those issues most urgent to its ex-slave constituency reflected these and other important tensions. From the end of the Civil War, Republican intervention in the South only obliquely reflected the consensus among black Southerners about a way forward out of slavery. The influence of those who had labored on the cotton and rice plantations before the war was far more palpable in local politics than in the body of policy emanating from the highest echelons of the national party, and at critical junctures the divergence between grassroots and national priorities generated ruptures and crises. But even on a local level one can identify some of the fault lines that would mark the Radical project in South Carolina throughout Reconstruction.

Historians have noted the focus on agitation over civil and political equality and the conspicuous absence of the land question in the early "colored conventions" dominated by propertied African Americans.[7] But while silence and evasion prevailed in some of the early meetings held under the auspices of the Republican leadership, in other arenas the urgency attached to the labor and land questions by freedpeople was unmistakable. The *New York Times* reported in November 1866 a "very large attendance" of freedpeople at a meeting held at the Freedman's Tabernacle in Sumter where "not a word was said about political rights, Negro suffrage or Negro equality." Instead the "first and last note of the occasion was on the same chord—a fair and remunerative wage for the services of the laborer, and the ways and means of saving the destitute multitude from starvation and death." From his attendance at the meeting the *Times* correspondent, "Q," concluded that a "spontaneous" but "general movement" was "now on foot among . . . blacks in many of the interior districts, designed to secure . . . a very material increase in the compensation paid to the laborer."[8]

Even more striking illustrations of the chasm that divided freedpeople and their professed allies in the Union military and federal agencies like the Freedmen's Bureau are to be found in the series of confrontations that erupted along the South Carolina coast through the mid-1860s. Early elation over the government's commitment to granting freedpeople title to the sea island plantations abandoned by white owners in the tumult of war gave way to consternation, and then to livid outrage, as federal troops and Bureau officials exerted their authority on the side of returning planters. Skirmishes erupted across the Lowcountry south of Charleston as former slaves took up arms to prevent restoration. Increasingly they came into conflict not only with former Confederates but with federal officials as well. Despite being inundated with reports of outrages against freedpeople throughout the summer of 1865, Brigadier-General James Chaplin Beecher, then attached to Charleston military headquarters, expressed his greatest indignation over the attempts by freedpeople on Wadmalaw Island to "prevent whites [i.e. returning planters] from coming ashore." In early 1866 Beecher banished the local Freedmen's Bureau agent from the island for "leading freedpeople astray," arrested the freedman identified as a ringleader in the incident, and called together the committee elected by former slaves to inform them that "the people on these islands are going to make cotton and have no time for public meetings." At Edisto freedpeople confronted a similar ban on meetings, ordered by then General—future Republican governor—Robert K. Scott.[9]

As the Wadmalaw incident suggests, the federal government's dedication to upholding the rights of freedpeople varied greatly, often reflecting the commitment of individual military and Freedmen's Bureau personnel, but more critical in the larger context was the consensus among Northern officials that the priority was to "make cotton"—to lend their efforts to restoring the profitability of the plantation economy. The grassroots, quasi-military organizations proliferating among freedpeople across the Lowcountry in the aftermath of emancipation stood as impediments to that aim, and the potential for a clash between their expansive notions of freedom and the more restrictive free labor commitment of the Republican leadership was inscribed in the politics of Reconstruction from the beginning.

Federal intervention in the sharp contest between black laborers and their former owners was characterized by extreme indifference and cruelty on some occasions and by bold and compassionate defense of freedpeople's newly attained rights on others. But by early 1866 it was clear that Republican state officials and the Charleston-based military command shared a conviction that restoration of the lands set aside in the Sherman reserve to their former owners was essential for compelling black laborers across the state to submit to contracting under white authority. In February, Governor James L. Orr wrote President Andrew Johnson to urge him to resolve the land question in favor of the planters. The "great difficulty" in convincing freedmen to contract for labor was their enduring "conviction that the lands of his former master were to be given him." This "delusion," which had not yet been "dispelled," was especially troublesome in the Lowcountry, where clashes yet seemed "impossible to overcome." As long as ownership of the land remained in dispute, Orr asserted, "so long the freedmen of the lowcountry will refuse to work for wages, and the freedmen of the upcountry will work discontentedly." Restoration alone would deliver a "solution" to the labor question—in Orr's view the only "real obstacle" to reconstruction on terms acceptable to the white Carolinians who'd elected him.[10]

The powerful mobilization that emancipation had detonated among freedpeople across the state complicated the governor's plans, however, ensuring that the military would be compelled to resort to force in carrying through restoration in the Lowcountry. Tragically, these clashes increasingly pitted coastal freed communities against black troops, many of whom had been recruited locally and redeployed from the interior at the insistence of native whites.[11] National developments conspired as well to frustrate plans for the wholesale reversal that conservative state officials envisioned in 1866. President Johnson's fall from grace, coinciding with the ascent of the Radical Republicans at Washington, reinvigorated grassroots mobilization at a critical juncture and seems to have had an especially profound effect in the interior and the Upcountry. While Union occupation along the coast had nurtured the extension of grassroots organization there over months and years prior to the war's conclusion, less favorable demographics combined with rural isolation and early exertions on the part of whites to constrain freedpeople's mobilization in the interior. Even there, however, passage of the Reconstruction Acts and the granting of the vote to black men shifted momentum dramatically, producing a "hothouse atmosphere of political mobilization" and a "vast expansion of the black political leadership" that left no part of the state untouched.[12]

This was most plainly reflected in the rapid spread of the Union Leagues, a development overseen by the national party and assisted by literate, committed organizers hailing from Charleston or the North, but driven forward on the ground by locally rooted individuals. Ministers, skilled artisans, Union Army veterans, and field hands with little wealth but enjoying exceptional standing in their communities, their main task in the eyes of Republican officials was to galvanize and deliver the black vote. And given the stakes involved, resident leaders took this aspect of their obligations seriously. Closely identified with an impoverished constituency whose vision of freedom encompassed both political equality and economic transformation, local leaders and the clubs and societies they organized reflected a plebeian militancy that often exceeded the bounds of Republican free labor propriety. Politics in the early period of Radical Reconstruction, Eric Foner writes, "was intimately tied to the freedmen's economic aspirations," and the party seemed then to have been divided between a minority who shared freedpeople's aspirations and others who gauged that the risk of alienating their only dependable Southern constituency outweighed the immediate need for restraining black expectations.[13]

Tensions between Republican leaders and the grassroots were evident from early on. Given the high proportion of white Northerners involved in the upper ranks of the party, these strains often took the form of intra-party racial antagonism, or in demands from freedpeople for officeholding in proportion to their numbers. But the evidence suggests that in the period before 1870, at least, fracture lines in the Republican ranks were more complex. A number of white conservatives, both Northern and native-born, attached themselves to the Republicans with the hope that they could steer the party toward a moderate course, and they seemed as alarmed by the prominence of genuine white Radicals as they were at the radical ferment among freedpeople.

J.P.M. Epping—before the war a minor slaveowner with questionable Union sympathies and later a Charleston-based U.S. provost marshal—became active in the state Republican Party, maneuvering constantly to prevent both the black rank-and-file and the more outspoken white Radicals from influencing Republican policy. He corresponded regularly with Governor Orr, attempting to convince him to affiliate with the Republicans and in May 1867 sought his support in an impending contest for the party leadership. Alarmed at the ascent of the Radical faction in the state organization, Epping called upon Orr to "assist us in this war, and to . . . consult with your friends in the upper Districts" to see whether any would join the Republicans to aid in heading off the Radicals' ascent.

Four months later Epping informed Orr of his advanced plans for dismantling the Union Leagues, charged by him with "teach[ing] agrarian doctrines [to] ignorant freedmen and hold[ing] out [to them] the prospect of obtaining property or Land and other plunder." He proposed to counter the radicalization by purging the state Union League president (Massachusetts-born Gilbert Pillsbury) and returning the "political machinery" to "safe capable hands." Through the governor, Epping aimed to convince the U.S. military command (led by General Edward Canby) to postpone the pending Constitutional Convention and thereby gain more time to "take the . . . machinery of the republican party . . . out of the hands of [the] gang of disorganizers and agrarianists" and turn it over to the "Conservative wing of the party."[14]

The success of Epping's strategy depended, in part, on taking advantage of divisions he perceived among freedpeople themselves. He drew a distinction, first, between the "better thinking and conservative negroes" and others (ostensibly) being "converted" to agrarianism and, second, between the "upcountry colored men" (whom he considered "alright") and radicalized freedpeople along the coast. While it is difficult to gauge whether Epping's reading of these fissures bore any semblance to reality, there can be little doubt that lowcountry mobilization served as the engine for radicalism across the state.[15]

Whether Epping's plan succeeded in undermining statewide mobilization, it is clear that by the late 1860s the social content of the Radical project had been trimmed. Strikes and other forms of laborers' militancy persisted intermittently (though less frequently) on the lowcountry plantations and especially in Charleston itself, but in the interior, Republicanism had been reduced to a holding operation as local leaders struggled to deliver their constituency at election time in the face of well-organized white paramilitary violence. In South Carolina, as throughout the South, it was by now clear to freedpeople that Reconstruction would not deliver any fundamental redistribution of land.[16]

The first substantial onslaught against developing grassroots radicalism had occurred in the run-up to the 1868 elections, when the Ku Klux Klan made its first organized foray into South Carolina. The Lowcountry would remain fairly impervious to white paramilitarism until 1876, and along the coast, Radicals had little trouble in turning out their constituency. But their experience contrasted sharply with the situation in the interior. There the Klan managed to establish a presence in ten Piedmont and upcountry districts at election time, murdering at least eight freedpeople in a campaign of intimidation that succeeded in blocking Republican victory. In Abbeville less than 20 percent of registered black voters appeared at the polls, and white conservatives carried two interior congressional districts. Upcountry leagues, which had experienced such rapid growth in 1867 and 1868, reportedly withered as "the great mass of Negro voters . . . faded out of the organization." Although the leagues would revive, and upcountry radicalism would reemerge under a variety of organizational forms throughout and beyond Reconstruction, the 1868 experience was a chastening one. In the long run white paramilitary terror would play a critical role in demoralizing black workers and shifting internal dynamics within the Republican Party in favor of Epping and other moderates.[17]

It was partly in response to this disconcerting outcome in the Upcountry that the Republican Party under Governor Robert K. Scott undertook the reorganization of the state militia, enrolling freedpeople in an effort to raise an armed force that could protect black suffrage and restore a Republican majority. Scott became the focus of widespread abuse from white conservatives outraged over his arming of a "negro militia."[18] The upcountry press was littered with reports of nighttime meetings and "negro drilling," along with complaints about the insolence that newly acquired arms seemed to encourage among former slaves now "thoroughly contaminated with false notions as to their rights," as ex-Governor Benjamin F. Perry put it. But their real cause for complaint became evident in the next elections in 1870 when, despite another concerted attempt at intimidation, freedpeople turned out en masse to return a Republican majority.[19]

Ironically, the Radicals' victory at the polls set the stage for the first major breach between Republican state officials and their grassroots constituency. Herbert Shapiro writes that the 1870 election "was the prelude to a major outbreak of terror" across the Upcountry, and before it was brought to an end by determined federal intervention, an intense period of white paramilitary violence once again decimated grassroots Republican organization—this time with more permanent repercussions. Freedman Sam Sturges, one of hundreds of victims of Klan terror, testified that his attackers "said their business was to break down these damned Union Leagues, and these radical parties," and the collective testimony of grassroots leaders attests to their success. In a menacing atmosphere marked by threat and intimidation, few whites had been willing to ally with the Republicans in the Upcountry, and of these many were now compelled to publish "cards" in the local press declaring their disaffiliation. Freedman Jack Johnson, from Laurens County, reported in 1871 that the party was "down out there now . . . for all the Republican men that have been the leaders . . . has left there." Sam Nuckles, a league organizer from Union County, reported that the party was "scattered and beaten and run out . . . just like scattered sheep everywhere." Baptist preacher and former Union League president Elias Hill told federal investigators that he and nearly two hundred freedpeople from the vicinity of Clay Hill in York County no longer "believe[d] it possible, from the past history and present aspect of affairs, for our people to live in this country peaceably," and had determined therefore to emigrate to Liberia. White conservatives, including prominent Klansmen, orchestrated "black and white meetings" at which they publicly pledged to curtail paramilitary violence in return for the dismantling of league organization.[20]

In this context, conservatives were elated—and freedmen despondent—at Governor Scott's response to the upsurge in Klan-driven violence in 1871. Secure in his office, and with a party grassroots in serious disarray, Scott seems to have settled on a policy of attempting to reach an accommodation with his conservative adversaries at the precise moment when Democrats aimed to pressure leading Republicans to disband the militias. Between gentlemanly negotiations, conservatives aggressively pursued the disarmament of freedpeople through paramilitary terror.[21] A series of confrontations between black militia units and upcountry whites (including an apparently unprovoked attack on a pair of white bootleggers and the hanging of militia leader Jim Wilkes by white paramilitaries at Carmel Hill) provided the pretext around which a deal was struck. The most notable element in Scott's response to these incidents was the dispatching of military aides to retrieve arms from the local militias at Chester and Rock Hill.

The injustice—and sheer peril—in Scott's concession was plainly apparent to freedpeople, and when the governor agreed in meetings with prominent Democrats to remove black trial justices and other officials considered noxious by conservatives and replace them with more acceptable individuals, indignation became palpable in the lower ranks of the party. Prominent conservative M. C. Butler, who later played a prominent role in the massacre of blacks at Hamburg, expressed satisfaction with Scott's judgment, crediting him with making "amends" for his past mistakes by "appointing good men to office," but black Republicans, in particular, were livid. They "bitterly denounced" Scott, threatening the governor with impeachment because of his failure to protect upcountry Radicals, and in an early exposé of Republican corruption charged him with being "criminally guilty" in a scandal that involved the selling off of horses intended for the militia.[22]

The confrontation over disarming the state militia not only revealed the growing chasm between the party's grassroots and those at the top of the state Republican administration but also demonstrated the difficulties of reorienting the party so that it might deliver tangible benefits to freedmen increasingly consigned to a purely electoral role. Divisions that first became apparent in the fight over the militia festered and multiplied, producing an almost chronic factionalism in which freedpeoples' votes were eagerly canvassed—but in which their social and economic interests featured tangentially, if at all. The chief beneficiary of the opposition to Governor Scott, for example, was the Speaker of the House Franklin J. Moses Jr., whose role as a lightning rod for black discontent over Scott's betrayal proved critical during his successful campaign for the governorship. Once in power, however, his own administration not only failed to encourage any serious revival of grassroots mobilization but sank deeper into the swirl of corruption that diverted state funds away from the urgent needs of the party grassroots, leaving the Republican project even more vulnerable to vilification by its adversaries. When, in 1874, his Columbia residence was besieged during streetfighting between Republican factions, the governor who had made his run for office on the basis of opposition to Scott's disbanding of the militias reportedly called upon one of the prominent white rifle clubs to come to his rescue.[23]

That freedpeople managed to hold together the Republican vote in such difficult circumstances is a testament both to their capacity for organization and their deep apprehension about the consequences of a conservative restoration. But by the time of Moses's election in 1872, there was little remaining of the impressive stores of confidence and optimism that had driven early mobilization in the Upcountry. This retreat was evident not only in the sharp decline in local confrontations over access to land and the terms of labor but also in the inability of freedpeople to hold elected officials to account. While the relationship between the Radical grassroots and elected representatives had been problematic from the outset, one critical effect of white paramilitary violence was the undermining of black workers' capacity to challenge "moderating tendencies" within the Republican Party. The already tenuous links between an expectant ex-slave community and moderating party officials weakened even further under the strain.[24]

In the Lowcountry these developments were mitigated to some extent. Long-standing traditions of collective organization, the weakness of white paramilitarism, and the proximity of an urban seaport and political hub all helped to sustain grassroots radicalism in the face of a deteriorating national context and a statewide retreat.[25] A series of dramatic labor strikes in Charleston revealed remarkable cleavages between black workers and their elected officials: Republicans frequently expressed "strong and forceful opposition" to efforts by the city's (mostly) black longshoremen and others to improve their wages and conditions and resist employers' attempts to victimize Radicals. In 1869 the city's tailors—overwhelmingly black—walked out for "their own special benefit," though the Democratic press was probably correct in asserting that they were "imitating the example set by the longshoremen." The planter William Middleton noted with some satisfaction that a "general strike among [Charleston's] negro laborers" in 1873 had "embarrassed Republican party officials," but their discomfiture did not seem to deter others, including female domestics. Labor militancy continued as a frequent feature of Charleston life and would persist even after the end of Reconstruction.[26]

The strength and militancy of black laborers in Charleston rendered it difficult for Republican officials to ignore their grievances while Reconstruction endured. But intense factionalism proliferated even in Georgetown, with its substantial black majority. And while competing Republican machines vied for the votes of black rice workers, a struggle over the spoils of office rather than any substantive differences lay at the root of the district's raucous antagonisms. Georgetown planters' foremost concern through the early 1870s was to reestablish control over their field laborers, and they reserved their greatest resentment for the "pestilential . . . northern nigga" William H. Jones, who reportedly "stir[red] up the negroes," visiting rice plantations and "rendering them dissatisfied with the terms of their contracts." An intense rivalry developed between Jones and his party rival, Baltimore-born James A. Bowley, erupting in armed clashes ("veritable civil war," according to one account) between Jones's plantation-based following and Bowley's supporters, concentrated in the town. Authorities reacted by deploying federal troops to occupy the town—much to the satisfaction of local whites. Despite their disdain for Jones, local planters seem to have overstated his radicalism: he was a close associate of Republican Congressman Joseph H. Rainey, formerly a free negro who had earlier expressed his clear opposition to land confiscation and reached an accommodation with conservatives. Jones's support among rice workers was reportedly paid for in cash, and there is little evidence that either faction pursued a course of action that benefited the black poor. When Wade Hampton campaigned in the district in 1876 he pitched his appeal for black votes on dissatisfaction over the collapse of the free school system under local Republicans.[27]

While Georgetown seems to demonstrate the willingness and ability of populist-inclined Republican officials to manipulate grassroots dissatisfaction to their own advantage, elsewhere, in the Lowcountry south of Charleston, freedpeople proved more capable of acting independently, coming closest to mounting a successful challenge to the rightward drift of Republican moderates. Daniel H. Chamberlain's governorship represented a return to the conciliatory approach to white conservatives that Scott had embarked on after 1870. Pledging to bring an end to the flagrant corruption evident during the Moses administration, Chamberlain intensified efforts aimed at forging a coalition with moderate, business-oriented Democrats based in Charleston and clustered around *News and Courier* editor Francis W. Dawson. But as

Thomas C. Holt suggests, neither aspect of this strategy offered solace to the party's black, working-class constituents, who while having paid the steepest price for corruption stood to gain little from Chamberlain's austerity.[28]

On the whole, Chamberlain's strategy accelerated Republican fragmentation and did so without delivering the stability or political longevity that he hoped it would deliver. His program of fiscal retrenchment left freedmen deeply embittered, believing it was enacted "at the expense of white and black Republicans," while the series of concessions he extended to white conservatives seemed only to encourage them to demand more. In particular the restrictions that Chamberlain imposed on the revived state militia in the face of renewed white paramilitary atrocities and his agreement to replace trial justices and other local officials with Democrats closely allied to the planters alienated black Republicans across the Lowcountry, and by 1875 the split in the Republican ranks had burst into the open. By the time he came up for reelection in 1876 the *New York World* reported that Chamberlain was "greatly disliked by the negroes . . . who more than once during the present campaign have hooted him from the hustings." It was "possible," editors speculated, that "his nomination may excite such dissatisfaction among the [Republican] rank and file . . . that the very evident change of sentiment among the better classes of the negroes toward the Democratic party will be supplemented by a fatal apathy on the part of the opposition."[29]

The demoralization resulting from these internal divisions took its toll on the Republican Party, fatally weakening it at a time when white conservatives—for many years utterly dejected about their prospects for ever regaining the upper hand in state affairs—began to sense that their moment was fast approaching. Their increasing inability to influence Republican policy drove freedmen from pillar to post in search of a corrective fix, but their efforts yielded little. By the early 1870s, grassroots dissatisfaction manifested itself in resentment at the disproportionate influence of Northern "carpetbaggers" in the state administration. Such anger over the exclusion of native Republicans could enhance the bargaining position of elected officials coveting administrative positions, but it had little or no potential for altering fundamental policy. Similarly, freedmen seem to have become increasingly receptive to complaints that the spoils of office were monopolized by white Republicans, or by light-skinned blacks, and while this was borne out by the facts, it was hopelessly inadequate as a basis for challenging the party's overall direction.[30]

The singular instance in which the Republican grassroots managed both to reassert the indivisibility of political and economic power and to challenge the conservative drift of the Republican leadership occurred during the series of "tramping strikes" that convulsed the lowcountry rice district below Charleston through the summer and early autumn of 1876. In challenging the Chamberlain administration, plantation field hands compelled locally elected Republican officials to take sides in a dispute between propertied whites and the party's mostly landless black constituency. The strikes first erupted in May after planters attempted to reduce the wages of the mostly female, casual laborers hired at peak seasons to aid with planting and the harvest but spread quickly, threatening the rice crop across the expansive plantation district lying between the Ashepoo and Combahee rivers.[31]

While the strikes have been explored in detail by Eric Foner and others, two features relevant to tensions in the Republican Party are worth highlighting: Chamberlain's role in the events and the telling intervention of local officials. The Beaufort and Colleton County planters who arrayed themselves against the strikers were closely associated with Democratic politics in the Lowcountry, comprising an important element in the constituency Chamberlain had hoped to win to an alliance. But the explosive labor conflict in the rice fields rendered this unlikely combination completely untenable. One veteran of the 1876 electoral campaign recalled Colleton as "probably the most fiercely determined county of the state," which had a "large number of high spirited, hot blooded, young men of old and once wealthy families" determined to resist "degradation in continuance of Republican and Negro rule." The county was in "a blaze of excitement," planter John Larescey later testified, recalling that he "did not know of a single white man in that whole county but what was a Democrat." J. Bennett Bissell, upon whose Combahee property the dispute first erupted, was among those who insisted on suppressing the strike at all costs. The largest rice planter in the district, he was prominently linked to white paramilitaries and to the planters' hard-line policy, making incessant demands upon Chamberlain and his Attorney General to crush the strike forcefully.[32]

Their policy of cooperating with Chamberlain seemed vindicated, for Charleston's business-oriented conservatives, during the early period of the rice strikes. Although he publicly expressed sympathy "with all who are struggling for a bare subsistence," the governor admonished strikers to avoid interfering with strikebreakers, declaring that it was "wrong to trouble any man who is willing to work, no matter how low the wages." In response to a direct request from Bissell, Chamberlain appointed R. H. Colcock as trial justice in Colleton, an appointment that the *News and Courier* heartily supported but one which outraged lowcountry Republicans, who charged that Colcock "had no interest in the laborers, and would do whatever the planters told him to do." The governor resisted appeals for the removal of a second trial justice identified by Beaufort's leading black Republican Robert Smalls as "a large planter . . . who issues checks to his laborers," but was less obliging to planter demands for "severe application of the law," hopeful that he could defuse the crisis without completely alienating the black, laboring-class constituency whose support he would desperately require at election time, and who were already deeply skeptical about the course he had set for the Republican Party. Overall, however, Chamberlain's efforts to "facilitate a settlement and to quiet the troubles" in the Lowcountry were "favorably spoken of" among prominent Democrats.[33]

Among freedpeople, by contrast, the perception that Chamberlain was going out of his way to mollify the strikers' adversaries combined with their growing general disaffection over Republican policy to produce an explosive confrontation. At the state Republican convention in Orangeburg, reporters found it "a matter of deep astonishment to see the deep-seated opposition to Chamberlain among the negroes of this county, as well as Barnwell, Colleton, and the upper part of Beaufort." Chamberlain was reported to have been "so persistently interrupted by his own party" that he stormed out of the convention "in a fit of disgust." Similarly, a meeting of Republicans at Barnwell turned down a resolution endorsing Chamberlain's candidacy, with observers noting that the attempt "did not take well with the negroes."[34]

With their large, assertive black majorities, Beaufort and Colleton counties constituted the epicenter of anti-Chamberlain sentiment in the 1876 campaign. Some measure of the anomaly this introduced in party alignment can be gleaned in correspondence sent to the governor in August, in which a Colleton conservative assured him that "amid some *seeming* opposition to yourself [here] among *Republicans* only; I want to assure you that [the] great majority of the Democrats will vote for you" and that "*You will carry Colleton* most respectfully." With white conservatives extending him their hearty support, however, Chamberlain was finding it increasingly difficult to get a hearing among lowcountry blacks. He was forced to withdraw from a meeting in Walterboro, in the heart of the strike district, after "colored republicans . . . would not allow him to speak."[35]

The deeply inscribed fault lines that the rice strikes had rendered transparent greatly weakened South Carolina Republicans just as they were compelled to face up to a powerful attempt to bring Reconstruction to an end. On one side, the *News and Courier* observed perceptively in a report from the strike district, "Republicans from the North are frightened by the storm they have raised." "[I]t has got beyond their control," editors reasoned, "and they can only smother it." With his hopes for building a bridge to white conservatives dashed after the Fourth of July massacre at Hamburg, Chamberlain had to be mindful of the deep anger prevailing among a large section of the party's black constituency. But freedpeople, no less than Republican moderates, faced a dilemma of their own. Dejected and often outraged by the behavior of their state leadership, black South Carolinians never enjoyed the luxury of undertaking party reform in a context of peace and stability: instead any decisions about the way forward would have to be made against the backdrop of an aggressive Democratic campaign aimed at reestablishing white supremacy, and the imperative to deliver votes for the Republicans was therefore overwhelming. The *Journal of Commerce* gloated, with an astute grasp of the quandary confronting freedpeople, that the Republican "faithful are at a loss. They have thrown Chamberlain overboard," the editors noted, "and are now themselves adrift."[36]

The difficulties were perhaps even more acute for locally elected Republican officials. The upper ranks of the lowcountry party apparatus proved only slightly more hospitable to rice laborers' assertiveness in 1876 than their Charleston counterparts had in the face of urban labor militancy several years earlier. The embrace of an increasingly coercive free labor vision was most evident in the record of the black Beaufort Republican Thomas Hamilton. A state representative and a rice planter of some means, Hamilton was Chamberlain's "champion" in the Lowcountry and at times his solitary supporter among local Republican officials, "dragging [the governor's case] before every meeting and pressing his claims for a re-nomination." A forceful opponent of the strike from the outset, Hamilton reminded rice workers gathered in a mass meeting at Crooked Hill that their interests were "identical with the owners of these plantations," urging them to abandon the strike and steer clear of the "hellish politicians" urging them on, who were "paupers themselves . . . and too poor to tell the truth." Caught between the insurgency unleashed by the strike and the growing momentum of the conservative campaign, Hamilton moved ever closer to an alliance with the lowcountry Democracy and by the end of the strike had "crossed over," abandoning the Republicans completely to align himself with the campaign for conservative restoration.[37]

Hamilton was not alone among lowcountry Republicans in bolting once the conservatives appeared to have gained the upper hand. Black Republican Thomas E. Miller later claimed to have been involved in negotiations with Wade Hampton to redraw lowcountry electoral boundaries, slicing off the interior of Beaufort County to carve out a new district (Hampton County) "with the objective of electing a Negro Democrat to the state Senate." Nathaniel B. Myers, a "well-to-do freeborn mulatto" stepped forward to stake his claim to the seat, abandoning the Republicans in an act that "destroyed his influence in Beaufort County."[38] The gulf between Republican officials and their black working-class constituents was most apparent in the upper ranks of the party, but even at the local level officials' ambivalence about the field hands' plight could rankle their constituents.

The problems that this created for grassroots morale, and the difficulties it introduced into the project of mounting an alternative to Chamberlain, can best be seen in the figure of northern-born (but Beaufort-based) Republican William J. Whipper. The governor's very public refusal to sign the commission that would have allowed Whipper to take his seat as circuit court judge won the approval of Chamberlain's Democratic admirers but provoked serious disaffection within Republican ranks. Still, the lowcountry Republican grassroots could be forgiven for their ambivalence about the outcome of this particular squabble: described by his biographer as one of the "wealthiest African Americans of the [antebellum] period" (who had, like Hamilton, plowed some of his capital into rice planting), Whipper had been dragged into court by his own field hands for nonpayment of wages.[39]

Deep divisions among the Republicans, with serious disaffection taking root among black workers across the Lowcountry contrasted with growing cohesion and increasing belligerence (including an impressive, unchecked paramilitary resurgence) on the Democratic side: these were the most salient features in the backdrop to the overthrow of Reconstruction in South Carolina in 1876 and 1877. Polarization in the Republican ranks divided a moderate leadership which accepted the conservatives' demand that the state should be ruled again by its "intelligence and property" from a largely propertyless black majority that had tasted power, briefly, in the early years of Reconstruction. In the fragmentation that ensued, many black elected officials either publicly endorsed Chamberlain's retreat from the Radical project or deserted the Republican Party entirely for a place in Wade Hampton's Democratic Party, a party unequivocally committed to white supremacy. With no practical alternative available to them, and in the face of massive intimidation, freedpeople voted almost unanimously for the Republican ticket, as they had in every election previously. The conservatives triumphed only by "run[ning] right over the fourteenth and fifteenth amendments," as Ben Tillman would later recall.[40]

Before Wade Hampton's vision of a paternalistic, post-Reconstruction social order gave way to Benjamin Tillman's more rigid and malicious hierarchy of race, a redeemed Palmetto state seemed briefly to offer space to those black politicians who shared the conservatives' sensibilities about the sanctity of property rights and its implications for suffrage and other salient questions. This new order rendered it safe for men like Charles N. Hunter to appear in front of black audiences and urge reconciliation and moderation. It allowed black and mulatto elites like J. H. Holloway, who had held themselves aloof from politics during the tempest of Reconstruction (possibly out of fear of risking their relationships with powerful whites) to present themselves—after the storm had passed—as sensible and unthreatening men of color, every bit as committed to social hierarchy as their white counterparts. To some extent, it provided room for ex-Republicans like Thomas Hamilton to find a home in the Democratic Party and, after an initial period of victimization, it even allowed individual Republicans to hold onto their offices where overwhelming black majorities made conservative victory unlikely. North of Charleston a "new Georgetown elite" emerged, composed of white men whose wealth derived from antebellum rice and cotton planting and others rooted in railroads, phosphates, and new industries. This new commercial leadership reached a fusion arrangement with Republicans that divided local offices between themselves and a section of black leadership whose main quality, it seems, was that they "did nothing to cause any friction between the whites and blacks." Even in the Lowcountry south of Charleston, Robert Smalls was able to hold onto his congressional seat through 1887 when, faced with a vote of no confidence from local Republicans, he also made his peace with the Democrats.[41]

Redemption is most commonly remembered for marking the end of Republican rule in the South—the final derailment of the project of Reconstruction that had been inaugurated by slave emancipation at the end of the Civil War. But it seems also to have marked a rupture in the long and troubled relationship between freedpeople and the party of emancipation. Not in the sense that—so long as they held the franchise—black people would desert the Republican ticket: except where third party movements presented a viable alternative in parts of the South in the late 1880s and 1890s, African Americans had little choice but to hold on and hope for better days. But Redemption did mark a breaking point in the sense that the great hopes that black working people had invested in the Radical project in the early period following emancipation seemed increasingly misplaced.

Among its important effects, the Democrats' spectacular, menacing 1876 campaign and Hampton's subsequent "victory"[42] exposed cleavages that had been present in the black community all along but which had intensified over the course of Reconstruction. A small minority of African Americans—some free before the war; others who had accumulated wealth and property in the years since—could consent to the strict division between political and economic equality that Republican moderates insisted on from the late 1860s onward. But for the vast majority of former slaves, this separation contradicted the vision of freedom they had carried with them since the end of slavery. "[N]o other group of working people in the United States has ever linked its aspirations so tightly or with such unanimity to a political party" as did freedpeople in the Reconstruction South, the late David Montgomery observed. "Nevertheless, the Republicans never became *their* party, in the sense of a party whose program and leadership were determined by black constituents."[43]

New opportunities for self-assertion would present themselves to black workers after 1877, but they would be fewer and further between. Within the black community, Redemption shifted initiative and momentum away from the ex-slave community and toward black elites, who more and more owed their status to an embrace of social hierarchy and laissez-faire economic principles. In a very real sense, the ascendancy of accommodation sealed by Booker T. Washington's celebrated speech at the Atlanta Exposition in 1895 was a product of historical circumstances that had been at work since the late 1860s. Its triumph marked not so much a new trend in black thinking as the eclipse of the black working-class politics that had flickered so brightly, yet fleetingly, in the remarkable historical juncture brought on by war and emancipation.

Notes

1. Charles N. Hunter to Hon. J. C. Pritchard, "Strictly Confidential," 21 April 1902, Charles N. Hunter Papers, DUSC. The most comprehensive treatment of Hunter's career is Haley, *Charles N. Hunter and Race Relations.*

2. Logan, *Negro in American Life*; Heather Cox Richardson, *Death of Reconstruction,* 5; Fairclough, *Better Day Coming,* xiii. The most forthright expression of this trend in recent scholarship can be found in Norrell, *Up from History.* From a perspective rooted in black nationalism, Steven Hahn (in *A Nation under Our Feet*) views the period between Redemption and World War I as one in which "black men and women were again reconfiguring the political landscape of the South and the nation" (414), pointing especially to a "remarkable 'thickening' of African-American civic and associational life" (461) in the South. Litwack, *Trouble in Mind* stands out as an obvious recent exception to this positive assessment. I offer an extended critique of this trend in Kelly, "No Easy Way Through."

3. Studies that explore these tensions in African American life include Meier, "Negro Class Structure and Ideology," 258–66, and *Negro Thought in America*; Painter, *Exodusters*;

Armstead L. Robinson, "Beyond the Realm of Social Consensus"; Gordon, *Caste and Class*; Kelly, "Industrial Sentinels."

4. "Among black Americans," Willard B. Gatewood writes, "the aristocrats of color in Charleston, South Carolina, more than those anywhere in the South, even in New Orleans, had a reputation for snobbery and colorphobia that persisted well into the twentieth century" (*Aristocrats of Color*, 80). See also Foner, *Reconstruction*, 101.

5. Thomas Holt writes that the "blindly uncompromising acts of the white power structure were to prove ultimately beneficial to the masses of freedmen. After all, no compromise could have possibly helped them, while the whites' intransigency forced the mulatto bourgeoisie into a political alliance with the ex-slaves, instead of with the white ruling classes, as happened in many Caribbean societies during the post-emancipation period" (*Black over White*, 22–23).

6. J. H. Holloway to Freeman Owens, in Holloway Scrapbook, ARI; Newsclipping from *Charleston News and Courier*, 1884, in Holloway Scrapbook, ARI; Foner, *Reconstruction*, 102.

7. On the relative silence concerning the freedpeoples' desire for land, see Holt, *Black over White*, 18. Foner qualifies this generalization slightly, singling out South Carolina for the degree of attention that the land question evoked and particularly for its initiative in setting up a Land Commission. See Foner, *Reconstruction*, 329.

8. *New York Times*, 30 November 1866. "Q" was almost certainly Julius L. Fleming, a native South Carolinian who published letters regularly in the Charleston press under the sobriquet "Juhl." See the entry for 17 November 1866 in Moore, *Juhl Letters*, 134–37.

9. For examples of outrages see James C. Beecher Journal, 19 July 1865; 13, 19, and 25 August 1865; 19 and 25 September 1865; 9 and 15 October 1865. Reports on Wadmalaw incident and the expulsion of freedman Samuel Johnson appear in Beecher Memorandum Book, 31 January, and 2 February 1866. All in James Chaplin Beecher Papers, DUSC. Scott's intervention is discussed in Saville, *Work of Reconstruction*, 93.

10. *New York Times*, 5 February 1866. See Sickles's "General Order No. 1" in the same issue.

11. On white hostility to black troops, see Zuczek, *State of Rebellion*, 19. For examples of planters' attitudes to their presence in the interior, see "Monthly Conclusion," June 1865, in Jacob Schirmer Diary, SCHS, and W. F. Robert to Governor Perry, ca. 1865–66, Benjamin F. Perry Papers, SHC.

12. Foner, *Reconstruction*, 285, 289. On the varying strength of black mobilization in the interior and the Lowcountry, see Saville, *Work of Reconstruction*, 16, and Kelly, "Labor and Place."

13. Foner, *Reconstruction*, 289. On the rise and evolution of the Union Leagues see Fitzgerald, *Union League Movement in the Deep South*, passim, and Saville, *Work of Reconstruction*, 186.

14. Epping, a German-American immigrant, appears in the 1850 Slave Schedules as a druggist owning $8000 in real estate and three slaves. By 1870 his assets had increased, to $11000 in real estate and $6000 in personal property. See *1850 Slave Schedules*, Roll M432-

850,p. 264a; and *U. S. Federal Census (1870)*, St. Luke's, Beaufort: Roll M593-1485, p. 83a. Quotes from J.P.M. Epping to Governor James L. Orr, 14 May 1867; Epping to Governor Orr, 23 Sept 1867; Epping to Governor Orr, 14 October 1867. All in Governor James Lawrence Orr Papers, SCDAH.

15. The scholarship of William C. Hine and Thomas Holt lends support to the suggestion that African Americans approached Reconstruction with a range of perspectives shaped by class, their status prior to the war, and other factors.

16. William McKee Evans uncovers a similar trajectory in North Carolina. "By 1868," he writes, "the idea of 'forty acres and a mule' was virtually dead. Accommodating themselves to the status quo, the Republicans undertook to promote political equality in a society characterized by equality in almost nothing else" (*Ballots and Fence Rails*, 251).

17. Williamson, *After Slavery*, 373. The best overview of Reconstruction era white paramilitarism in South Carolina is Shapiro, "Ku Klux Klan during Reconstruction"; West, *Reconstruction Ku Klux Klan in York County*; Zuczek, *State of Rebellion*.

18. Ostensibly these militia were open to "all males between the ages of eighteen and forty-five," both white and black, but it was the determined policy of the Democrats by this point to boycott all state institutions, and in any case whites in South Carolina (as elsewhere) were repulsed by the idea of serving in a "mixed militia." Thus, as Peggy Lamson writes, for all intents and purposes, the militia was almost exclusively black. Whites universally referred to them as the "negro militia" (see *Glorious Failure*, 86). On Reconstruction era state militias generally, see Singletary, *Negro Militia and Reconstruction*.

19. Zuczek, *State of Rebellion*, 18.

20. Shapiro, "Ku Klux Klan during Reconstruction," 40. See also Sam Sturges Testimony, South Carolina, 3: 1950; Lewis Merrill Testimony, South Carolina, 3: 1480; Jack Johnson Testimony, South Carolina, 2: 1168; Sam Nuckles Testimony, South Carolina, 2: 1161; Elias Hill Testimony, South Carolina, 3: 1410; James R. Bratton Testimony, South Carolina, 3: 1361–62. All in U.S. Congress, *Testimony Taken by the Joint Select Committee.*

21. *New York Herald*, 13 March 1871, cited in Shapiro, "Ku Klux Klan during Reconstruction," 44.

22. Matthew C. Butler Testimony, South Carolina, 2: 1191, U.S. Congress, *Testimony Taken by the Joint Select Committee*; West, *Reconstruction Ku Klux Klan in York County*, 62; R. B. Elliott to Governor Scott, 1 April 1870, in Governor Robert K. Scott Papers, SCDAH. On Scott's meetings with conservatives, see *Macon Weekly Telegraph*, 21 March 1871.

23. West, *Reconstruction Ku Klux Klan in York County*, 62; Henry T. Thompson, *Ousting the Carpetbagger*, 70.

24. See Foner, *Reconstruction*, 344.

25. See Kelly, "Labor and Place," passim.

26. William C. Hine, "Black Organized Labor in Reconstruction Charleston," 512; *Charleston Daily Courier*, 14 October 1869; William Middleton to Henry Middleton, 13 September 1873, cited in Shick and Doyle, "South Carolina Phosphate Boom," 15. Hine (512) detects "a fairly distinct gap between the politicians and the postwar organized labor force that was largely unskilled and had only recently been freed from slavery."

27. T. P. Bailey to Thomas Jefferson McKie, 20 February 1871, 27 March 1871, Thomas Jefferson McKie Papers, DUSC; Rogers, *History of Georgetown* County, 448–60, 442.

28. Holt, *Black over White*, 153.

29. Gillette, *Retreat from Reconstruction*, 316; *New York World*, 16 September 1876. On Chamberlain and the content of his retrenchment policies see also Camejo, *Racism, Revolution, Reaction*, 159; Foner, *Reconstruction*, 543–44. On the tensions between Chamberlain and the Republican electorate see also Tindall, *South Carolina Negroes*, 11; Simkins and Woody, *South Carolina during Reconstruction*, 477; Williamson, *After Slavery*, 401–2.

30. It is likely the Democratic press exaggerated these tensions, though they were evident on the stump after 1874. Holt suggests that the color issue "was really only the visible tip of a deeper schism in the postwar Negro leadership [manifesting] subtle but distinct differences in outlook and emphasis between the largely mulatto bourgeoisie and the black peasantry, with the urban-based slaves and ex-slave domestics constituting something of a swing group" (*Black over White*, 17).

31. The seminal treatment of the 1876 strikes is Foner, "Emancipated Worker." For an extended treatment that emphasizes division between Republican moderates and the grassroots, see Kelly, "Black Laborers, the Republican Party, and the Crisis of Reconstruction."

32. Alfred B. Williams, *Hampton and His Red Shirts*, 331; "Testimony of John Larescey," U.S. Congress, *Papers in the Case of Tillman vs. Smalls*, 191; information on Bissell is included in Linder, *Historical Atlas of the Rice Plantations*, 86.

33. Chamberlain's telegram to Colleton Sheriff Terry is quoted in "Troubles in Colleton," *Charleston News and Courier*, 27 May 1876. Planter Robert Fishburne discusses Colcock's appointment in his testimony in U.S. Congress, *Papers in the Case of Tillman vs. Smalls*, 197. See also William Stone to Governor Chamberlain, 24 May 1876, Telegrams Received, Governor Chamberlain Papers, SCDAH. Fuller's appointment is discussed in Robert Smalls to Governor Chamberlain, 24 August 1876, Governor Chamberlain Papers, SCDAH. Democratic approval of Chamberlain is expressed in "Latest News from the Combahee and Ashepoo Rice Fields," *Charleston News and Courier*, 27 May 1876.

34. "High Times at Orangeburg," Charleston *Journal of Commerce*, 23 August 1876.

35. S. G. Welch to Governor Chamberlain, 23 August 1876, Letters Received, Box 14, Folder 8, Governor Chamberlain Papers, SCDAH. The assurances offered to Chamberlain by this individual contradict a number of other accounts of sentiment among Colleton Democrats. There were, across the state, some who favored gradualism and continued stability under Chamberlain to the prospects of race war seemingly contained in the white paramilitary campaign.

36. *Charleston News and Courier*, 23 September 1876; "High Times at Orangeburg," Charleston *Journal of Commerce*, 23 August 1876.

37. Hamilton's support for Chamberlain is discussed in *Port Royal Standard and Commercial*, 31 August 1876, and the *Charleston News and Courier*, 17 July 1876, where Hamilton is described as a "formidable obstacle" to the "elements of probable opposition to [Chamberlain's] renomination." Alfred B. Williams (44) credits Hamilton with carrying a Beaufort meeting for Chamberlain when "the real majority of the negroes seemed hostile." The

transcript of Hamilton's speech at the Crooked Hill meeting appears in the *Charleston News and Courier*, 30 May 1876. Hamilton's letter to the *News and Courier* appears under the heading "Indignation Meetings" on 25 July 1876. Republican denunciation of Hamilton's role appears in the *News and Courier*, 1 August 1876.

38. After conservatives regained power, Hampton would attempt to make good on his pledge, dividing interior Beaufort from the coast and renaming the new district Hampton County, but Myers's desertion would go unrewarded. Having rid themselves of the Republican threat, "straight-outs" felt under no compulsion to allow even the much-attenuated back political representation that Miller and Myers had sought, making it "impossible for men of Myers' stamp of the Negro race" to hold office on behalf of the Democrats. See Tindall, *South Carolina Negroes*, 23–24.

39. *Charleston News and Courier*, 2 June 1876; Holt, *Black over White*, 161–62, cited in Montgomery, *Citizen Worker*, 126. Before his journey southward, David Zimmerman writes, Whipper had "amassed a sizable fortune" in Pennsylvania business ventures, which included "land holdings in Pennsylvania and Canada, lumberyards, railroad cars, and a steam ship on Lake Erie." See Zimmerman, "William Whipper."

40. *Columbus Enquirer-Sun*, 30 December 1902.

41. On fusion arrangements in Georgetown, see Rogers, *History of Georgetown County*, 464–78. Rogers writes that Robert B. Anderson, a school superintendent prominent in local Republican politics, was known for having spoken out "against leaving the control of the [local] normal and industrial school . . . under the control of a board of Northerners who did not teach the students to be in sympathy 'with the great interests of the South.' Anderson wanted his race to be educated, but he wanted an education that would fit the Negro into a southern society" (477–78). On Smalls's maneuvering in the late 1880s see Gelston, "Radical Versus Straight-Out," 234.

42. The most thorough modern study of the 1876 results in South Carolina concludes that "Chamberlain, who lost the election according to the count of ballots actually cast, would probably have won had the election not been so corrupt." See King, "Counting the Votes," 190.

43. Montgomery, *Citizen Worker*, 118.

Afterword

ERIC FONER

When one reaches a certain age as a historian, an odd phenomenon sets in. The scholar realizes that he has made the transition from young Turk to elder statesman. Approaches once considered cutting edge are now viewed by one's students as old hat. I think Professor Holt and I are the only contributors to this volume old enough to remember the excitement, the liberating power, produced by the first appearance of the works of E. P. Thompson, Eric Hobsbawm, Herbert Gutman, and other pioneers of the "new social history."[1] Today, my graduate students consider this the "old" history, which scholars need to move beyond. In writing about Reconstruction, I suppose I now represent the old school. But this process is altogether natural. As I wrote more than twenty years ago at the beginning of *Reconstruction: America's Unfinished Revolution*, nothing is more essential to the study of history than reinterpretation. Or, as Oscar Wilde put it: the only thing we owe to history is to rewrite it.

My book appeared at the end of an incredibly creative thirty-year period of scholarship on Reconstruction. Although the critique of the Dunning School can be traced back to W.E.B. Du Bois's *Black Reconstruction in America* in the 1930s, and even earlier to the works of John R. Lynch and others, the modern revisionist wave began with the appearance in 1960 of Eric McKitrick's *Andrew Johnson and Reconstruction* and, for Reconstruction in the South, Joel Williamson's *After Slavery*.[2] By the time my book appeared, the traditional interpretation of Reconstruction had been laid to rest, and in dozens of outstanding monographs the building blocks had been created for a new overall account of the era.[3]

Of course, the rewriting of Reconstruction's history did not stop in 1988. A few years ago, Thomas Brown edited a volume, *Reconstructions*, surveying recent trends in historiography.[4] The essays in this collection demonstrate that the reinterpretation of Reconstruction is continuing apace. What impresses me about the individual contributions is how they reflect an expansion of historians' approaches, or to put it more precisely, a series of expansions that hold out the promise of reconceptualizing Reconstruction. One can begin with the expansion of the source base available to scholars brought about by the digital revolution. When I began work on Reconstruction, the World Wide Web did not exist (nor did e-mail, so that scholars wasted a lot less of their time than nowadays). I was used to writing on an electric typewriter (those who have never heard of this device can probably see one at the Smithsonian Institution). "High tech" meant consulting documents on microfilm or microfiche. Midway through my research, the Kaypro II appeared. I wrote my book on this precursor of today's laptop computer (the size of a small suitcase), on 5¼ inch floppy disks, each of which held about twenty pages of typed text. My book consisted of a very large stack of these disks.

Several of the contributions illustrate how digitalized sources make possible the kinds of investigations previously all but impossible. Susan O'Donovan uses the records of the Freedman's Savings Bank to probe the occupational and family structure of the post-emancipation black community of Wilmington, North Carolina. Michael Fitzgerald locates Alabama Ku Klux Klansmen in the manuscript census of 1860 and 1870, enabling him to sketch the "ruinous impact" of the Civil War on what became an embittered group of violent young men. When I wrote *Freedom's Lawmakers* in the early 1990s, I searched the manuscript census for black officials.[5] This was a laborious process, made somewhat easier by finding names in the printed indexes compiled by a publishing company associated with the Mormon Church and then locating each entry on the relevant reel of microfilm. Today, that research could be done at home in an afternoon. Numerous other sources for the Reconstruction era are also now available and searchable online, including congressional debates and documents (among them the indispensable Ku Klux Klan hearings), plantation records, and nineteenth-century newspapers.

Of course, historical sources are only as useful as the questions historians ask of them. And these essays reveal several ways in which historians' approaches to Reconstruction have expanded in recent years. One is a new emphasis on the diversity of the post-emancipation experience. Several essays exemplify the value of looking carefully at Reconstruction at the local level. This may make generalization more difficult, but it gives us a far richer sense of the texture of life in the postwar South. O'Donovan's study of Wilmington shows that the black community there differed from its counterparts in plantation areas in economic structure, exposure to new ideas, and family stability. Erik Mathisen examines in detail how issues relating to citizenship, loyalty, and property rights were debated in Mississippi. Brian Kelly (building on the work of Thomas Holt) stresses how careful attention to the class divisions and political dynamics within the black population help explain the collapse of Reconstruction in South Carolina. James Illingworth relates how grassroots agitation for political rights and economic justice among African Americans and their white allies in New Orleans predated Radical Reconstruction. Bruce Baker focuses on Reconstruction in Greenville, South Carolina, and J. Michael Rhyne on Kentucky (a state that remained in the Union during the Civil War, but experienced its own version of Reconstruction afterward).

Then there is the expansion of Reconstruction's cast of characters itself. Some of the best recent work on that era has introduced gender as a key category of analysis, examining changes in gender roles and relations resulting from the Civil War and emancipation among both white and black women. O'Donovan sees the family as central to the early emergence and long persistence of black political activism in Wilmington. Rhyne discusses the extreme risks taken by freedwomen in combating Kentucky's oppressive apprenticeship system, which represented a dire threat to postwar black families. Holt notes that in Jamaica, British emancipators assumed that freedom carried with it specific definitions of gender roles, with women remaining at home to look after their families—something denied them in slavery—while men entered the wage-labor force. A gendered division of social space was to be part of the legacy of emancipation. These essays suggest that in the United States, too, women experienced emancipation and its aftermath differently from men in significant ways, and that patriarchal assumptions were built into black men's understanding of freedom.

My book on Reconstruction paid some attention to gender issues, in discussions of the post-emancipation black family and the Reconstruction era women's rights movement. (It may well have been the first survey of the era to discuss the career of Victoria Woodhull.) But more recent studies, such as books by Laura Edwards, LeeAnn Whites, and others, have placed far more emphasis on the interrelationship of gender, race, labor, and politics. One of the most interesting of these is Thavolia Glymph's *Out of the House of Bondage*, which examines the difficult, sometimes violent transformation in relations between black and white women, exploring freedwomen's struggles to create new gender roles at a time when many white women were attempting to recreate antebellum lives of privilege in dramatically changed circumstances. Another important work is Martha Jones's *All Bound Up Together*, which examines the debate within black organizations over the role and rights of women. Jones demonstrates how the abolitionist discourse of equal rights affected discussions of the "woman question" in black churches and societies. All this scholarship asks us to expand our definition of politics beyond the electoral arena to the many locations where struggles for power occur, thereby opening the door to the inclusion of women in political history.[6]

Baker's paper builds on a different kind of expansion of the cast of characters. His indicates that the era witnessed a profound transformation in the lives of upcountry white Southerners, a group neglected in most histories of Reconstruction. Baker's call for an approach to Reconstruction that integrates the experience of poor whites and former slaves suggests an agenda that few historians, as yet, have attempted.

These essays also embody an expansion of the chronological definition of Reconstruction. My book began Reconstruction in 1863 and ended in 1877, although it noted that the process of adjustment to the end of slavery continued well beyond the latter date. Since then, the chronological boundaries of Reconstruction have continued to expand. Steven Hahn's *A Nation under Our Feet* begins with black political ideas under slavery as the seedbed of Reconstruction politics and takes the story of rural black politics down to the twentieth century.[7] Several essays here reflect this broadened definition of Reconstruction: Kelly takes his story to 1900; Baker to 1878; O'Donovan begins her essay in 1898 and works her way backward to the Reconstruction era.

The implication of this chronological redefinition is significant. Historians now recognize Reconstruction as part of the long trajectory of Southern and national history, not a bizarre aberration unrelated to what came before or after, as the Dunning School saw it. We now have what might be called a Long Reconstruction, like the long civil rights movement (which begins in the 1930s or 1940s) or the long nineteenth century (1789–1914). Of course, this expansion was anticipated by Du Bois, who used the dates 1860–1880 for *Black Reconstruction* and began his book with a chapter on slavery.

Several essays illustrate the value of this chronological redefinition. The expanded chronology allows Kelly to demonstrate the result of the collapse of Reconstruction for South Carolina's black population. However significant as a national and regional turning point, the year 1877 did not mark the end of black politics. Black political power ebbed and flowed for at least another generation, as people found new organizational expressions for their aspirations. Kelly traces the rise of a more conservative black politics, anticipating Booker T. Washington's outlook. Elsewhere, blacks took advantage of splits among whites to ally with dissident Democrats or Populists, as O'Donovan shows.

Taking the story into the 1890s also allows for comparison with other parts of the country. As O'Donovan notes, the retreat from universal suffrage was not confined to the South in these years. Still to be fully studied are the history of black-white relations in the Knights of Labor, the Farmers' Alliance, and the Populist Party, and how, whatever the limitations of these movements, black activists sought to use them to achieve local gains.

To understand history, E. H. Carr observed in *What Is History*, study the historian.[8] Reconstruction historiography has always reflected the preoccupations of the era in which it was written. Four of the essays here, by Jonathan Bryant, Michael Fitzgerald, Susan O'Donovan, and J. Michael Rhyne, examine the role of violence—both organized and day-to-day—in Reconstruction, especially in the undermining of blacks' political power and economic aspirations. Illingworth shows how the New Orleans riot (or "massacre" as he calls it) of 1866 "decapitated" the city's white Radical leadership. In the post-9/11 era, it is perhaps not surprising that historians are turning their attention to homegrown American terrorism. Recent books on Reconstruction aimed at an audience outside the academy have tended to infuse their subjects with drama by focusing on violent confrontations (rather than, for example, the operations and accomplishments of Reconstruction governments). One thinks of works like Nicholas Lemann's *Redemption* on the violent overthrow of Reconstruction in Mississippi; Stephen Budiansky's *Bloody Shirt*, a survey of violence during the entire period; and two recent books on the Colfax Massacre, the single bloodiest incident in an era steeped in terrorism by the Ku Klux Klan and kindred white supremacist groups.[9]

Also reflecting today's preoccupations is a more bittersweet assessment of the Reconstruction governments. Kelly condemns South Carolina's Republican leadership for factionalism, fragmentation, and failing to serve the interests of their grassroots black constituency. Gregory Downs sees Reconstruction as doomed from the outset by Northern Republicans' rapid demobilization of the Union army and general fiscal retrenchment. Fitzgerald, in previous work on Alabama and a recent overall account of Reconstruction, *Splendid Failure*, is far more critical of the South's Republican government than I have been, emphasizing how corruption and factionalism undermined their effectiveness and legitimacy.[10] Fitzgerald's call in the Brown volume for an "ethical recalibration" of Reconstruction studies that would downplay the era's idealism, not only in the South but also on the national level, perhaps reflects in part an understandable cynicism about politics in the age of George W. Bush, when that collection appeared.[11]

On the other hand, Kelly's paper mentions that the advent of Radical Reconstruction in Washington invigorated grassroots mobilization in South Carolina. And the collapse of Reconstruction in the state in 1876 was intimately related to national politics. This points to the most glaring absence in the collection: national politics. No essay mentions the name Charles Sumner, or for that matter, Frederick Douglass. None of the contributions discusses the titanic battle between Andrew Johnson and Congress that led to the rewriting of our laws and constitution in ways that still reverberate in the twenty-first century.

To ask for attention to these national debates and changes does not mean homogenizing the study of Reconstruction or losing sight of its local diversity. Mathisen demonstrates the value of looking closely at the legal history of Reconstruction, at how definitions of citizenship and loyalty were played out at the local level. Downs details the difficulties faced by representatives of the federal government, such as Freedmen's Bureau agents, in establishing their authority in North Carolina. The legal historian Linda Tverdy is currently examining how national civil rights legislation was implemented at the local level (also in North Carolina), highlighting the inherent conflict between a national standard of equal civil rights and a local legal culture still governed by the common law, with its traditional emphasis on status and hierarchy.[12]

Despite, or because of, the proliferation of new approaches, the question remains how to synthesize current insights into a coherent new account of Reconstruction. Holt suggests one possible way forward. As I have noted, Reconstruction historiography has always spoken directly to current concerns. The Dunning School, with its emphasis on the alleged horrors of Republican Reconstruction, provided scholarly legitimation for Jim Crow, black disenfranchisement, and the now long-departed solid Democratic South. The revisionist school arose in tandem with the civil rights movement. What I have termed the "post-revisionist" writing of the 1970s reflected disappointment with what seemed to be the limits of civil rights activism, especially in terms of the economic status of black Americans.[13] Today, issues central to Reconstruction are still "relevant": terrorism, the rights of citizens, the possibilities of interracial politics, the relationship between political and economic democracy, the limits of presidential power, and American empire. Downs, indeed, refers directly to the American occupation of Iraq and Afghanistan as a way of understanding the challenges facing the postwar "occupation" of the American South.[14]

The newly empowered national state created by the Civil War and Reconstruction could be used for all kinds of purposes. Shortly before the end of the war, Francis E. Spinner, the Treasurer of the United States (whose signature adorned every greenback issued by the federal government, itself a key expression of the expansion of national power), made this point in a different way: "What a school we have kept, and what a lesson we have taught the Secesh in particular and mankind in general. The thing to be feared now is, that we will be running around the world with a chip on our shoulder. If we can avoid this, a glorious future is ours."[15]

The warning reverberates in our own time. Ironically, as Downs argues, the national state was simply too weak during Reconstruction to impose its will effectively in the South. But even during Reconstruction the reborn Union began to project its power against Native Americans in the West and other peoples abroad. As the struggle between Johnson and Congress reached its climax, the United States acquired Alaska, one part of an imperial agenda long advocated by Secretary of State William H. Seward. President Grant attempted to annex the Dominican Republic. In other words, if recent events have placed the question of the origins of American empire back on historians' agendas, part of the answer lies during Reconstruction.

But the question is more complex than simply territorial acquisition. The emancipation of the slaves greatly strengthened empire's ideological underpinning. In his excellent study of the British movement to abolish the slave trade, Christopher Brown shows how abolition created a stash of moral capital (the title of his book) that Britain expended throughout the nineteenth century.[16] The very act of abolition demonstrated irrefutably Britain's noble motives as it expanded its imperial holdings in Africa and elsewhere. So, too, emancipation in the United States gave new meaning to Jefferson's description of the United States as an "empire of liberty," a notion somewhat tarnished before the Civil War by the powerful presence of slavery. With emancipation, advocates of an imperial mission insisted, it could no longer be denied that American expansionism meant the expansion of freedom. And current political rhetoric shows that this conception remains alive and well today. Indeed, it is striking how commentators across the political spectrum, from Glenn Beck to President Obama, have assimilated the struggle against slavery and the civil rights movement into an overall narrative of American history that seeks to convince the world of our nation's commitment to "freedom." Yet it is also worth remembering that veterans of the struggle against slavery and for equal rights for black Americans were among those who argued in 1898 that an empire cannot be a democratic republic. The abolitionist legacy flowed into anti-imperialism as well as American empire.[17]

Other aspects of the contested legacy of emancipation and Reconstruction offer fruitful areas for research. One is how the language of slavery and antislavery was appropriated by the courts to legitimize liberty of contract jurisprudence. The memory of slavery played a large role in the era's judicial discourse. Yet the courts seemed to understand slavery not as a complex system of economic, political, social, and racial power, but as little more than the denial of the laborer's right to choose his livelihood and bargain for compensation. The identification of freedom of labor with freedom of contract was enshrined in successive decisions of state and federal courts that struck down state laws regulating economic enterprise as an interference with the right of the free laborer to choose his employment and working conditions and of the entrepreneur to utilize his property as he saw fit. "Liberty of contract," not equality before the law for blacks, came to be defined as the meaning of the Fourteenth Amendment. For decades, the courts viewed state regulation of business enterprise as a paternalistic insult to free labor, a throwback to the thinking characteristic of slavery.

By the same token, however, the labor movement adopted and expanded the Reconstruction era language of equal citizenship (even though by and large it did little to address the plight of the former slaves). Labor spokesmen referred to the Thirteenth Amendment as a "glorious labor amendment" that enshrined the dignity of labor in the Constitution. Reaching back across the divide of the Civil War, labor defined employers as a new "slave power," called for the "emancipation and enfranchisement of all who labor," and spoke of an "irrepressible conflict between the wage system of labor and the republican system of government."[18]

All this raises the question of the historical "memory" of Reconstruction, a subject recently examined by Baker in *What Reconstruction Meant*, which shows how in South Carolina politicians used a particular understanding of Reconstruction as a weapon in the construction of the Jim Crow South.[19] In this white supremacist narrative, the Redeemers and Red Shirts took on heroic status. A counternarrative survived in black communities, Baker shows, to be rediscovered in the 1930s by Southern radicals who found in Reconstruction a model for the interracial cooperation they hoped to bring to the twentieth-century South.

There is much more to be done on how the "memory" of Reconstruction affected subsequent American history. The decline of Reconstruction helped to inscribe a racialized version of empire, illustrating the long-term consequences of the failure of the vision of equality that for a time animated Reconstruction. One wonders how ideas about Reconstruction and its alleged abuses affected policymakers in the U.S.-occupied Philippines or, later, Cuba, Haiti, and the Dominican Republic, as they dealt with non-white subjects.

In this regard, American historians can learn a great deal from a recent book by two Australian scholars, Marilyn Lake and Henry Reynolds, *Drawing the Global Colour Line*.[20] They point out that the late nineteenth and early twentieth centuries were a time of global concern about nonwhite immigration, a global assumption of the white man's burden, and a global sense of fraternity among self-described "Anglo-Saxon" nations, including Australia, New Zealand, Canada, the United States, and South Africa. Political leaders in these countries studied and copied each other's racial policies. South Africa was influenced by American segregation in implementing its own system of racial apartheid. Australia, the United States, and Canada borrowed from each other in implementing Chinese exclusion. The "bible" of those who implemented such measures, Lake and Reynolds write, was James Bryce's *American Commonwealth*, and especially his account of Reconstruction as a time of corruption and misgovernment caused by the enfranchisement of the former slaves. Bryce's account "proved" that blacks, coolies, aborigines, et cetera, were unfit to be citizens. It was frequently invoked by the founders of Australia's federal nation in support of their vision of a White Australia, and by white South Africans to rationalize apartheid. In the 1893 edition of his book, Bryce noted the similarities between the 1890 Mississippi literacy test, a key step in black disenfranchisement, and the Franchise of Ballot Act of 1892 in Cape Colony. Both were ostensibly nonracial laws, in deference to metropolitan authorities (in Washington and London) still rhetorically committed to the idea of equal rights among citizens or subjects but willing to allow the exclusion of "unfit" persons from the ballot on other grounds. Around the world, the "key history lesson" (as Lake and Reynolds put it) of Reconstruction was taken to be the impossibility of multiracial democracy.[21]

Holt takes this question of Reconstruction and empire even further, juxtaposing the problem of slavery and freedom in the nineteenth century with the globalization of labor and capital in our own time and the spread, even in the heart of the American metropolis, of slave-like conditions of labor. Like *Drawing the Global Colour Line*, Holt's essay suggests the need to breach the boundary of the nation-state that has defined the history of Reconstruction, like so much else in American historical writing. This is, to be sure, a difficult task. But it holds out the promise of a truly new account of Reconstruction, one fully embedded in the long processes of American and global history.

Notes

1. The key works, among many others, were Edward P. Thompson, *Making of the English Working Class*; Hobsbawm, *Labouring Men*; and Gutman, "Work, Culture, and Society."

2. Du Bois, *Black Reconstruction*; Lynch, *Facts of Reconstruction*; McKitrick, *Andrew Johnson*; Williamson, *After Slavery*.

3. Among many others, these works included Carter, *When the War Was Over*; Ronald F. Davis, *Good and Faithful Labor*; Drago, *Black Politicians and Reconstruction in Georgia*; Fields, *Slavery and Freedom on the Middle Ground*; Harris, *Day of the Carpetbagger*; Litwack, *Been in the Storm So Long*; Powell, *New Masters*; Rable, *But There Was No Peace*.

4. Thomas J. Brown, ed., *Reconstructions*.

5. Foner, *Freedom's Lawmakers*.

6. Edwards, *Gendered Strife and Confusion*; Whites, *Gender Matters*; Glymph, *Out of the House of Bondage*; Martha S. Jones, *All Bound Up Together*.

7. Hahn, *A Nation under Our Feet*.

8. Carr, *What Is History?*

9. Lemann, *Redemption*; Budiansky, *Bloody Shirt*; Keith, *Colfax Massacre*; Lane, *The Day Freedom Died*.

10. Fitzgerald, *Urban Emancipation* and *Splendid Failure*.

11. Fitzgerald, "Reconstruction Politics."

12. Tverdy's work is in a dissertation-in-progress at Columbia University.

13. Foner, "Reconstruction Revisited," 83.

14. Jeremi Suri's recent *Liberty's Surest Guardian* makes the comparison between Reconstruction and the occupation of Iraq explicit.

15. Day, *Man on a Hill Top*, 299.

16. Christopher L. Brown, *Moral Capital*.

17. Beisner, *Twelve Against Empire*.

18. See the discussion in Foner, *Story of American Freedom*, 116–30.

19. Baker, *What Reconstruction Meant*.

20. Lake and Reynolds, *Drawing the Global Colour Line*.

21. Ibid., 6–10, 50–65.

Bibliography

Primary Sources

Adjutant General's Office, 1762–1984. Records. National Archives and Records Administration Record Group 94. Washington, D.C.

Beecher, James Chaplin. Papers. Duke University Special Collections. Durham, N.C.

Bullock, Governor Rufus. Papers. Georgia Department of Archives and History. Atlanta, Ga.

Bureau of Refugees, Freedmen, and Abandoned Lands. Records. National Archives and Records Administration Record Group 105. Washington, D.C.

Chamberlain, Governor Daniel H. Papers. South Carolina Department of Archives and History. Columbia, S.C.

Durant, Thomas Jefferson. Papers. New York Historical Society Library.

Fleming, Walter Lynwood. Papers. New York Public Library. New York, N.Y.

Greenville County (South Carolina) Board of County Commissioners. *Minute Book, 1873–1883*. http://www.greenvillecounty.org.

Haddock, T. M., comp. *Haddock's Wilmington, N.C., Directory, and General Advertiser, Containing a General and Business Directory of the City, Historical Sketch, State, County, City Government, &c., &c.* Wilmington, N.C.: P. Heinseberger, 1871.

Hart, Joel Tanner. Papers. Filson Historical Society. Louisville, Ky..

Hayes, John W. Papers. Catholic University Archives. Washington, D.C.

Historical Census Browser. University of Virginia: Geospatial and Statistical Data Center. http://www.fisher.lib.virginia.edu/collections/stats/histcensus/index.html.

Historical United States Census Data Browser, using data from The Ninth Census of the United States: 1870. Ann Arbor, Mich. Inter-university Consortium for Political and Social Research. http://www.fisher.lib.virginia.edu/census/.

Holloway Scrapbook. Avery Research Institute. Charleston, S.C.

Howard, Betty. Diary, 1865–1866. Filson Historical Society. Louisville, Ky.

Humphries, Governor Benjamin. Correspondence and Papers. Mississippi Department of Archives and History. Jackson, Miss.

Hunter, Charles N. Papers. Duke University Special Collections. Durham, N.C.

Irwin, David, ed. *The Code of the State of Georgia, 1867*. Atlanta: Steam Press, 1867.

League of Nations. *Convention on Certain Questions Relating to the Conflict of Nationality Law*. The Hague: League of Nations, 13 April 1930. Treaty Series, vol. 179, p. 89, No. 4137. http://www.unhcr.org/refworld/docid/3ae6b3b00.html.

McKie, Thomas Jefferson. Papers. Duke University Special Collections. Durham, N.C.

New Georgia Encyclopedia, s.v. "Jackson, Henry Rootes." http://www.georgiaencyclopedia.org/nge/Article.jsp?id=h-865&hl=y.

———. S.v. "Johnson, James." http://www.georgiaencyclopedia.org/nge/Article.jsp?id=h-2814.

The New-Orleans Riot: Its Official History (The Tribune Tracts, No. 1). New York: *New York Tribune*, 1866.

Office of the Comptroller of the Currency. Records. National Archives and Records Administration Record Group 101. Washington, D.C.

Orr, Governor James Lawrence. Papers. South Carolina Department of Archives and History. Columbia, S.C.

Perry, Benjamin F. Papers. Southern Historical Collection. Wilson Library, University of North Carolina at Chapel Hill.

Schirmer, Jacob. Diary. South Carolina Historical Society. Charleston, S.C.

Scott, Governor Robert K. Papers. South Carolina Department of Archives and History. Columbia, S.C.

Sharkey, Governor William Lewis. Correspondence and Papers. Mississippi Department of Archives and History. Jackson, Miss.

Shoemaker, Isaac. Diary. Duke University Special Collections. Durham, N.C.

Stagg, J.C.A., ed. *The Papers of James Madison Digital Edition*. Charlottesville: University of Virginia Press, Rotunda, 2010. http://www.rotunda.upress.virginia.edu/founders/default.xqy?keys=JSMN-search-1-1&mode=deref.

State of Louisiana Republican Party. *Proceedings of the Convention of the Republican Party of Louisiana, Held at Economy Hall, New Orleans, September 23, 1865; and of the Central Executive Committee of the Friends of Universal Suffrage*. New Orleans: The Tribune, 1865.

State of Mississippi. *Journal of the Proceedings and Debates in the Constitutional Convention of the State of Mississippi*. Jackson: E. M. Yerger, 1865.

State of South Carolina. *Acts and Joint Resolutions of the General Assembly of the State of South Carolina Passed at the Regular Session of 1870–71*. Columbia, S.C.: Republican Printing Co., 1871.

Stone, Amherst Willoughby. Vertical File. Georgia Historical Society. Savannah, Ga.

Switzler, William. F. *Report on the Internal Commerce of the United States*. Washington, D.C.: Government Printing Office, 1886.

Tift, Nelson. *The Condition of Affairs in Georgia: Statement of the Hon. Nelson Tift to the Reconstruction Committee of the House of Representatives, Washington, 18 February 1869*. 1869. Reprint, New York: Books for Libraries Press, 1971.

United States Army Continental Commands, 1821–1920. Records. National Archives and Records Administration Record Group 393. Washington, D.C.

United States, Bureau of the Census. *Agriculture of the United States in 1860*. Washington: Government Printing Office, 1864.

———. *Agriculture Schedule, 1860 manuscript census returns*. Chatham County, Ga.

———. *Compendium of the Ninth Census*. Washington, Government Printing Office, 1872.

———. *Population Schedule, 1870 manuscript census returns*. Chatham County, Ga.

United States, Congress. *House Executive Documents*. H.R. Rep., 39th Cong., 1st Sess., No. 11, Ser. 1255. Washington, D.C.: Government Printing Office, 1866.

———. *Message from the President of the United States, Transmitting Report of the Commissioner of the Bureau of Refugees, Freedmen, and Abandoned Lands*. H.R. Rep., 39th Cong., 1st Sess., H.R. Doc. No. 11, Ser. 1255. Washington, D.C.: Government Printing Office, 1866.

———. *Papers in the Case of Tillman vs. Smalls*. U.S. H.R. Rep., 45th Cong., Misc. H.R. Doc. No. 11. Washington, D.C.: Government Printing Office, 1878.

———. *Report of the Joint Committee on Reconstruction*. 39th Cong., 1st Sess., pt. 3, H.R. Rep. No. 30. Washington, D.C.: Government Printing Office, 1866.

———. *Report on the Condition of the South, by Carl Schurz*. 39th Cong., 1st Sess. Exec. Doc. No. 2. Washington, D.C.: Government Printing Office, 1865.

———. *Testimony Taken by the Joint Select Committee to Inquire into the Condition of Affairs in the Late Insurrectionary States*. 42nd Cong., 2nd Sess., No. 41, Pts. 3–5: South Carolina, vols. 1–3. Washington, D.C.: Government Printing Office, 1872.

———. *United States Statutes at Large*. 121 vols. Washington, D.C.: Government Printing Office, 1937–.

United States, Department of Labor: Office of Policy Planning and Research. *The Negro Family: The Case for National Action*. Washington: The Superintendent of Documents, 1965.

United States, Department of State. *Executive Documents Published by the Order of the House of Representatives during the First Session of the Thirty-Ninth Congress 1865–66*. Washington D.C.: Government Printing Office, 1866.

———. *Human Trafficking and Modern-day Slavery, USA, 2011*. http://www.gvnet.com/humantrafficking/USA.htm.

———. *Trafficking in Persons Report, 2011*. http://www.state.gov/j/tip/rls/tiprpt/.

United States, Navy Department. *Report of the Secretary of the Navy, with an Appendix Containing Reports from Officers*. Washington: Government Printing Office, 1865.

United States, War Department. *Examination and Survey of Wilmington Harbor and Cape Fear River, North Carolina*. H.R. Rep., House Executive Docs., 56th Cong., 2nd Sess., No. 180, Ser. 4148. Washington: Government Printing Office, 1900.

———. *Report of Brevet Major General O. O. Howard, Commissioner Bureau of Refugees, Freedmen, and Abandoned Lands to the Secretary of War, Oct. 20, 1869*. Washington: Government Printing Office, 1869.

———. *The War of the Rebellion: A Compilation of the Official Records of the Union and Confederate Armies*. Washington: Government Printing Office, 1880–1901.

Warren, C. J. "Dissenting Opinion." Supreme Court of the United States, 356 U.S. 44, Perez v. Brownell [No. 44]; Decided 31 March 1958.

Wilmington Chamber of Commerce. *Wilmington, North Carolina: Past Present, and Future, History of Its Harbor with Detailed Reports of the Work for Improving and Restoring the Same, Now Being Conducted by the U.S. Government, Resources and Advantages as an Entrepôt for Western Cities, Harbor of Refuge, and Coaling Depot for the Navy and Merchant Marine*. Wilmington, N.C.: J. A. Englehard, 1872. http://www.docsouth.unc.edu/nc/wilming72/wilming72.html.

Wright, Donald P. *A Different Kind of War: The United States Army in Operation Enduring Freedom (OEF), October 2001–September 2005*. Washington: Government Printing Office, 2010.

Secondary Sources

Abbott, Martin. *The Freedmen's Bureau in South Carolina, 1865–1872*. Chapel Hill: University of North Carolina Press, 1967.

Aleinikoff, T. Alexander, and Douglas Klusmeyer, eds. *From Migrants to Citizens: Membership in a Changing World*. Washington, D.C.: Carnegie Endowment for International Peace, 2000.

———. "Plural Nationality: Facing the Future in a Migratory World." In *Citizenship Today: Global Perspectives and Practices*, edited by T. Alexander Aleinikoff and Douglas Klusmeyer, 63–88. Washington, D.C.: Carnegie Endowment for International Peace, 2001.

Alexander, Roberta Sue. *North Carolina Faces the Freedmen: Race Relations during Presidential Reconstruction, 1865–1867*. Durham: Duke University Press, 1985.

Anderson, Benedict R. O'G. *Imagined Communities: Reflections on the Origin and Spread of Nationalism*. London: Verso, 1991.

Andrews, Sidney. *The South since the War: As Shown by Fourteen Weeks of Travel and Observation in Georgia and the Carolinas*. Boston: Ticknor and Fields, 1866.

Aptheker, Herbert. *American Negro Slave Revolts*. New York: International Publishers, 1943.

Armstrong, Thomas F. "From Task Labor to Free Labor: The Transition along Georgia's Rice Coast, 1820–1880." *Georgia Historical Quarterly* 64, no. 4 (Winter 1980): 432–47.

Arnesen, Eric. *Waterfront Workers of New Orleans: Race, Class, and Politics, 1863–1923*. Urbana: University of Illinois Press, 1991.

Astor, Aaron. *Rebels on the Border: Civil War, Emancipation, and the Reconstruction of Kentucky and Missouri*. Baton Rouge: Louisiana State University Press, 2012.

Ayers, Edward L. *The Promise of the New South: Life after Reconstruction*. New York: Oxford University Press, 1992.

———. "Exporting Reconstruction." In *What Caused the Civil War? Reflections on the*

South and Southern History, edited by Edward L. Ayers, 145–66. New York: W. W. Norton, 2005.

———. "The First Occupation." *New York Times*, 29 May 2005.

Baker, Bruce E. *What Reconstruction Meant: Historical Memory in the American South*. Charlottesville: University of Virginia Press, 2007.

Ball, Charles. *Fifty Years in Chains*. Mineola, N.Y.: Dover Books, 1970.

Balogh, Brian. *A Government out of Sight: The Mystery of National Authority in Nineteenth-Century America*. New York: Cambridge University Press, 2009.

Bao, Xiaolan. "Sweatshops in Sunset Park: A Variation of the Late 20th Century Chinese Garment Shops in New York City." *International Labor and Working Class History* 61 (2002): 69–90.

Bardaglio, Peter W. *Reconstructing the Household: Families, Sex, and the Law in the Nineteenth-Century South*. Chapel Hill: University of North Carolina Press, 1995.

Barney, William L. *The Secessionist Impulse: Alabama and Mississippi in 1860*. Princeton, N.J.: Princeton University Press, 1974.

Barton, Keith C. "'Good Cooks and Washers': Slave Hiring, Domestic Labor, and the Market in Bourbon County, Kentucky." *Journal of American History* 84, no. 2 (1997): 436–60.

Batson, Mann. *The Upper Part of Greenville County, South Carolina*. Taylors, S.C.: Faith Printing Co., 1993.

Bayly, Christopher A. *Empire and Information: Intelligence Gathering and Social Communication in India, 1780–1870*. Cambridge, U.K.: Cambridge University Press, 1996.

Beckert, Sven. *The Monied Metropolis: New York City and the Consolidation of the American Bourgeoisie, 1850–1896*. New York: Cambridge University Press, 2001.

Behrend, Justin. "Rebellious Talk and Conspiratorial Plots: The Making of a Slave Insurrection in Civil War Natchez." *Journal of Southern History* 77, no. 1 (February 2011): 17–52.

Beisner, Robert L. *Twelve Against Empire: The Anti-Imperialists 1898–1900*. New York: McGraw Hill, 1968.

Bell, Caryn Cossé. *Revolution, Romanticism, and the Afro-Creole Protest Tradition in Louisiana 1718–1868*. Baton Rouge: Louisiana State University Press, 1997.

Bell, Karen B. "The Ogeechee Troubles: Federal Land Restoration and the 'Lived Realities' of Temporary Proprietors, 1865–1868." *Georgia Historical Quarterly* 85, no. 3 (Fall 2001): 375–97.

Bensel, Richard Franklin. *Yankee Leviathan: The Origins of Central State Authority in America, 1859–1877*. New York: Cambridge University Press, 1990.

Bercaw, Nancy. *Gendered Freedoms: Race, Rights, and the Politics of Household in the Delta, 1861–1875*. Gainesville: University Press of Florida, 2003.

Berlin, Ira, Barbara J. Fields, Thavolia Glymph, Joseph P. Reidy, and Leslie S. Rowland, eds. *Freedom: A Documentary History of Emancipation, 1861–1867, Series 1, Volume 1: The Destruction of Slavery*. New York: Cambridge University Press, 1985.

Berlin, Ira, Joseph P. Reidy, and Leslie S. Rowland, eds. *Freedom: A Documentary History of Emancipation, Series 2: The Black Military Experience*. New York: Cambridge University Press, 1982.

Berlin, Ira, and Leslie F. Rowland, eds. *Families and Freedom: A Documentary History of African-American Kinship in the Civil War Era*. New York: New Press, 1997.

Bessel, Richard. *Germany 1945: From War to Peace*. New York: Harper/HarperCollins, 2009.

Bickel, Alexander M. *History of the Supreme Court of the United States: The Judiciary and Responsible Government: 1910–1921*. Vol. 9. New York: Macmillan, 1984.

Bleser, Carol K. Rothrock. *The Promised Land: A History of the South Carolina Land Commission, 1869–1890*. Columbia: University of South Carolina Press, 1969.

Bolster, W. Jeffrey. *Black Jacks: African American Seamen in the Age of Sail*. Cambridge, Mass.: Harvard University Press, 1997.

Bonacich, Edna, and David V. Waller. "The Role of U.S. Apparel Manufacturers in the Globalization of the Industry in the Pacific Rim." In *Global Production: The Apparel Industry in the Pacific Rim*, edited by Edna Bonacich, Lucie Cheng, Norma Chinchilla, Nora Hamilton, and Paul Ong, 80–102. Philadelphia: Temple University Press, 1994.

Bradley, Mark L. *Bluecoats and Tar Heels: Soldiers and Civilians in Reconstruction North Carolina*. Lexington: University Press of Kentucky, 2009.

Brock, W. R. *An American Crisis: Congress and Reconstruction, 1865–67*. London: Macmillan and Co., 1963.

Brooks, Ethel. "The Ideal Sweatshop: Gender and Transnational Protest." *International Labor and Working-Class History* 61, no. 1 (Spring 2002): 91–111.

Brown, Christopher L. *Moral Capital: Foundations of British Abolitionism*. Chapel Hill: University of North Carolina Press, 2006.

Brown, Elsa Barkley. "Negotiating and Transforming the Public Sphere: African American Political Life in the Transition from Slavery to Freedom." *Public Culture* 7, no. 1 (Fall 1994): 107–46.

Brown, Henry Box. *Narrative of the Life of Henry Box Brown*. Edited by Richard Newman. New York: Oxford University Press, 2002.

Brown, Thomas J., ed. *Reconstructions: New Perspectives on the Postbellum United States*. New York: Oxford University Press, 2006.

Buchanan, Thomas C. *Black Life on the Mississippi: Slaves, Free Blacks, and the Western Steamboat World*. Chapel Hill: University of North Carolina Press, 2004.

Budiansky, Stephen. *Bloody Shirt: Terror after Appomattox*. New York: Viking, 2008.

Burnett, Edmund Cody. "Hog Raising and Hog Driving in the Region of the French Broad River." *Agricultural History* 20, no. 2 (1946): 86–103.

Butler, Benjamin F. *Butler's Book: A Review of His Legal, Political, and Military Career*. Boston: A. M. Thayer and Co. 1892.

Bynum, Victoria E. *The Free State of Jones: Mississippi's Longest Civil War*. Chapel Hill: University of North Carolina Press, 2001.

———. *The Long Shadow of the Civil War: Southern Dissent and Its Legacies*. Chapel Hill: University of North Carolina Press, 2010.

Camejo, Peter. *Racism, Revolution, Reaction, 1861–1877: The Rise and Fall of Radical Reconstruction*. New York: Pathfinder Press, 1976.

Capers, Gerald M. *Occupied City: New Orleans under the Federals, 1862–1865*. Lexington: University of Kentucky Press, 1965.

Carr, E. H. *What Is History?* New York: Alfred A. Knopf, 1962.

Carter, Dan T. "The Anatomy of Fear: The Christmas Day Insurrection Scare of 1865." *Journal of Southern History* 42, no. 3 (1976): 345–64.

———. *When the War Was Over: The Failure of Self-Reconstruction in the South, 1865–1867*. Baton Rouge: Louisiana State University Press, 1985.

Cecelski, David S. *The Waterman's Song: Slavery and Freedom in Maritime North Carolina*. Chapel Hill: University of North Carolina Press, 2001.

Cecelski, David S., and Timothy B. Tyson, eds. *Democracy Betrayed: The Wilmington Race Riot of 1898 and Its Legacy*. Chapel Hill: University of North Carolina Press, 1998.

Cimbala, Paul A. *Under the Guardianship of the Nation: The Freedmen's Bureau and the Reconstruction of Georgia, 1865–1870*. Athens: University of Georgia Press, 1997.

Cimbala, Paul A., and Randall M. Miller, eds. *The Freedmen's Bureau and Reconstruction: Reconsiderations*. New York: Fordham University Press, 1999.

Clavin, Matthew J. *Toussaint Louverture and the American Civil War: The Promise and Peril of a Second Haitian Revolution*. Philadelphia: University of Pennsylvania Press, 2010.

Click, Patricia C. *Time Full of Trial: The Roanoke Island Freedmen's Colony 1862–1867*. Chapel Hill: University of North Carolina Press, 2001.

Clifton, James M. "Twilight Comes to the Rice Kingdom: Postbellum Rice Culture on the South Atlantic Coast." *Georgia Historical Quarterly* 62, no. 2 (Summer 1978): 146–54.

Coclanis, Peter. *The Shadow of a Dream: Economic Life and Death in the South Carolina Lowcountry, 1670–1920*. New York: Oxford University Press, 1991.

Coclanis, Peter. "Slavery, African-American Agency, and the Worlds We Have Lost." *Georgia Historical Quarterly* 79, no. 4 (Winter 1995): 873–84.

Coleman, Kenneth, and Charles Stephen Gurr, eds. *Dictionary of Georgia Biography*. Athens: University of Georgia Press, 1983.

Condon, John Joseph Jr. "Manumission, Slavery, and Family in the Post-Revolutionary Rural Chesapeake: Anne Arundel County, Maryland, 1781–1831." PhD diss., University of Minneapolis, 2001.

Conway, Alan. *The Reconstruction of Georgia*. Minneapolis: University of Minnesota Press, 1966.

Cooper, Frederick, Thomas C. Holt, and Rebecca J. Scott. *Beyond Slavery: Explorations of Race, Labor, and Citizenship in Postemancipation Societies*. Chapel Hill: University of North Carolina Press, 2000.

Coulter, E. Merton. *The Civil War and Readjustment in Kentucky*. Chapel Hill: University of North Carolina Press, 1926.

———. *The South during Reconstruction, 1865–1877*. Baton Rouge: Louisiana State University Press, 1947.

Cullen, Jim. "'I's a Man Now': Gender and African American Men." In *Divided Houses: Gender and the Civil War*, edited by Catherine Clinton and Nina Silber, 76–91. New York: Oxford University Press, 1992.

Darnton, Robert. "An Early Information Society: News and the Media in Eighteenth-Century Paris." *American Historical Review* 105 (February 2000): 1–35.

David, C. A. *Greenville of Old, Vol. I*. Edited by Suzanne J. Case and Sylvia Lanford Marchant. Greenville, S.C.: Historic Greenville Foundation, 1998.

Davis, David Brion. *The Problem of Slavery in the Age of Revolution, 1770–1823*. Ithaca: Cornell University Press, 1975.

———. *Slavery and Human Progress*. New York: Oxford University Press, 1984.

Davis, Lenwood D., and Janet L. Sims-Wood, comps. *The Ku Klux Klan: A Bibliography*. Westport, Conn.: Greenwood Press, 1984.

Davis, Ronald F. *Good and Faithful Labor: From Slavery to Sharecropping in the Natchez District, 1860–1890*. Westport, Conn.: Greenwood Press, 1982.

Dawson, Joseph G. *Army Generals and Reconstruction: Louisiana 1862–1877*. Baton Rouge: Louisiana State University Press, 1994.

Day, Sarah J. *The Man on a Hill Top*. Philadelphia: Ware Bros., 1931.

Dean, Sidney. *Eulogy Pronounced in the City Hall, Providence, April 19, 1865, on the Occasion of the Funeral Solemnities of Abraham Lincoln*. Providence: H. H. Thomas and Co., 1865.

De Forest, John William. *A Union Officer in the Reconstruction*. Edited by James H. Croushore and David Morris Potter. 1948. Reprint, Baton Rouge: Louisiana State University Press, 1997.

Dennett, John Richard. *The South As It Is, 1865–1866*. Edited by Henry M. Christman. New York: Viking Press, 1965.

Dewey, David Rich. *Financial History of the United States*. New York: Longman, Green and Co., 1922.

Deyle, Steven. *Carry Me Back: The Domestic Slave Trade in American Life*. New York: Oxford University Press, 2005.

Downs, Gregory P. *Declarations of Dependence: The Long Reconstruction of Popular Politics in the South, 1861–1908*. Chapel Hill: University of North Carolina Press, 2011.

Drago, Edmund L. *Black Politicians and Reconstruction in Georgia*. Baton Rouge: Louisiana State University Press, 1982.

Dubois, Laurent. *A Colony of Citizens: Revolution and Slave Emancipation in the French Caribbean, 1787–1804*. Chapel Hill: University of North Carolina Press, 2003.

Du Bois, W.E.B. *Black Reconstruction in America, 1860–1880*. 1935. Reprint, New York: Free Press, 1999.

———. "The Freedman's Bureau." *Atlantic Monthly* 87 (1901): 354–65.

Dunaway, Wilma A. *The First American Frontier: Transition to Capitalism in Southern Appalachia, 1700–1860*. Chapel Hill: University of North Carolina Press, 1996.

Duncan, Randall P. "Wilmington, North Carolina: The Historical Development of a Port City." *Annals of the Association of American Geographers* 58 (September 1968): 441–51.

———. *Reconstruction, Political and Economic, 1865–1877*. New York: Harper and Brothers, 1907.

Edwards, Laura F. "Enslaved Women and the Law: Paradoxes of Subordination in the Post-Revolutionary Carolinas." *Slavery and Abolition* 26 (August 2005): 305–23.

———. *Gendered Strife and Confusion: The Political Culture of Reconstruction*. Urbana: University of Illinois Press, 1997.

———. "'The Marriage Covenant Is the Foundation of All Our Rights': The Politics of Slave Marriages in North Carolina after Emancipation." *Law and History Review* 14, no. 1 (1996): 81–124.

Eelman, Bruce. *Entrepreneurs in the Southern Upcountry: Commercial Culture in Spartanburg, 1845–1880*. Athens: University of Georgia Press, 2008.

Einhorn, Robin. *Property Rules: Political Economy in Chicago, 1833–1872*. Chicago: University of Chicago Press: 1991.

Elkins, Stanley M. *Slavery: A Problem in American Institutional and Intellectual Life*. 2nd ed. Chicago: University of Chicago Press, 1968.

Emberton, Carole. "Reconstructing Loyalty: Love, Fear, and Power in the Postwar South." In *The Great Task Remaining before Us*, edited by Paul A. Cimbala and Randall M. Miller, 173–82. New York: Fordham University Press, 2010.

Evans, David Owen. *Social Romanticism in France, 1830–1848*. New York: Octagon, 1969.

Evans, P. S. *Funeral Elegy on Abraham Lincoln, Delivered before the Military Authorities in Norfolk, Va., Wednesday, April 19th, 1865*. Norfolk, Va.: Office of the Old Dominion, 1865.

Evans, William McKee. *Ballots and Fence Rails: Reconstruction on the Lower Cape Fear*. 1967. Reprint, Athens: University of Georgia Press, 1995.

Fairclough, Adam. *Better Day Coming: Blacks and Equality, 1890–2000*. New York: Viking Books, 2001.

Farmer, Mary J. "'Because They Are Women': Gender and the Virginia Freedmen's Bureau's 'War on Dependency.'" In *The Freedmen's Bureau and Reconstruction: Reconsiderations*, edited by Paul A. Cimbala and Randall M. Miller, 161–92. New York: Fordham University Press, 1999.

Farmer-Kaiser, Mary J. *Freedwomen and the Freedmen's Bureau: Race, Gender, and Public Policy in the Age of Emancipation*. New York: Fordham University Press, 2010.

Faulkner, Carol. *Women's Radical Reconstruction: The Freedmen's Aid Movement*. Philadelphia: University of Pennsylvania Press, 2004.

Fellman, Michael. *Inside War: The Guerrilla Conflict in Missouri during the American Civil War.* New York: Oxford University Press, 1989.

Fenn, Elizabeth A. "'A Perfect Equality Seemed to Reign': Slave Society and Jonkonnu." *North Carolina Historical Review* 65 (April 1988): 127–53.

Ferleger, Herbert Ronald. *David A. Wells and the American Revenue System, 1865–1870.* Philadelphia: Porcupine Press, 1977.

Fett, Sharla M. *Working Cures: Healing, Health, and Power on Southern Slave Plantations.* Chapel Hill: University of North Carolina Press, 2007.

Fields, Barbara Jeanne. *Slavery and Freedom on the Middle Ground: Maryland during the Nineteenth Century.* New Haven: Yale University Press, 1985.

Filkins, Dexter. *The Forever War.* New York: Alfred A. Knopf, 2008.

Finley, Randy. *From Slavery to Uncertain Freedom: The Freedmen's Bureau in Arkansas, 1865–1869.* Fayetteville: University of Arkansas Press, 1996.

Fischer, Roger A. "A Pioneer Protest: The New Orleans Street-Car Controversy of 1867." *Journal of Negro History* 53, no. 3 (July 1968): 219–33.

Fitzgerald, Michael W. "Emancipation and Military Pacification: The Freedmen's Bureau and Social Control in Alabama." In *The Freedmen's Bureau and Reconstruction: Reconsiderations,* edited by Paul A. Cimbala and Randall M. Miller, 45–66. New York: Fordham University Press, 1999.

———. "The Ku Klux Klan: Property Crime and the Plantation System in Reconstruction Alabama." *Agricultural History* 71, no. 2 (1997): 186–206.

———. "Reconstruction Politics and the Politics of Reconstruction." In *Reconstructions: New Perspectives on the Postbellum United States,* edited by Thomas J. Brown, 91–116. New York: Oxford University Press, 2006.

———. *Splendid Failure: Postwar Reconstruction in the American South.* Chicago: Ivan R. Dee, 2007.

———. *The Union League Movement in the Deep South: Politics and Agricultural Change during Reconstruction.* Baton Rouge: Louisiana State University Press, 1989.

———. *Urban Emancipation: Popular Politics in Reconstruction Mobile 1860–1890.* Baton Rouge: Louisiana State University Press, 2002.

Fleming, Walter L. *Civil War and Reconstruction in Alabama.* New York: Columbia University Press, 1905.

Follett, Richard, Eric Foner, and Walter Johnson. *Slavery's Ghost: The Problem of Freedom in the Age of Emancipation.* Baltimore: John Hopkins University Press, 2012.

Foner, Eric. "The Emancipated Worker." In *Nothing but Freedom: Emancipation and Its Legacy,* 74–110. Baton Rouge: Louisiana State University Press, 1983.

———. *Freedom's Lawmakers: A Directory of Black Officeholders during Reconstruction.* Baton Rouge: Louisiana State University Press, 1993.

———. *Free Soil, Free Labor, Free Men: The Ideology of the Republican Party before the Civil War.* 1970. Reprint, New York: Oxford University Press, 1995.

———. *Nothing but Freedom: Emancipation and its Legacy.* Baton Rouge: Louisiana State University Press, 1983.

———. *Reconstruction: America's Unfinished Revolution, 1863–1877*. New York: Harper and Row, 1988.

———. "Reconstruction Revisited." *Reviews in American History* 10, no. 4 (December 1982): 82–100.

———. *The Story of American Freedom*. New York: W. W. Norton, 1998.

Ford, Lacy K., Jr. *Origins of Southern Radicalism: The South Carolina Upcountry, 1800–1860*. New York: Oxford University Press, 1988.

Formwalt, Lee W. "The Camilla Massacre of 1868: Racial Violence as Political Propaganda." *Georgia Historical Quarterly* 71, no. 3 (Fall 1987): 399–426.

Frankel, Noralee. *Freedom's Women: Black Women and Families in Civil War Era Mississippi*. Bloomington: Indiana University Press, 1999.

Franklin, John Hope. *Reconstruction after the Civil War*. Chicago: University of Chicago Press, 1961.

Gates, Merrill E., ed. *Men of Mark in America: Ideals of American Life Told in Biographies of Eminent Living Americans*. Washington D.C.: Men of Mark Publishing Co., 1906.

Gatewood, Willard B. *Aristocrats of Color: The Black Elite, 1880–1920*. Arkansas: University of Arkansas Press, 2000.

Gelston, Arthur Lewis. "Radical Versus Straight-Out in Post-Reconstruction Beaufort County." *South Carolina Historical Magazine* 75, no. 4 (October 1974): 225–37.

Gerteis, Louis S. *From Contraband to Freedman: Federal Policy toward Southern Blacks: 1861–1865*. Westport, Conn.: Greenwood Press, 1973.

Gillette, William. *Retreat from Reconstruction, 1869–1879*. Baton Rouge: Louisiana State University Press, 1980.

Gilmore, Glenda Elizabeth. *Gender and Jim Crow: Women and the Politics of White Supremacy in North Carolina, 1896–1920*. Chapel Hill: University of North Carolina Press, 1996.

Glymph, Thavolia. *Out of the House of Bondage: The Transformation of the Plantation Household*. New York: Cambridge University Press, 2008.

Gordon, Fon Louise. *Caste and Class: The Black Experience in Arkansas, 1880–1920*. Athens: University of Georgia Press, 1995.

Green, William A. *British Slave Emancipation: The Sugar Colonies and the Great Experiment, 1830–1865*. Oxford: Clarendon Press, 1976.

Grimsley, Mark. *The Hard Hand of War: Union Military Policy towards Southern Civilians, 1861–1865*. Cambridge, U.K.: Cambridge University Press, 1995.

Guha, Ranajit. *Elementary Aspects of Peasant Insurgency in Colonial India*. 1983. Reprint, Durham: Duke University Press, 1999.

Gutman, Herbert G. *The Black Family in Slavery and Freedom, 1750–1925*. New York: Random House, 1976.

———. "*Work, Culture, and Society in Industrializing America, 1815–1919*." *American Historical Review* 78, no. 3 (June 1973): 531–88.

Hadden, Sally E. *Slave Patrols: Law and Violence in Virginia and the Carolinas*. Cambridge, Mass.: Harvard University Press, 2001.

Hahn, Steven, "'Extravagant Expectations' of Freedom: Rumour, Political Struggle, and the Christmas Insurrection Scare of 1865 in the American South." *Past and Present* 157, no. 1 (November 1997): 122–58.

———. *A Nation under Our Feet: Black Political Struggles in the Rural South from Slavery to the Great Migration*. Cambridge, Mass.: Harvard University Press, 2003.

———. *Roots of Southern Populism: Yeoman Farmers and the Transformation of the Georgia Upcountry, 1850–1890*. New York: Oxford University Press, 1985.

Hahn, Steven, with Steven F. Miller, Susan E. O'Donovan, John C. Rodrigue, and Leslie S. Rowland, eds. *Freedom: A Documentary History of Emancipation, 1861–1867, Series 3, Volume 1: Land and Labor, 1865*. Chapel Hill: University of North Carolina Press, 2008.

Haley, John H. *Charles N. Hunter and Race Relations in North Carolina*. Chapel Hill: University of North Carolina Press, 1987.

Hamilton, Daniel W. "The Confederate Sequestration Act." *Civil War History* 52, no. 4 (2006): 373–408.

Haraway, Donna. "A Manifesto for Cyborgs: Science, Technology, and Socialist Feminism in the 1980s." In *Feminism/Postmodernism*, edited by Linda J. Nicholson, 190–223. New York: Routledge, 1990.

Hardin, Stephanie. "Climate of Fear: Violence, Intimidation, and Media Manipulation in Reconstruction Mobile, 1865–1876." *Gulf Coast Historical Review* 2, no. 1 (1986): 39–52.

Harris, William C. *The Day of the Carpetbagger: Republican Reconstruction in Mississippi*. Baton Rouge: Louisiana State University Press, 1979.

———. *Presidential Reconstruction in Mississippi*. Baton Rouge: Louisiana State University Press, 1967.

Hild, Matthew. *Greenbackers, Knights of Labor, and Populists: Farmer-Labor Insurgency in the Late-Nineteenth-Century South*. Athens: University of Georgia Press, 2007.

Hine, William C. "Black Organized Labor in Reconstruction Charleston." *Labor History* 25, no. 4 (Fall 1984): 504–17.

Hinks, Peter P. *To Awaken My Afflicted Brethren: David Walker and the Problem of Antebellum Slave Resistance*. University Park: University of Pennsylvania Press, 1997.

Hitchcock, William I. *The Bitter Road to Freedom: A New History of the Liberation of Europe*. New York: Free Press, 2008.

Hobsbawm, Eric J. *Labouring Men: Studies in the History of Labour*. London: Weidenfeld and Nicolson, 1964.

Hodes, Martha. *White Women, Black Men: Illicit Sex in the 19th-Century South*. New Haven: Yale University Press, 1997.

Hogue, James K. *Uncivil War: Five New Orleans Street Battles and the Rise and Fall of Radical Reconstruction*. Baton Rouge: Louisiana State University Press, 2006.

Hollandsworth, James G., Jr. *The Louisiana Native Guards: The Black Military Experience during the Civil War*. Baton Rouge: Louisiana State University Press, 1995.

Holt, Thomas. *Black over White: Negro Political Leadership in South Carolina during Reconstruction*. Urbana: University of Illinois Press, 1977.

———. *Children of Fire: A History of African Americans*. New York: Hill and Wang, 2010.

———. *The Problem of Freedom: Race, Labor and Politics in Jamaica and Britain, 1832–1938*. Baltimore: Johns Hopkins University Press, 1992.

———. "Review of Steven Hahn, *A Nation Under our Feet: Black Political Struggles in the Rural South from Slavery to the Great Migration*." *Journal of American History* 91, no. 3 (December 2004): 981–82.

———. "Whither Now and Why?" In *The State of Afro-American History: Past, Present and Future*, edited by Darlene Clark Hine, 1–10. Baton Rouge: Louisiana State University Press, 1986.

Honey, Michael. "Race, Class, and Power in the New South: Racial Violence and the Delusions of White Supremacy." In *Democracy Betrayed: The Wilmington Race Riot of 1898 and Its Legacy*, edited by David S. Cecelski and Timothy B. Tyson, 163–84. Chapel Hill: University of North Carolina Press, 1998.

Honig, Bonnie. *Democracy and the Foreigner*. Princeton: Princeton University Press, 2001.

Hormats, Robert D. *The Price of Liberty: Paying for America's Wars*. New York: Times Books, 2007.

House, Albert V. "Deterioration of a Georgia Rice Plantation during Four Years of Civil War." *Journal of Southern History* 9, no. 1 (February 1943): 98–113.

Houzeau, Jean-Charles. *My Passage at the New Orleans Tribune: A Memoir of the Civil War Era*. Edited by David C. Rankin. Translated by Gerard F. Denault. Baton Rouge: Louisiana State University Press, 1984.

Howard, Oliver Otis. *Autobiography of Oliver Otis Howard*. New York: Baker and Taylor Co., 1907.

Howard, Victor B. *Black Liberation in Kentucky: Emancipation and Freedom, 1862–1884*. Lexington: University Press of Kentucky, 1983.

Huff, Archie Vernon, Jr. *Greenville: The History of the City and County in the South Carolina Piedmont*. Columbia: University of South Carolina Press, 1995.

Hughes, Langston. *Montage of a Dream Deferred*. New York: Henry Holt, 1951.

Hunter, Tera W. *To 'Joy My Freedom: Southern Black Women's Lives and Labors after the Civil War*. Cambridge, Mass.: Harvard University Press, 1997.

Isaacs, I. J., comp. *Wilmington Up-To-Date: The Metropolis of North Carolina Graphically Portrayed, Compiled Under the Auspices of the Chamber of Commerce, also a Series of Comprehensive Sketches of Representative Business Enterprises*. Wilmington, N.C.: W. L. de Rossett, Jr., Printer, 1902. http://www.docsouth.unc.edu/nc/uptodate/uptodate.html.

John, Richard R. "Ruling Passions: Political Economy in Nineteenth-Century America." In *Ruling Passions: Political Economy in Nineteenth-Century America*, edited by Richard R. John, 1–20. University Park: Pennsylvania State University Press, 2006.

———. *Spreading the News: The American Postal System from Franklin to Morse*. Cambridge, Mass.: Harvard University Press, 1995.

Johnson, Walter. *Soul by Soul: Life inside the Antebellum Slave Market*. Cambridge, Mass.: Harvard University Press, 2001.

Jones, Jacqueline. *Labor of Love, Labor of Sorrow: Black Women and the Family, from Slavery to the Present*. New York: Basic Books, 1985.

———. *Saving Savannah: The City and the Civil War*. New York: Alfred A Knopf, 2008.

Jones, Martha S. *All Bound Up Together: The Woman Question in African-American Public Culture, 1830–1900*. Chapel Hill: University of North Carolina Press, 2007.

Jordan, Winthrop D. *Tumult and Silence at Second Creek: An Inquiry into a Civil War Slave Conspiracy*. Baton Rouge: Louisiana State University Press, 1993.

Joseph, Peniel E. *Waiting 'Til the Midnight Hour: A Narrative History of Black Power in America*. New York: Henry Holt and Co., 2007.

Jung, Moon-Ho. *Coolies and Cane: Race, Labor, and Sugar in the Age of Emancipation*. Baltimore: Johns Hopkins University Press, 2006.

Kaye, Anthony E. *Joining Places: Slave Neighborhoods in the Old South*. Chapel Hill: University of North Carolina Press, 2007.

Keith, Lee Anna. *The Colfax Massacre: The Untold Story of Black Power, White Terror, and the Death of Reconstruction*. New York: Oxford University Press, 2008.

Kelly, Brian. "Black Laborers, the Republican Party, and the Crisis of Reconstruction in Lowcountry South Carolina." *International Review of Social History* 51, no. 3 (December 2006): 375–414.

———. "Industrial Sentinels Confront the 'Rabid Faction': Black Elites, Black Workers and the Labor Question in the Jim Crow South." In *The Black Worker: Race, Labor and Civil Rights since Emancipation*, edited by Eric Arnesen, 94–121. Urbana: University of Illinois, 2007.

———. "Introduction to the Illinois Edition." In *Labor, Free and Slave: Workingmen and the Anti-Slavery Movement in the United States*, edited by Bernard Mandel, xxxii–xxxiv. 1955. Reprint, Urbana: University of Illinois Press, 2007.

———. "Labor and Place: The Contours of Grassroots Black Mobilization in Reconstruction South Carolina." *Journal of Peasant Studies* 35, no. 4 (October 2008): 653–87.

———. "No Easy Way Through: Race Leadership and Black Workers at the Nadir." *Labor: Studies in the Working-Class History of the Americas* 7, no. 3 (2010): 79–93.

———. "Review of Steven Hahn, *A Nation under Our Feet: Black Political Struggles in the Rural South from Slavery to the Great Migration*." *Labor: Studies in the Working-Class History of the Americas* 1, no. 3 (Fall 2004): 145–47.

Kenzer, Robert C. "The Black Businessman in the Postwar South: North Carolina, 1865–1880." *Business History Review* 63 (Spring 1989): 61–87.

Kerber, Linda K. *No Constitutional Right to Be Ladies: Women and the Obligations of Citizenship*. New York: Hill and Wang, 1998.

———. "The Stateless as the Citizen's Other: A View from the United States." *American Historical Review* 112, no. 1 (2007): 1–34.

Keyssar, Alexander. *The Right to Vote: The Contested History of Democracy in the United States*. New York: Basic Books, 2000.

Kiernan, James Patrick. "The Manumission of Slaves in Colonial Brazil, Paraty, 1789–1822." PhD diss., New York University, 1976.

Kimmel, Michael. *Manhood in America: A Cultural History*. New York: Free Press, 1996.

King, Ronald F. "Counting the Votes: South Carolina's Stolen Election of 1876." *Journal of Interdisciplinary History* 32, no. 2 (Autumn 2001): 169–91.

Kramer, Paul A. *The Blood of Government: Race, Empire, the United States, and the Philippines*. Chapel Hill: University of North Carolina Press, 2006.

Lake, Marilyn, and Henry Reynolds. *Drawing the Global Colour Line: White Men's Countries and the International Challenge of Racial Equality*. New York: Cambridge University Press, 2008.

Lamson, Peggy. *The Glorious Failure: Black Congressman Robert Brown Elliott and the Reconstruction in South Carolina*. New York: W. W. Norton, 1973.

Lane, Charles. *The Day Freedom Died: The Colfax Massacre, the Supreme Court, and the Betrayal of Reconstruction*. New York: Henry Holt and Co., 2008.

Latour, Bruno. *Reassembling the Social: An Introduction to Actor-Network Theory*. New York: Oxford University Press, 2007.

Law, John. *After Method: Mess in Social Science Research*. New York: Routledge, 2004.

Lemann, Nicholas. *Redemption: The Last Battle of the Civil War*. New York: Farrar, Strauss and Giroux, 2006.

Lichtenstein, Alex. "Roots of Black Nationalism? Review of Steven Hahn, *A Nation under Our Feet: Black Political Struggles in the Rural South from Slavery to the Great Migration*." *American Quarterly* 57, no. 1 (March 2005): 261–69.

———. "Was the Emancipated Slave a Proletarian?" *Reviews in American History* 26, no. 1 (March 1998): 124–45.

Light, Donald W. "From Migrant Enclaves to Mainstream: Reconceptualizing Informal Economic Behavior." *Theory and Society* 33, no. 6 (December 2004): 705–37.

Lincoln, Abraham. *The Collected Works of Abraham Lincoln*. 9 vols. New Brunswick, N.J.: Rutgers University Press, 1953–55.

Linder, Suzanne Cameron. *Historical Atlas of the Rice Plantations of the ACE River Basin—1860*. Columbia: South Carolina Department of Archives and History, 1995.

Linebaugh, Peter, and Rediker, Marcus. *The Many-Headed Hydra: Sailors, Commoners, and the Hidden History of the Revolutionary Atlantic*. Boston: Beacon Press, 2000.

Litwack, Leon F. *Been in the Storm So Long: The Aftermath of Slavery*. New York: Vintage Books, 1980.

———. *Trouble in Mind: Black Southerners in the Age of Jim Crow*. New York: Alfred Knopf, 1998.

Livingston, David N. *Putting Science in its Place: Geographies of Scientific Knowledge*. Chicago: University of Chicago Press, 2003.

Logan, Rayford W. *The Negro in American Life and Thought: The Nadir, 1877–1901*. New York: Dial Press, 1954.

Lucas, Marion B. *A History of Blacks in Kentucky, Volume 1: From Slavery to Segregation, 1760–1891*. Frankfort: Kentucky Historical Society, 1992.

———. "Kentucky Blacks: The Transition from Slavery to Freedom." *Register of the Kentucky Historical Society* 91, no. 4 (1993): 403–19.

Ludden, David. *An Agrarian History of South Asia*. New York: Cambridge University Press, 1999.

Lynch, John R. *The Facts of Reconstruction*. New York: Neale, 1913.

Magdol, Edward. *A Right to the Land: Essays on the Freedmen's Community*. Westport, Conn.: Greenwood Press, 1977.

Martin, Jonathan D. *Divided Mastery: Slave Hiring in the American South*. Cambridge, Mass.: Harvard University Press, 2004.

Mathisen, Erik Thomas. "Pledges of Allegiance: State Formation in Mississippi between Slavery and Redemption." PhD diss., University of Pennsylvania, 2009.

McCrary, Peyton. *Abraham Lincoln and Reconstruction: The Louisiana Experiment*. Princeton, N.J.: Princeton University Press, 1978.

———. "The Political Dynamics of Black Reconstruction." *Reviews in American History* 12, no. 1 (March 1984): 51–57.

McDuffie, Jerome A. "Politics in Wilmington and New Hanover County, North Carolina, 1865–1900: The Genesis of a Race Riot." PhD diss., Kent State University, 1979.

McFeely, William S. *Grant: A Biography*. 1982. Reprint, New York: W. W. Norton, 2003.

———. *Yankee Stepfather: General O. O. Howard and the Freedmen*. New York: W. W. Norton and Co., 1970.

McGerr, Michael E. *The Decline of Popular Politics: The American North, 1865–1928*. New York: Oxford University Press, 1986.

McKinney, Gordon B. *Southern Mountain Republicans, 1865–1900: Politics and the Appalachian Community*. Chapel Hill: University of North Carolina Press, 1978.

McKitrick, Eric L. *Andrew Johnson and Reconstruction*. Chicago: University of Chicago Press, 1960.

Megginson, W. J. *African-American Life in South Carolina's Upper Piedmont, 1780–1900*. Columbia: University of South Carolina Press, 2005.

Meier, August. "Negro Class Structure and Ideology in the Age of Booker T. Washington." *Phylon* 23 (Fall 1962): 258–66.

———. *Negro Thought in America, 1880–1915: Racial Ideologies in the Age of Booker T. Washington*. Ann Arbor: University of Michigan Press, 1963.

Melville, Herman. *Battle-Pieces and Aspects of War*. New York: Harper and Brothers, 1866.

Messner, William F. *Freedmen and the Ideology of Free Labor*. Lafayette: University of Southwestern Louisiana, 1978.

Joseph C. Miller. "From Group Mobility to Individual Movement: The Colonial Effort to Turn Back History." In *Angola on the Move: Transport Routes, Communications, and History*, edited by Beatrix Heintze and Achim von Oppen, 243–62. Frankfurt am Main: Otto Lembeck Verlag, 2008.

Miller, Randall M. "The Freedmen's Bureau and Reconstruction: An Overview." In *The Freedmen's Bureau and Reconstruction: Reconsiderations*, edited by Paul A. Cimbala and Randall M. Miller, xiii–xxxii. New York: Fordham University Press, 1999.

Miller, Wilbur R. *Revenuers and Moonshiners: Enforcing Federal Liquor Law in the Mountain South, 1865–1900*. Chapel Hill: University of North Carolina Press, 1991.

Mintz, Sidney W. *Caribbean Transformations*. Chicago: Aldine, 1974.

———. *Sweetness and Power: The Place of Sugar in Modern History*. New York: Viking Press, 1985.

Mobley, Joe A. *James City: A Black Community in North Carolina 1863–1900*. Raleigh: North Carolina Division of Archives and History, 1981.

Mohr, Clarence. *On the Threshold of Freedom: Masters and Slaves in Civil War Georgia*. Baton Rouge: Louisiana State University Press, 1986.

Moneyhon, Carl. "The Failure of Southern Republicanism, 1867–1876." In *The Facts of Reconstruction: Essays in Honor of John Hope Franklin*, edited by Eric Anderson and Alfred A. Moss, 99–119. Baton Rouge: Louisiana State University Press, 1991.

———. *The Impact of the Civil War and Reconstruction on Arkansas: Persistence in the Midst of Ruin*. Baton Rouge: Louisiana State University Press, 1994.

Montgomery, David. *Beyond Equality: Labor and the Radical Republicans, 1862–1872*. Urbana: University of Illinois Press, 1981.

———. *Citizen Worker: The Experience of Workers in the United States with Democracy and the Free Market during the Nineteenth Century*. New York: Cambridge University Press, 1993.

Moore, John Hammond, ed. *The Juhl Letters to the Charleston Courier: A View of the South 1865–1871*. Athens: University of Georgia Press, 1974.

Morgan, Edmund S. *Inventing the People: The Rise of Popular Sovereignty in England and America*. New York: Norton, 1988.

Nelson, Scott Reynolds. *Iron Confederacies: Southern Railways, Klan Violence, and Reconstruction*. Chapel Hill: University of North Carolina Press, 1999.

Nicolay, John G., and John Hay. *Abraham Lincoln: A History*. New York: The Century, 1890.

Norrell, Robert J. *Up from History: The Life of Booker T. Washington*. Cambridge, Mass.: Bellknap Press of Harvard University, 2009.

Novak, William J. "The Myth of the 'Weak' American State." *American Historical Review* 113 (June 2008): 752–72.

———. *The People's Welfare: Law and Regulation in Nineteenth-Century America*. Chapel Hill: University of North Carolina Press, 1996.

O'Donovan, Susan Eva. *Becoming Free in the Cotton South*. Cambridge, Mass.: Harvard University Press, 2007.

———. "Universities of Social and Political Change: Slaves in Jail in Antebellum America." In *Buried Lives: Incarcerated in Early America*, edited by Michele Lise Tarter and Richard Bell, 124–46. Athens: University of Georgia Press, 2012.

O'Leary, Cecelia Elizabeth, *To Die For: The Paradox of American Patriotism*. Princeton, N.J.: Princeton University Press, 1999.

Osthaus, Carl. R. *Freedmen, Philanthropy, and Fraud: A History of the Freedman's Savings Bank*. Urbana: University of Illinois Press, 1976.

Otten, James T. "Disloyalty in the Upper Districts of South Carolina during the Civil War." *South Carolina Historical Magazine* 75, no. 2 (1974): 95–110.

Painter, Nell Irvin. *Exodusters: Black Migration to Kansas after Reconstruction*. New York: W. W. Norton, 1976.

———. Comment on Armstead L. Robinson, "The Difference Freedom Made." In *The State of Afro-American History: Past, Present and Future*, edited by Darlene Clark Hine, 80–88. Baton Rouge: Louisiana State University Press, 1986.

Patterson, Orlando. *Slavery and Social Death: A Comparative Study*. Cambridge, Mass.: Harvard University Press, 1982.

Penningroth, Dylan C. *The Claims of Kinfolk: African American Property and Community in the Nineteenth-Century South*. Chapel Hill: University of North Carolina Press, 2003.

Perman, Michael. "Eric Foner's Reconstruction: A Finished Revolution." *Reviews in American History* 17, no. 1 (March 1989): 73–78.

———. *Reunion Without Compromise: The South and Reconstruction, 1865–1868*. Cambridge, U.K.: Cambridge University Press, 1973.

———. *The Road to Redemption: Southern Politics, 1869–1879*. Chapel Hill: University of North Carolina Press, 1984.

Powell, Lawrence N. *New Masters: Northern Planters during the Civil War and Reconstruction*. New Haven: Yale University Press, 1980.

Prather, H. Leon, Sr. "We Have Taken a City: A Centennial Essay." In *Democracy Betrayed: The Wilmington Race Riot of 1898 and Its Legacy*, edited by David Cecelski and Timothy B. Tyson, 15–42. Chapel Hill: University of North Carolina Press, 1998.

———. *We Have Taken a City: The Wilmington Racial Massacre and Coup of 1898*. Wilmington, N.C.: Dram Tree Books, 2006.

Rabinowitz, Howard N. *Race Relations in the Urban South, 1865–1890*. 1978. Reprint, Athens: University of Georgia Press, 1996.

———, ed. *Southern Black Leaders of the Reconstruction Era*. Urbana: University of Illinois Press, 1982.

Rable, George C. *But There Was No Peace: The Role of Violence in the Politics of Reconstruction*. Athens: University of Georgia Press, 1984.

Rachleff, Marshall. "David Walker's Southern Agent." *Journal of Negro History* 62 (January 1977): 100–103.

Rachleff, Peter. *Black Labor in Richmond, 1865–1890*. Urbana: University of Illinois Press, 1989.

Rainwater, Lee, and William L. Yancey. *The Moynihan Report and the Politics of Controversy: A Trans-Action Social Science and Public Policy Report*. Cambridge, Mass.: MIT Press, 1967.

Rankin, David C. "The Origins of Black Leadership in New Orleans during Reconstruction." *Journal of Southern History* 40, no. 3 (August 1974): 417–40.

Ransom, Roger L., and Richard Sutch. *One Kind of Freedom: The Economic Consequences of Emancipation*. Cambridge, U.K.: Cambridge University Press, 1977.

Rashid, Ahmed. *Descent into Chaos: The United States and the Failure of Nation Building in Pakistan, Afghanistan, and Central Asia*. New York: Viking Press, 2008.

Rawick, George P., ed. *The American Slave: A Composite Autobiography, Supplement, Series 1*. 12 vols. Westport, Conn.: Greenwood Press, 1977.

Reed, Emily Hazen. *Life of A. P. Dostie, or The Conflict of New Orleans*. New York: W. P. Tomlinson, 1868.

Reid, Whitelaw. *After the War: A Southern Tour, May 1, 1865 to May 1, 1866*. London: S. Low, Son, and Marston, 1866.

Renda, Mary A. *Taking Haiti: Military Occupation and the Culture of U.S. Imperialism, 1915–1940*. Chapel Hill: University of North Carolina Press, 2000.

Reynolds, Donald E. "The New Orleans Riot of 1866, Reconsidered." *Louisiana History* 5, no. 1 (Winter 1964): 5–27.

———. *Texas Terror: The Slave Insurrection Panic of 1860 and the Secession of the Lower South*. Baton Rouge: Louisiana State University Press, 2007.

Reynolds, John S. *Reconstruction in South Carolina, 1865–1877*. Columbia, S.C.: State Co., 1905.

Rhyne, J. Michael. "'Conduct . . . Inexcusable and Unjustifiable': Bound Children, Battered Freedwomen, and the Limits of Emancipation in Kentucky's Bluegrass Region." *Journal of Social History* 42, no. 2 (2008): 319–40.

———. "A 'Murderous Affair in Lincoln County': Politics, Violence, and Memory in a Civil War Era Kentucky Community." *American Nineteenth Century History* 7, no. 3 (2006): 337–59.

———. "'We Are Mobed and Beat': Regulator Violence Against Free Black Households In Kentucky's Bluegrass Region, 1865–1867." *Ohio Valley History* 2, no. 1 (2002): 30–42.

Richardson, Heather Cox. *The Death of Reconstruction: Race, Labor, and Politics in the Post-Civil War North, 1865–1901*. Cambridge, Mass.: Harvard University Press, 2001.

Richardson, James D., ed. and comp. *A Compilation of the Messages and Papers of the Presidents, 1789–1897*. 21 Vols. Washington: Government Printing Office, 1896–1899.

Ripley, C. Peter. *Slaves and Freedmen in Civil War Louisiana*. Baton Rouge: Louisiana State University Press, 1976.

Robinson, Armstead L. "Beyond the Realm of Social Consensus: New Meanings of Reconstruction for American History." *Journal of American History* 68, no. 2 (September 1981): 276–97.

———. "The Difference Freedom Made: The Emancipation of Afro-Americans." In *State of Afro-American History: Past, Present, and Future*, edited by Darlene Clark Hine, 51–74. Baton Rouge: Louisiana State University Press, 1986.

Robinson, Cedric J. *Black Marxism: The Making of the Black Radical Tradition*. Chapel Hill: University of North Carolina Press, 2000.

Rodrigue, John C. "Black Agency after Slavery." In *Reconstructions: New Perspectives on the Postbellum United States*, edited by Thomas J. Brown, 40–65. New York: Oxford University Press, 2006.

———. *Reconstruction in the Cane Fields: From Slavery to Free Labor in Louisiana's Sugar Parishes, 1862–1880*. Baton Rouge: Louisiana State University Press, 2001.

Rogers, George C., Jr. *The History of Georgetown County, South Carolina*. Columbia: University of South Carolina Press, 1970.

Rosen, Hannah. "'Not That Sort of Women': Race, Gender, and Sexual Violence during the Memphis Riot of 1866." In *Sex, Love, Race: Crossing Boundaries in North American History*, edited by Martha Hodes, 267–93. New York: New York University Press, 1999.

Rosen, Robert N. *A Short History of Charleston*. Columbia: University of South Carolina Press, 1997.

Ross, Robert J. S. *Slaves to Fashion: Poverty and Abuse in the New Sweatshops*. Ann Arbor: University of Michigan Press, 2004.

Rubin, Hyman. *South Carolina Scalawags*. Columbia: University of South Carolina Press, 2006.

Ryan, James G. "The Memphis Riots of 1866: Terror in a Black Community during Reconstruction." *Journal of Negro History* 62, no. 3 (July 1977): 243–57.

Sassen, Saskia. *The Global Cities: New York, London, Tokyo*. Princeton: Princeton University Press, 2001.

———. *Globalization and Its Discontents: Essays on the New Mobility of People and Money*. New York: The New Press, 1998.

Saville, Julie. *The Work of Reconstruction: From Slave to Wage Laborer in South Carolina, 1860–1870*. New York: Cambridge University Press, 1994.

Schmidt, James D. *Free to Work: Labor Law, Emancipation, and Reconstruction, 1815–1880*. Athens: University of Georgia Press, 1998.

Schwalm, Leslie A. *A Hard Fight for We: Women's Transition from Slavery to Freedom in South Carolina*. Urbana: University of Illinois Press, 1997.

Schwartz, Stuart B. "The Manumission of Slaves in Colonial Brazil: Bahia, 1684–1745." *Hispanic American Historical Review* 54, no. 4 (1974): 606–35.

Schweninger, Loren. *Black Property Owners in the South, 1790–1915*. 1990. Reprint, Urbana: University of Illinois Press, 1997.

Scott, James C. *Domination and the Arts of Resistance: Hidden Transcripts*. New Haven: Yale University Press, 1990.

———. *Weapons of the Weak: Everyday Forms of Peasant Resistance*. New Haven: Yale University Press, 1985.

Scott, Rebecca J. "The Battle over the Child: Child Apprenticeship and the Freedmen's Bureau in North Carolina." *Prologue* 10, no. 2 (1978): 101–13.

———. *Degrees of Freedom: Louisiana and Cuba after Slavery*. Cambridge, Mass.: Harvard University Press, 2005.

Sears, Richard D. *Camp Nelson, Kentucky: A Civil War History*. Lexington: University Press of Kentucky, 2002.

Sefton, James E. *The United States Army and Reconstruction, 1865–1877*. Baton Rouge: Louisiana State University Press, 1967.

Sellers, James Benson. *Slavery in Alabama*. Tuscaloosa: University of Alabama Press, 1950.

Shapiro, Herbert. "The Ku Klux Klan during Reconstruction: The South Carolina Episode." *Journal of Negro History* 49, no. 1 (January 1964): 34–55.

Sharkey, Robert P. *Money, Class, and Party: An Economic Study of Civil War and Reconstruction*. Baltimore: Johns Hopkins Press, 1959.

Sherman, William T. *Memoirs of General William T. Sherman*. New York: D. Appleton, 1887.

Shick, Tom W., and Don H. Doyle, "The South Carolina Phosphate Boom and the Stillbirth of the New South, 1867–1920." *South Carolina Historical Magazine* 86, no. 1 (January 1985): 1–12, 14–15, 17–31.

Shugg, Roger W. *Origins of Class Struggle in Louisiana*. 1938. Reprint, Baton Rouge: Louisiana State University Press, 1968.

Simkins, Francis Butler, and Robert Hilliard Woody. *South Carolina during Reconstruction*. Chapel Hill: University of North Carolina Press, 1932.

Simpson, Brooks D. "Ulysses S. Grant and the Freedmen's Bureau." In *The Freedmen's Bureau and Reconstruction: Reconsiderations*, edited by Paul A. Cimbala and Randall M. Miller, 1–28. New York: Fordham University Press, 1999.

———. *Ulysses S. Grant, Triumph over Adversity, 1822–1865*. New York: Houghton Mifflin, 2000.

Singletary, Otis A. *Negro Militia and Reconstruction*. New York: McGraw-Hill, 1963.

Skowronek, Stephen. *Building a New American State: The Expansion of National Administrative Capacities, 1877–1920*. New York: Cambridge University Press, 1982.

Smith, Julia Floyd. *Slavery and Rice Culture in Low Country Georgia, 1750–1860*. Knoxville: University of Tennessee Press, 1991.

Somers, Dale A. "Black and White in New Orleans: A Study in Urban Race Relations." *Journal of Southern History* 40, no. 1 (February 1974): 19–42.

Stanley, Amy Dru. *From Bondage to Contract: Wage Labor, Marriage, and the Market in the Age of Slave Emancipation*. New York: Cambridge University Press, 1998.

Stewart, W. H. *Reminiscence of Elder W. H. Stewart, with Sketches and Skeletons of His Sermons*. Jackson, Miss.: n.p., 1894.

Strickland, John Scott. "Traditional Culture and Moral Economy: Social and Economic Change in the South Carolina Low Country, 1865–1910." In *The Countryside in the*

Age of Capitalist Transformation, edited by Steven Hahn and Jonathan Prude, 141–78. Chapel Hill: University of North Carolina Press, 1985.

Summers, Mark Wahlgren. *A Dangerous Stir: Fear, Paranoia, and the Making of Reconstruction*. Chapel Hill: University of North Carolina Press, 2009.

———. *The Press Gang: Newspapers and Politics, 1865–1878*. Chapel Hill: University of North Carolina Press, 1994.

Suri, Jeremi. *Liberty's Surest Guardian: American Nation-Building from the Founders to Obama*. New York: Simon and Schuster, 2011.

Sutherland, Daniel E. *A Savage Conflict: The Decisive Role of Guerrillas in the American Civil War*. Chapel Hill: University of North Carolina Press, 2009.

Syrett, John. *The Civil War Confiscation Acts: Failing to Reconstruct the South*. New York: Fordham University Press, 2005.

Takagi, Midori. *"Rearing Wolves to Our Own Destruction": Slavery in Richmond, Virginia 1782–1865*. Charlottesville: University Press of Virginia, 1999.

Tannenbaum, Frank. *Slave and Citizen: The Negro in the Americas*. New York: Alfred A. Knopf, 1947.

Taylor, Joe Gray. *Louisiana Reconstructed, 1863–1877*. Baton Rouge: Louisiana State University Press, 1974.

Thomas, Herbert A., Jr. "Victims of Circumstances: Negroes in a Southern Town, 1865–1880." *Register of the Kentucky Historical Society* 71, no. 3 (1973): 253–71.

Thompson, Edward P. *The Making of the English Working Class*. London: Victor Gollancz, 1963.

Thompson, Henry T. *Ousting the Carpetbagger from South Carolina*. Columbia: R. L. Bryan, 1927.

Thornton, J. Mills, III. "Fiscal Policy and the Failure of Reconstruction in the Lower South." In *Region, Race, and Reconstruction: Essays in Honor of C. Vann Woodward*, edited by James M. McPherson and J. Morgan Kousser, 349–94. New York: Oxford University Press, 1982.

Tindall, George B. *South Carolina Negroes, 1877–1900*. Chapel Hill: University of North Carolina Press, 1952.

Tourgée, Albion W. *Bricks without Straw: A Novel*. Edited by Carolyn L. Karcher. Durham: Duke University Press, 2009.

———. *A Fool's Errand: By One of the Fools*. New York: Fords, Howard and Hulbert, 1879.

Towers, Frank. *The Urban South and the Coming of the Civil War*. Charlottesville: University Press of Virginia, 2004.

Tregle, Joseph G., Jr. "Thomas J. Durant, Utopian Socialism, and the Failure of Presidential Reconstruction in Louisiana." *Journal of Southern History* 45, no. 4. (November 1979): 485–512.

Trelease, Allen. *White Terror: The Ku Klux Conspiracy and Southern Reconstruction*. New York: Harper and Row, 1971.

Turtle, Gordon Bruce. "Slave Manumission in Virginia, 1782–1806: The Jefferson Dilemma in the Age of Liberty." MA thesis, University of Alberta, 1991.

Vandal, Gilles. "Black Utopia in Early Reconstruction New Orleans: The People's Bakery as a Case-Study." *Louisiana History* 38, no. 4 (Fall 1997): 437–52.

———. "Origins of the New Orleans Riot of 1866, Revisited." *Louisiana History* 22, no. 2 (Spring 1981): 135–65.

Wade, Richard C. *Slavery in the Cities: The South 1820–1860*. London: Oxford University Press, 1964.

Waldrep, Christopher. *The Many Faces of Judge Lynch: Extralegal Violence and Punishment in America*. New York: Palgrave MacMillan, 2002.

———. *Roots of Disorder: Race and Criminal Justice in the American South, 1817–80*. Urbana: University of Illinois Press, 1998.

Waller, Altina L. "Community, Class, and Race in the Memphis Riot of 1866." *Journal of Social History* 18, no. 2 (Winter 1984): 233–46.

Wells, David Ames. *Our Burden and Our Strength*. Boston: Gould and Lincoln, 1864.

———. *The Theory and Practice of Taxation*. New York: D. Appleton, 1900.

West, Jerry Lee. *The Reconstruction Ku Klux Klan in York County, South Carolina*. York County, S.C.: McFarland, 2002.

Whalen, Carmen Teresa. *From Puerto Rico to Philadelphia: Puerto Rican Workers and Postwar Economies*. Philadelphia: Temple University Press, 2001.

———. "Sweatshops Here and There: The Garment Industry, Latinas, and Labor Migrations." *International Labor and Working Class History* 61 (2002): 45–68.

Wharton, Vernon Lane. *The Negro in Mississippi, 1865–1890*. 1947. Reprint, New York: Harper and Row, 1965.

Whites, LeeAnn. *Gender Matters: Civil War, Reconstruction, and the Making of the New South*. New York: Palgrave and Macmillan, 2005.

Wiener, Jonathan M. *Social Origins of the New South: Alabama, 1860–1885*. Baton Rouge: Louisiana State University Press, 1978.

Williams, Alfred B. *Hampton and His Red Shirts: South Carolina's Deliverance in 1876*. Charleston, S.C.: Walker, Evans, and Cogswell Co., 1935.

Williams, Heather Andrea. *Self-Taught: African American Education in Slavery and Freedom*. Chapel Hill: University of North Carolina Press, 2005.

Williamson, Joel. *After Slavery: The Negro in South Carolina during Reconstruction, 1861–1877*. Chapel Hill: University of North Carolina Press, 1965.

———. *The Crucible of Race: Black-White Relations in the American South since Emancipation*. New York: Oxford University Press, 1984.

Wilson, Joseph. *The Black Phalanx*. New York: Arno Press, 1968.

Wilson, Mark R. *The Business of Civil War: Military Mobilization and the State, 1861–1865*. Baltimore: Johns Hopkins University Press, 2008.

Wooley, Robert Howard. "Race and Politics: The Evolution of the White Supremacy Campaign of 1898 in North Carolina." PhD diss., University of North Carolina at Chapel Hill, 1977.

Wright, George C. *Racial Violence in Kentucky, 1865–1940: Lynchings, Mob Rule, and "Legal Lynchings."* Baton Rouge: Louisiana State University Press, 1990.

Wyatt-Brown, Bertram. "The Changing Faces of Honor in National Crises." Paper prepared for Johns Hopkins History Seminar. Baltimore: Johns Hopkins University, Fall 2005.

———. "Honor, Shame and Iraq in American Foreign Policy." Paper prepared for Workshop on Humiliation and Violent Conflict. New York: Columbia University, November 2004.

Zimmerman, David. "William Whipper and the Black Abolitionist Tradition." http://www.muweb.millersville.edu/~ugrr/resources/columbia/whipper.html.

Zuczek, Richard. *State of Rebellion: Reconstruction in South Carolina*. Columbia: University of South Carolina Press, 1996.

Contributors

Bruce E. Baker is lecturer on American history at Newcastle University. He is the author of *What Reconstruction Meant: Historical Memory in the American South* and *This Mob Will Surely Take My Life: Lynchings in the Carolinas, 1871–1947* and a number of articles on topics relating to the history of the American South. He is co-editor of the journal *American Nineteenth Century History*.

Jonathan M. Bryant is associate professor of history at Georgia Southern University. He has been fascinated by the nineteenth-century American South since childhood. He is currently working on the story of the slave ship *Antelope* and the illegal slave trade in the nineteenth-century Atlantic World.

Gregory P. Downs is associate professor of history at City College of New York (CUNY) and the author of *Declarations of Dependence: The Long Reconstruction of Popular Politics in the South, 1861–1908*. He is currently at work on a study of the transition from Civil War to Reconstruction. His collection of short stories, *Spit Baths*, won the Flannery O'Connor Award.

Michael W. Fitzgerald earned his PhD from the University of California, Los Angeles and is currently professor of history at St. Olaf College. He authored *The Union League Movement in the Deep South*, *Urban Emancipation: Popular Politics in Reconstruction Mobile*, and *Splendid Failure: Postwar Reconstruction in the American South*. He is currently finishing a full-scale history of Alabama after the Civil War.

Eric Foner is DeWitt Clinton Professor of History at Columbia University and among the most prominent historians of this generation. He has published widely and is a distinguished scholar of the American Civil War and

Reconstruction. His *Reconstruction: America's Unfinished Revolution, 1863–1877*—awarded the Bancroft Prize, the Parkman Prize, and the Los Angeles Times Book Award, among others—remains among the most influential studies in modern American historiography. His most recent book, *The Fiery Trial: Abraham Lincoln and American Slavery*, won the Bancroft Prize, the Pulitzer Prize for History, and the Lincoln Prize.

Thomas C. Holt, the James Westfall Thompson Professor of American and African American History at the University of Chicago, is a distinguished scholar of U.S. Reconstruction and a pioneer in the comparative study of slave emancipation in the Atlantic World. He is the author of *Black over White: Negro Political Leadership* in *South Carolina during Reconstruction*, *The Problem of Freedom: Race, Labor, and Politics in Jamaica and Britain, 1832–1938*, and *Children of Fire: A History of African Americans*, and co-author of *Beyond Slavery: Explorations of Race, Labor, and Citizenship in Postemancipation Societies.*

James Illingworth was born in Sheffield, U.K., and completed his undergraduate studies at the University of Edinburgh. He is currently working toward a PhD in history from the University of California, Santa Cruz. His dissertation, *Revolution in the Urban South: New Orleans, 1830–1877*, examines the actions and experiences of the urban popular classes during the Civil War period.

Brian Kelly is director of the After Slavery Project and a reader in U.S. history at Queen's University Belfast. His first book, *Race, Class, and Power in the Alabama Coalfields, 1908–21*, won a number of awards, including the Frances Butler Simkins and the H. L. Mitchell Prizes from the Southern Historical Association. He has published widely on labor and race and is completing a study of black political mobilization in Reconstruction South Carolina.

Erik Mathisen is lecturer in American studies at the University of Portsmouth in the United Kingdom. A graduate of the University of Pennsylvania, he is currently working on a book entitled *American Crucible: Citizens, Slaves, and the Politics of Loyalty in Civil War America.*

Susan Eva O'Donovan is associate professor of history at the University of Memphis. She is a former editor of the Freedmen and Southern Society Project; coeditor of the documentary history *Land and Labor, 1865*; and author of

Becoming Free in the Cotton South, which was awarded the James A. Rawley Prize by the Organization of American Historians. With Bruce E. Baker she is co-editor of the journal *American Nineteenth Century History.*

J. Michael Rhyne is associate professor of history at Urbana University in Ohio. He received his PhD from the University of Cincinnati, where he completed a dissertation under Wayne K. Durrill's direction that focused on the problem of freedom in the Bluegrass Region. He has published articles in *Ohio Valley History, American Nineteenth Century History,* and the *Journal of Social History.*

Index

Abell, Edmund, 51
Abolition movement, 227
Addison, Jennie, 122
African Americans, divisions among, 200, 205
African American soldiers, 37, 40–41, 59, 90, 111; in conflict with freedpeople, 203; trespassing, 40; veterans, 35, 40–41, 72; veterans attacked by whites, 106, 125, 133
Agency: limits of, 8, 116; of African Americans, 7, 116, 199
Alabama, counties: Conecuh, 150; Coosa, 150; Limestone, 150; Sumter, 150
Alabama, towns, Tuscaloosa, 152
Allen, James M., 168
Aman, Benjamin, 186
American Missionary Association, 88
Amnesty Proclamation, 39, 81–82, 146
Anderson, Benedict, 23
Andrews, Sidney, 106
Appalachia, 159–61
Apprenticeship, of African American children, 11, 39, 88–89, 95–96n25, 106, 128–30
Arkansas, 145
Arkansas, towns, Little Rock, 191
Arnesen, Eric, 45, 50
Arterburn, Harrison, 127–28
Ashepoo River, 211
Avery, Columbus, 150
Ayers, Edward, 101
Ayres, Walter, 127

Baird, Absalom, 39, 47–48
Baker, Anna, 87
Baker, Bruce E., 228
Ball, Charles, 184, 189
Banks, for freedpeople, 44
Banks, Lewis, 42
Banks, Nathaniel, 38, 45
Barbers, African American, 41, 189
Barney, William, 155
Batson, George, 183
Bavis, Kate, 182
Baxley, Reddin, 68
Bayly, Christopher, 189
Beadford, Josephine, 129–30
Beale, Howard K., 6
Beecher, James Chaplin, 202
Belgium, 41
Bell, Caryn Cossé, 50, 53
Berlin, Ira, 22
Bernard, Harry, 182
Berrien, George, 68
Bickel, Alexander, 30
Bissell, J. Bennett, 211
Black Codes, 1, 47, 50, 108
Bligh, D. F., 135
Blue Ridge, 160
Blythe, Absalom, 163
Board of Indian Commissioners, 103
Bourne, W. R., 132
Bowden, Julia, 186–87, 192
Bowley, James A., 209
Bozeman, D. B., 150
Bradley, Aaron, 61
Branford, Peter, 125
Brazil, 23
Bricks without Straw (1880), 115–17
Bridgewater, James H., 136
Brisbane, Albert, 41
Broad River, 161, 162

Brock, William R., 5
Brown, A. Benson, 136
Brown, Christopher, 227
Brown, Henry Box, 184, 189
Brown, Silas, 182
Brown, Thomas J., 221
Brown Fellowship Society, 201
Bryan, B. C., 182
Bryant, Julian E., 82
Bryce, James, 229
Buchanan, Thomas, 36
Budiansky, Stephen, 225
Bullock, Rufus, 60, 65, 70
Butler, Benjamin, 37
Butler, M. C., 207

Cailloux, Andre, 43
Caldwell, James, 41
Calhoun, Allen, 192
Canada, 229
Canby, Edward, 38, 205
Cape Fear River, 179, 182, 184, 187, 191
Caraway, James, 189
Carr, E. H., 225
Carruthers, Robert, 126
Cecelski, David, 36
Chamberlain, Daniel H., 209–13
Champion Compress, 185
Chase, John, 52
Cheves, John R., 70–71
Children, as workers, 27
Chirac, Jacques, 17
Churches, African American, as targets of violence, 47
Churchill, Emily, 127–28
Citizenship: denied to freedpeople, 82; for former Confederates, 83; of freedpeople, 17, 22; lack of, 29; and loyalty, 82; and relationship to the state, 78; and slavery, 24
Civil rights movement, 6, 200
Civil War: effects on north Alabama, 150; financing of, 110–11
Clark, Charles, 81
Cleapot, Charles E., 188
Cobb, A. L., 170
Colcock, R. H., 211
Combahee River, 211
Committee of Public Safety, in Savannah, 63
Confederate veterans, 47; favoring land reform, 167; in Ku Klux Klan, 144, 154; response to defeat, 2
Confiscation, 81
Congo Square, 51
Congressional legislation: Civil Rights Act of 1866, 50, 107; Confiscation Act of 1862, 80, 92–93; Ku Klux Act of 1871, 145, 147; Reconstruction Acts of 1867, 49–51, 108, 151, 165, 203
Congressional Reconstruction, 151, 155
Constitutional amendments: Thirteenth Amendment, 18–19, 48, 122, 124, 137, 228; Fourteenth Amendment, 1, 3, 107, 151, 214, 228; Fifteenth Amendment, 214
Constitutional conventions: Alabama (1868), 151; Louisiana (1864), 48; Louisiana (1866), 36, 49; Louisiana (1868), 52–53; Mississippi (1865), 83; South Carolina (1868), 165, 205
Conway, Thomas, 39, 46–47
Corn, sold to drovers, 162
Corruption, 39
Coulter, E. Merton, 149
Council, Lucy, 113
Crete, 112
Cromwell, Robert, 42
Cuba, 4, 229
Culture of poverty, 32n11

Darnton, Robert, 190
Davis, Augustus, 182
Davis, David Brion, 22, 59
Davis, James, 186
Dawson, Francis W., 209
De Forest, John W., 167
Democracy, definition of, 31
Deportation, of *sans papiers* from France, 17
Desegregation, 52
Deserters, from Confederate army, 150, 164
Disarming, of freedpeople, 91, 125, 132–33, 207
Distilling, federal tax on, 170–71
Domestic servants, 128–30, 133, 186, 190, 209
Dominican Republic, 227, 229
Donaldson, R. S., 90
Dooner, James, 61, 64–65, 67
Dostie, A. P., 48–49
Dougherty, William, 35, 41
Douglass, Frederick, 226
Drovers, 161–63; decline of, 169–70

Du Bois, W.E.B., 4–5, 7–8, 11, 117, 171, 221, 224
Dubois, Laurent, 17
Dumas, Francis, 42
Dunaway, Wilma, 161
Dunn, Oscar J., 41, 42, 44, 48
Durant, Thomas J., 41, 43–44, 48–50

Education, 52
Edwards, Laura, 129, 223
Egalitarianism, 2
Eggin, Collin, 129–30
Eight-hour movement, 50
Elections: Alabama (1870), 155; Georgia (1868), 60; Louisiana (April 1868), 52; national (November 1868), 155; North Carolina (November 1865), 106; South Carolina (1870), 206; South Carolina (1876), 212, 215; South Carolina (April 1868), 166; South Carolina (November 1868), 205
Emancipation, in French territories (1848), 15
Epping, J.P.M., 204, 206
Evans, John J., 131
Evans, William McKee, 5

Families: and citizenship, 18; of freedpeople, violence toward, 87; loyalty to, 79
Farley, Solomon, 62, 67
Farmer, Mary J., 131
Farmers' Alliance, 225
Fields, Barbara Jeanne, 132
Fisk, Clinton B., 88, 124–26
Fitch, Henry, 66–68
Fitzgerald, Archie, 89
Fitzgerald, Jane, 89
Fitzgerald, Michael, 36, 225
Flanders, Benjamin, 43
Fleming, Walter L., 149
Florida, towns, Tallahassee, 180
Foner, Eric, 4, 11, 22, 155, 201, 204, 211; *Reconstruction: America's Unfinished Revolution*, 6–7, 144, 149
Fool's Errand (1879), *A*, 115
Ford, James C., 122
Ford, Lacy K., 162
Fourier, Charles, 41
Franchise of Ballot Act of 1892 (Cape Colony), 229
Franklin, John Hope, 6
Freedman's Savings and Trust Company, records of, 179–82
Freedmen Aid Association, 44
Freedmen's Bureau, 39, 47, 83, 85, 88, 114, 124, 202; distribution of rations by, 104; enforcing contracts, 71, 98, 129; lack of sufficient military support for, 100, 108, 112–13, 131, 136, 165; reauthorization of, 107; responsibilities of, 103, 105; understaffed, 102, 105
Freedmen's Tabernacle, 201
Freedom, meaning of for freedpeople, 3, 228
Free labor ideology, 5–6, 59, 73, 99–100, 104, 204
Free people of color, 41–42, 200–201
French Broad River, 161
French West Africa, 4
Friends of Universal Suffrage, 42–43
Fullerton, Joseph, 39

Gardner, Samuel, 183
Garibaldi, Giuseppe, 98, 112
Garmany, J. W., 163
Georgia, counties: Bryan, 62–63; Liberty, 62–63
Georgia, towns: Atlanta, 36; Burroughs, 73; Miller's Station, 62–64, 67–68, 70; Savannah, 58–63, 65, 69, 73
Gilbert, Anderson, 135–36
Gill, Nelson, 89
Glymph, Thavolia, 223
Goodloe, William Cassius, 125–26
Governors: of Alabama, 148, 155; of Georgia, 60, 65, 70; of Louisiana, 38; of Mississippi, 81, 83–84, 90–91; of North Carolina, 106; of South Carolina, 203–4, 206–9, 211
Graham, John S., 127
Grant, Ulysses S., 80, 227
Grapevine telegraphs, 189
Green, Lewis, 189
Guadeloupe, 15
Guerrilla warfare, during Civil War, 150, 164
Gutman, Herbert, 123, 221
Gwinn, Emma, 135

Hahn, Michael, 38, 49
Hahn, Steven, 47, 143, 145, 155, 190, 192; *A Nation under Our Feet*, 7–8, 36, 224
Haiti, 229
Hall, Henry, 180
Halloway, William, 150

Hamilton, Thomas, 213–15
Hampton, Wade, 209, 213–15
Haraway, Donna, 184
Haskell, Joseph, 71
Heath, Edward, 51
Helm, Henry, 135–36
Henderson, W. F., 113
Herron, Andrew, 51
Hill, Elias, 206
Hillebrandt, Hugo, 98–99; biography of, 111–12
Hinton, Archer, 52
Historical memory of Reconstruction, 228
Historiography of Reconstruction, 3–8, 20–21, 117–18, 143, 155, 167, 171, 199–200; comparative history of emancipation, 3–4; Dunning School, 6, 11, 118, 149, 221, 224, 226; "Long Reconstruction," 224; and new social history, 221; post-revisionist, 4, 225–26; Reconstruction as labor history, 6, 8; revisionist, 6–7, 221, 226
Hobsbawm, Eric, 221
Hogue, James, 39
Holden, William, 106
Holloway, J. H., 200–201, 215
Holt, Thomas C., 3–4, 10, 200, 210
Honig, Bonnie, 31
Houston, George, 68
Houzeau, Jean-Charles, 41, 43
Howard, Betty, 128
Howard, H. C., 131
Howard, Oliver Otis, 3, 46, 102–3, 105, 114–15, 124
Howard University, 103
Hungary, 98, 112
Hunter, Charles N., 199–200, 215
Hunter, Tera, 36

Immigrants, 26, 38, 61, 98, 130
Imperialism, 228–29
Industrialization, 6
Insurrection: African Americans charged with, 64–70; by African Americans, 15, 58; by African Americans, fear of, 59, 74n4, 91, 154; Christmas Insurrection Scare of 1865, 46, 60, 90–91, 154
Isabelle, Robert H., 43
Italy, 98, 112

Jackson, Henry Rootes, 63, 66–69, 72
Jamaica, 4, 27
James, Horace, 104
Jeffers, Stephen, 132
Johnson, Andrew, 50, 100, 106–7, 124, 146, 226; leniency to Confederates, 1, 37, 203
Johnson, Jack, 206
Johnson, James, 66–67
Johnson, William B., 166
Joint Committee on Reconstruction, 67, 88
Joint Committee on Retrenchment, 111
Jones, Amanda, 192
Jones, Edward, 187–88
Jones, Hannah, 133–34
Jones, Joseph, 192
Jones, Martha, 223–24
Jones, Solomon, 161–63
Jones, William H., 209
Jonkonnu festival, 189

Kaufmann, Julius, 61, 67–69
Kennedy, E. D., 126
Kennedy, Hugh, 38–39, 45, 47
Kentucky, Camp Nelson, 136
Kentucky, counties: Bath, 132; Boyle, 126, 136; Jefferson, 126–27; Lincoln, 126, 135–37; Mercer, 125–26, 136; Montgomery, 131; Rockcastle, 136; Spencer, 130; Woodford, 127
Kentucky, towns: Covington, 133; Crab Orchard, 136; Cynthiana, 127; Danville, 132, 136; Frankfort, 133; Lexington, 131, 133; Louisville, 122, 126, 129, 133; Maysville, 127, 133; Mount Sterling, 131; Paris, 133; Portland, 133; Taylorsville, 130; Yellmanville, 133
Keyssar, Alex, 30
Kidder Lumber Company, 185
King, Martin Luther, Jr., 21
Knights of Labor, 190, 193, 225
Knights of the White Camelia, 144, 154
Kossuth, Lajos, 98, 112
Ku Klux Klan, 132, 166, 170, 205–7

Labor, coolie, 24, 179
Labor communes, 44
Labor contracts, 41, 203; disputes over, 68–70, 74n9, 90, 151, 153; with freedpeople, 46, 68, 106
Labor migration, 27
Land ownership, 68, 71, 161; by African Americans, 2–3, 125, 132, 201; conflict over, 68, 74n9
Land reform, 44, 46–47, 52, 82, 90, 93, 201, 203–4; failure of, 73, 167, 205; opposed by some Republicans, 209
Larescy, John, 211

Leavel, Hayden, 90
Lemann, Nicholas, 225
Leslie, C. P., 167
Lewis, John, 47
Liberia, emigration to, 206
Lincoln, Abraham, 37
Livingston, David, 193
Livingston, James, 89
Local government, 9, 39, 84, 169; courts used by Democrats, 65; in Jefferson City, Louisiana, 38; in New Orleans, 38, 45, 48, 51; opposing Republicans, 168; participation in by African Americans, 177, 201, 207, 215; treatment of freedpeople, 91
Logan, Rayford, 199
Louisiana, 137
Louisiana, Fort Banks, 40
Louisiana, parishes: Jefferson, 40–41, 46; Lafourche, 40; Rapides, 38; St. Mary's, 53; Terrebonne, 44
Louisiana, towns: Algiers, 35, 52; Baton Rouge, 44; Clinton, 46; Monroe, 46
Louisiana Association of Workingmen, 44
Louisiana Equal Rights League, 43
Louisiana Native Guards, 42, 51
Lowcountry, 202–3, 208–14
Lowery, James, 183
Loyal League, 61–62

Madison, James, 22
Manhood: of freedmen, 123, 135, 141n22; of white men, 123
Manly, Alex, 176, 183
Manumission, 22–23
Maryland, violence in, 132
McCary, Robert, Jr., 42
McIntosh, Rosser, 182
McKinney, Gordon B., 159
McKitrick, Eric, 221
Meade, George, 64
Mears, Edward, 182
Melville, Herman, 109
Mendel, Emanuel, 61
Merchants, 42
Middleton, J. Motte, 61, 71
Middleton, William, 208
Migration: of African Americans from Kentucky, 137; of African Americans from Wilmington, N.C., 176–77; from countryside to towns, 40, 47, 131, 133
Military occupation, 37, 41, 63, 78–80, 101–2, 106, 150, 203, 209, 226; troop levels, 108–9
Military Reconstruction, 102
Militia units: of freedmen, 60, 72, 206, 210; of whites, 78, 91
Miller, Joseph C., 190
Miller, Thomas E., 213
Miller, Wilbur R., 170
Miller, William, 62
Ministers: African American, 42, 47, 132, 203; African American, Baptist, 206; African American, Methodist, 193
Mintz, Sidney, 27
Mississippi, counties: Adams, 81; DeSoto, 80, 88; Hinds, 83; Jones, 93; Monroe, 87; Noxubee, 91; Pike, 92; Tippah, 84; Yazoo, 90
Mississippi, towns: Holly Springs, 89; Jackson, 83; Natchez, 85; Ripley, 85; Vicksburg, 77, 81
Mississippi River, 87
Mitchell, John, 38
Moneyhon, Carl, 145
Monroe, John, 48, 51
Montgomery, David, 216
Moore, John W., 183
Moore, Samuel, 150
Morse, Andrew, 38
Moses, Franklin J., Jr., 208–9
Moynihan, Daniel Patrick, 21
Myers, Nathaniel B., 213–14

National Equal Rights League, 46
Naval stores, 179
Navassa Guano Company, 185
Neille, Hannah, 129
Newland, Lavina, 130
Newspapers, 59, 65, 70, 178, 206; accounts of racial conflicts, 63; African American, 176, 183; and fear of insurrection by African Americans, 90; *Charleston News and Courier*, 209, 211–12; *L'Union*, 41; *New Orleans Tribune*, 41–44, 50–51; reporting of Ogeechee Insurrection, 69; *Savannah Daily Advertiser*, 66; *Savannah Daily Herald*, 59; *Savannah Morning News*, 60, 65, 69–70; *Savannah Republican*, 58, 65
North Carolina: Fort Fisher, 109; Green River Cove, 161; Roanoke Island, 104; western, 159, 185
North Carolina, counties: Brunswick, 185; New Hanover, 177, 182, 191

North Carolina, towns: Charlotte, 105; Fayetteville, 185; Greensboro, 104, 111–12; Hendersonville, 164; Kinston, 111–12; Lexington, 113; New Bern, 114, 184; Raleigh, 102–3; Washington, 184; Wilmington, 107, 109; Wilmington, economy of after the Civil War, 184–86; Wilmington, industries, 186; Wilmington, shipping, 185–86
Nuckles, Sam, 206
Nullification Crisis, 164

Ogeechee Home Guard, 72
Orr, James L., 203–4
Outlaw bands, 92, 112, 123, 126, 131, 164

Painter, Nell Irvin, 8
Paramilitary units, of whites, 60–61, 63, 72, 208, 210
Patterson, Orlando, 22
Patton, George, 126
Pearne, W. H., 42
Pearson, James, 180
People's Bakery, 44
Perman, Michael, 7, 156
Perry, Benjamin F., 164, 166, 170, 206
Piedmont, 160, 168, 205
Pillsbury, Gilbert, 204
Plantations: Grove Hill, 71; Grove Point, 70–71; Prairie, 61, 64, 68, 71; Southfield, 61, 64, 68, 71
Planters, 147–48, 150, 153, 202–3, 211
Police: African American, 190; interference with elections, 51, 61; violence towards African Americans, 38, 47, 51
Poor whites, 12
Populist Party, 225
Port Royal Experiment, 202
Potter, George L., 83
Prather, H. Leon, 194n1
Presidential Reconstruction, 78, 83, 90
Price, George W., Jr., 183, 193
Price, George W., Sr., 193
Price, Peter, 98, 100
Prostitution, by freedwomen, 40, 134

Quinby, Isaac F., 80
Quince, Harriet, 183

Rabinowitz, Howard, 6
Rachleff, Peter, 36
Railroads, and segregation, 51; as employers of African American men, 182, 186, 189; Blue Ridge Railroad, 168; bonds for, 168; effects on economy of the South, 12; Greenville and Columbia Railroad, 162; Pennsylvania Railroad, 168; Richmond and Atlanta Air Line Railroad, 168–69; Spartanburg and Union Railroad, 168; Wilmington and Weldon Railroad, 185, 189
Rainey, Joseph H., 209
Randolph, Ryland, 152
Read, J. W., 127
Redemption, 178
Redemption, in S.C., 160, 167, 209, 214
Reid, Whitelaw, 2
Religious conflict, 85
Republican Party: conflict within, 159, 204, 207, 209–10, 212; failures of, 6; in Louisiana, founding of, 43; as trade union, 46;
Republican Party, in South Carolina, 159–72; Radicals, 2, 10, 65, 67, 204–5
Revenue agents, 166
Revolution, French, 17, 41
Revolution, Haitian, 41, 59, 90
Reynolds, Donald, 49
Rice, 10, 70, 73
Richardson, Heather Cox, 73
Right to vote, 30; for African American men, 37–38, 42–43, 48, 50–51, 60, 107, 151, 177, 203; removed from Confederates, 51–52, 107
Robbins, Morris S., 183
Robinson, Armstead, 12
Rodrigue, John, 53
Rumors, 46, 90–91
Runion, James M., 163, 165–66, 168
Russell, Philip M., Jr., 64, 66, 69
Ryan, Augustus, 129

Salesday, 161
Saluda River, 160–61
Sans papiers, deportation of, from France, 17
Sassen, Saskia, 26
Savannah River, 60, 162
Schools, African American, as targets of violence, 47, 136
Scott, Robert K., 202, 206–7, 209
Scott, Shelton, 130
Scott, Stephen, 135
Scott, Tom, 168

Segregation, of streetcars in New Orleans, 51
Sequestration Act of 1861 (CSA), 81
Seward, William H., 227
Sexual assault, of African American women by white men, 123, 132, 135
Shapiro, Herbert, 206
Sharkey, William, 83, 91
Sherman's Special Field Orders No. 15, 3, 71–72, 93, 202
Shields, Marion, 91
Shoemaker, Isaac, 81
Sibley, Caleb, 74
Silva, Frank, 187
Slaveholders, 146–51
Slavery, historiography of, 20–21
Slaves, as contrabands, 37
Slave trade: domestic, 191; international, 18–19, 25, 27
Smalls, Robert, 212, 215
Smith, Alfred B., 66
Smith, Ephraim, 182
Smith, William H., 148, 155
Smuggling, 80
Smyth, Jonathan H., 182–83
Snider, Eli, 130
Soloman, Hardy, 168
Soulié, Bernard, 42
South Africa, 229
South Carolina, 4, 90; Dark Corner, 165; Edisto Island, 202; Jones Gap, 160, 162, 164; Saluda Gap, 160–61; Wadmalaw Island, 202
South Carolina, counties: Anderson, 160, 162, 165; Barnwell, 212; Beaufort, 211–14; Colleton, 211–12; Hampton, 213; Laurens, 160, 206; Union, 162, 206; York, 206
South Carolina, towns: Abbeville, 180, 205; Beaufort, 212–14; Carmel Hill, 207; Charleston, 199–200, 203–5, 208–10; Chester, 207; Clay Hill, 206; Crooked Hill, 213; Frog Level, 163; Georgetown, 209, 215; Greenville, 164, 168–69; Merrittsville, 161; Orangeburg, 212; Rock Hill, 207; Sumter, 201; Walterboro, 212
South Carolina Land Commission, 167
Spinner, Francis E., 227
Stampp, Kenneth, 6
State, 77, 101, 170, 226; historical roots of, 23–24, 29–30; weakness of, 9, 99, 111
State government, in Mississippi, 79, 83
Stevens, Thaddeus, 1–2, 92–93, 154
Stewart, W. H., 137
Stone, Amherst W., 66–67
Stoneman, George, 164
Stoneman's Raid, 164
Strikes, 205; Charleston tailors (1869), 208; considered as insurrection, 67; New Orleans waterfront (1865), 35, 45; New Orleans waterfront (1867), 52; over wages, 35, 46; South Carolina rice workers (1876), 211–13
Sturges, Sam, 206
Subsistence strategies, 73
Sumner, Charles, 102, 226
Sutherland, Alfred, 129
Sutherland, Daniel, 165
Sutherland, Harriet, 129
Sweatshops, 18–19, 24–27, 32n8
Swope, Joseph, 135–36

Tannenbaum, Frank, 17, 28
Taxation, white complaints about, 167
Texas, 108, 150, 163
Theft: from African Americans by whites, 90, 92, 112, 123, 132, 135; from whites by African Americans, 64, 72, 82, 145, 153
Thompson, E. P., 221
Thornton, J. Mills, III, 167
Tillman, Ben, 178, 214
Tourgée, Albion W., 115–17
Trelease, Allen, 144, 147, 155
Trent River, contraband camp at, 114–15
Trévigne, Paul, 41
True, C. J., 127
Tucker, Henry, Sr., 192
Turlingland, W. B., 183
Tverdy, Linda, 226

United States Army: demobilization of, 108–11; in Ogeechee Insurrection, 64; protecting freedpeople, 72; supporting revenue agents, 170–71
Union Convention, of Mississippi (1851), 84
Unionists: after Civil War, 84–85, 107, 115, 136–37, 159, 164–65; during Civil War, 38, 79, 81, 150; murdered by Regulators, 131, 136
Union League, 8, 165–66, 189, 203–6
Union Reform party, 163
Union soldiers: attacks upon, 112; demobilization of, 105; veterans, 103, 203
Upcountry, 166, 203, 205, 208–9

Vagrancy, 106, 126
Vandal, Gilles, 44, 49
Violence against African Americans, 165; against children, 11, 130, 141n22; as labor control, 52, 104, 122, 151, 165; against men, 106, 135; whipping, 132, 136; against women, 11, 127, 133, 141n22
Violence, riots: Camilla Riot (1868), 65, 75n20; Charleston Riot (1866), 49; Colfax Massacre (1873), 225; Hamburg Massacre (1876), 207, 213; Memphis Riot (1866), 49, 107; New Orleans Massacre (1866), 36, 47–50, 107; Wilmington Riot (1898), 107, 176
Virginia, towns, Richmond, 36

Wagoner, Charles, 187
Walker, David, 189
Wall St. Baptist Church, 85–86
Warmouth, Henry Clay, 43–44
Warren, Earl, 29
Washington, Booker T., 200, 224; Atlanta Compromise speech (1895), 216
Waterfront workers, 32, 52, 179, 186, 208
Watson, J.W.C., 84–85
Wells, David Ames, 110
Wells, James Madison, 38–39, 44, 47–48
Whig party, 147
Whipper, William J., 213
Whites, LeeAnn, 223
Whittlesey, Eliphalet, 103–6, 113
Wilfong, George, 66
Wilkes, Jim, 207
Williams, Arthur, 63–65
Williams, Ellen, 193
Williamson, Joel, 221
Women, African American, 11, 40
Woodhull, Victoria, 223
Workers: agricultural, 35; agricultural, African American, 39, 46, 53; urban, 35, 40; white, 50; white, men, 37, 45; women, 27; women, African American, 36
Workers' cooperatives, New Orleans, 44
Worth, Jonathan, 106
Wright, Dennis, 182
Wright, George C., 137
Wyatt-Brown, Bertram, 101

NEW PERSPECTIVES ON THE HISTORY OF THE SOUTH

Edited by John David Smith

"In the Country of the Enemy": The Civil War Reports of a Massachusetts Corporal, edited by William C. Harris (1999)

The Wild East: A Biography of the Great Smoky Mountains, by Margaret L. Brown (2000; first paperback edition, 2001)

Crime, Sexual Violence, and Clemency: Florida's Pardon Board and Penal System in the Progressive Era, by Vivien M. L. Miller (2000)

The New South's New Frontier: A Social History of Economic Development in Southwestern North Carolina, by Stephen Wallace Taylor (2001)

Redefining the Color Line: Black Activism in Little Rock, Arkansas, 1940–1970, by John A. Kirk (2002)

The Southern Dream of a Caribbean Empire, 1854–1861, by Robert E. May (2002)

Forging a Common Bond: Labor and Environmental Activism during the BASF Lockout, by Timothy J. Minchin (2003)

Dixie's Daughters: The United Daughters of the Confederacy and the Preservation of Confederate Culture, by Karen L. Cox (2003)

The Other War of 1812: The Patriot War and the American Invasion of Spanish East Florida, by James G. Cusick (2003)

"Lives Full of Struggle and Triumph": Southern Women, Their Institutions, and Their Communities, edited by Bruce L. Clayton and John A. Salmond (2003)

German-Speaking Officers in the United States Colored Troops, 1863–1867, by Martin W. Öfele (2004)

Southern Struggles: The Southern Labor Movement and the Civil Rights Struggle, by John A. Salmond (2004)

Radio and the Struggle for Civil Rights in the South, by Brian Ward (2004; first paperback edition, 2006)

Luther P. Jackson and a Life for Civil Rights, by Michael Dennis (2004)

Southern Ladies, New Women: Race, Region, and Clubwomen in South Carolina, 1890–1930, by Joan Marie Johnson (2004)

Fighting Against the Odds: A Concise History of Southern Labor Since World War II, by Timothy J. Minchin (2004; first paperback edition, 2006)

"Don't Sleep With Stevens!": The J. P. Stevens Campaign and the Struggle to Organize the South, 1963–1980, by Timothy J. Minchin (2005)

"The Ticket to Freedom": The NAACP and the Struggle for Black Political Integration, by Manfred Berg (2005; first paperback edition, 2007)

"War Governor of the South": North Carolina's Zeb Vance in the Confederacy, by Joe A. Mobley (2005)

Planters' Progress: Modernizing Confederate Georgia, by Chad Morgan (2005)

The Officers of the CSS Shenandoah, by Angus Curry (2006)

The Rosenwald Schools of the American South, by Mary S. Hoffschwelle (2006; first paperback edition, 2014)

Honor in Command: Lt. Freeman S. Bowley's Civil War Service in the 30th United States Colored Infantry, edited by Keith Wilson (2006)

A Black Congressman in the Age of Jim Crow: South Carolina's George Washington Murray, by John F. Marszalek (2006)

The Spirit and the Shotgun: Armed Resistance and the Struggle for Civil Rights, by Simon Wendt (2007; first paperback edition, 2010)

Making a New South: Race, Leadership, and Community after the Civil War, edited by Paul A. Cimbala and Barton C. Shaw (2007)

From Rights to Economics: The Ongoing Struggle for Black Equality in the U.S. South, by Timothy J. Minchin (2008)

Slavery on Trial: Race, Class, and Criminal Justice in Antebellum Richmond, Virginia, by James M. Campbell (2008; first paperback edition, 2010)

Welfare and Charity in the Antebellum South, by Timothy James Lockley (2008; first paperback edition, 2009)

T. Thomas Fortune the Afro-American Agitator: A Collection of Writings, 1880–1928, by Shawn Leigh Alexander (2008; first paperback edition, 2010)

Francis Butler Simkins: A Life, by James S. Humphreys (2008)

Black Manhood and Community Building in North Carolina, 1900–1930, by Angela Hornsby-Gutting (2009; first paperback edition, 2010)

Counterfeit Gentlemen: Manhood and Humor in the Old South, by John Mayfield (2009; first paperback edition, 2010)

The Southern Mind Under Union Rule: The Diary of James Rumley, Beaufort, North Carolina, 1862–1865, edited by Judkin Browning (2009; first paperback edition, 2011)

The Quarters and the Fields: Slave Families in the Non-Cotton South, by Damian Alan Pargas (2010; first paperback edition, 2011)

The Door of Hope: Republican Presidents and the First Southern Strategy, 1877–1933, by Edward O. Frantz (2011; first paperback edition, 2012)

Painting Dixie Red: When, Where, Why, and How the South Became Republican, edited by Glenn Feldman (2011; first paperback edition, 2014)

After Freedom Summer: How Race Realigned Mississippi Politics, 1965–1986, by Chris Danielson (2011; first paperback edition, 2013)

Dreams and Nightmares: Martin Luther King Jr., Malcolm X, and the Struggle for Black Equality in America, by Britta Waldschmidt-Nelson (2012)

Hard Labor and Hard Time: Florida's "Sunshine Prison" and Chain Gangs, by Vivien M. L. Miller (2012)

Ain't Scared of Your Jail: Arrest, Imprisonment, and the Civil Rights Movement, by Zoe A. Colley (2013; first paperback edition, 2014)

After Slavery: Race, Labor, and Citizenship in the Reconstruction South, edited by Bruce E. Baker and Brian Kelly (2013; first paperback edition, 2014)

Stinking Stones and Rocks of Gold: Phosphate, Fertilizer, and Industrialization in Postbellum South Carolina, by Shepherd W. McKinley (2014)

The Path to the Greater, Freer, Truer World: Southern Civil Rights and Anticolonialism, 1937–1955, by Lindsey R. Swindall (2014)

CPSIA information can be obtained at www.ICGtesting.com
Printed in the USA
LVOW12s0150140315

430525LV00003B/3/P

9 780813 060972